Critical Survey of Poetry
Avant-Garde Poets

Editor

Rosemary M. Canfield Reisman
Charleston Southern University

SALEM PRESS
A Division of EBSCO Publishing, Ipswich, Massachusetts

Cover photo:
E.E. Cummings (© Bettmann/Corbis)

Copyright © 2012, by Salem Press, A Division of EBSCO Publishing, Inc.
All rights in this book are reserved. No part of this work may be used or reproduced in any manner whatsoever or transmitted in any form or by any means, electronic or mechanical, including photocopy, recording, or any information storage and retrieval system, without written permission from the copyright owner except in the case of brief quotations embodied in critical articles and reviews or in the copying of images deemed to be freely licensed or in the public domain. For information address the publisher, Salem Press, at csr@salempress.com.

ISBN: 978-1-42983-646-3

CONTENTS

Contributors iv

Avant-Garde Poetry 1

Guillaume Apollinaire 4
Louis Aragon 15
John Ashbery 26
Ted Berrigan 41
André Breton 46
Paul Celan 54
Jean Cocteau 63
E. E. Cummings 74
Sergei Esenin 85
Barbara Guest 94
Zbigniew Herbert 99
Kenneth Koch 110
Amy Lowell 120
Stéphane Mallarmé 131
Alice Notley 140
Frank O'Hara 146
Pierre Reverdy 155
James Schuyler 165
Delmore Schwartz 175
Jaroslav Seifert 186
Gertrude Stein 197
Tristan Tzara 210
César Vallejo 220
Anne Waldman 233
Dean Young 240

Checklist for Explicating a Poem 246
Bibliography 249
Guide to Online Resources 252
Geographical Index 256
Category Index 257
Subject Index 260

CONTRIBUTORS

Peter Baker
Southern Connecticut State University

Franz G. Blaha
University of Nebraska-Lincoln

John Carpenter
University of Michigan

Peter Carravetta
Queens College, City University of New York

Steven E. Colburn
Largo, Florida

J. Madison Davis
Pennsylvania State College-Behrend College

Frank Day
Clemson University

Lloyd N. Dendinger
University of South Alabama

Robert DiYanni
Pace University

Lillian Doherty
University of Maryland

Lee Hunt Dowling
University of Houston

Desiree Dreeuws
Sunland, California

Lawrence S. Friedman
Indiana University

Elaine Gardiner
Topeka, Kansas

Scott Giantvalley
California State University, Dominguez Hills

Daniel L. Guillory
Millikin University

Sarah Hilbert
Pasadena, California

David Harrison Horton
Patten College

Tracy Irons-Georges
Glendale, California

Maura Ives
Texas A&M University

Philip K. Jason
United States Naval Academy

Jeffry Jensen
Pasadena, California

Irma M. Kashuba
Chestnut Hill College

Rebecca Kuzins
Pasadena, California

John D. Lyons
University of Massachusetts, Dartmouth

Rado Pribic
Lafayette College

Thomas Rankin
Concord, California

Mark Rich
Cashton, Wisconsin

Roy Seeger
University of South Carolina, Aiken

Twyla R. Wells
Lima, Ohio

Scott D. Yarbrough
Charleston Southern University

AVANT-GARDE POETRY

While the term "avant-garde" may have first been used during the French Revolution as a military term meaning "vanguard," it has been applied in many other contexts, including both political and literary. Its literary application came later than its other uses, around the beginning of the twentieth century. The avant-garde movement of the twentieth century is difficult to define, as earlier avant-garde artistic trends were more focused. The twentieth century literary avant-garde movement, in contrast, had no single driving force.

This diversity of approach can be seen in the various literary and artistic movements that began during the early decades of the twentieth century, including Dadaism, Surrealism, and Futurism. The development of each of these movements took place in the public square, where each avant-garde movement had to push forward, with poets in the position of defining, shaping, and advancing new forms and fending off the dismissal and resistance of traditionalists. The avant-garde poet fights not only society, but his or her own conditioning and education, and for that reason, is often seen as the advance foot soldier. He or she fires the first shot. Poets such as Walt Whitman, Charles Baudelaire, Arthur Rimbaud, Guillaume Apollinaire, André Breton, Jean Cocteau, E. E. Cummings, Gertrude Stein, Tristan Tzara, and John Ashbery have all had something memorable, puzzling, or provocative to say. As avant-garde poets, they seek to probe, confront, and make nuisances of themselves. An avant-garde literary movement may appear first in one form in one country and eventually appear in another, where it may serve an entirely different purpose from where it started. The artist or poet becomes what the culture requires of him or her; the motivations may be the same, but the end result is completely upside down. Avant-garde literature feeds on the beast that it inhabits. Poets found in repressive environments use their surroundings as springboards to fully vent their startling views.

Poets who wish to look at any situation, any human thought, in a new way have been called radicals and trailblazers. They do not hope to make observations easy for themselves or the reader; rather, they wish to bring clarity through confusion, exposure through obfuscation. The desire to make more of what has come before is as old as literature itself. For every movement that demands unification via adherence to agreed-upon standards or rules, there are outsiders, extremists, and troublemakers who resist, who create outside the lines and outside the norms. Some do it with new thought patterns, while others seek to invent new forms and constructs to reveal a path to wisdom. Visual presentation and language are two of the most obvious means of expressing fresh ways of looking at the world, at society, and at the very core of existence.

In contemporary poetry, there have been several vibrant movements or schools that have taken a metaphorical sledgehammer to traditional modes of expression. In a very real sense, each of these movements flowed into another. There are examples of avant-garde poetry in every culture in every part of the world. Rebellion is a natural outgrowth of stagnation, of repression, of a so-called natural order in literary terms. Straight lines do not exist in the chaos of avant-garde creativity, but this does not mean that connections do not exist. One can speak of French Symbolism and German Romanticism in the same breath and not be out of line, and there is an almost direct path from the French Symbolists of the nineteenth century to the French Dadaists and Surrealists of the twentieth century. There are threads everywhere, in all literary movements, generations, and pillars of tradition. So it is not such a leap of faith to see in the avant-garde movement the urge to reveal something heretofore unsaid in Romanticism, Transcendentalism, or Metaphysical poetry. It is the inspiration; it is the experience that connects the wellspring of poetic purpose. It is the motive that puts the avant-garde poets into the same pregnant pool of creativity. For all the differences between radical movements of poetry, it is their shared need to rattle the very foundations that places them in the same discussion at the same literary table.

The Avant-Garde Century

It can be argued that of all the literary forms, poetry has been controlled by tradition for the longest. With this in mind, when change comes to poetry, it is a major event. By the twentieth century, poetry was ripe not just for revolution but for a mind-altering transformation. Faced with all the horrors of the new century, poets seemed to understand that new languages and landscapes were needed for poetry to speak to the current conditions. With chaos and mass slaughter the new norm, poetry had to be pulled up by its roots and radically altered. Each of the avant-garde forms that emerged during the twentieth century—Dadaism, Imagism, Futurism, Surrealism, Objectivism, the Beat movement, Language poetry, concrete poetry, modernism, and more—found a method of expression that was unique, different, and necessary for the moment. By definition, avant-garde poets make waves, and in so doing they provoke the wrath of the establishment, causing many to question the very meaning of what constitutes poetry. For some poets, the avant-garde is a direct threat to the very existence of poetry. For them, poetry is marginalized by change and chaos. The poetic mainstream can only hope to hold on to its standing in the community by stamping out the fires of change. Poetry becomes scarier, more isolated, and more misunderstood when it encourages growth, stimulation, and divergence.

It can be said that poetry came into a golden age during the nineteenth century. In the beginning, the English Romantic poets took the literary world by storm, with the likes of Samuel Taylor Coleridge, John Keats, Percy Bysshe Shelley, Lord Byron, and William Wordsworth all turning away from the conservatism of the previous era. By the middle of the century, the French Symbolists were changing the face of poetry with taboo subject matter and free forms of verse, beginning with Charles Baudelaire, who was prosecuted for the supposedly scandalous topics in his collection *Les fleurs du mal* (1857, 1861, 1868; *The Flowers of Evil*, 1931), and continuing with the radical Symbolist poetry of Arthur Rimbaud, Paul Verlaine, and Stéphane Mallarmé. Out of these developments came the Surrealist poets of the 1920's and beyond. The two world wars gave rise to a radical poetic response to the visible chaos and horrors. Whether motivated by political, psychological, or linguistic factors, poets from around the globe were exercising their desire to bring attention to a world gone mad.

Each new literary movement pushes its way onto the world stage, hoping for the chance to leave a lasting impression. Several literary avant-garde movements entered at historical crossroads. In all likelihood, it is during a time of upheaval, when the social and political environment is in disarray or crumbling, that new literary and art forms will emerge. These movements are seen as a cure for what ails the current situation, self-confidence being a necessity. The movement may even appear aggressively bombastic in its approach, as self-confidence can turn into self-righteousness on occasion. These qualities will feed into the energy that is necessary to do battle with the decaying mainstream, strike a blow against the current status quo, and speak out against all derelict responses to the ever-expanding chaos of the moment.

Jeffry Jensen

BIBLIOGRAPHY

Bürger, Peter. *Theory of the Avant-Garde*. Translated by Michael Shaw. Minneapolis: University of Minnesota Press, 1984. Suggests that avant-garde innovators are looked upon as outsiders because they attempt to discount what already exists.

Clinton, Alan. "An Ocean View of the Avant-Garde." *Extrapolation* 44, no. 4 (Winter, 2003): 446-455. Explores the similarities between avant-garde poetry and science fiction literature.

"Introduction: Poetics of Avant-Garde Poetries." *Poetics Today* 20, no. 4 (Winter, 1999): 545-547. Argues that poetry was the most inventive art form of the twentieth century.

Noland, Carrie, and Barrett Watten, eds. *Diasporic Avant-Gardes: Experimental Poetics and Cultural Displacement*. New York: Palgrave Macmillan, 2009. A collection of essays that reflect on how both avant-garde and diasporic poets have been fighting against the same larger societal norms.

O'Neil, Mary Anne. "The Fortunes of Avant-Garde Poetry." *Philosophy and Literature* 25, no. 1 (April, 2001): 142-154. Contrasts the reception of French poetry at the beginning of the twentieth century with that of the avant-garde poets of the twenty-first century.

GUILLAUME APOLLINAIRE

Born: Rome, Italy; August 26, 1880
Died: Paris, France; November 9, 1918
Also known as: Wilhelm Apollinaris; Guillelmus Apollinaris de Kostrowitzki

PRINCIPAL POETRY
Le Bestiaire, 1911 (*Bestiary*, 1978)
Alcools: Poèmes, 1898-1913, 1913 (*Alcools: Poems, 1898-1913*, 1964)
Calligrammes, 1918 (English translation, 1980)
Il y a, 1925
Le Guetteur mélancolique, 1952
Tendre comme le souvenir, 1952
Poèmes à Lou, 1955
Œuvres poétiques, 1956

OTHER LITERARY FORMS

Besides poetry, Guillaume Apollinaire (ah-pawl-ee-NEHR) wrote a number of prose works. Among the most significant of his short stories and novellas are *L'Enchanteur pourrissant* (1909; "the putrescent enchanter"), published by Henry Kahnweiler and illustrated with woodcuts by André Derain; *L'Hérésiarque et Cie.* (1910; *The Heresiarch and Co.*, 1965), a contender for the Prix Goncourt; and *Le Poète assassiné* (1916; *The Poet Assassinated*, 1923). They are contained in the Pléiade edition, *Œuvres en prose* (1977), edited by Michel Décaudin.

Apollinaire collaborated on numerous plays and cinema scripts. His best-known individual works in these genres are two proto-Surrealist plays in verse: *Les Mamelles de Tirésias* (pr. 1917; *The Breasts of Tiresias*, 1961), first published in the magazine *SIC* in 1918, and *Couleur du temps* (the color of time; pr. 1918), which first appeared in the *Nouvelle Revue française* in 1920. They are available in the Pléiade edition of *Œuvres poétiques*. Apollinaire also published a great deal of art criticism and literary criticism in journals, newspapers, and other periodicals. In 1913, the articles published before that year were collected in *Peintres cubistes: Méditations esthétiques* (*The Cubist Painters: Aesthetic Meditations*, 1944). In 1918, *Mercure de France* published his famous manifesto "L'Esprit nouveau et les poètes" ("The New Spirit and the Poets"), which later appeared, along with many other articles, in *Chroniques d'art, 1902-1918* (1960), edited by L. C. Breunig. This collection has been translated into English as *Apollinaire on Art: Essays and Reviews, 1902-1918* (1972).

Achievements

After Guillaume Apollinaire, French poetry was never the same again. Writing at the end of the long Symbolist tradition, a tradition very apparent in his early works, Apollinaire moved into a new perception of the world and of poetry. In the world of his mature verse, spatial and temporal relations are radically altered. Apollinaire's was one of the first voices in French poetry to attempt to articulate the profound discontinuity and disorientation in modern society. At the same time, however, his works reflect hope, frequently ecstatic, in the promise of the future.

Apollinaire's sense of radical discontinuity was reflected in his formal innovations, analyzed in considerable depth by Jean-Claude Chevalier in *Alcools d'Apollinaire* (1970). Immediately before the publication of *Alcools*, Apollinaire went through the volume and removed all punctuation, a device that he continued to use in most of his later works. His most notable poems, such as "Zone," "Liens" ("Chains"), and "Les Fenêtres" ("Windows"), use free verse with irregular rhyme and rhythm; his most startling works are the picture poems of *Calligrammes*, a form that he falsely claimed to have invented. They consist of verses arranged to give both a visual and an auditory effect in an effort to create simultaneity.

Like the cubists and other modern painters who sought to go beyond the traditional boundaries of space and time, Apollinaire desired to create the effect of simultaneity. This ambition is evident in "Zone," with its biographical, geographical, and historical discontinuity. In this single poem, the poet leaps from his pious childhood at the Collège Saint-Charles in Monaco to the wonders of modern aviation and back to the "herds" of buses "mooing" on the streets of Paris. Perhaps his most obvious achievement in simultaneity, though less profound, is in "Lundi rue Christine" ("Monday in Christine Street"), which records overheard bits of conversation in a "sinistre brasserie," a low-class café-restaurant that Apollinaire had frequented as early as 1903.

The friend and collaborator of many important painters during the exciting years in Paris just before World War I, Apollinaire began associating with artists when he met Pablo Picasso in 1904, after which he frequented the famous Bateau-Lavoir on the rue Ravignan with Max Jacob, André Derain, Maurice Vlaminck, Georges Braque, and others. After 1912, he moved into the world of art criticism, not always appreciated by the artists themselves, as critic Francis Steegmuller has noted. Not unrelated to this interest was Apollinaire's tumultuous liaison with Marie Laurencin from 1907 to 1912. He frequently inspired works and portraits by artists, including Laurencin, Henri Rousseau, and Picasso. Apollinaire's own works further testify to his links with painters: *Bestiary* was illustrated by Raoul Dufy, and "Windows" was the introductory poem to the catalog of the Robert Delaunay exhibit in 1912. His poems often parallel the work of the painters in their spirit of simultaneity; in their subjects, such as the *saltimbanques* of Picasso; and in their moods, such as those of Marc Chagall's dreamworld and inverted figures.

After 1916, Apollinaire became the *chef d'école*, the leader of a new generation of poets and painters. Among them were Pierre Reverdy, Philippe Soupault, Jean Cocteau, André Breton, and Tristan Tzara. His own works appeared in the most avant-garde journals: Reverdy's *Nord-Sud*, Picabia's *391*, and Albert Birot's *SIC*. His lecture "The New Spirit and the Poets" called poets to a new prophetic vision, imploring them to create prodigies with their imagination like modern Merlins. Like Paul Claudel, Apollinaire regarded the poet as a creator. The modern poet, he believed, must use everything for his (or her) creation: new discoveries in science, in the subconscious and the dreamworld, and in the cinema and visual arts.

The Surrealists, in their desire to revolutionize art and literature, saw in Apollinaire their precursor. It was he who coined the word *surréaliste*, in the preface to his drama in verse *The Breasts of Tiresias*. In it, he explains that an equivalent is not always an imitation, even as the wheel, though intended to facilitate transportation, is not a reproduction of the leg. Apollinaire conveys his message with a lighthearted tone, employing incongruous rhythms, parody, and sexual imagery. This is essentially the technique he employs in his most avant-garde poetry, and *The Breasts of Tiresias* echoes poems from "Ondes" ("Waves," the first part of *Calligrammes*) such as "Zone," "Le Brasier" ("The Brazier"), "Les Fiançailles" ("The Betrothal"), and "Le Larron" ("The Thief"). Thus, Apollinaire indicated the path to follow in revolutionizing poetry, although much of his work was in some respects traditional. Like Victor Hugo, he served subsequent poets chiefly as a guide rather than as a model, but it was his "esprit nouveau" that gave considerable impetus to a new form of modern poetry.

Biography

Born in Rome on August 26, 1880, Guillaume Albert Wladimir Alexandre Apollinaire de Kostrowitzky was an illegitimate child; in "The Thief," he says that his "father was a sphinx and his mother a night." In reality, his mother was a Polish adventurer of noble ancestry, Angelique Kostrowicka, known in Paris mostly as "Olga." His father's identity has never been definitively ascertained. The most plausible supposition points to Francesco Flugi d'Aspermont, who was from a noble Italian family that included many prelates. This theory is based on the careful investigation of biographer Marcel Adéma. Apollinaire's mysterious and involved parentage haunted the poet throughout his life, leaving unmistakable marks on his character and works.

Apollinaire received his only formal education at the Collège of Saint-Charles in Monaco and the Collège Stanislas at Cannes, from 1890 to 1897, where he acquired a solid grounding in religious and secular knowledge. Although his Catholic training was to remain firmly implanted in his memory and is evident in his poetry, he moved away from any outward adherence to religious beliefs after 1897. In 1899, he arrived in Paris, his home for most of the next nineteen years of his life and the center and inspiration of his literary activity. First, however, he made a significant trip to Germany's Rhineland in 1901, as tutor to Gabrielle, the daughter of the viscountess of Milhau. There, he met and fell in love with Annie Playden, Gabrielle's English governess. This ill-fated romance and the beauty of the Rhineland inspired many of Apollinaire's early poems, which were later published in *Alcools*.

Apollinaire's return to Paris coincided with the beginning of friendships with artists and writers such as André Salmon, Alfred Jarry, Max Jacob, and especially Picasso. In 1903, he began his collaboration on many periodicals, which he continued throughout his lifetime. Most of his prose and poetry was first published in such journals, many of which—such as *Le Festin d'Esope* and *La Revue immoraliste*—were of very short duration. His works appeared under several pseudonyms, of which "Apollinaire" was the most significant. Others included "Louise Lalame," "Lul," "Montade," and "Tyl." In 1907, he met Marie Laurencin, an artist, whose talent Apollinaire tended to exaggerate. Their liaison continued until 1912 and was an inspiration and a torment to both of them. During this period, Apollinaire was deeply marked by the false accusation that he was responsible for the theft of the *Mona Lisa* from the Louvre. A series of six poems in *Alcools*, "À la Santé" ("At the Santé") describes his brief stay in the prison of La Santé in Verlainian imagery.

The year 1912 marked Apollinaire's break with Laurencin and his definite espousal of modern art, of which he became a staunch proponent. During the two years preceding World War I, he gave lectures and wrote articles on modern art and prepared *Alcools* for publication. The beginning of the war, in 1914, was to Apollinaire a call to a mission. Although not a French citizen until the year 1916, he embraced with great enthusiasm his *métier de soldat* as an artilleryman and then as an infantryman, according an almost mystical dimension to his military service. His poetry of these first two years reveals the exaltation of war and the idealization of two women, "Lou" (Louise de Coligny-Châtillon) and Madeleine Pagès, to whom he was briefly engaged.

Wounded in the head in 1916, Apollinaire required surgery and was then discharged from the service. He returned to the world of literature and art with numerous articles, lectures, two plays, and a volume of poetry, *Calligrammes*. In May of 1918, he married Jacqueline Kolb ("Ruby"), the "jolie rousse" ("pretty redhead") of the last poem in *Calligrammes*. The marriage was of short duration, however, as Apollinaire died of Spanish influenza on November 9 of the same year.

ANALYSIS

In his poetic style, Guillaume Apollinaire might be characterized as the last of the Symbolists and the first of the moderns. He is considered a revolutionary and a destroyer, yet the bulk of his work shows a deep influence of traditional symbolism, especially biblical, legendary, and mythical. Very knowledgeable in Roman Catholic doctrine from his years with the Marianists at Monaco and Cannes, he uses extensive biblical imagery: Christ, the Virgin Mary, and the Holy Spirit in the form of a dove.

Robert Couffignal has analyzed Apollinaire's religious imagery in detail and considers his comprehension of the Bible to be "a cascade of superficial weavings." Scott Bates sees the Last Judgment, with its apocalyptic implications, as central to Apollinaire's works. The concept of messianism and the advent of a new millennium is evident in both the early works and the war poems, which predict a new universe. In the Symbolist tradition, the poet is the seer of the new kingdom.

Many of Apollinaire's symbols are from the realm of legend and myth. Rosemonde, the idealized woman of the Middle Ages, is present in several poems, though she appears also as a prostitute. In "Merlin et la vielle femme" ("Merlin and the Old Woman"), the medieval seer foreshadows Apollinaire's vision of the future. Ancient mythology is the source for Orpheus, under whose sign *Bestiary* is written. Orpheus is also the symbol of Christ and the poet, as is Hermès Trismègiste. Ancient Egypt appears in frequent references to the Nile, the Israelites in bondage, and Pharaoh, the image of the poet himself. The fantastic abounds in Apollinaire's works: ghosts, diabolic characters, and phantoms, as found, for example, in "La Maison des Morts" ("The House of the Dead") and especially in the short stories.

Much of Apollinaire's early symbolism is directed toward the quest for self-knowledge; his choice of the name Apollinaire is a clue to his search. Though it was the name of his maternal grandfather and one of the names given to him at baptism, he seems to have chosen it for its reference to Apollo, the god of the sun. Indeed, solar imagery is central to his poetry, and the introductory poem of *Alcools*, "Zone," ends with the words "Soleil cou coupé" ("Sun cut throat"). Bates argues that the violent love-death relationship between the sun and night, with its corresponding symbolism, is as crucial to the interpretation of Apollinaire as it is to a reading of Gérard de Nerval or Stéphane Mallarmé. Along with love and death is death and resurrection. Apollinaire chooses the phoenix as a sign of rebirth and describes his own psychological and poetic resurrection in "The Brazier" and "The Betrothal," poems that he regarded as among his best. Fire seems to be his basic image, with its multiple meanings of passion, destruction, and purification.

Passion as a flame dominated Apollinaire's life and poetry. Of the many women whom he loved, five in particular incarnated his violent passion and appear in his work: Playden and Laurencin in *Alcools*; Lou, Madeleine, and Jacqueline in *Calligrammes* and in several series of poems published after his death. Apollinaire is capable of expressing tender, idealistic love, as in the "Aubade chantée à Lætare un an passé" ("Aubade Sung to Lætare a Year Ago") section of the "La Chanson du mal-aimé" ("The Song of the Poorly Loved") and in "La Jolie Rousse" ("The Pretty Redhead"), which closes *Calligrammes*. In most cases, Apollinaire is the *mal-aimé*, and as he himself says, he is much less the poorly beloved than the one who loves poorly. His first three loves ended violently; his last was concluded by his death. Thus, the death of love is as important as its first manifestation, which for him resembles the shells bursting in the war.

Autumn is the season of the death of love, wistfully expressed in such nostalgic works as "L'Adieu" ("The Farewell") and "Automne" ("Autumn"). Because the end of love usually involved deep suffering for him, the image of mutilation is not uncommon. The beloved in "The Song of the Poorly Loved" has a scar on her neck, and the mannequins in "L'Émigrant de Landor Road" ("The Emigrant from Landor Road") are decapitated, much like the sun in "Zone." Apollinaire perceives love in its erotic sense, and in many cases he resorts to arcane symbolism, as in the seven swords in "The Song of the Poorly Loved." "Lul de Faltenin" ("Lul of Faltenin") is also typical, with its subtle erotic allusions. Such themes are more overt in Apollinaire's prose; indeed, Bates has compiled a glossary of erotic symbolism in the works of Apollinaire.

Apollinaire was both a lyric poet and a storyteller. In the lyric tradition, he writes of his emotions in images drawn from nature. His work is particularly rich in flora and fauna. *Bestiary* shows his familiarity with and affection for animals and his ability, like the fabulists, to see them as caricatures of people. *Alcools*, as the title indicates, often evokes grapes and wine; it also speaks of fir trees (in "Les Sapins") and falling leaves. "Zone" contains a catalog of birds, real and legendary. The Seine comes alive in Apollinaire's ever-popular "Le Pont Mirabeau" ("Mirabeau Bridge"). In *Calligrammes*, the poet often compares the explosion of shells to bursting buds.

Apollinaire was the author of many short stories, and he maintains a narrative flavor in his poetry. "The House of the Dead" was originally a short story, "L'Obituaire," and it reads like one. Many of the picture poems in *Calligrammes* tell a story; "Paysage" ("Landscape"), for example, portrays by means of typography a house, a tree, and two lovers, one of whom smokes a cigar that the reader can almost smell. Apollinaire's technique often involves improvisation, as in "Le Musicien de Saint-Merry" ("The Musician of Saint-Merry"). Although he claims almost total spontaneity, there are revised versions of many of his poems, and he frequently borrowed from himself, rearranging both lines and poems. In particular, Apollinaire tells stories of the modern city, imitating its new structures as Arthur Rimbaud did in his innovative patterns, and like Charles Baudelaire, Apollinaire peoples his verse with the forgotten and the poor, the prostitutes and the clowns.

Apollinaire had a remarkable sense of humor, displayed in frequent word-plays, burlesques, and parodies. The briefest example of his use of puns is the one-line poem "Chantre" ("Singer"): "Et l'unique cordeau des trompettes marines" ("and the single string of marine trumpets"). *Cordeau*, when read aloud, might be *cor d'eau*, or "horn of water," another version of a marine trumpet, as well as *corps d'eau* ("body of water") or even *cœur d'eau* ("heart of water"). The burlesque found in his short stories appears in poetry as dissonance, erotic puns, and irreverent parodies, such as in "Les Sept Epées" ("The Seven Swords") as well as in "The Thief," a poem that Bates interprets as parodying Christ. Apollinaire's lighthearted rhythm and obscure symbolism tend to prevent his verse from becoming offensive and convey a sense of freedom, discovery, and surprise.

BESTIARY

Bestiary is one of the most charming and accessible of Apollinaire's works. The idea for the poem probably came from Picasso in 1906, who was then doing woodcuts of animals. In 1908, Apollinaire published in a journal eighteen poems under the title "La Marchande des quatre saisons ou le bestiaire moderne" (the costermonger or the modern bestiary). When he prepared the final edition in 1911, with woodcuts by Raoul Dufy, he added twelve poems and replaced the merchant with Orpheus. According to mythology, Orpheus attracted wild beasts by playing on the lyre he had received from Mercury. He is the symbol of Gnosis and Neoplatonic Humanism and is also identified with Christ and poetry, in a mixture of mystical and sensual imagery.

Apollinaire himself wrote the notes to the volume and uses as its sign a δ (the Greek letter delta) pierced by a unicorn. He interprets it to mean the delta of the Nile and all the legendary and biblical symbols of ancient Egypt, also suggesting a *D* for Deplanche, the publisher, in addition to the obvious sexual symbolism. He added the motto "J'émerveille" ("I marvel"), thus giving a fantastic aura to the work. Roger Little sees in the volume a "delicious and malicious" wit, with metamorphoses, syncretism, pride in poetry, carnal love, and mysticism. Like all Apollinaire's early works, it is full of self-analysis. In "La Souris" ("The Mouse"), the poet speaks of his twenty-eight years as "mal-vécus" ("poorly spent").

The animals represent human foibles; the peacock, for example, displays both his best and, unbeknownst to him, his worst. They also speak of love: the serpent, the Sirens, the dove, and Orpheus himself. They point to God and things divine: the dove, the bull, or, again, Orpheus. They speak of poetry: the horse, the tortoise, the elephant, and the caterpillar. For Apollinaire, poetry is a divine gift. He concludes his notes by observing that poets seek nothing but perfection, which is God himself. Poets, he says, have the right to expect after death the full knowledge of God, which is sublime beauty.

ALCOOLS

The most analyzed and the best known of Apollinaire's works is *Alcools*, a slender volume published in 1913 with the subtitle *Poèmes, 1898-1913*. A portrait of Apollinaire, an etching by Picasso, serves as the frontispiece. Apollinaire chose fifty-five of the many poems he had written from his eighteenth to his thirty-third year and assembled them in an order that has continued to fascinate and baffle critics. Michel Décaudin says that the order in *Alcools* is based entirely on the aesthetic and sentimental affinities felt by the author, or their discrete dissonances. Very few poems have dates, other than "Rhénanes" (September, 1901, to May, 1902) and "At the Santé" (September, 1911); nevertheless, critics have succeeded in dating many, though not all, of the poems.

The poems have several centers, though not all of those from one group appear together. More than twenty were inspired by Apollinaire's trip to the Rhineland in 1901, including the nine in the cycle "Rhénanes." Several of these poems and some others, such as "The Song of the Poorly Loved," "Annie," and "The Emigrant from Landor Road," refer to his unhappy love affair with Playden. These poems and an interview with her as Mrs. Postings in 1951 by Robert Goffin and LeRoy Breunig are the only sources of information about this significant period in Apollinaire's life. Three poems, "Mirabeau Bridge," "Marie," and "Cors de chasse" ("Hunting Horns"), scattered throughout the volume, refer to Laurencin.

The poems exhibit great variety in form, tone, and subject matter. They range from the one-line "Chantre" to the seven-part "The Song of the Poorly Loved," the longest in the collection. Most of them have regular rhyme and rhythm, but "Zone" and "Vendémiaire," the first and the last, give evidence of technical experimentation. The poems range from witty ("The Synagogue") to nostalgic ("Autumn," "Hunting Horns") and from enigmatic ("The Brazier") to irreverent ("The Thief"). Critics have arranged them in various ways. Bates, for example, sees the volume as a "Dionysian-Apollonian dance of life in three major symbols: fire, shadow, alcools."

Apollinaire chose the beginning and concluding poems of the collection, "Zone" and "Vendémiaire," with great care. "Zone" is overtly autobiographical in a Romantic-Symbolist ambience, yet its instant leaps in space and time make it very modern. Also modern is the image of the city, where Apollinaire can see beauty in a poster, a traffic jam, and a group of frightened Jewish immigrants. The city is also the central focus in the concluding poem, "Vendémiaire" (the name given the month of vintage, September 22-October 21, in the revolutionary calendar), a hymn to the glory of Paris. The poet exuberantly proclaims his immortality and omnipresence: "I am drunk from having swallowed all the universe." Bates sees the end of the poem as a hymn to joy reminiscent of Walt Whitman and Friedrich Nietzsche.

The bizarre juxtapositions, the inner borrowings of lines from one poem to the next, and the absence of punctuation provoked various responses from critics. Cubists hailed Apollinaire as a great poet. Georges Duhamel, writing in the June 15, 1913, issue of *Mercure de France*, called the volume a junk shop. Critics such as Adéma, Décaudin, and Marie-Jeanne Durry analyze *Alcools* with depth and scholarship. They discover many platitudes and much mediocrity but find it redeemed by what Steegmuller identifies as a spirit of freedom.

CALLIGRAMMES

Intended as a sequel to *Alcools*, *Calligrammes* is much more unified than *Alcools*, yet its importance was seen only much later. It consists of six parts. The first part, "Waves," is the most innovative and was written before World War I in the frenzied stimulation of artistic activity in Paris. The other five contain poems inspired by the war and by the poet's love for Lou, Madeleine, and—in the final poem—his future wife, Jacqueline.

Philippe Renaud sees the difference between *Alcools* and "Waves" as one of nature rather than degree. Even the most enigmatic poems of *Alcools* follow a familiar plan, he maintains, whereas in "Waves" the reader is in unfamiliar territory, disoriented in space and time. In "Waves" one feels both the insecurity and the indefiniteness that can only be called modern art. The introductory poem, "Chains," uses the elements recommended by Apollinaire in "The New Spirit and the Poets" yet remains anchored in the past. It leaps from the Tower of Babel to telegraph wires in disconcerting juxtapositions, speaking of humankind's eternal, frustrating quest for unity. In "The Windows," the window opens like an orange on Paris or in the tropics and flies on a rainbow across space and time.

Beginning with "Waves" and throughout *Calligrammes*, Apollinaire uses what he calls ideograms, or picture poems. They are the most attractive pieces in the book, though not necessarily the most original. They became excellent vehicles for the war poems, where brevity and wit are essential. The theme of war dominates the majority of poems in *Calligrammes*. The war excited Apollinaire, promising a new universe. He experienced exhilaration as he saw shells exploding, comparing them in the poem "Merveilles de la guerre" ("Wonders of War") to constellations, women's hair, dancers, and women in childbirth. He saw himself as the poet-hero, the omnipresent seer, the animator of the universe. In "La Tête étoilée" ("The Starry Head"), his wound was a crown of stars on his head.

Apollinaire was as dependent on love as he was on air, and he suffered greatly in the solitary trenches of France. His brief romance with Lou was intense and violent, as his pun on her name in "C'est Lou qu'on la nommait" ("They Called Her Lou") indicates; instead of "Lou," the word *loup* (which sounds the same in French but means "wolf") is used throughout the poem. In his poems to Madeleine, he devours images like a starving man. The anthology ends serenely as he addresses Jacqueline, "la jolie rousse," the woman destined to be his wife, as poetry was destined to be his life. This final poem is also his poetic testament, in which he bequeaths "vast and unknown kingdoms, new fires and the mystery of flowers to anyone willing to pick them."

OTHER MAJOR WORKS

LONG FICTION: *L'Enchanteur pourrissant*, 1909; *Le Poète assassiné*, 1916 (*The Poet Assassinated*, 1923).

SHORT FICTION: *L'Hérésiarque et Cie.*, 1910 (*The Heresiarch and Co.*, 1965).

PLAYS: *Les Mamelles de Tirésias*, pr. 1917 (*The Breasts of Tiresias*, 1961); *Couleur du temps*, pr. 1918; *Casanova*, pb. 1952.

NONFICTION: *Peintres cubistes: Méditations esthétiques*, 1913 (*The Cubist Painters: Aesthetic Meditations*, 1944); *Chroniques d'art, 1902-1918*, 1960 (*Apollinaire on Art: Essays and Reviews, 1902-1918*, 1972).

MISCELLANEOUS: *Œuvres complètes*, 1966 (8 volumes); *Œuvres en prose*, 1977 (Michel Décaudin, editor).

BIBLIOGRAPHY

Adéma, Marcel. *Apollinaire.* Translated by Denise Folliot. New York: Grove Press, 1955. This is the prime source of biographical material, the bible of scholars researching the poet and his epoch.

Bates, Scott. *Guillaume Apollinaire.* Rev. ed. Boston: Twayne, 1989. This book offers detailed erudite analyses of Apollinaire's major works and informed judgments on his place in French literature and in the development of art criticism. It emphasizes the importance to the entire world of Apollinaire's vision of a cultural millennium propelled by science and democracy and implemented by poetry. Included are a chronology, a twenty-six-page glossary of references, notes, and selected bibliographies of both primary and secondary sources.

Bohn, Willard. *The Aesthetics of Visual Poetry: 1914-1928.* New York: Cambridge University Press, 1986. Chapter 3, "Apollinaire's Plastic Imagination," reveals the lyric innovations that Apollinaire brought to visual poetry with *Calligrammes*: new forms, new content, multiple figures in a unified composition, a dual sign system used to express a simultaneity, and a difficulty of reading that mirrors the act of creation. Chapter 4, "Toward a Calligrammar," offers a sophisticated structural and statistical analysis of the calligrammes to demonstrate metonymy as the principal force binding the visual tropes, whereas metaphor and metonymy occur evenly in the verbal arena.

_____. *Apollinaire and the Faceless Man: The Creation and Evolution of a Modern Motif.* Rutherford, N.J.: Fairleigh Dickinson University Press, 1991. Traces the history of Apollinaire's faceless man motif as a symbol of the human condition, from its roots in the poem "Le Musicien de Saint-Mercy" to its dissemination to the arts community through the unproduced pantomime "A quelle heure un train partira-t-il pour Paris?"

_____. *Apollinaire and the International Avant-Garde.* Albany: State University of New York Press, 1997. Chronicles the early artistic and critical reception of Apollinaire in Europe, North America, and Latin America. Especially interesting is the discussion of Argentina, exported through the Ultraism of Jorge Luis Borges, and Apollinaire's place in the revolutionary circles of Mexico.

Cornelius, Nathalie Goodisman. *A Semiotic Analysis of Guillaume Apollinaire's Mythology in "Alcools."* New York: Peter Lang, 1995. Examines Apollinaire's use of linguistic and mythological fragmentation and reordering to mold his material into an entirely new system of signs that both encompasses and surpasses the old. Chapters give close semiotic readings of four poems: "Claire de lune," "Le Brasier," "Nuit rhëane," and "Vendémaine."

Couffignal, Robert. *Apollinaire.* Translated by Eda Mezer Levitine. Tuscaloosa: University of Alabama Press, 1975. This is a searching analysis of some of Apollinaire's best-known works, including "Zone," strictly from the Roman Catholic point of view. It traces his attitude toward religion from his childhood to his death. The book contains a chronology; translations of ten texts, both poems and prose, with the author's comments; a bibliographical note; and an index.

Matthews, Timothy. *Reading Apollinaire: Theories of Poetic Language*. New York: Manchester University Press, 1987. Uses a variety of historical, biographical, and stylistic approaches to offer an accessible point of entry into often difficult texts. Matthews's detailed discussion of *Alcools* focuses heavily on "L'Adieu" and "Automne malade," which allows for a reading that may be transferred to the rest of the book. His chapter "Poetry, Painting, and Theory" offers a solid historical background that leads directly into his examination of *Calligrammes*.

Shattuck, Roger. *The Banquet Years*. Rev. ed. New York: Vintage Books, 1968. In the two long chapters devoted to Apollinaire, "The Impresario of the Avant-garde" and "Painter-Poet," the author gives a year-by-year and at times even a month-by-month account of his life, loves, friends, employment, writings, and speeches. The tone is judicial, the critical judgments fair and balanced. Includes a bibliography and an index.

Steegmuller, Francis. *Apollinaire: Poet Among the Painters*. New York: Farrar, Straus, 1963. This is an exhaustive, extremely well-documented, unbiased, and highly readable biography. Contains a preface, translations, numerous photographs and illustrations, two appendixes, notes, and an index.

Irma M. Kashuba
Updated by David Harrison Horton

LOUIS ARAGON

Born: Paris, France; October 3, 1897
Died: Paris, France; December 24, 1982

PRINCIPAL POETRY
Feu de joie, 1920
Le Mouvement perpétuel, 1925
La Grande Gaîté, 1929
Persécuté persécuteur, 1931
Hourra l'Oural, 1934
Le Crève-coeur, 1941
Brocéliande, 1942
Les Yeux d'Elsa, 1942
En Français dans le texte, 1943
Le Musée grévin, 1943
La Diane française, 1945
Le Nouveau Crève-coeur, 1948
Les Yeux et la mémoire, 1954
Le Roman inachevé, 1956
Elsa, 1959
Les Poètes, 1960
Le Fou d'Elsa, 1963
Les Chambres, 1969
Aux abords de Rome, 1981
Les Adieux, et autres poèmes, 1982

OTHER LITERARY FORMS

Louis Aragon (ah-rah-GAWN) was one of the most prolific French authors of the twentieth century, and although lyric poetry was his first medium, to which he always returned as to a first love, he also produced many novels and volumes of essays. As a young man, he participated in the Surrealist movement, and his works of this period defy classification. In addition to the exercises known as automatic writing, which had a considerable impact on his mature style in both prose and poetry, he wrote a number of Surrealist narratives combining elements of the novel (such as description and dialogue) and the essay. The most important of these, *Le Paysan de Paris* (1926; *Nightwalker*, 1970), is a long meditation on the author's ramblings in his native city and on the "modern sense of the mythic" inspired by its streets, shops, and parks.

In the 1930's, after his espousal of the Communist cause, Aragon began a series of

Louis Aragon
(Library of Congress)

novels under the general title of *Le Monde réel* (1934-1944), which follow the tenets of Socialist Realism. These are historical novels dealing with the corruption of bourgeois society and the rise of Communism. His later novels, however, beginning with *La Semaine sainte* (1958; *Holy Week*, 1961), show greater freedom of form and lack the explicit "message" characteristic of Socialist Realism; these later works incorporate an ongoing meditation on the novel as a literary form and on its relation to history and biography.

An important characteristic of Aragon's style that cuts across all his works of fiction and poetry is the use of spoken language as a model: His sentences reproduce the rhythms of speech, full of parentheses, syntactic breaks, and interjections, and his diction, especially in prose, is heavily interlarded with slang. This trait is true to some extent even of his essays, although the latter tend to be more formal to both diction and rhetorical strategy. His nonfiction works are voluminous, for he was an active journalist for much of his life, producing reviews and essays on politics, literature, and the visual arts for a variety of Surrealist and then Communist publications.

Achievements

Like most writers who have taken strong political stands, Louis Aragon was, during the course of his lifetime, the object of much praise and blame that had little to do with the literary value of his work. This was especially true of his series of novels, *Le Monde réel*, which was hailed by his fellow Communists as a masterpiece and criticized by most non-Communist reviewers as contrived and doctrinaire. He was, with André Breton, one of the leaders of the Surrealist movement; his poetry after the mid-1940's combined elements of Romanticism and modernism, but his style evolved in a direction of its own and cannot be identified with that of any one school.

After his Surrealist period, during which he wrote for an intellectual elite, Aragon sought to make his work accessible to a wider public and often succeeded. The height of his popularity was achieved in the 1940's, when his poems played an important role in the French Resistance: written in traditional meters and using rhyme, so that they might more easily be sung, they became rallying cries for French patriots abroad and in occupied France. (Many of Aragon's poems have, in fact, been set to music by writers of popular songs, including Léo Ferré and George Brassens.) Beginning in the late 1950's, Aragon's work became much less overtly political, which contributed to its acceptance by non-Communist critics. At the time of his death in 1982, Aragon was considered even by his political opponents as a leading man of letters. Writers of lesser stature have been elected to the French Academy, but Aragon never applied for membership, and it is hard to imagine such an ardent advocate of commoners, who used slang liberally in his own work, sitting in judgment on the purity of the French language.

For Aragon, who wrote his first "novel" at age six (and dictated a play to his aunt before he could write), writing was like breathing, a vital activity coextensive with living. He was a novelist whose eye (and ear) for telling detail never dulled, a poet whose lyric gifts did not diminish with age.

Biography

Until late in life, Louis Aragon was reticent about his childhood, and many biographical notices describe it as idyllic; in fact, his family (which consisted of his grandmother, mother, and two aunts) was obsessed with a concern for appearances that caused the boy considerable pain. The illegitimate son of a prominent political figure, Louis Andrieux, who chose the name Aragon for his son and acted as his legal guardian, Aragon was reared as his mother's younger brother, and although as a boy he guessed much of the truth, it was not until his twentieth year that he heard it from his mother (at the insistence of his father, who had previously insisted on her silence). Since his maternal grandfather had also deserted the family, his mother, Marguérite Toucas-Masillon, supported them all as best she could by painting china and running a boardinghouse. According to his biographer, Pierre Daix, the circumstances of Aragon's childhood left him with an instinctive sympathy for outsiders, especially women, and a great longing to be accepted as a full member of a group. This longing was first satisfied by his friendship with André Breton and later by Aragon's adherence to the Communist Party. (Indeed, his deep need to "belong" may help to account for his unswerving loyalty to the party throughout the Stalinist era.)

Breton, whom he met in 1917, introduced Aragon to the circle of poets and artists that was to form the nucleus of the Dadaist and Surrealist movements. Horrified by the carnage of World War I (which Aragon had observed firsthand as a medic), these young people at first embraced the negative impulse of Dada, an absurdist movement founded in Zurich by Tristan Tzara. Their aim was to unmask the moral bankruptcy of the society that had tolerated such a war. Realizing that a philosophy of simple negation was ultimately sterile, Breton and Aragon broke away from the Dadaists and began to pursue the interest in the subconscious, which led them to Surrealism. Through the technique of automatic writing, they tried to suppress the rational faculty, or "censor," which inhibited free expression of subconscious impulses.

Politically, the Surrealists were anarchists, but as they became increasingly convinced that profound social changes were necessary to free the imagination, a number of them, including Aragon, joined the French Communist Party. At about the same time (1928), Aragon met the Russian poet Vladimir Mayakovsky and his sister-in-law, the novelist Elsa Triolet, at the Coupole, a Paris café. As Aragon put it, describing his meeting with Elsa many years later, "We have been together ever since" (literally, "We have not left each other's side"). In Elsa, Aragon found the "woman of the future," who could be her husband's intellectual and social equal while sharing with him a love in which all the couple's aspirations were anchored. Aragon celebrated this love in countless poems spanning forty years; some of the most ecstatic were written when the two were in their sixties. Elsa introduced Aragon to Soviet Russia, which they visited together in the early 1930's; she also took part with him in the French Resistance during World War II, publishing clandestine newspapers and maintaining a network of antifascist intellectuals. Although he followed the "party line" and tried to rationalize the Soviet pact with the Nazis, Aragon was an ardent French patriot; he was decorated for bravery in both world wars and wrote hymns of praise to the French "man (and woman) in the street," who became the heroes of the Resistance.

After the war, Aragon redoubled his activities on behalf of the Communist Party, serving as editor of the Communist newspaper *Ce Soir* and completing his six-volume novel *Les Communistes* (1949-1951). In 1954, he became a permanent member of the Central Committee of the French Communist Party, and in 1957, the Soviet Union awarded him its highest decoration, the Lenin Peace Prize. He was vilified by many of his fellow intellectuals in France for failing to criticize Stalin; not until 1966, during the much-publicized trial of two Soviet writers, Andrei Sinyavsky and Yuli Daniel, did he venture to speak out against the notion that there could be a "criminality of opinion." In 1968, he joined with the French Communist Party as a whole in condemning the Russian invasion of Czechoslovakia. Throughout his life, Aragon continued to produce a steady stream of poetry, fiction, and essays. His wife's death in 1970 was a terrible blow, but he survived it and went on to write several more books in the twelve years that were left to him.

ANALYSIS

Despite the length of Louis Aragon's poetic career and the perceptible evolution of his style in the course of six decades, there is a remarkable unity in the corpus of his poetry. This unity results from stylistic as well as thematic continuities, for even when he turned from free verse to more traditional metric forms, he managed to preserve the fluency of spoken language. In fact, his most highly structured verse has some of the qualities of stream-of-consciousness narrative. There are a variety of reasons for this. Aragon began to write as a very young boy and continued writing, steadily and copiously, throughout his life. As critic Hubert Juin has observed, Aragon never needed to keep a journal or diary because "his work itself was his journal," into which he poured his eager questions and reflections on what most closely concerned him.

This confessional impulse was reinforced and given direction in Aragon's Surrealist period by experiments with automatic writing, a technique adapted for literary use primarily by Breton and Philippe Soupault. By writing quickly without revising and by resisting the impulse to edit or censor the flow of words, the Surrealistis hoped to tap their subconscious minds and so to "save literature from rhetoric" (as Juin puts it). Literature was not all they hoped to save, moreover, for "rhetoric" had poisoned the social and political spheres as well; in liberating the subconscious, Aragon and his friends sought to break old and unjust patterns of thought and life. They also expected this powerful and hitherto untapped source to fuel the human imagination for the work of social renewal. Although Aragon repudiated the Surrealist attitude (which was basically anarchistic) when he embraced Communism as the pattern of the future, he never lost the stylistic freedom that automatic writing had fostered, nor did he become complacent about the "solution" he had found. Like his relationship with his wife, in which his hopes for the future were anchored, Aragon's Communism was a source of pain as well as of fulfillment: the deeper his love and commitment, the greater his vulnerability. Thus, poetry remained for him, as it had been in his youth, a form of questioning in which he explored the world and his relation to it.

There were, nevertheless, perceptible changes in Aragon's style during the course of his career. After the Dadaist and Surrealist periods, when he wrote mainly free verse (although there are metrically regular poems even in his early collections), Aragon turned to more traditional prosody—including rhyme—in the desire to make his verses singable. At the same time, he sought to renew and broaden the range of available rhymes by adopting new definitions of masculine and feminine rhyme based on pronunciation rather than on spelling. He also applied the notion of enjambment to rhyme, allowing not only the last syllable of a line but also the first letter or letters of the following line to count as constituent elements of a rhyme. Partly as a result of the conditions under which they were composed, Aragon's Resistance poems are for the most part short and self-contained, although *Le Musée grévin* (the wax museum) is a single long poem, and the pieces in *Brocéliande* are linked by allusions to the knights of the Arthurian cycle, whom Aragon saw as the symbolic counterparts of the Resistance fighters.

Aragon's postwar collections are more unified, and beginning with *Les Yeux et la mémoire* (eyes and memory), they might almost be described as book-length poems broken into short "chapters" of varying meters. Many of these "chapters," however, can stand alone as finished pieces; good examples are the love lyrics in *Le Fou d'Elsa* (Elsa's madman), some of which have been set to music, like the war poems, and the vignette from *Le Roman inachevé* (the unfinished romance) beginning "Marguerite, Madeleine, et Marie," which describes Aragon's mother and aunts—whom he thought of as his sisters—dressing for a dance. Within his longer sequences, Aragon skillfully uses shifts of meter to signal changes of mood and does not hesitate to lapse into prose when occasion warrants—for example, when, in *Le Roman inachevé*, he is suddenly overwhelmed by the weariness and pain of old age: "The verse breaks in my hands, my old hands, swollen and knotted with veins." Such disclaimers to the contrary, Aragon was never in greater control of his medium than in these poems of his old age, culminating in *Elsa, Le Fou d'Elsa*, and *Les Chambres* (the rooms). *Le Fou d'Elsa* is perhaps his greatest tour de force, a kind of epic (depicting the end of Muslim rule in Spain, with the fall of Granada in 1492) made up of hundreds of lyric pieces, along with some dialogue and prose commentary. As Juin has remarked, Aragon tends to alternate between two tones, the epic and the elegiac, and *Le Fou d'Elsa* is a perfect vehicle for both. The grand scale of the book gives full sweep to Aragon's epic vision of past and future regimes, while the inserted lyrics preserve the reduced scale proper to elegy.

To appreciate the texture of Aragon's poetry—his characteristic interweaving of image and theme, diction and syntax—it is necessary to examine a few of his poems in detail. Choosing one poem from each of the three distinct phases of his career (the Surrealist, Resistance, and postwar periods), all dealing with his central theme, the love of a woman, makes it possible to demonstrate both the continuities and the changes in his poetry during the greater part of his career. All three poems are in his elegiac vein, the mode easiest to examine at close range and the most fertile for Aragon. The occasional false notes in his verse tend to be struck when he assumes the triumphalist pose of the committed Marxist. When he speaks of his wife, his very excesses suggest a shattering sincerity, especially when the subject is separation, age, or death.

"POEM TO SHOUT IN THE RUINS"

"Poème à crier dans les ruines" ("Poem to Shout in the Ruins"), although addressed to a woman, is not addressed to Elsa, whom Aragon had yet to meet when it was written. The poem records the bitterness of an affair that has recently ended and from which the poet seems to have expected more than his lover did. Like most of Aragon's work, the poem is heavily autobiographical; the woman involved was American heir Nancy Cunard, with whom Aragon had lived for about a year, and the allusions to travel throughout the poem recall trips the couple had taken together. Although the poem opens with a passage that might be described as expository, and although it moves from particular details to a general observation and closes with a sort of reprise, it strikes the reader as more loosely organized than it actually is. This impression results from its rhythm being that of association—the train of thought created when a person dwells on a single topic for a sustained period of time. Because the topic is unhappy love and the bitterness of rejection, the process of association takes on an obsessive quality, and although the resulting monologue is ostensibly addressed to the lover, the title suggests that neither she nor anyone else is expected to respond. The overall effect, then, is that of an interior monologue, and its power stems not from any cogency of argument (the "rhetoric" rejected by the Surrealists) but from the cumulative effects of obsessive repetition. Thus, the speaker's memories are evoked in a kind of litany ("I remember your shoulder/ I remember your elbow/ I remember your linen."); later, struck by the realization that memory implies the past tense, he piles up verbs in the *passé simple* (as in "Loved Was Came Caressed"), the tense used for completed action.

The lack of a rhetorical framework in the poem is paralleled by the absence of any central image or images. Although many arresting images appear, they are not linked in any design but remain isolated, reinforcing the sense of meaninglessness that has overwhelmed the speaker. The "little rented cars" and mirrors left unclaimed in a baggage room evoke the traveling the couple did together, which the speaker now sees as aimless. Some of the details given remain opaque because they have a private meaning that is not revealed ("Certain names are charged with a distant thunder"); others seem to be literary allusions, such as Mazeppa's ride (described in a poem by George Gordon, Lord Byron) and the bleeding trees, which to a reader who knows the works of Dante suggest that poet's "wood of the suicides." (Not until many years later did Aragon reveal that he had attempted suicide after the breakup with Cunard.)

The use of such arcane personal and literary allusions was a legacy of the Symbolist movement; as a young man, Aragon admired both Arthur Rimbaud and Stéphane Mallarmé, two of the most gifted Symbolists. The Surrealist approach to imagery evolved directly out of Symbolism in its more extreme forms, such as "Le Bateau ivre" ("The Drunken Boat") of Rimbaud and the *Chants de Maldoror* (1869) of Comte de Lautréamont. Despite its hopelessness, "Poem to Shout in the Ruins" conveys the almost hallucinatory power the Surrealists saw in imagery: its ability to charge ordinary things with mystery by appealing to the buried layers of the subconscious. "Familiar objects one by one were taking on . . . the ghostly look of escaped prisoners. . . ." The poem also suggests, however, that Aragon is not content merely to explore his subconscious; he hungers for a real connection to a real woman. In his desperate desire to prolong the liaison, he tries fitfully to make a "waltz" of the poem and asks the woman to join him, "since *something* must still connect us," in spitting on "what we have loved together." Despite its prevailing tone of negation and despair, the poem anticipates two central themes of Aragon's mature works: the belief that love between man and woman should be infinitely more than a source of casual gratification and the awareness of mortality (which the finality of parting suggests). This awareness is not morbid but tragic—the painful apprehension of death in a man whose loves and hopes were lavished on mortal existence.

"Elsa's Eyes"

"Les Yeux d'Elsa" ("Elsa's Eyes"), the opening poem in the collection of that name, is a good example of the metrically regular pieces Aragon produced in the 1940's (and continued to produce, together with free verse, until the end of his life). It is particularly characteristic in that, while each stanza has internal unity, the stanzas do not follow one another in a strictly necessary order; like those of a folk song or lyrical ballad, they offer a series of related insights or observations without logical or narrative progression. Many of Aragon's mature poems *do* exhibit such a progression (notably "Toi qui es la rose"—"You Who Are the Rose"), but in most cases it is subordinated to the kind of associative rhythm observed in "Poem to Shout in the Ruins."

The imagery of "Elsa's Eyes" is more unified than that of the earlier poem. Taking his wife's eyes as the point of departure, the poet offers a whole array of metaphors for their blueness (sky, ocean, wildflowers), brilliance (lightning, shooting stars), and depth (a well, far countries, and constellations). The last four stanzas are more closely linked than the preceding ones and culminate in an apocalyptic vision of Elsa's eyes surviving the end of the world. The poem as a whole, however, cannot be said to build to this climax; its power stems from the accumulation of images rather than from their arrangement. It should be noted that Aragon's Surrealist formation is still very much in evidence here, not only in the hallucinatory quality of his images but also in their obvious connection with subconscious desires and fears. The occasional obscurities are no longer the result of a deliberate use of private or literary allusions; Aragon was already writing with a wider public in mind. Nevertheless, he continued to evoke his own deepest desires and fears in language whose occasional ambiguity reflects the ambiguity of subconscious impulses.

A relatively new departure for Aragon in this period, the serious use of religious imagery, is reflected in the references to the Three Kings and the Mother of the Seven Sorrows in "Elsa's Eyes." Although reared a Catholic, Aragon became an atheist in his early youth and never professed any religious faith thereafter. During World War II, however, he was impressed by the courage of Christian resisters and acquired a certain respect for the faith that sustained them in the struggle against fascism. For his own part, Aragon began to use the vocabulary of traditional religion to extol his wife. Thus, for example, in "Elsa's Eyes," Elsa is described as the Mother of the Seven Sorrows, an epithet of the Virgin Mary; at the same time, Elsa is assimilated by natural forces and survives the cataclysm of the last stanza like a mysterious deity. This is partly attributable to Aragon's rediscovery, at about this time, of the courtly love tradition in French poetry, in which the lady becomes the immediate object of the knight's worship, whether as a mediatrix (who shows the way to God) or as a substitute for God himself. Repeatedly in Aragon's postwar poetry, Elsa is endowed with godlike qualities, until, in *Le Fou d'Elsa*, a virtual apotheosis takes place: The "holy fool" for whom the book is named (a Muslim, not a Christian) is convicted of heresy for worshiping a woman—Elsa—who will not be born for four centuries.

Whenever he was questioned on the subject, Aragon insisted that his aim was not a deification of Elsa but the replacement of the transcendent God of traditional religions with a "real" object, a woman of flesh and blood who could serve as his partner in building the future. Thus, Elsa's madman tells his judge, "I can say of her what I cannot say of God: She exists, because she *will be*." At the same time, the imagery of "Elsa's Eyes" clearly indicates that on some level there is an impulse of genuine worship, compounded of love, fear, and awe, in the poet's relation to his wife; he turned to the courtly tradition because it struck a deep chord in him. From the very first stanza, Elsa is identified with forces of nature, not all of which are benevolent: "Your eyes are so deep that in stooping to drink/ I saw all suns reflected there/ All desperate men throw themselves there to die." In most of the early stanzas, emphasis is laid on her grief (presumably over the effects of war), which only enhances her beauty, but the insistence on her eyes also suggests that, like God, she is all-seeing. Aragon himself often referred to his wife as his conscience, and Bernard Lecherbonnier has suggested in *Le Cycle d'Elsa* (1974) that the circumstances of Aragon's upbringing created in him, first in regard to his mother and later in regard to his wife, "an obsession with self-justification that permitted the myth of god-as-love to crystallize around the person, and in particular the eyes, of Elsa." Such an attitude is especially suggested by the final images of the poem, that of "Paradise regained and relost a hundred times" and that of Elsa's eyes shining over the sea after the final "shipwreck" of the universe.

"You Who Are the Rose"

An attitude of worship can also be seen in "You Who Are the Rose," from the collection *Elsa*, but it is tempered considerably by the vulnerability of the rose, the central image around which the poem is built. Its tight construction makes this a somewhat uncharacteristic poem for Aragon, yet his technique is still that of association and accumulation rather than logical or rhetorical development. As in "Poem to Shout in the Ruins," short syntactic units give the impression of spoken (indeed, in this poem, almost breathless) language. With an obsessiveness reminiscent of the earlier poem, the speaker worries over the flowering of the rose, which he fears will not bloom "this year" because of frost, drought, or "some subterranean sickness." The poem has a clear dramatic structure: The tension of waiting builds steadily, with periodic breaks or breathing spaces marked by the one-line refrain "*(de) la rose*," until the miraculous flowering takes place and is welcomed with a sort of prayer. The images that accumulate along the way, evoked by the poet in a kind of incantation designed to call forth the rose, are all subordinated to this central image of flowering, yet by their startling juxtaposition and suggestiveness, they clearly reflect Aragon's Surrealist background. Thus, the dormant plant is compared to "a cross contradicting the tomb," while two lines later its roots are "like an insinuating hand beneath the sheets caressing the sleeping thighs of winter." The use of alliteration is excessive—as when six words beginning with *gr-* appear in the space of three lines—and although this serves to emphasize the incantatory quality of the verse, to hostile critics it may look like simple bad taste. Hubert Juin, a friendly critic, freely acknowledges that a certain kind of bad taste is evident in Aragon; he ascribes it to the poet's "epic" orientation, his desire to include as much of the world as possible in his design, which precludes attention to every detail. It seems more to the point to recall that for the Surrealists, editing was a kind of dishonesty; by writing rapidly and not revising, they sought to lay bare what was most deeply buried in their psyches. What often saves Aragon from *préciosité*, or literary affectation, is the realism of this stream-of-consciousness technique. Caught up in the speaker's own anxiety or fantasy, the reader does not stop to criticize the occasional banalities and lapses of taste; he follows in the poet's wake, eager to see where the train of thought will lead.

The poignancy of "You Who Are the Rose," as of so many of Aragon's late poems, stems from the contrast between his exaggerated hopes—still virtually those of a young man—and the fact of old age, which threatens to deprive him of his wife and of his poetic voice. There is also, in some of his later work, a hint of sadness (although never of disillusionment) at the failure of Communism to fulfill its promise within his own lifetime. It is worth noting that in France the rose has long been associated with Socialist ideals; the poet's fear for his wife in "You Who Are the Rose" may be doubled by a tacit fear that the promise of Marxism will not be fulfilled. The two fears are related, moreover, because Aragon saw the harmony between husband and wife as the hope of the future, the cornerstone of a just and happy (Communist) society. His anguish is that of the idealist who rejects the possibility of transcendence: His "divinity" is mortal, like him. This helps to account for the fact that he continued to write with undiminished passion until the very end of his life, for poetry held out the only prospect of immortality in which he believed. The rose is mortal, but she has a name, and the poet can conjure with it (as his conclusion emphasizes: "O rose who are your being and your name"). What is more, Elsa Triolet was herself a writer, and in the preface to an edition combining her own and her husband's fiction, she described their mutually inspired work as the best possible memorial to their love. Aragon will probably be remembered primarily as the poet of Elsa—"Elsa's Madman," perhaps, in his anguished self-disclosure—but above all as Elsa's troubadour, an ecstatic love poet who insists on the possibility of earthly happiness because he has tasted it himself.

OTHER MAJOR WORKS

LONG FICTION: *Anicet: Ou, le panorama*, 1921; *Les Aventures de Télémaque*, 1922 (*The Adventures of Telemachus*, 1988); *Le Paysan de Paris*, 1926 (*Nightwalker*, 1970); *Les Cloches de Bâle*, 1934 (*The Bells of Basel*, 1936); *Le Monde réel*, 1934-1944 (includes *Les Cloches de Bâle*, 1934; *Les Beaux Quartiers*, 1936; *Les Voyageurs de l'impériale*, 1942; and *Aurélien*, 1944); *Les Beaux Quartiers*, 1936 (*Residential Quarter*, 1938); *Les Voyageurs de l'impériale*, 1942 (*The Century Was Young*, 1941); *Aurélien*, 1944 (English translation, 1947); *Les Communistes*, 1949-1951; *La Semaine sainte*, 1958 (*Holy Week*, 1961); *La Mise à mort*, 1965; *Blanche: Ou, L'oubli*, 1967; *Théâtre/roman*, 1974.

SHORT FICTION: *Servitude et grandeur de français*, 1945; *Le Mentir-vrai*, 1981.

NONFICTION: *Le Traité du style*, 1928; *Pour une réalisme socialiste*, 1935; *L'Homme communiste*, 1946, 1953; *Introduction aux littératures soviétiques*, 1956; *J'abats mon jeu*, 1959; *Les Deux Géants: Histoire parallèle des États-Unis et de l'U.R.S.S.*, 1962 (with André Maurois; 5 volumes; partial translation *A History of the U.S.S.R. from Lenin to Khrushchev*, 1964); *Entretiens avec Francis Crémieux*, 1964; *Écrits sur l'art moderne*, 1982.

BIBLIOGRAPHY

Adereth, M. *Aragon: The Resistance Poems*. London: Grant & Cutler, 1985. A brief critical guide to Aragon's poetry.

_____. *Elsa Triolet and Louis Aragon: An Introduction to Their Interwoven Lives and Works*. Lewiston, N.Y.: Edwin Mellen Press, 1994. An introductory biography of Triolet and Aragon and their lives together including critical analysis of their work and a bibliography.

Becker, Lucille Frackman. *Louis Aragon*. New York: Twayne, 1971. An introductory biography of Aragon and critical analysis of selected works. Includes bibliographic references.

Benfey, Christopher, and Karen Remmler, eds. *Artists, Intellectuals, and World War II: The Pontigny Encounters at Mount Holyoke College, 1942-1944*. Amherst: University of Massachusetts Press, 2006. Contains a chapter on Aragon, Gustave Cohen, and the poetry of the Resistance. Provides a general perspective on World War II literature.

Josephson, Hannah, and Malcolm Cowley, eds. *Aragon, Poet of the French Resistance*. New York: Duell, Sloan and Pearce, 1945. A study of Aragon's poetic works produced between 1939 and 1945.

Lillian Doherty

JOHN ASHBERY

Born: Rochester, New York; July 28, 1927

PRINCIPAL POETRY
Turandot, and Other Poems, 1953
Some Trees, 1956
The Tennis Court Oath, 1962
Rivers and Mountains, 1966
Selected Poems, 1967
The Double Dream of Spring, 1970
Three Poems, 1972
Self-Portrait in a Convex Mirror, 1975
Houseboat Days, 1977
As We Know, 1979
Shadow Train, 1981
A Wave, 1984
Selected Poems, 1985
April Galleons, 1987
Flow Chart, 1991
Hotel Lautrémont, 1992
Three Books: Poems, 1993
And the Stars Were Shining, 1994
Can You Hear, Bird: Poems, 1995
The Mooring of Starting Out: The First Five Books of Poetry, 1997
Wakefulness: Poems, 1998
Girls on the Run: A Poem, 1999
Your Name Here, 2000
As Umbrellas Follow Rain, 2002
Chinese Whispers, 2002
Where Shall I Wander, 2005
A Worldly Country: New Poems, 2007
Notes from the Air: Selected Later Poems, 2007
Collected Poems, 1956-1987, 2008
Planisphere: New Poems, 2009

OTHER LITERARY FORMS

Although known mainly as a poet, John Ashbery has produced a number of works in various genres. *A Nest of Ninnies* (1969) is a humorous novel about middle-class American life written by Ashbery in collaboration with James Schuyler. His plays include *The Compromise: Or, Queen of the Carabou* (pr. 1956) and *Three Plays* (1978). He also produced a volume of art criticism, *Reported Sightings: Art Chronicles, 1957-1987* (1989). His Charles Eliot Norton Lectures (given at Harvard University) were collected as *Other Traditions* (2000), an engaging volume of literary criticism about six eccentric poets.

Achievements

John Ashbery won three major literary awards for *Self-Portrait in a Convex Mirror:* the National Book Award in Poetry, the Pulitzer Prize, and the National Book Critics Circle Award. Ashbery is a member of the Academy of Arts and Sciences and the American Academy of Arts and Letters (since 1980) and served as chancellor for the Academy of American Poets (1988-1999). He has been honored with two Guggenheim Fellowships, two Fulbright Fellowships, and two National Endowment for the Arts grants. He won the Yale Series of Younger Poets award (1955) for *Some Trees*, Union League Civic and Arts Poetry Prize (1966), an Award in Literature from the American Academy of Arts and Letters (1969), the Shelley Memorial Award (1973), the Levinson Prize (1977), the Jersome J. Shestack Poetry Award (1983), and the Bollingen Prize from Yale University (1985). In 1982, Ashbery was awarded the Fellowship of the Academy of American Poets. In 1985, he was named a winner of both a MacArthur Prize Fellowship and a Lenore Marshall Poetry Prize. He received the Commonwealth Award in Literature (1986), the Ruth Lilly Poetry Prize (1992), the Frost Medal from the Poetry Society of America (1995), the Gold Medal for Poetry from the American Academy of Arts and Letters (1997), the prestigious Antonio Feltrinelli Prize from the Accademia Nazionale dei Lincei in Rome (1992), the Bingham Poetry Prize (1998), the Wallace Stevens Award (2001), and the Griffin Poetry Prize (2008). In 2002, he was made an officer of the French Legion of Honor by presidential decree.

Biography

Born in Rochester, New York, in 1927, John Lawrence Ashbery grew up in rural Sodus, New York. He attended Deerfield Academy and Harvard University, where he became friends with poet Kenneth Koch. Ashbery received his B.A. from Harvard in 1949 and his M.A. from Columbia University in 1951. After leaving university life, Ashbery worked for various publishers in New York City until he moved to Paris in 1955. He remained in Paris until 1965, writing for the *New York Herald Tribune*, *Art International*, and *Art News*. From 1965 until 1972, Ashbery worked as executive editor for *Art News* in New York, before becoming a distinguished professor of writing at the Brooklyn College campus of the City University of New York. He has also taught at Harvard University. Ashbery became the Charles P. Stevenson, Jr., Professor of Languages and Literature at Bard College in 1990.

Analysis

As a brief review of his biography would suggest, John Ashbery has had a considerable amount of exposure to the world of art and to the language of art criticism. Ashbery spent a full decade of his life in Paris, the art capital of Europe, where he read deeply in French poetry and immersed himself in the day-to-day life of French culture. Readers of Ashbery's poetry, then, should not be surprised to encounter references to art and occasional snatches of the French language as part of the poetic texts. For example, one of his poems is entitled "Le Livre est sur la table." There are other titles in German, Latin, and Russian, and the poetry as a whole bristles with references from every department of highbrow, middlebrow, and lowbrow culture, including cartoons ("Daffy Duck in Hollywood"), silent movies ("The Lonedale Operator"), literature ("Sonnet," "A Long Novel," and "Thirty-seven Haiku"), history ("The Tennis Court Oath"), and linguistics ("The Plural of 'Jack-in-the-Box'").

Because of its unpredictable style and subject matter, Ashbery's poetry has managed to infuriate, befuddle, amuse, delight, and instruct its readers. His work remains some of the most difficult verse produced, for he refuses to provide the reader with a poetic "reality" that is any less complex than the "reality" of the world outside poetry. Ashbery cannot be simplified or paraphrased because his work has no "content" in the ordinary sense. His poetry is "about" the act of knowing, the process of imagining, the curious associational leaps made by the human mind as it experiences any given moment in time. To read Ashbery is to be teased into a whole range of possible meanings without finally settling on a single one. Although this openness might confuse the reader at the outset, the process of reading Ashbery becomes more pleasurable on each encounter. New meanings appear, and Ashbery's voice comes to seem strangely present, as if he were intoning directly into the reader's ear. These poems are filled with little verbal cues and signals aimed directly at the reader; many of the poems depend on a complicated dialogue or interplay between the author and the reader (a technique he exploits masterfully in *Three Poems*). Thus his work is a kind of half-poetry, always requiring an active reader to make it whole. Ashbery achieves his trademark effect of apparent intimacy while simulating the very process of thought itself.

How Ashbery came to create this new kind of poetry is actually a subchapter in the general history of art and culture in the twentieth century. Certainly he benefited mightily from his study of other artists and thinkers. During his formative years in Paris, he absorbed the French language and the famous paintings of the Louvre while immersing himself in all kinds of printed matter: cheap pamphlets and paperback novels bought from the bookstalls, as well as journalistic prose (in French and English) and the rarefied language of art criticism (which he himself was producing).

In addition, it is clear that a strong line of influence connects Ashbery with writers such as Gertrude Stein, who used disjointed syntax and unorthodox grammar as part of her Surrealistic poetry. He owes a clear debt also to Wallace Stevens, who taught him how to philosophize in poetry and also how to approach subjects obliquely. Stevens, also, was a great lover of French Impressionist painting and Symbolist poetry. From W. H. Auden, who chose Ashbery's *Some Trees* for the Yale Series of Younger Poets, Ashbery learned a conversational naturalness and a lyrical or musical way of phrasing. It might be argued that Ashbery, as a literate artist, was influenced by all the great thinkers of the century, but these poetic debts seem particularly obvious, especially in the early books. He probably learned something from Ludwig Wittgenstein's idea of language as a game, just as he must have responded to Jackson Pollock's expressionist paintings, which use paint in much the same way that Ashbery uses words. Something of the sheer shock value and unpredictability of musicians such as Igor Stravinsky, John Cage, and Anton Webern must have touched him also, since Ashbery is clearly fond of similar effects in his own poems.

These debts to the artistic pioneers of the twentieth century are most obvious in Ashbery's earlier books—that is, those preceding the publication of *Three Poems: Some Trees, The Tennis Court Oath*, and *Rivers and Mountains*. All these books are relatively short and compact, typically containing one long or major poem, often positioned near the end of the volume.

Ashbery's characteristic wonder and inventiveness has proven a hallmark of the several volumes published since 1990. During that period, Ashbery wrote and published more and wrote more of the highest quality than at any other time in his career. With Ashbery, there is no limit to the possibilities inherent in human life and to the sheer fun of the mind's response to them. Regular readers of Ashbery will begin to inhabit a world that is larger, more unpredictable, and infinitely more interesting than anything they have known before.

SOME TREES

Typical of Ashbery's early poems are "The Instruction Manual" from *Some Trees* and the title poem from *Rivers and Mountains*, each of which forces the reader to perform another kind of imaginative leaping, one that is different from the mere shock of the surreal. In "The Instruction Manual," the speaker is bored with his job of writing an instruction manual on the uses of a new metal and, instead, falls into a prolonged aesthetic daydream on the city of Guadalajara, Mexico, which he has never visited. He invents this city in magical detail for the rest of the poem. In like manner, the places described on a map and the map itself become utterly indistinguishable in "Rivers and Mountains," as if Ashbery were suggesting that one's most vivid moments are those that have been rescued or resurrected by the fertile powers of the poetic imagination. Ashbery always emphasizes the primacy of the imagination. In his view, the most vivid reality occurs in the poem itself, because that is the precise point where the inner and outer (spiritual and sensory) experiences of life actually intersect.

Two more early poems bear analysis here, because they also illustrate the poetic techniques favored in many of Ashbery's later poems. "Le Livre est sur la table" and "The Picture of Little J. A. in a Prospect of Flowers" (both from *Some Trees*) are magnificent feats of imaginative power, and each operates on the same principle of aesthetic meditation. In each poem, the poet looks at reality through a work of art, or as if it were a work of art (in "The Picture of Little J. A. in a Prospect of Flowers" a photograph is the medium). The effect is largely the same, because the world is always transformed and made into a work of art by the conclusion of the poem. Stevens is probably the model for this kind of poem, exemplified by his "Thirteen Ways of Looking at a Blackbird" and "A Study of Two Pears." Other poets, particularly William Carlos Williams, Marianne Moore, and Elizabeth Bishop, were to involve themselves passionately in the writing of aesthetically oriented poems, and one can look to some of their pioneering work to explain the sureness and control of Ashbery's similar efforts.

In "Le Livre est sur la table," Ashbery offers the reader a number of aesthetic propositions to contemplate, the most important of which is the notion that beauty results from a certain emptiness or from the placement of an object in an unusual or unaccustomed position. In both instances, the viewer is forced to see the object in a new way. Ashbery again underlines the power of the imagination, giving the example of an imaginary woman who comes alive in her stride, her hair, and her breasts as she is imagined. Most important of all is the artist who creates small artistic catalysts, new and strange relationships that haunt the perceiver with their beauty. Neither the sea nor a simple birdhouse can make for innovative art but placing them together in a fundamental relationship changes them forever:

> The young man places a bird-house
> Against the blue sea. He walks away
> And it remains. Now other
> Men appear, but they live in boxes.

The men in the boxes are the nonartists, who do not realize that the newly created sea is a highlighted thing. All along, the sea has been "writing" a message (with its waves and lines), but only the "young man" (the artist) can read it.

The other "young man," or artist figure, in *Some Trees* is Ashbery himself, described in the snapshot that serves as the aesthetic focal point for the autobiographical poem "The Picture of Little J. A. in a Prospect of Flowers." This little fellow has a head like a mushroom and stands comically before a bed of phlox, but he has the makings of a poet precisely because he appreciates the value of words—especially lost words, those tip-of-the-tongue utterances and slips of the tongue, in which the speaker strains to specify clear meaning. "The Picture of Little J. A. in a Prospect of Flowers" is a typical Ashbery performance, not merely because of its high aesthetic theme but also because of its inclusion of low comedy, irony, and parody. The epigraph—taken from Boris Pasternak's autobiography *Okhrannaya gramota* (1931; *Safe Conduct*, 1945 in *The Collected Prose*

Works)—seemingly contradicts the rest of the poem in what is the first of many jokes (Dick and Jane of childhood books become Dick and Genevieve, conversing in complicated Elizabethan sentences). Childhood is full of jokes and embarrassments, like standing in front of the clicking shutter of a camera, but childhood can also be the beginning of the artist's journey: The poem ends by praising the imagination and its ability to rescue this early phase of life through the power of words. "The Picture of Little J. A. in a Prospect of Flowers" is a bittersweet portrait of a self-conscious and precocious young man who was destined to become a great artist.

THE TENNIS COURT OATH

In *The Tennis Court Oath*, the reader encounters the long quasi-epical poem entitled "Europe," a work related in overall form to T. S. Eliot's *The Waste Land* (1922) and to similar efforts by Ezra Pound, Hart Crane, and Williams. In the most general terms, "Europe" here means the accumulated cultural wealth of European history and its ability—or inability—to help the creative artist in the twentieth century. The decay, or "wasteland," of Europe is juxtaposed to or "intercut" (in film terms) with a trivial story of two travelers, Pryor and Collins, whose unheroic status stands in sharp contrast to the old order. As the poem begins, the poet registers all these complex feelings, while focusing on the shocking blueness of the morning sky, here presented surrealistically:

> To employ her
> construction ball
> Morning fed on the
> light blue wood
> of the mouth

The wrecking ball of construction crews is one of the most visible symbols of the typical cityscape, suggesting simultaneously the twin processes of destruction and re-creation. The sudden, destructive impact of the steel ball approximates the elemental power of the morning light as it, too, rearranges and alters the city and all of its facets. The bystander is left openmouthed and speechless, like the sky itself. This analysis does not fully explicate Ashbery's lines, because, like all dream imagery, they resist final explication. One can describe their suggestiveness and allusiveness, but the dream itself remains a mystery, as does this purely perceived moment of an ordinary morning in the city.

THREE POEMS

Some of the poet's greatness is evident on nearly every page of *Three Poems*, the book that many critics cite as Ashbery's masterpiece. The long, meditative work consists of three interlocking prose poems, "The New Spirit," "The System," and "The Recital," and totals 118 densely packed pages of text. Most of that text is written in prose, a highly interactive prose that constantly urges the reader forward, raises questions, voices doubts and suspicions, and generally plunges the reader headlong into a highly meditative process of thinking and reflecting. *Three Poems* is Ashbery at his most difficult and most satisfying, even though there is virtually no story or tidy paraphrase that can be made of the reading experience itself. Nevertheless, a few elusive details do emerge, and one dimly begins to realize that *Three Poems* is an oblique narrative that in general terms charts a deep relationship between two lovers, one that somehow founders, so that the narrator grows more and more self-possessed. The narrator becomes less and less likely to address the familiar "you" who is called upon again and again in the opening pages of the book. By the end, the "you" has virtually disappeared, as if the loss of love might be charted by the absence of the "you" from pages where only the "I" can finally dominate.

The form of *Three Poems* deserves some attention, because the poems are cast in the form of prose, though their imagery, tonal shifts, and complicated rhythms all suggest poetic (not prosaic) form. To complicate matters even further, Ashbery originally published the second section of the work, "The System," in the *Paris Review* in 1971, the year before the whole work appeared in the form of a book. Ashbery specifically allowed "The System" to be published as a prose work, so by titling the whole three-part composition *Three Poems*, he seems to be teasing the reader again on the simplest level and at the same time calling attention to the arbitrariness of literary labels and taxonomy. As if all those complications were not enough, Ashbery carries the joke further by inserting several poems (or at least texts that look like poems) into the longer work. What counts in the end is the sustained act of mediation and empathy with the narrator that these manipulations of typeface and marginal format will induce in the reader.

The reader, facing *Three Poems*, has a Herculean task to perform: absorbing a long, oblique narrative that requires constant reflection, analysis, and thoughtful mediation. The difficulty is an intentional by-product of Ashbery's stated goal on the first page of the book: to leave out as much as possible in order to create a newer and truer form of communication. Any love story the reader could have encountered would have finally become banal; what Ashbery gives, however, cannot grow stale. To read *Three Poems* is to invent on every page the pain and exaltation that make up the essence of a love story. In that way, the "private" person of the book remains mysterious, as all lovers essentially must remain. Thus, one cannot summarize Ashbery's love story, but one can experience it vicariously.

In "The System," the second and most difficult part of the poem, the narrator becomes utterly preoccupied with himself. In "The New Spirit," even small details of urban life were associated with something the beloved had said or done; here, however, the details and the lover have disappeared. Instead, the narrator is trapped in a kind of mental labyrinth, or "system." In one memorable passage, he imagines the members of the human race boarding a train, which is, of course, their whole life. No one has any idea where the train is going or how fast it is moving. The passengers are ignorant of their journey and—the narrator insists—ignorant of their fundamental situation. The very core of their being is ignorance, yet they fail to recognize this crucial fact. Hence, the narrator views them with contempt.

Three Poems concludes on a lighter note, literally on notes of music, which offer a kind of deliverance for the narrator, who has been trapped in the labyrinth of his doleful thoughts. "The Recital" is important because Ashbery often sees music as an analogue to poetry. Indeed, at one point, he had planned to become a musician, and music has remained a rich source of inspiration throughout his career. The power of music and its essential abstractness make a powerful appeal to the narrator, who at this juncture is exhausted by his Hamlet-like speculations. The poem ends, and with it the whole book, with a description of the power of music (and of art)—the power to inspire new beginnings and new possibilities. In a final jest, Ashbery offers the reader an ending that is actually a beginning: "There were new people watching and waiting, conjugating in this way the distance and emptiness, transforming the scarcely noticeable bleakness into something both intimate and noble." With this brilliant virtuoso effect, Ashbery concludes a poem that is at once a continuance of the great Western tradition of meditative writing (one that includes Saint John of the Cross and Sir Thomas Browne)—and a dramatically arresting rendition of how it feels to be alive in the last decades of the twentieth century. The old and the new come together in a synthesis that is as disturbing, fascinating, and elusive as the century that produced it.

Having reached a kind of artistic plateau with *Three Poems*, Ashbery's career took a new direction. In many ways, *Three Poems* occupies the kind of position in his life that *The Waste Land* did for Eliot. Both works explore psychological traumas and deeply sustained anguish; both plumb the depths of despair until a kind of spiritual nadir is reached. After Eliot completed *The Waste Land*, his work took on a new, spiritual dimension, culminating in the complex Christian poem he called *Four Quartets* (1943). Ashbery's work also changed after the publication of *Three Poems*, but he has not embraced Christian or even theistic belief; he has always insisted on a kind of agnostic or even atheistic vision of life, in which art supplants all conventional notions of divinity. Nevertheless, like Eliot, he has passed through the proverbial dark night of the soul, and his work after *Three Poems* is somehow more confident, less self-consciously experimental, and less opaque. The newer poetry is still impossible to paraphrase, but it is much more accessible and more readable (at least on first sight) than the most extravagant of the early poems, and its subject matter generally seems more central to human experience.

SELF-PORTRAIT IN A CONVEX MIRROR

All these tendencies culminate in a book that won the National Book Award, the Pulitzer Prize, and the National Book Critics Circle Award: *Self-Portrait in a Convex Mirror*. Those prizes and the book itself helped put Ashbery on the literary map, so that he could no longer be summarily dismissed as an eccentric aesthete turning out brilliant but inaccessible work. Readers began to look more closely at what Ashbery was saying and to embrace his message (however complex) as never before.

"Self-Portrait in a Convex Mirror," the title poem, is a brilliant piece of autobiographical writing that does not reveal gritty details of Ashbery's personal life so much as his opinions about art and its power to transform the artist. Self-portraits are as old as art itself, but Ashbery as an art critic and former expatriate had encountered some especially powerful examples of the genre. He must have encountered the great self-portraits of Rembrandt van Rijn and Vincent van Gogh, but the particular work that inspired this poem is a famous masterpiece of the High Renaissance, *Self-Portrait in a Convex Mirror* (1524) by Parmigianino (Girolamo Francesco Maria Mazzola), which hangs in the Kunsthistorisches Museum in Vienna. Ashbery tells the reader that he encountered Parmigianino's famous painting in the summer of 1959, during a visit to Vienna. Parmigianino's self-portrait is uniquely circular in overall form and, as the title suggests, resulted from the artist's close inspection of his visage in a convex mirror, an optical device that creates interesting distortions of scale and distance. Parmigianino's hand, for example, is grossly exaggerated and dominates the foreground of the painting, while his head seems undersized and nearly childlike. It is possible that the Italian artist's childlike appearance appealed to Ashbery because it reminded him of the snapshot of little John Ashbery that had inspired his earlier, much shorter autobiographical lyric, "The Picture of Little J. A. in a Prospect of Flowers."

It is in the nature of self-portraits, then, to conceal and reveal simultaneously—hence the appropriateness of the convex mirror, whose powers of transformation and distortion apply equally to Parmigianino and Ashbery. The poet begins the poem by quoting and paying homage to Giorgio Vasari, the first great art critic. (Ashbery too had been an art critic at the time he saw the painting in Venice.) Vasari explains the complicated arrangements that preceded Parmigianino's actual painting: the use of a barber's convex mirror and the necessity of having a carpenter prepare the circular wooden substratum of the painting. These operations are mere preliminaries, however, to the much more important work of the eyes themselves once the painting has been set up. The eyes cannot penetrate the artificial depth created by this strange mirroring device; therefore, everything that results is a kind of speculation—a word that derives from the Latin word for mirror, *speculum*, as Ashbery points out. Thus in the self-portrait one kind of "mirroring" leads to another; what one sees is not precisely what is there. To hold the paradox in the mind is to enter the world of the artist.

The argument that Ashbery then goes on to develop may perhaps be summarized by the adagelike statement that stability (or order) can be maintained in the presence of instability (or chaos). The movements of time, weather, table tennis balls, and tree branches are all potential elements for the synthesizing and harmonizing power of art, no matter if it distorts something in the process. Perhaps the greatest distortion is that of stability; the stable simply cannot be found in nature, as Isaac Newton showed through his laws of thermodynamics. It is only in the mirror of art (a symbol also favored by William Shakespeare) that stability, order, and form may thrive. Since all art is by definition artificial, then, stability also is an artifice.

Nevertheless, artistic stability is all the artist and the race of human beings can rely on to reveal meaning in an otherwise meaningless space. So Parmigianino's Renaissance painting, like all art, is applicable to all future generations, and Ashbery borrows Parmigianino's technique of mirroring until the world seems to spin around him in a merry-go-round of papers, books, windows, trees, photographs, and desks, and "real life" itself becomes a kind of trick painting. Addressing the Italian master, Ashbery admits that the "uniform substance" or order in his life derives from the Italian genius: "My guide in these matters is your self."

He goes on to quote a contemporary art critic, Sydney Freedberg, who finds the idealized beauty and formal feeling of Parmigianino's self-portrait to depend on the very chaos Ashbery had earlier described. For Freedberg this instability is a collection of bizarre, unsettling aspects of reality that somehow the painting enfolds and harmonizes.

Readers might at this point recall similar discussions—though in radically different language—by John Keats, especially in his great meditation on art, "Ode on a Grecian Urn," which asks the reader to accept art precisely because it transforms the chaos and changeability of human life. Ultimately, this process results in a complete fusion of truth (or reality) and beauty (or art), in Keats's formulation. Ashbery is not Keats, but one has to note the similar posture of the two poets, both contemplating the power of art, both commencing with an art object (the Grecian urn and the Italian self-portrait) and concluding on a note of affirmation. For Ashbery, the power of art is not only magnificent but terrifying, like a pistol primed for Russian roulette with only one bullet in the chamber. Art has the potential to "kill" our old perceptions. Some people might consider this power to be only a dream, but for Ashbery the power remains, and art becomes a kind of "waking dream" in the same unhappy world of human beings that Keats evokes in "Ode on a Grecian Urn." Even in the city, which Ashbery imagines as an insect with multifaceted eyes, art somehow survives. He envisions each person as a potential artist holding a symbolic piece of chalk, ready to begin a new self-portrait.

HOUSEBOAT DAYS

Ashbery continues with this more accessible (and essentially more affirmative) kind of poetry in *Houseboat Days*, the title poem of which likens the mind and its vast storehouse of memory to a boardinghouse that is open to everyone, taking in boarders of every possible type and description. This metaphorical way of describing the sensory, intellectual, and imaginative powers of human beings is a valuable clue for understanding another poem in the volume, one of Ashbery's wittiest and most polished performances, "Daffy Duck in Hollywood," a poem that manages to be tender, lyrical, comic, outrageous, and serious without losing its sense of direction.

An obscure opera serves as a kind of grid or structural framework for this rather freewheeling poem. The poem begins with a stupefyingly absurd collection of mental odds and ends, the flotsam and jetsam of a highly cultured and sophisticated mind that also appreciates the artifacts of popular culture: an Italian opera, Rumford's Baking Powder, Speedy Gonzales, Daffy Duck, Elmer Fudd, the Gadsden Purchase, Anaheim(California), pornographic photographs, and the comic-strip character Skeezix. All these apparent irrelevancies are entirely relevant, because they illustrate the random nature of the mind, its identity as a stream of consciousness. However, these items are also a kind of dodge or subterfuge to block out images of a significant other, possibly a lover. Because of the odd way the mind works through the principle of association, however, these same cartoonlike images also remind the narrator of that other person.

As in so many of his other poems, Ashbery is again insisting that the only reality is the one human beings make, and he concludes by wisely noting that no one knows all the dimensions of this mental life or where the parts fit in. The goal, in Ashbery's opinion, is to keep "ambling" on; thus, each person might remain "intrigued" and open to all the extravagant invitations of life. The mind, with its interminable image making, is strangely cut off from life, but when used properly (that is, aesthetically) it can lay hold of the abundant and unanticipated gifts that always surround and endow impoverished human beings.

A WAVE

This optimistic vein is apparent in most of *A Wave* but especially in the title poem, which seems to contrast crests of positive feelings with troughs of despair. The poem is a long discursive work in which Ashbery creates variations on one essential theme: that a fundamental feeling of security (not to be confused with superficial happiness), a deep and abiding sense of the goodness of life, can, in fact, sustain the person through the pain that life inevitably brings. In this poem, human beings do have final control of their destiny because they are supported by something powerfully akin to older notions of grace or faith. Having this power or "balm," as Ashbery terms it, no one is ever really stripped of autonomy: "we cannot be really naked/ Having this explanation."

APRIL GALLEONS

This mood of sustained hope continues in the exquisitely lyrical *April Galleons*, a book that, like *Houseboat Days*, relies on the metaphor of a boat as a vehicle for psychological as well as physical travel. Included is "Ice Storm," a poem that is highly original yet somehow manages to echo Robert Frost (especially "Birches" and "Design"). As Frost did in "Birches," Ashbery describes winter ice in glittering detail. As Frost did in "Design," Ashbery questions the fate of small things that are out of their accustomed places, such as the rose he stumbles on, growing beside a path entirely out of season. However, none of these matters disturbs him fundamentally, because he is beginning to get his "bearings in this gloom and see how [he] could improve on the distraught situation all around me, in the darkness and tarnished earth."

AND THE STARS WERE SHINING

Ashbery's wit and virtuosity are often noted by critics, yet his humanity and intelligence are equally important facets of his work. In *And the Stars Were Shining*, this fact becomes readily apparent when in many of the poems his wisdom of age is blended with a great and tender sadness and bursts of wit and vitality. The title poem harks back to the long poems of another age—Roman numerals mark its sections and its cadences recall a past era—but its direct and relaxed language brings it firmly into the late twentieth century. There are fifty-seven more poems in the volume, displaying Ashbery's characteristic wryness and filled with tragicomic snapshots of our time. The works are also philosophical, as he endeavors to find amusement as well as pain in his autumnal themed poems, including the title poem and "Token Resistance."

YOUR NAME HERE

The title of *Your Name Here* aptly hints at the volume's rambunctious, arbitrary themes and pell-mell performances: Poems include "Frogs and Gospels," "Full Tilt," "Here We Go Looby," "Amnesia Goes to the Ball," and "A Star Belched." While his poetic themes are capricious and whimsical, Ashbery's language is intricate, tightly constructed, rhythmic, and sinuous, with a serious undercurrent of memory, time, loss, angst, and desire. Thus, his tone is at once melancholic and comedic, best demonstrated in "What Is Written."

WHERE SHALL I WANDER

Ashbery is reported to have once said that his ambition was "to produce a poem that the critic cannot even talk about." Most of Ashbery's readers would probably agree that he has satisfied this ambition, although some of the poems in *Where Shall I Wander* are more accessible. For example, "Interesting People of Newfoundland" is quite easy to talk about, with its roll call of characters like Larry, who performed foolishly on street corners, and the Russian who said he was a grand duke—and may have been. Doc Hanks was a good "sawbones" when he was not completely drunk; even half drunk he could perform "decent cranial surgery." Walsh's department store had teas and little cakes and rare sherries from all over. The population was small: "But for all that/ we loved each other and had interesting times." Altogether different in conception, "Novelty Love Trot" is hardly transparent, but it musters some explicable philosophical commentary. The poet's taste in books runs to biographies and cultural studies; in music, he likes Liszt's Consolations, "though I've never been consoled/ by them." In the poet's view, for most people, religion is about going to Hell: "I'm probably the only American/ / who thinks he's going to heaven," but first there is "the steep decline/ into a declivity."

The title of the prose piece "From China to Peru" comes from the first two lines of Samuel Johnson's *The Vanity of Human Wishes* (1749), an imitation of Juvenal's tenth satire: "Let observation with extensive view,/ Survey Mankind, from China to Peru." The vanity of the title stands out clearly in Ashbery's version as the speaker finds himself "taunted" for his dark woolen suit when he arrives at some trivial social occasion where the men appear dressed "to go off on a safari." His only recourse is to the bar, where the "unnerving" events around him make him eager for the cocktail hour. The coherence of this satire then dissolves into a typical Ashbery riff on Japan declaring war on Austro-Hungary and his failure to track down a weather report. "The Red Easel" has a rhymed counterpart in "The Bled Weasel," a *jeu d'esprit* that exemplifies the kind of opaque collection of apparently random lines that frustrates so many readers. No weasel appears in the poem but a caterpillar shows up, "Erect on its parasol," while "Glowworms circulated/ under the trees, confirmed [whatever 'confirmed' means] by whimpering Dobermans." This frivolity collapses, appropriately, in a "crazy quilt of expired pageantry."

A WORLDLY COUNTRY

The title poem of *A Worldly Country*, written in long lines worked into couplets, tells of a city that is riotous by day, with "insane clocks" and "the scent of manure in the municipal parterre." Chickens and geese enjoy the leftover bonbons, but even though "all hell broke loose" in the day, all was calm again by evening. The poet's musings lead him to a moral: "And just as waves are anchored to the bottom of the sea/ we must reach the shallows before God cuts us free." In "Autumn Tea Leaves," it is a partial eclipse that violates the normal day, but the poet cannot discern "what is special about this helix." These phenomena raise questions: What blanket will be sufficient for a freezing night? The dancers who celebrated the celestial occasion revealed "faces/ and senses of humor." However, when it all ended, who knows how many cakes were served, "or leaves collected/ in the hollow of a stump"?

In the fifteen four-line stanzas of "Phantoum," the second line of each stanza is repeated as the first line of the next, with other patterns sneaked in as the stanzas proceed. For example, in stanza 5, the second line, "The auks were squawking, the emus shrieking," becomes line 1 of stanza 6. Little Orphan Annie's adoptive father, Daddy Warbucks, makes a guest appearance in stanza 9 ("Daddy Warbucks was sad, but kept his reasons to himself") with no appreciable gain to the plotless but amiable verses.

A line from Auden's poem "At Last the Secret Is Out" provides the title "The Handshake, the Cough, the Kiss," and it is tempting to interpret the secret as Auden's homosexuality. Even though nothing in the poem speaks directly to a sexual theme, stanza 3 encourages speculation: "We risked it anyway,/ out on the ice where it darkens/ and seems to whisper/ from down below. Watch out, it's the Snow Queen. . . ." The poem then evolves into the poet's reminiscences of childhood in the unnamed "port city of his birth," where he was something of a boy wonder, "the local amateur historian." Rambling thoughts about childhood and the city lead to an apparent climax to the poet's relationship with a coworker in the television industry, a man identified only as "him": "look,/ if that's all you can bring to the table, why are we here?" The speaker concludes his critique by lamenting "an academy/ where losers file past, and the present is unredeemed,/ and all fruits are in season." The poems in this volume show no fading of the wit and bright phrasing of the works first published nearly half a century earlier.

OTHER MAJOR WORKS

LONG FICTION: *A Nest of Ninnies*, 1969 (with James Schuyler).

PLAYS: *Everyman*, pr. 1951; *The Heroes*, pr. 1952; *The Compromise: Or, Queen of the Carabou*, pr. 1956; *The Philosopher*, pb. 1964; *Three Plays*, 1978.

NONFICTION: *The Poetic Medium of W. H. Auden*, 1949 (senior thesis); *Reported Sightings: Art Chronicles, 1957-1987*, 1989; *Other Traditions*, 2000; *John Ashbery in Conversation with Mark Ford*, 2003; *Selected Prose*, 2004.

TRANSLATIONS: *Melville*, 1960 (of Jean-Jacques Mayoux); *Murder in Montarte*, 1960 (of Noel Vixon); *The Deadlier Sex*, 1961 (of Genevieve Manceron); *Alberto Giacometti*, 1962 (of Jacques Dupin); *The Landscape Is Behind the Door*, 1994 (of Pierre Martory); *Giacometti: Three Essays*, 2002 (of Dupin); *The Recitation of Forgetting*, 2003 (of Franck André Jamme).

EDITED TEXT: *Best American Poetry, 1988*, 1988.

BIBLIOGRAPHY

Ashbery, John. "John Ashbery in Conversation with Mark Ford." Interview by Mark Ford. In *Seven American Poets in Conversation: John Ashbery, Donald Hall, Anthony Hecht, Donald Justice, Charles Simic, W. D. Snodgrass, Richard Wilbur*, edited by Peter Dale, Philip Hoy, and J. D. McClatchy. London: Between the Lines, 2008. Ashbery talks about his life and works, including his influences.

_____. "A Kind of Musical Spa." Interview by Craig Burnett. *Frieze* 85 (September, 2004). Ashbery identifies and discusses some of his favorite writers—Ronald Firbank, André Breton, and Frank O'Hara. He praises Guy Maddin's films and says he hated writing art criticism.

Bloom, Harold, ed. *John Ashbery: Comprehensive Research and Study Guide*. Philadelphia: Chelsea House, 2004. Overview of Ashbery's published work, discussing his form, complex linguistics, and vision.

Herd, David. *John Ashbery and American Poetry*. New York: Palgrave, 2000. Herd chronicles Ashbery's poetic career, analyzing his continuities, differences, and improvements over time.

Lehman, David. *The Last Avant-Garde: The Making of the New York School of Poets*. New York: Doubleday, 1998. Chronicle of New York School of poets, closely tracing Ashbery's life and analyzing elements contributing to the backdrop of his poetry.

MacArthur, Marit J. *The American Landscape in the Poetry of Frost, Bishop, and Ashbery: The House Abandoned*. New York: Palgrave Macmillan, 2008. Examines the poetry of Ashbery, Robert Frost, and Elizabeth Bishop, noting that all three had the subject of the abandoned house.

Malinowska, Barbara. *Dynamics of Being, Space, and Time in the Poetry of Czesław Miłosz and John Ashbery*. New York: Peter Lang, 2000. Malinowska provides a challenging discussion of poetic visions of reality in the works of Miłosz and Ashbery. She works with Martin Heidegger's philosophy of phenomenology and applies key Heideggerian terms—Dasein, space, time, and culture—to explore the reality created by or alluded to in their writings. Jargon heavy but useful.

Milne, Ira Mark, ed. *Poetry for Students*. Vol. 28. Detroit: Thomson/Gale Group, 2008. Contains an analysis of Ashbery's "Self-Portrait in a Convex Mirror."

Shoptaw, John. *On the Outside Looking Out: John Ashbery's Poetry*. Cambridge, Mass.: Harvard University Press, 1994. Abundant and detailed information about Ashbery's life, publication history, and manuscripts make the book valuable. It offers an intriguing but perhaps overworked and insufficiently proven argument that Ashbery's elusiveness derives from his homosexuality.

Vendler, Helen. "Toying with Words." Review of *Plainsphere*. *The New York Times Book Review*, December 13, 2009, p. 14. Vendler reviews the collection dedicated to Ashbery's partner, David Kermani. She notes his wordplay and praises his lyric poems.

Vincent, John Emil. *John Ashbery and You: His Later Books*. Athens: University of Georgia Press, 2007. Examines *And the Stars Were Shining*, *Your Name Here*, and other later works by Ashbery.

Daniel L. Guillory; Philip K. Jason; Sarah Hilbert
Updated by Frank Day

TED BERRIGAN

Born: Providence, Rhode Island; November 15, 1934
Died: New York, New York; July 4, 1983

PRINCIPAL POETRY
The Sonnets, 1964, 2000
Living with Chris, 1965 (with Joe Brainard)
Bean Spasms, 1967 (with Ron Padgett)
Many Happy Returns to Dick Gallup, 1967
Doubletalk, 1969 (with Anselm Hollo)
In the Early Morning Rain, 1970
Memorial Day, 1971 (with Anne Waldman)
Train Ride, 1971
Back in Boston Again, 1972 (with Padgett and Tom Clark)
The Drunken Boat, 1974
A Feeling for Leaving, 1975
Red Wagon, 1976
Nothing for You, 1977
So Going Around Cities: New and Selected Poems, 1958-1979, 1980
In a Blue River, 1981
A Certain Slant of Sunlight, 1988 (Alice Notley, editor)
Selected Poems, 1994
Great Stories of the Chair, 1998
The Collected Poems of Ted Berrigan, 2005 (edited by Notley, with Anselm Berrigan and Edmund Berrigan)

OTHER LITERARY FORMS

Ted Berrigan (BEHR-ih-gan) is primarily known as a poet. However, he has edited collections of poetry as well as works about poetry, including a book by underground artist and poet Tom Veitch, *Literary Days: Selected Writings* (1964), which he edited with Ron Padgett. He founded and was the primary editor for the poetry press C Press in New York for several years, publishing collections by such poets as Kenward Elmslie, Dick Gallup, Joe Ceravolo, Michael Brownstein, and his frequent collaborator Padgett. He also served as the organizer of and an instructor for the very successful St. Mark's Poetry Project in New York City.

ACHIEVEMENTS

Ted Berrigan's most famous collection, *The Sonnets*, won the Poetry Foundation Award and placed Berrigan on the literary map of American poetry. In 1967, he won a

Poetry Foundation Grant and a National Anthology of Literature Award for an interview with John Cage. He supported and influenced a number of rising stars of poetry through his work with the C Press and through his work with the St. Mark's Poetry Project. Like such contemporaries as poets Padgett and Frank O'Hara, Berrigan believed in wedding the everyday to the ephemeral, and as an artist, editor, and teacher, he significantly influenced a generation of poets to come. He was awarded a Community Arts Project (CAPS) grant in 1977 for his collection *Nothing for You*. In 1979, he received a National Endowment for the Arts grant.

BIOGRAPHY

Born in Providence, Rhode Island, in 1934, Edmund Joseph Michael Berrigan, Jr., briefly attended Providence College before joining the U.S. Army and serving during the Korean War. Although he never engaged in combat, Berrigan spent three years in the U.S. Army. He subsequently attended the University of Tulsa in Oklahoma, earning a B.A. in 1959 and an M.A. in 1962. In Tulsa, he met young poets and future collaborators Padgett and Joe Brainard, who would be among Berrigan's closest friends for the rest of his life.

In 1960, Berrigan moved to New York to make the connections needed for success in the poetry world. There he met Sandra Alper, also a poet. They married, eventually having two children, David and Kate. The New York City poetry scene in the early 1960's was particularly vital, featuring not only the established poets O'Hara and Kenneth Koch but also younger poets such as Berrigan and his friend Padgett; in all they were part of the New York School of poetry. Although Berrigan may not have been as influential as his friend O'Hara, he was nevertheless essential to the group.

In 1964, Berrigan published *The Sonnets*, which established his reputation and his career. That same year, he began *C* magazine and then C Press, where he published the works of many of his friends as well as those of new poets who shared his sensibilities. In 1966, he helped organize the Poetry Project at St. Mark's Church-in-the-Bowery, where he would teach workshops and support the project for years to come.

Berrigan was a visiting lecturer in the prestigious University of Iowa writing program from 1968 to 1969; he also taught for short periods at a number of colleges, including the University of Michigan, Yale University, Buffalo University, Northeastern Illinois University, and the University of Essex. Berrigan became known as a particularly gifted and insightful teacher and was often sought out for advice. While at Michigan in 1971, he divorced his first wife and married his student, the poet Alice Notley, with whom he would have two sons, Anselm (named for Berrigan's friend, poet Anselm Hollo) and Edmund. Although Berrigan remained prolific throughout his career, his reputation was largely founded on his work during the 1960's and early 1970's. He died of hepatitis in 1983 at the age of forty-eight. His health had been compromised by recurring episodes of methamphetamine abuse.

Analysis

Ted Berrigan was an integral part of the New York School of poetry and the general movement toward expressionism in American poetry. Loosely put, works of literary expressionism focus more on the personal than the abstract and more on the day to day than the political. From an aesthetic point of view, expressionist works tend to follow the free-associative quality of everyday speech rather than the more rigid and uniform rules of more traditional forms. In the 1950's and early 1960's, literary expressionism manifested itself in three primary forms in American literature: the works of the confessional poets (including Robert Lowell, Elizabeth Bishop, and Sylvia Plath), which focused on the personal experience; the literature of the Beat writers (including novelist Jack Kerouac and poet Allen Ginsberg), which emphasized energetic and "spontaneous" creativity in writing; and the works of the New York School, which combined approaches from each of the former schools while generating its own voice. The first poet associated with the New York School was O'Hara, whose literary reputation quickly rose before his untimely death at the age of forty. While showing the influence of O'Hara and other New York School poets in his appreciation of the everyday reality of life, Berrigan also brought to the movement a lyrical sensibility and a wry sense of humor.

In his poetry, Berrigan demonstrated his conversance with a diversity of poetic forms and styles. He composed in free verse with long lines, short lines, and spaced lines; he wrote sonnets and prose poetry. The scattered spacing of his famous early poem "Tambourine Life" (anthologized in *The Young American Poets*, 1968), for example, contributes to the expressionistic, "take life by the horns" attitude of the poem. Additionally, his tendency to be more lyrical and imagistic than other members of the New York School is on display in poems such as "Sonnet LXXIV" (from *The Sonnets*), in which he writes that ". . . The only travelled sea/ that I still dream of/ is a cold black pond, where once/ on a fragrant evening fraught with sadness/ I launched a boat frail as a butterfly."

Despite his departure from the familiar, however, Berrigan is often at his most successful and his most touching when he sticks to the common truths, as shown in his poem "Words for Love" (from *Many Happy Returns to Dick Gallup*), where the speaker states, ". . . If/ I sometimes grow weary, and seem still, nevertheless// my heart still loves, will break." More than any spontaneous or expressionist style, however, the content that informed Berrigan's poetry throughout his entire career largely consisted of the personal and everyday. Such a focus is, in a way, a democratization of poetry: One does not have to have read important philosophy, consider world religions, or participate in armed conflicts to write poems. Berrigan seems to address his focus in poetry in "Around the Fire" (from *So Going Around Cities*), where the speaker claims, ". . . I'm interested in/ anything. Like I could walk out the door right now and go some-/ where else. I don't have any center in that sense. . . ." However, he goes on to say, "My heart and my head feel exactly the same."

Humor is an essential part of Berrigan's oeuvre as well, as shown in "Hearts" (from *Nothing for You*), with its wry sendup of conflicting poetic traditions:

> At last I'm a real poet I've written a
> ballade a sonnet a poem in spontaneous
> prose and even a personal poem   I can use
> punctuation or not and it doesn't even
> matter . . .

Many of Berrigan's greatest strengths are brought together in his elegies, from the everyday listing of the dead in "People Who Died" (from *In the Early Morning Rain*), including his grandfather, father, O'Hara, folksinger Woody Guthrie, Kerouac, and Beat icon Neal Cassady, to the masterful elegy "Frank O'Hara" (from *Red Wagon*), which unites his sense of humor, his lyrical sensibilities, and his personal loss:

> You are dead. And you'll never
> write again about the country, that's true.
> But the people in the sky really love
> to have dinner & take a walk with you.

THE SONNETS

Berrigan's first book published other than through private means, *The Sonnets*, was the one that would cement his career and stay with him for the rest of his life. The poems making up this 1964 collection are each fourteen lines long but eschew other requirements of the form, such as iambic pentameter, formalized rhyme schemes, and a turn (or *volta*), where the theme changes or develops in the latter part of the poem. Furthermore, Berrigan forgoes the traditional focus of sonnets—courtly love—and tackles a variety of subjects. "Sonnet XV" is about Marilyn Monroe's death; others are about writing, friendship, and sex. The humor and expressionism that became Berrigan hallmarks are made manifest in "Sonnet LII," in which the narrator states, "It is a human universe: & I/ is a correspondent. . . ." The personal and emotional appeal of his later poetry is on full display in the sonnets as well, as shown when Berrigan's narrator calls out in "Sonnet XVII," "Dear, be the tree your sleep awaits/ Sensual, solid, still, swaying alone in the wind." Furthermore, although *The Sonnets* are not solely concerned with love, many of them do deal with romantic love, albeit in Berrigan's idiosyncratic way.

PERSONAL POEMS

Berrigan titled a number of his poems "Personal Poems" in the earlier years of his career; many later poems also very clearly detail facts of the narrator's personal life and world. The influence of Berrigan's friend O'Hara seems more prevalent in such poems. "Personal Poem #9" (from *Many Happy Returns to Dick Gallup*), for example, begins, "It's 8:54 a.m. in Brooklyn it's the 26th of July/ and it's probably 8:54 in Manhattan but

I'm/ in Brooklyn   I'm eating English muffins and drinking/ Pepsi . . . ," very much echoing O'Hara's famous "The Day Lady Died," which starts "It is 12:20 in New York a Friday." As his poetry grew and matured, Berrigan avoided the trap of self-indulgence that makes such poetry problematic; instead, the personal nature of his poems makes the poet more accessible and human to the reader. This transformation is manifested in "Ann Arbor Song" (from *In the Early Morning Rain*), a 1969 poem in which a complaint about having to attend a reading becomes an elegy for Kerouac and a contemplation of the nature of loss. "I won't be at this boring poetry reading/ again!" begins the speaker, who then goes on to say, "Anne won't call me here again,/ To tell me that Jack is dead." Despite the speaker's sense of loss—not only of his friend but also of his life at that time in itself—he will not "cry for Jack here again."

OTHER MAJOR WORKS

NONFICTION: *On the Level Everyday: Selected Talks on Poetry and the Art of Living*, 1997 (Joel Lewis, editor).

PLAYS: *Seventeen: Plays*, 1964 (with Ron Padgett).

EDITED TEXTS: *Literary Days: Selected Writings*, 1964 (with Padgett); *Fits of Dawn*, 1965 (with Joseph Ceravolo).

BIBLIOGRAPHY

Berrigan, Ted. *On the Level Everyday: Selected Talks on Poetry and the Art of Living*. Edited by Joel Lewis. Jersey City, N.J.: Talisman House, 1997. A collection of speeches, notes, and commentaries by Berrigan on the craft of poetry and the writing process.

Lopez, Tony. "'Powder on a Little Table': Ted Berrigan's Sonnets and 1960's Poems." *Journal of American Studies* 36, no. 2 (August, 2002): 281-292. A thorough discussion of Berrigan's *The Sonnets* that investigates his technical use of the form as well as his development away from simply writing "personal" poetry.

Padgett, Ron. *Ted: A Personal Memoir of Ted Berrigan*. Great Barrington, Mass.: The Figures Press, 1993. Padgett was a friend and a frequent collaborator with Berrigan; this memoir is particularly insightful into Berrigan's creative process as well as his generosity to fellow poets.

Rifkin, Libbie. "'Worrying About Making It': Ted Berrigan's Social Poetics." *Contemporary Literature* 38, no. 4 (Winter, 1997): 640-671. A long article that examines Berrigan in terms of his influence on other poets, considering his work with *C* magazine and his development of social support groups of poets.

Waldeman, Anne, ed. *Nice to See You: An Homage to Ted Berrigan*. Minneapolis: Coffee House Press, 1991. A collection of letters, memoirs, and journal entries about Berrigan's life and work by such poets and literary lights as Ron Padgett, Clark Coolidge, Tom Clark, and Robert Creeley, as well as by Berrigan himself.

Scott D. Yarbrough

ANDRÉ BRETON

Born: Tinchebray, France; February 19, 1896
Died: Paris, France; September 28, 1966

PRINCIPAL POETRY
Mont de piété, 1919
Clair de terre, 1923
L'Union libre, 1931 (*Free Union*, 1982)
Le Revolver à cheveux blancs, 1932
L'Air de l'eau, 1934
Fata Morgana, 1941 (English translation, 1982)
Pleine marge, 1943
Young Cherry Trees Secured Against Hares, 1946
Ode à Charles Fourier, 1947 (*Ode to Charles Fourier*, 1970)
Poèmes, 1948
Poésie et autre, 1960
Selected Poems, 1969
Poems of André Breton, 1982 (includes *Free Union* and *Fata Morgana*, among other selected poems)

OTHER LITERARY FORMS

André Breton (bruh-TOHN) published many experimental works during his career, some of which were written in collaboration with friends. *Les Champs magnétiques* (1921; *The Magnetic Fields*, 1985), the first Surrealist text to employ the technique of what came to be called automatic writing, was done with Philippe Soupault. *L'Immaculée Conception* (1930; immaculate conception), an attempt to simulate the thought processes of various types of insanity, was written with Paul Éluard. Among the basic Surrealist documents were several works by Breton alone, such as *Poisson soluble* (1924; soluble fish) and *Les Vases communicants* (1932; *Communicating Vessels*, 1990), which mixed lyrical elements with philosophical speculations cast in the form of prose, as well as the numerous polemical manifestos such as *Manifeste du surréalisme* (1924; *Manifesto of Surrealism*, 1969) and *Second Manifeste du surréalisme* (1930; *Second Manifesto of Surrealism*, 1969). Breton's numerous essays were also collected in three volumes: *Les Pas perdus* (1924; the lost steps), *Point du jour* (1934; *Break of Day*, 1999), and *Perspective cavalière* (1970). Convenient selections from Breton's prose in English translation have appeared in *Les Manifestes du surréalisme* (1955; *Manifestoes of Surrealism*, 1969), translated by Richard Seaver and Helen R. Lane, and *What Is Surrealism? Selected Writings* (1978), edited by Franklin Rosemont.

Achievements

Above all, André Breton will be remembered as the founder and leader of the Surrealist movement. Of all the avant-garde movements that rocked the foundations of the arts at the beginning of the twentieth century, Surrealism has had perhaps the greatest and longest-lived impact. Surrealism, created in Paris in 1924 by Breton and a small group of friends, was the last inheritor of a long series of "isms," including Dadaism, German expressionism, French and Spanish cubism, Italian Futurism, and Anglo-American Imagism and Vorticism, which attempted to transform the conception of the world through artistic innovation. Under the leadership of Breton, Surrealism became the most mature expression of this developing sensibility, not only because of its relatively well developed underlying philosophy—which was both far-reaching and systematic in nature—but also because it eventually came to have the greatest international scope of all these movements and because it stimulated the production of a vast body of work of great diversity in all the major artistic genres—poetry, fiction, drama, philosophy, painting, sculpture, and film.

Biography

André Breton was born on February 19, 1896, in Tinchebray, a small inland town in the old French province of Normandy. The family soon moved, however, to the fishing port of Lorient, in Brittany, on the Atlantic coast of France. This seaside environment was particularly important later in the poet's life. When Breton first began to write in 1914, his highly imaginative lyrical poems expressed the wondrous abundance of nature and were often filled with images of sea life and other details evoking the maritime setting of his youth—which contrasted sharply with his life in Paris.

Breton was an only child, and his parents seemingly had an unusually strong influence on his personality. His father, who was a merchant, seems almost a prototype of the complacent, self-satisfied bourgeois that the Surrealists were later to attack as the epitome of the social conformity they rejected. Breton's mother, whom he described as straitlaced, puritanical, and harsh in her response to any suggestion of impropriety, must have also been responsible, to a large degree, for his later hatred of restraint and his provocative attitude toward anything he considered conventional.

Being the only child of a comfortably situated family, Breton had much attention lavished on him, and naturally, his parents had great ambitions for him. He attended school in Paris from 1907 until his graduation in 1912, entering the Sorbonne in 1913 to study medicine. This contact with medicine was also important for the later development of the poet and is reflected in Breton's diverse poetic vocabulary. Even more important, however, was the experience that resulted when Breton was sent to work at the neurological center of the hospital at Nantes during World War I instead of into combat. Breton's experiences as a medical assistant during the war—first at Nantes and later at the psychiatric center at Saint-Dizier, to which he was transferred in 1917—introduced the young, impressionable poet to the bizarre aberrations of mental illness.

During this period, Breton was exposed not only to the diverse forms of mental illness from which the soldiers suffered but also to the theories on which the practical measures used to treat them were based. Among the most important of these theories were those of Jean-Martin Charcot, Sigmund Freud, and Pierre Janet, each of which contributed an important element to the formulation of Breton's view of the operation, structure, and purpose of the human mind. From Charcot's work, Breton learned of the unlocking of the will through the use of hypnosis and saw some of the dramatic cures it was able to effect. From Freud's work, he learned about the existence of the unconscious, its role in determining mental health, and the method of dream interpretation by which one could reveal its secrets to the dreamer. From Janet's work, he learned about the existence of "psychic automatism" and the means by which it might be evoked—which eventually resulted in his own experiments with automatic writing.

These influences were reflected in three important ways in Breton's later work. First, they resulted in the two important prose experiments in automatic writing that he produced: *The Magnetic Fields*, written with Philippe Soupault, and *Poisson soluble*, which Breton created alone. The second product of his wartime experience was the novel *Nadja* (1928; English translation, 1960), which describes the encounter of an autobiographical persona with a mysterious woman who suffers a bizarre and debilitating psychosis. The third product of these influences was *L'Immaculée Conception*, a series of writings undertaken with Paul Éluard, with the purpose of simulating, in verbal form, the thought processes of various types of insanity.

Following the war, Breton came under the influence of Dadaism, which by then had moved its base of operation from Zurich to Paris. The heyday of Dada in Paris was brief, however, lasting from January of 1920 until July of 1923. In the meantime, beginning in May of 1921, Breton and some of his friends were forming a new group whose optimistic attitude toward life, experiments with new methods of literary composition, and increasingly systematic philosophical orientation was in marked contrast to Dada's attitude of nihilistic despair. Breton later called this period the intuitive phase of Surrealism, a phase that extended from May of 1921 until October of 1924, when the first *Manifesto of Surrealism* was published. The publication of this first manifesto established, in an explicit way, a new aesthetic and a profoundly optimistic, imaginative conception of the world which its author, Breton, named Surrealism. The intense period of Surrealist creative activity, which began at that time and continued unabated until the appearance of the *Second Manifesto of Surrealism* in 1930, Breton was later to call the reasoning phase of Surrealism. This period culminated in the appearance of *Communicating Vessels*, a series of lyrical philosophical discourses expressing in mature, fully developed form the central ideas of the Surrealist philosophy and aesthetic.

The period following 1930, the year of the second manifesto, was characterized by two developments. One of these was the Surrealists' increasing involvement with the

Communist International movement. The second development was, in a direct sense, an outgrowth of the first, for it was also during this period that Surrealism was disseminated on a worldwide scale and gained adherents outside Western Europe in many places where it was seen as the artistic concomitant of Marxist revolutionary philosophy. This period, which might be called, with some small injustice, the dogmatic phase of Surrealism, lasted until the outbreak of World War II. In 1941, Breton left France and lived for five years in New York. When he returned to Paris in 1946, Surrealism was effectively dead, although with those few friends of the original group who still remained, and with the growing support of countless other self-acknowledged "Surrealists" in many other countries where their dream had been carried, Breton lived on as the universally acknowledged magus of Surrealism until his death on September 28, 1966, in Paris.

Analysis

André Breton's poetry forms a relatively small though important part of his total literary output, being dwarfed in quantity by his lengthy experiments in prose and his numerous polemical writings. His poetry, from the first published collection, *Mont de piété* (mount of piety), to his last major poetic work, *Ode to Charles Fourier*, shows a remarkable consistency of style. As a poet, Breton is best known for his remarkable imagery—which, at its best, expresses the powerful ability of the imagination to reconcile basic human drives and desires with the material conditions of reality and, at its worst, lapses into bizarre forms of irrationality that are incomprehensible to all but the poet himself.

In general terms, Breton's poetic imagery is characterized by comparisons that yoke together extremely disparate objects; by the sudden, sometimes violent shifting of context as the poet moves from one image to the next; and by an extremely indirect method of expressing comparisons between objects. It is these three qualities, above all, that give his poetic imagery the appearance of being spontaneous rather than deliberate. As critics have shown, however, much to Breton's credit as a poet, this initial impression is a misleading one.

Breton's imagery is reinforced by other prominent aspects of his style, one of which might be called devices of syntactic derangement. These devices range from the use of simple paradoxes involving logical and semantic contradictions, to syntactic ambiguity involving multiple or imprecise grammatical modification, to much more unsettling contradictions of reference—where the referent of a speech act is left unidentified, is deliberately misidentified, or is made ambiguous.

One other important element of Breton's style that helps support the dramatic effect of his poetic images on his readers is his diction, which is characterized by two principal traits. The first of these is the extremely wide range of his vocabulary, which frequently includes the use of words from anatomical, zoological, botanical, and technical contexts that are unfamiliar to most readers of poetry. The second important trait of his diction is the tendency to use words in specialized, atypical ways that emphasize (and often create) their figurative meanings over their denotations. These qualities have two important effects on Breton's work: The first helps make possible his imagery of violent contrasts, and the second is, to a large degree, responsible for the great difficulty his readers and translators encounter searching for paraphrasable or translatable meaning in his work.

Another element of Breton's style is his use of recurring themes and symbolic motifs, such as the revolver as a synecdochic image for rebellion or revolt of any kind. These recurring thematic and symbolic elements in Breton's work can frequently be used as contextual clues for interpreting his most difficult works.

The poetry of Breton expresses three key ideas—the liberating power of the imagination, the transformation of the material world into a utopian state, and the exploration of human potentiality through love—which recur, with increasing elaboration, throughout the course of his work and constitute the essence of his Surrealist vision.

POWER OF IMAGINATION

Breton's faith in the liberating power of the human imagination, although suggested and influenced by his contact with modern psychoanalytic thought, especially that of Freud on the operations of the unconscious, goes far beyond the notion of simply releasing the bound or "repressed" energies that is the therapeutic basis of psychoanalytic practice. For Breton, the unconscious is not an enclosed inner space, or reservoir, of trapped energy; it is, rather, the way out of the everyday world of material reality into the realm of the surreal. According to the Surrealists, this realm—where human reason and imagination no longer struggle against each other but function in harmony—is the ultimate reality, and each person's goal in life is to seek out continually the signs of this reality, which, when directly experienced, is capable of transforming the life of the person. Although Breton envisioned the realm of the surreal as accessible to all men who seek it, it was especially important for the artist, whose goal was to capture the fleeting traces of *le merveilleux* (the marvelous) in his writing.

The Surrealists recommended a number of different methods for attaining this experience. Two, in particular, are frequently used and referred to in Breton's work: the surrendering of the person to the *hasard objectif* ("objective chance") of the universe, and the evocation of the "primary processes" of the unconscious through such procedures as automatic writing. The first of these methods is illustrated well in "Au regard des divinités" ("In the Eyes of the Gods"), one of Breton's early poems from *Clair de terre* (the light of Earth):

> Shortly before midnight near the landing-stage
> If a dishevelled woman follows you, pay no attention.
> It's the blue. You need fear nothing of the blue.

> There'll be a tall blonde vase in a tree.
> The spire of the village of melted colors
> Will be your landmark. Take it easy,
> Remember. The dark geyser that hurls fern-tips
> Towards the sky greet
> Greets you.

This poem reads like, and in fact is intended to be, a set of instructions for encountering the marvelous through the technique of objective chance.

Breton's other primary technique for evoking the marvelous—using the unfettered association of ideas in the unconscious to produce automatic writing —is illustrated by "Au beau demi-jour" ("In the Lovely Half-light"), a poem from *L'Air de l'eau* (air of the water):

> In the lovely half-light of 1934
> The air was a splendid rose the colour of red mullet
> And the forest when I made ready to enter it
> Began with a tree that had cigarette-paper leaves
> For I was waiting for you. . . .

UTOPIAN IDEAL

Breton believed not only in the power of the creative imagination to transform the life of individuals but also in the possibility of transforming society itself into a Socialist utopia, and he came to believe that the Communist International movement was a means to that end. Breton's association with the Communist Party, which began about 1930, was an increasingly divisive force among the French Surrealists. Many who were willing to accept Surrealism's aesthetic and philosophical premises did not believe that this view of life could ever transform the material world of nations and societies. Breton saw this resistance against political involvement as an indication of insufficient commitment, while those who resisted engagement countered by emphasizing the restrictive nature of the Communist Party, its repressive disciplinary practices, and its hostility to artistic activity that did not directly further the interests of the party itself. Regardless of the problems it created for him, Breton never gave up this utopian faith, as the choice of subject for his last major poetic work, *Ode to Charles Fourier*, makes clear.

TRANSFORMATIVE POWER OF LOVE

The third key idea that informs Breton's poetry is one that, like his belief in the liberating power of the imagination, was shared by many of the Surrealists: the belief that romantic love was the means by which humans might establish an enduring link between the mundane world of material reality and the limitless, eternal world of surreality. At times, the mere presence of the beloved is enough to evoke such a response, and some of

Breton's most moving poetry deals with this experience. The idea is expressed in two principal forms in Breton's love poetry. The first is the belief in woman as muse: The beloved becomes the source of contact with the realm of surreality, where, Breton's friend Paul Éluard (the greatest of the Surrealist love poets) wrote, "all transformations are possible." This belief is clearly expressed in two of Breton's best poems: the famous "catalog-poem""Free Union," which celebrates the magical connection between the poet's beloved and the unspoiled world of nature, and"Fata Morgana," which celebrates the ecstatic elation of the poet at the advent of a new love. The second form taken by this belief in the magical power of love is the equation of poetic creation itself with sexual love, as in "Sur la route de San Romano" ("On the Road to San Romano"): "Poetry is made in a bed like love/ Its rumpled sheets are the dawn of things."

It was these three ideas—together with the support of countless writers, scattered across the world, who identified themselves with the Surrealist ideal—that sustained Breton throughout a career that lasted more than fifty years. Although Breton died in 1966, the beliefs that he helped to formulate and that he expressed so brilliantly in his own poetry continue to exist.

OTHER MAJOR WORKS

LONG FICTION: *Nadja*, 1928 (English translation, 1960).

NONFICTION: *Les Champs magnétiques*, 1921 (with Philippe Soupault; *The Magnetic Fields*, 1985); *Manifeste du surréalisme*, 1924 (*Manifesto of Surrealism*, 1969); *Les Pas perdus*, 1924; *Poisson soluble*, 1924; *Légitime Défense*, 1926; *Le Surréalisme et la peinture*, 1928, 1945, 1965; *L'Immaculée Conception*, 1930 (with Paul Éluard); *Second Manifeste du surréalisme*, 1930 (*Second Manifesto of Surrealism*, 1969); *Les Vases communicants*, 1932 (*Communicating Vessels*, 1990); *Point du jour*, 1934 (*Break of Day*, 1999); *Qu'est-ce que le surréalisme?*, 1934 (*What Is Surrealism?*, 1936); *L'Amour fou*, 1937 (*Mad Love*, 1987); *Prolégomènes à un troisième manifeste du surréalisme ou non*, 1942 (*Prolegomena to a Third Surrealist Manifesto or Not*, 1969); *Arcane 17*, 1944 (*Arcanum*, 1994); *Situation du surréalisme entre les deux guerres*, 1945; *Les Manifestes du surréalisme*, 1955 (*Manifestoes of Surrealism*, 1969); *Perspective cavalière*, 1970; *What Is Surrealism? Selected Writings*, 1978.

BIBLIOGRAPHY

Aspley, Keith. *Surrealism: The Road to the Absolute*. 3d ed. Chicago: University of Chicago Press, 1986. Updated with a new introduction. A critical history of Surrealist literature.

Balakian, Anna. *André Breton: Magus of Surrealism*. New York: Oxford University Press, 1971. A biography by an expert in Surrealist art and literature.

Benedikt, Michael. *The Poetry of Surrealism: An Anthology*. Boston: Little, Brown, 1975. With introduction, critical notes, and translations.

Breton, André. *Conversations: The Autobiography of Surrealism*. Translated and with an introduction by Mark Polizzotti. New York: Paragon House, 1993. Collection of interviews with Breton.

Carrouges, Michel. *André Breton and the Basic Concepts of Surrealism*. Tuscaloosa: University of Alabama Press, 1974. Biography and an introduction to Surrealism with bibliographic references.

Caws, Mary Ann. *André Breton*. Rev. ed. New York: Twayne, 1996. Caws provides practical analysis of individual works. The French is ably translated into readable English.

Petterson, James. *Poetry Proscribed: Twentieth-Century (Re)visions of the Trials of Poetry in France*. Lewisburg, Pa.: Bucknell University Press, 2008. Examines the relationship among poetry, politics, and culture in France, with a chapter on Breton.

Polizzotti, Mark. *Revolution of the Mind: The Life of André Breton*. New York: Farrar, Straus and Giroux, 1995. A thorough biography of the artist and poet highlighting his lifelong adherence to Surrealist principles even at the expense of personal relationships. With an extensive bibliography and index.

Steven E. Colburn

PAUL CELAN
Paul Antschel

Born: Czernowitz, Romania (now Chernivtsi, Ukraine); November 23, 1920
Died: Paris, France; April, 1970
Also known as: Paul Ancel

PRINCIPAL POETRY
Der Sand aus den Urnen, 1948
Mohn und Gedächtnis, 1952
Von Schwelle zu Schwelle, 1955
Gedichte: Eine Auswahl, 1959
Sprachgitter, 1959 (*Speech-Grille*, 1971)
Die Niemandsrose, 1963
Gedichte, 1966
Atemwende, 1967 (*Breathturn*, 1995)
Ausgewählte Gedichte: Zwei Reden, 1968
Fadensonnen, 1968 (*Threadsuns*, 2000)
Lichtzwang, 1970 (*Lightduress*, 2005)
Schneepart, 1971 (*Snow Part*, 2007)
Speech-Grille, and Selected Poems, 1971
Nineteen Poems, 1972
Selected Poems, 1972
Gedichte: In zwei Bänden, 1975 (2 volumes)
Zeitgehöft: Späte Gedichte aus dem Nachlass, 1976
Paul Celan: Poems, 1980 (revised as *Poems of Paul Celan*, 1988)
Gedichte, 1938-1944, 1985
Sixty-five Poems, 1985
Last Poems, 1986
Das Frühwerk, 1989
Gesammelte Werke in sieben Bänden, 2000 (7 volumes)
Glottal Stop: 101 Poems, 2000

OTHER LITERARY FORMS

The literary reputation of Paul Celan (TSEHL-on) rests exclusively on his poetry. His only piece of prose fiction, if indeed it can be so described, is "Gespräch im Gebirg" (1959), a very short autobiographical story with a religious theme. Celan also wrote an introductory essay for a book containing works by the painter Edgar Jené; this essay, entitled *Edgar Jené und der Traum vom Traume,* (1948; *Edgar Jené and the Dream About the Dream*, 1986), is an important early statement of Celan's aesthetic theory. Another, more oblique, statement of Celan's poetic theory is contained in his famous speech, "Der Meridian" (1960), given on his acceptance of the prestigious Georg Büchner Prize. (An English translation of this speech, "The Meridian," was published in the Winter, 1978, issue of *Chicago Review*.)

Achievements

Paul Celan is considered an "inaccessible" poet by many critics and readers. This judgment, prompted by the difficulties Celan's poetry poses for would-be interpreters seeking traditional exegesis, is reinforced by the fact that Celan occupies an isolated position in modern German poetry. Sometimes aligned with Nelly Sachs, Ernst Meister, and the German Surrealists, Celan's work nevertheless stands apart from that of his contemporaries. A Jew whose outlook was shaped by his early experiences in Nazi-occupied Romania, Celan grew up virtually trilingual. The horror of his realization that he was, in spite of his childhood experiences and his later residence in France, a German poet was surely responsible in part for his almost obsessive concern with the possibilities and the limits of his poetic language. Celan's literary ancestors are Friedrich Hölderlin, Arthur Rimbaud, Stéphane Mallarmé, Rainer Maria Rilke, and the German expressionists, but even in his early poems his position as an outsider is manifest. Celan's poems, called Hermetic by some critics because of their resistance to traditional interpretation, can be viewed sometimes as intense and cryptic accounts of personal experience, sometimes as religious-philosophical discussions of Judaism, its tradition and its relation to Christianity. Many of his poems concern themselves with linguistic and poetic theory to the point where they cease to be poems in the traditional sense, losing all contact with the world of physical phenomena and turning into pure language, existing only for themselves. Such "pure" poems, increasingly frequent in Celan's later works, are largely responsible for the charge of inaccessibility that has been laid against him. Here the reader is faced with having to leave the dimension of conventional language use, where the poet uses language to communicate with his audience about subjects such as death or nature, and is forced to enter the dimension of metalanguage, as Harald Weinrich calls it, where language is used to discuss only language—that is, the *word* "death," and not death itself. Such poems are accessible only to readers who share with the poet the basic premises of an essentially linguistic poetic theory.

In spite of all this, much of Celan's poetry can be made accessible to the reader through focus on the personal elements in some poems, the Judaic themes in others, and by pointing out the biblical and literary references in yet another group.

Biography

Paul Celan was born Paul Ancel, or Antschel, the only child of Jewish parents, in Czernowitz, Romania (now Chernivtsi, Ukraine), in Bukovina, situated in the foothills of the Carpathian Mountains. This region had been under Austrian rule and thus contained a sizable German-speaking minority along with a mix of other nationalities and ethnic groups. In 1918, just two years before Celan's birth, following the collapse of the Austro-Hungarian Empire, Bukovina became part of Romania. Thus, Celan was reared in a region of great cultural and linguistic diversity, the tensions of which energized his poetry.

Little is known of Celan's early childhood, but he appears to have had a very close relationship with his mother and a less satisfying relationship with his father. Positive references to his mother abound in his poems, whereas his father is hardly mentioned. After receiving his high school diploma, the young Celan went to study medicine in France in 1938, but the war forced his return in the following year to Czernowitz, where he turned to the study of Romance languages and literature at the local university. In 1940, his hometown was annexed by the Soviet Union but was soon occupied by the Germans and their allies, who began to persecute and deport the Jewish population. Celan's parents were taken to a concentration camp, where they both died, while the young man remained hidden for some time and finally ended up in a forced-labor camp. These events left a permanent scar on Celan's memory, and it appears that he had strong feelings of guilt for having survived when his parents and so many of his friends and relatives were murdered. After Soviet troops reoccupied his hometown, he returned there for a short time and then moved to Bucharest, where he found work as an editor and a translator. In 1947, his first poems were published in a Romanian journal under the anagrammatic pen name Paul Celan. In the same year, he moved to Vienna, where he remained until 1948, when his first collection of poetry, *Der Sand aus den Urnen*, was published.

After moving to Paris in the same year, Celan began to frequent avant-garde circles and was received particularly well by the poet Yvan Goll and his wife. Unfortunately, this friendship soured after Goll's death in 1950, when Goll's wife, Claire, apparently jealous of Celan's growing reputation as a poet, accused him of having plagiarized from her husband. A bitter feud resulted, with many of the leading poets and critics in France and Germany taking sides. During this period, Celan also began his work as a literary translator, which was to be a major source of both income and poetic inspiration for the rest of his life. He translated from the French—notably the writings of Rimbaud, Paul Valéry, and Guillaume Apollinaire—as well as the poetry of William Shakespeare, Emily Dickinson, and Marianne Moore from the English and the works of Aleksandr Blok, Sergei Esenin, and Osip Mandelstam from the Russian.

In the following years, Celan married a French graphic artist, Gisèle Lestrange, and published his second volume of poetry, *Mohn und Gedächtnis* (poppy and memory), containing many poems from his first collection, *Der Sand aus den Urnen*, which he had withdrawn from circulation because of the large number of printing mistakes and editorial inaccuracies it contained. *Mohn und Gedächtnis* established his reputation as a poet, and most of his subsequent collections were awarded prestigious literary prizes.

Celan remained in Paris for the rest of his life, infrequently traveling to Germany. During his later years, he appears to have undergone many crises both in his personal and in his creative life (his feud with Claire Goll is only one such incident), and his friends agree that he became quarrelsome and felt persecuted by neo-Nazis, hostile publishers, and critics. His death in April of 1970, apparently by suicide—he drowned in the Seine—was the consequence of his having arrived, in his own judgment, at a personal and artistic dead end, although many critics have seen in his collections *Lightduress*, *Snow Part*, and *Zeitgehöft*, published post humously, the potential beginning of a new creative period.

Analysis

Paul Celan's poetry can be viewed as an expressive attempt to cope with the past—his personal past as well as that of the Jewish people. Close friends of the poet state that Celan was unable to forget anything and that trivial incidents and cataclysmic events of the past for him had the same order of importance. Many of his poems contain references to the death camps, to his dead parents (particularly his mother), and to his changing attitude toward the Jewish religion and toward God. In his early collections, these themes are shaped into traditional poetic form—long, often rhymed lines, genitive metaphors, sensuous images—and the individual poems are accessible to conventional methods of interpretation. In his later collections, Celan employs increasingly sparse poetic means, such as one-word lines, neologisms, and images that resist traditional interpretive sense; their significance can often be intuited only by considering Celan's complete poetic opus, a fact that has persuaded many critics and readers that Celan's poems are nonsense, pure games with language rather than codified expressions of thoughts and feelings that can be deciphered by applying the appropriate key.

Mohn und Gedächtnis

Mohn und Gedächtnis, Celan's first collection of poetry (discounting the withdrawn *Der Sand aus den Urnen*), was in many ways an attempt to break with the past. The title of the collection is an indication of the dominant theme of these poems, which stress the dichotomy of forgetting—one of the symbolic connotations of the poppy flower—and remembering, by which Celan expresses his wish to forget the past, both his own personal past and that of the Jewish race, and his painful inability to erase these experiences from his memory. Living in Paris, Celan believed that only by forgetting could he begin a new life—in a new country, with a non-Jewish French wife, and by a rejection of his past poetic efforts, as indicated by the withdrawal of his first collection.

Mohn und Gedächtnis is divided into four parts and contains a total of fifty-six poems. In the first part, "Der Sand aus den Urnen" ("Sand from the Urns"), Celan establishes the central theme of the collection: The poet "fills the urns of the past in the moldy-green house of oblivion" and is reminded by the white foliage of an aspen tree that his mother's hair was not allowed to turn white. Mixed with these reflections on personal losses are memories of sorrows and defeats inflicted on the Jewish people; references to the conquest of Judea by the Romans are meant to remind the reader of more recent atrocities committed by foreign conquerors.

The second part of *Mohn und Gedächtnis* is a single poem, "Todesfuge" ("Death Fugue"), Celan's most widely anthologized poem, responsible in no small part for establishing his reputation as one of the leading contemporary German poets. "Death Fugue" is a monologue by the victims of a concentration camp, evoking in vivid images the various atrocities associated with these camps. From the opening line, "Black milk of daybreak we drink it at sundown . . ."—one of the lines that Claire Goll suggested Celan had plagiarized from her husband—the poem passes on to descriptions of the cruel camp commander who plays with serpent-like whips, makes the inmates shovel their own graves, and sets his pack of dogs on them. From the resignation of the first lines, the poem builds to an emotional climax in the last stanza in which the horror of the cremation chambers is indicated by images such as "he grants us a grave in the air" and "death is a master from Germany." Although most critics have praised the poem, some have condemned Celan for what they interpret as an attempt at reconciliation between Germans and Jews in the last two lines of the poem. Others, however, notably Theodor Adorno, have attacked "Death Fuge" on the basis that it is "barbaric" to write beautiful poetry after, and particularly about, Auschwitz. A close reading of this long poem refutes the notion that Celan was inclined toward reconciliation with the Germans—his later work bears this out—and it is hard to imagine that any reader should feel anything but horror and pity for the anonymous speakers of the poem. The beautifully phrased images serve to increase the intensity of this horror rather than attempting to gloss it over. "Death Fugue" is both a great poem and one of the most impressive and lasting documents of the plight of the Jews.

"Auf Reisen" ("Travel"), the first poem of the third part of the collection, again indicates Celan's wish to leave the past behind and to start all over again in his "house in Paris." In other poems he makes reference to his wife, asking to be forgiven for having broken with his heritage and married a Gentile. As the title of the collection suggests, the poppy of oblivion is not strong enough to erase the memory of his dead mother, of his personal past, and of his racial heritage. In poems such as "Der Reisekamerad" ("The Traveling Companion") and "Zähle die Mandeln" ("Count the Almonds"), the optimistic view of "Travel" is retracted; in the former, the dead mother is evoked as the poet's constant travel companion, while in the latter, he acknowledges that he must always be counted among the "almonds." The almonds (*Mandeln*) represent the Jewish people and are an indirect reference also to the Russian Jewish poet Osip Mandelstam, whose work Celan had translated. The irreconcilable tension between the wish to forget and the inability to do so completely is further shown in "Corona," a poem referring to Rainer

Maria Rilke's "Herbsttag" ("Autumn Day"). Whereas the speaker of Rilke's poem resigns himself to the approaching hardships of winter, Celan converts Rilke's "Lord: it is time" into the rebellious "it is time that the stone condescended to bloom."

The poems in *Mohn und Gedächtnis* are not, for the most part, innovative in form or imagery, although the long dactylic lines and the flowery images of the first half begin to give way to greater economy of scope and metaphor in the later poems. There is a constant dialogue with a fictional "you" and repeated references to "night," "dream," "sleep," "wine," and "time," in keeping with the central theme of these poems. Celan's next collections show his continued attempts to break with the past, to move his life and his poetry to new levels.

VON SCHWELLE ZU SCHWELLE

In *Von Schwelle zu Schwelle* (threshold to threshold), Celan abandoned his frequent references to the past; it is as if the poet—as the title, taken from a poem in *Mohn und Gedächtnis*, suggests—intended to cross over a threshold into a new realm. Images referring to his mother, to the persecution of the Jews, to his personal attitude toward God, and to his Jewish heritage are less frequent in this volume. Many German critics, reluctant to concentrate on Celan's treatment of the Holocaust, have remarked with some relief his turning away from this subject toward the problem of creativity, the possibilities of communication, and the limits of language. Indeed, if one follows most German critics, *Von Schwelle zu Schwelle* was the first step in the poet's development toward "metapoetry"—that is, poetry that no longer deals with traditional *materia poetica* but only with poetry itself. This new direction is demonstrated by the preponderance of terms such as "word" and "stone" (a symbol of speechlessness), replacing "dream," "autumn," and "time." For Celan, *Von Schwelle zu Schwelle* constituted a more radical attempt to start anew by no longer writing about—therefore no longer having to think about—experiences and memories that he had been unable to come to grips with in his earlier poems.

SPEECH-GRILLE

Speech-Grille is, as the title suggests, predominantly concerned with language. The thirty-three poems in this volume are among Celan's finest, as the enthusiastic critical reception confirmed. They are characterized by a remarkable discipline of expression, leading in many cases to a reduction of poetry to the bare essentials. Indeed, it is possible to see these poems as leading in the direction of complete silence. "Engführung" ("Stretto"), perhaps the finest poem in the collection and one of Celan's best, exemplifies this tendency even by its title, which is taken from musical theory and refers to the final section of a fugue. A long poem that alludes to "Death Fugue," it is stripped of the descriptive metaphors that characterized that masterpiece, such as the "grave in the air" and "the black milk of daybreak"; instead, experience is reduced to lines such as "Came,

came./ Came a word, came/ came through the night,/ wanted to shine, wanted to shine/ Ash./ Ash, ash./ Night."

DIE NIEMANDSROSE

Celan's attempt to leave the past behind in *Speech-Grille* was not completely successful; on the contrary, several poems in this collection express sorrow at the poet's detachment from his Jewish past and from his religion. It is therefore not surprising that Celan's next collection, *Die Niemandsrose* (the no-one's rose), was dedicated to Mandelstam, a victim of Joseph Stalin's persecutions in the 1930's. One of the first poems in this collection makes mention of the victims of the concentration camps: "There was earth inside them, and/they dug." Rather than concentrating on the horrors of camp existence, the poem discusses the possibility of believing in an omnipotent, benevolent God in the face of these atrocities; this theme is picked up again in "Zürich, zum Storchen" ("Zurich, the Stork Inn"), in which Celan reports on his meeting with the Jewish poet Nelly Sachs: "the talk was of your God, I spoke/ against him." Other poems contain references to his earlier work; the "house in Paris" is mentioned again, and autumn imagery, suggesting the memory of his mother, is used more frequently. Several other poems express Celan's renewed and final acceptance of his Jewish heritage but indicate his rejection of God, culminating in the blasphemous "Psalm," with its bitter tribute: "Praised be your name, no one."

LATER YEARS

Celan's poetry after *Die Niemandsrose* became almost inaccessible to the average reader. As the title *Breathturn* indicates, Celan wanted to go in entirely new directions. Most of the poems in Celan's last collections are very short; references to language and writing become more frequent, and striking, often grotesque, portmanteau words and other neologisms mix with images from his earlier poems. There are still references to Judaism, to an absent or cruel God, and—in a cryptic form—to personal experiences. In the posthumously published *Snow Part*, the reader can even detect allusions to the turbulent political events of 1968. The dominant feature of these last poems, however, is the almost obsessive attempt to make the language of poetry perform new, hitherto unimagined feats, to coerce words to yield truth that traditional poetic diction could not previously force through its "speech-grille." It appears that Celan finally despaired of ever being able to reach this new poetic dimension. The tone of his last poems was increasingly pessimistic, and his hopes, expressed in earlier poems, of finding "that ounce of truth deep inside delusion," gave way to silence in the face of the "obstructive tomorrow." It is the evidence of these last poems, more than any police reports, which make it a certainty that his drowning in the Seine in 1970 was not simply the result of an accident.

Celan's poetry can be understood only by grasping his existential dilemma after

World War II as a Jewish poet who had to create his poetry in the German language. Desperate to leave behind everything which would remind him of his own and his people's plight, he nevertheless discovered that the very use of the German language inevitably led him back to his past and made a new beginning impossible. Finally, the only escape he saw still open to him was to attempt to abandon completely the conventions of German lyric poetry and its language, to try to make his poetry express his innermost feelings and convictions without having to resort to traditional poetic diction and form. Weinrich suggests that Celan, like Mallarmé before him, was searching for the "absolute poem," a poem that the poet creates only as a rough sketch and that the reader then completes, using private experiences and ideas, possibly remembered pieces of other poems. If this is true, Celan must have ultimately considered his efforts a failure, both in terms of his poetic intentions and in his desire to come to terms with his personal and his Jewish past.

OTHER MAJOR WORKS

SHORT FICTION: "Gespräch im Gebirg," 1959.

NONFICTION: *Edgar Jené und der Traum vom Traume*, 1948 (*Edgar Jené and the Dream About the Dream*, 1986); *Collected Prose*, 1986.

TRANSLATIONS: *Der goldene Vorhang*, 1949 (of Jean Cocteau); *Bateau ivre/Das trunkene Schiff*, 1958 (of Arthur Rimbaud); *Gedichte*, 1959 (of Osip Mandelstam); *Die junge Parzel/La jeune Parque*, 1964 (of Paul Valéry); *Einundzwanzig Sonette*, 1967 (of William Shakespeare).

MISCELLANEOUS: *Prose Writings and Selected Poems*, 1977; *Selected Poems and Prose of Paul Celan*, 2001.

BIBLIOGRAPHY

Baer, Ulrich. *Remnants of Song: Trauma and the Experience of Modernity in Charles Baudelaire and Paul Celan*. Stanford, Calif.: Stanford University Press, 2000. Baer sees a basis for comparison of the nineteenth and the twentieth century poets. Bibliographical references, index.

Bernstein, Michael André. *Five Portraits: Modernity and the Imagination in Twentieth-Century German Writing*. Evanston, Ill.: Northwestern University Press, 2000. Compared with Celan are four other German poets and philosophers: Rainer Maria Rilke, Robert Musil, Martin Heidegger, and Walter Benjamin. Includes bibliographical references, index.

Chalfen, Israel. *Paul Celan*. New York: Persea Books, 1991. A biography of Celan's youth and early career. Includes bibliographical references.

Colin, Amy D. *Paul Celan: Holograms of Darkness*. Bloomington: Indiana University Press, 1991. An overview of Celan's cultural background as well as postmodernist textual analysis.

Del Caro, Adrian. *The Early Poetry of Paul Celan: In the Beginning Was the Word.* Baton Rouge: Louisiana State University Press, 1997. A detailed treatment of the early volumes *Mohn und Gedächtnis* (1952) and *Von Schwelle zu Schwelle* (1955).

Felstiner, John. *Paul Celan: Poet, Survivor, Jew.* 1995. Reprint. New Haven, Conn.: Yale University Press, 2001. Illuminates the rich biographical meaning behind much of Celan's spare, enigmatic verse. Includes bibliographical references, illustrations, map, index.

Hillard, Derek. *Poetry as Individuality: The Discourse of Observation in Paul Celan.* Lewisburg, Pa.: Bucknell University Press, 2009. An examination of individuality in the writings of Celan. Touches on philosophy and the psychology of knowledge.

Rosenthal, Bianca. *Pathways to Paul Celan.* New York: Peter Lang, 1995. An overview of the varied and often contradictory critical responses to the poet. Illustrated; includes bibliographical references, index.

Tobias, Rochelle. *The Discourse of Nature in the Poetry of Paul Celan: The Unnatural World.* Baltimore: The Johns Hopkins University Press, 2006. Provides critical analysis of Celan's poetry in terms of its relationship to the natural world.

Wolosky, Shira. *Language and Mysticism: The Negative Way of Language in Eliot, Beckett, and Celan.* Stanford, Calif.: Stanford University Press, 1995. A useful comparative study that helps to place Celan in context. Bibliographical references, index.

Franz G. Blaha

JEAN COCTEAU

Born: Maisons-Laffitte, France; July 5, 1889
Died: Milly-la-Forêt, France; October 11, 1963

PRINCIPAL POETRY
La Lampe d'Aladin, 1909
Le Prince frivole, 1910
La Danse de Sophocle, 1912
Le Cap de Bonne-Espérance, 1919
L'Ode à Picasso, 1919
Escales, 1920
Poésies, 1917-1920, 1920
Discours du grand sommeil, 1922
Vocabulaire, 1922
Plain-Chant, 1923
Poésie, 1916-1923, 1924
L'Ange Heurtebise, 1925
Cri écrit, 1925
Prière mutilée, 1925
Opéra, 1927
Morceaux choisis, 1932
Mythologie, 1934
Allégories, 1941
Léone, 1945
Poèmes, 1945
La Crucifixion, 1946
Anthologie poétique, 1951
Le Chiffre sept, 1952
Appogiatures, 1953
Clair-obscur, 1954
Poèmes, 1916-1955, 1956
Gondole des morts, 1959
Cérémonial espagnol du phénix, 1961
Le Requiem, 1962

OTHER LITERARY FORMS

Jean Cocteau (kawk-TOH) was a formidable artist in many genres and very prolific. Among his seven novels, little read today, the most important is *Les Enfants terribles*

Jean Cocteau
(National Archives)

(1929; *Enfants Terribles*, 1930, also known as *Children of the Game*). Among his many plays, some of the most notable are *Orphée* (pr. 1926; *Orpheus*, 1933), *La Voix humaine* (pr., pb. 1930; *The Human Voice*, 1951), *La Machine infernale* (pr., pb. 1934; *The Infernal Machine*, 1936), *Les Parents terribles* (pr., pb. 1938; *Intimate Relations*, 1952), and *La Machine à écrire* (pr., pb. 1941; *The Typewriter*, 1948). In the opinion of many critics, Cocteau's greatest achievements were in the cinema. His masterpieces—which he both wrote and directed—include *Le Sang d'un poète* (1930; *The Blood of a Poet*, 1949), *La Belle et la bête* (1946; *Beauty and the Beast*, 1947), *Les Parents terribles* (1948; *Intimate Relations*, 1952), *Les Enfants terribles* (1950), *Orphée* (1950; *Orpheus*, 1950), and *La Testament d'Orphée* (1959; *The Testament of Orpheus*, 1968). Cocteau also wrote scenarios for ballets by various composers, notably for Erik Satie's *Parade* (1917), for Darius Milhaud's *Le Boeuf sur le toit* (1920), and for *Les Mariés de la tour Eiffel* (1921; *The Wedding on the Eiffel Tower*, 1937), which had music by Les Six. Cocteau also collaborated on two opera-oratorios, *Odipus-Rex* (1927) with Igor Stravinsky, and *Antigone* (1922; English translation, 1961) with Arthur Honegger. Cocteau's nonfiction includes a variety of idiosyncratic autobiographical and critical works.

Achievements

Jean Cocteau was one of the most remarkable figures in twentieth century art. Extremely versatile, he unified his diverse interests by seeing them as merely different aspects of *poésie: poésie de roman* (poetry of the novel), *poésie de théâtre* (poetry of the drama), *poésie cinématographique* (poetry of the film), and even *poésie graphique* (poetry of drawing). Curiously, with poetry as the metaphorical center of Cocteau's artistic achievement, critics are still uncomfortable with his accomplishments as a poet. Some consider him a central figure through whom the major currents of art in the early 1900's passed, while others regard him as a dilettante, interested only in stylishness and facile demonstrations of his considerable talents, lacking substance under the sparkling facade. Many of his contemporaries were uncertain of his importance because he remained always on the periphery of "serious" art. Looking back, however, it is clear that, at the very least, Cocteau's poetry is another brilliant aspect of one of the most versatile artistic minds of the century and that it has been underrated largely because of the difficulty in grasping Cocteau in all his variety.

Biography

Jean Cocteau was born in a prosperous suburb of Paris to Georges and Eugénie Lecomte Cocteau, a cultivated bourgeois couple who exposed Jean, his brother Paul, and their sister Marthe to the fine arts. When at their suburban home, the children played on the grounds of a nearby castle designed by François Mansart. When in Paris—Cocteau would always consider himself a Parisian above all—his family lived with his grandparents, whose house contained classical busts, vases, a painting by Eugène Delacroix, and drawings by Jean-Auguste-Dominique Ingres. Cocteau's grandfather was a cellist and would often be visited by the renowned violinist Pablo de Sarasate. Some of Cocteau's fondest memories of his early life were of trips to the circus, the ice palace, and the theater, especially the Comédie-Française. Years later, in his own drama, he would attempt to duplicate the lighting or brilliancy of theatrical events in his memory and would discover from lighting technicians that it had been technically impossible to do such things when he was a child. Time had increased the splendor of his memories, including those of the castle and of his grandparents' house. He thus began to perceive his own life as having mythological dimensions, as even his personal experiences had become exaggerated and distorted over time.

In 1899, Cocteau's father committed suicide as a result of financial problems. Cocteau became an indifferent student at the Petit Lycée Condorcet and, later, at the Grand Condorcet. Like many creative personalities, he found the institutional atmosphere oppressive. Besides having a weak constitution, which often led to legitimate absences, he was frequently truant. During his illnesses, he often had his German governess stitching doll clothes for his model theater. One of his closest childhood friends was Réné Rocher, later to become a director, who spent much time with Cocteau and his miniature theaters. After a trip with his mother to Venice, Cocteau began study for his baccalaureate, had his first love affair (with Madeleine Carlier, ten years his senior), and became more involved with the theater—meeting Edouard de Max, who acted opposite Sarah Bernhardt. Quite naturally, with all this to entertain him, Cocteau failed the examination.

On April 4, 1908, de Max sponsored a reading of Cocteau's poetry, by de Max, Rocher, and other prominent actors and actresses, at the Théâtre Fémina. Because the event was attended by many of the elite of Paris, including several leading literary critics, Cocteau became instantly well known. Subsequently, he became acquainted with such literary notables as Edmond Rostand, Marcel Proust, Charles-Pierre Péguy, Catulle Mendès, and Jules Lemaître. He became quite enamored of Comtesse Anna de Noailles and tried to write poetry like hers, with a refined sensibility and enhanced sensuality. He was one of three founders of a literary magazine, *Schéhérazade*, which was dedicated to poetry and music, and rented a room at the Hôtel Biron, where Auguste Rodin and his secretary, Rainer Maria Rilke, were also staying.

When Cocteau was introduced to the great impresario Sergei Diaghilev of the Ballets Russes, he begged Diaghilev to permit him to write ballets. Diaghilev eventually said "Étonne-moi!" ("Astonish me!"), and Cocteau took this injunction as an order to give shape to the rest of his life's work. His first ballet, *Le Dieu bleu* (1912), was not successful, though Diaghilev produced it for the coronation of George V. Convinced the music was at fault, Cocteau began to associate with Igor Stravinsky, living with him for a while. During this period, Cocteau was also trying to defend himself against the accusation of Henri Ghéon in the *Nouvelle Revue française*, who charged that he was an entirely derivative poet. Around 1914, Cocteau underwent what he called a "molting," breaking free of the influence of Rostand and the Comtesse de Noailles and moving toward his eventual association with Max Jacob and Guillaume Apollinaire.

As World War I broke out, Cocteau attempted to enlist but was rejected for health reasons. Illegally, he became an ambulance driver on the Belgian front, but after being discovered, he was sent back to Paris. These experiences would later form a large part of his novel *Thomas l'imposteur* (1923; *Thomas the Impostor*, 1925). Back in Paris, he met Amedeo Modigliani and Pablo Picasso and introduced the latter to Diaghilev, thereby creating the association that would produce Erik Satie's 1917 ballet *Parade*, with scenario by Cocteau, costumes and set by Picasso, and choreography by Léonide Massine. *Parade* created a scandal with its atonal music and extraordinary set and costumes. Only the presence of Apollinaire, in uniform and wearing a bandage over his head wound, kept the outraged spectators from attacking the creators of the ballet. Cocteau responded vigorously, attacking the musical influences of Claude Debussy, Richard Wagner, and Stravinsky and linking himself with the composers known as Les Six (Georges Auric, Louis Durey, Arthur Honegger, Darius Milhaud, Francis Poulenc, and Germaine Tailleferre).

In 1919, Cocteau met and fell in love with Raymond Radiguet, who was fifteen, handsome, and a poetic genius—or so Cocteau believed. Radiguet caused Cocteau to reevaluate his aesthetics and move toward a simpler, classic style; thus inspired, he found new energy and created a number of new works, including *Le Grand écart* (1923; *The Grand Écart*, 1925) and the volume of poems *Plain-Chant*. Radiguet, however, died of typhoid in December, 1923, and Cocteau was devastated. Diaghilev tried to shake Cocteau from his despair by taking him on a trip to Monte Carlo. The trip itself did little good, however, and the discovery of opium there proved to be Cocteau's only solace. His addiction eventually provoked his friends and family to persuade him to enter a sanatorium in 1925. There, he came under the influence of Jacques Maritain, the Catholic philosopher, who briefly restored Cocteau's faith in religion. He was able to pick up the pieces of this life and create such works as *L'Ange Heurtebise*, *Orpheus*, and *Children of the Game*. He even patched up his friendship with Stravinsky and wrote the words for Stravinsky's oratorio *Oedipus-Rex*.

In the 1930's, Cocteau seemed inexhaustible, even though he suffered a bout with typhoid in 1931. Plays, poems, songs, ballets, art criticism, and even a column for *Ce soir* poured forth from his pen. He took a trip around the world in imitation of Jules Verne's *Le Tour du monde en quatre-vingt jours* (1873; *Around the World in Eighty Days*, 1873). He became the manager of the bantamweight boxer Alphonse Theo Brown. Perhaps the most important of his activities during this period was his first attempt at *poésie cinématographique*, when he wrote and directed *The Blood of a Poet*.

Cocteau, always controversial, found himself caught between his artistic enemies and new political ones during the Nazi occupation of France. He was viciously attacked in the press. His play *The Typewriter* was banned. He never backed off, however, even when beaten by a group of French fascists for failing to salute the flag.

After the war, Cocteau found himself a "grand old man" of the artistic world, but he refused to rest on his laurels and continued arousing controversy. He traveled and wrote plays, journals, and films. He made recordings and designed frescoes for the city hall at Menton, the Chapel of St. Pierre at Villefranche-sur-Mer, the Chapel of Notre Dame in London, the Church of Saint Blaise-des-Simples in Milly-la-Forêt, and the Chapel of Notre-Dame-de-Jerusalem at Fréjus. He also designed fabrics, plates, and posters. He was made a member of the Royal Belgian Academy and the French Academy in 1955 and received an honorary doctorate of letters from Oxford University in 1956. He died on October 11, 1963, shortly after hearing of the death of his friend Edith Piaf.

ANALYSIS

Jean Cocteau's first three books of poetry enjoyed the kind of success that works that essentially flatter the prevailing literary establishment are prone to have. He was instantly praised and compared to various great poets, present and past, yet never aroused the outrage or bewilderment provoked by significant breakthroughs. Very much a salon poet and dandy, Cocteau had yet to discover his own voice. *La Lampe d'Aladin* contained poems dedicated to the various actors and actresses who had read them at Cocteau's "debut" in the Théâtre Fémina. Like much of the poetry of the early 1900's, the poems of this first volume seem self-serving, overly and insincerely emotional, and very immature, though occasionally some charming cleverness may emerge.

Le Prince frivole

Cocteau's second collection, *Le Prince frivole* (the frivolous prince), is little better than the first. Its title came to be applied to its author, and Cocteau would later refer to the book as elevating him to the "Prince du Ridicule." The creation of poetry here is still an amusing game. Cocteau rather dutifully insists on melancholy in many of the works, but it comes off as posing, even though it may be indicative of an indefinable feeling that all the praise he was receiving was undeserved.

La Danse de Sophocle

After the publication of *La Danse de Sophocle*, the inadequacy of Cocteau's artistic commitment was brought home to him in a review by Henri Ghéon in *Nouvelle Revue française* (André Gide may have had a hand in its authorship). Ghéon pointed out the derivative qualities of Cocteau's three books and implied that the poet was immature, frivolous, and greatly overestimated. Ghéon said that Cocteau was undeniably gifted but that he had not devoted himself to his gift. The review was more important in Cocteau's life than the book itself, though one can see in *La Danse de Sophocle* the beginning of Cocteau's lifelong interest in the eternal truths found in ancient Greek mythology and literature. The review provoked Cocteau to understand "that art and poetry aren't a game, but a descent into a mine, down toward the firedamp and danger."

Le Cap de Bonne-Espérance

Cocteau did not publish another collection of poetry until seven years later, after working for the Ballets Russes, associating with a more radical set of artists, and after his experiences in World War I. Later, when republishing his works, he ignored the earlier three books and dated his beginnings as a poet from *Le Cap de Bonne-Espérance* (the Cape of Good Hope), which was inspired by his association with the aviator Roland Garros. Garros would take Cocteau on daily flights from Villacoublay. He performed numerous acrobatics with Cocteau in the plane, and the poet was inspired by the sensation of flying and the view of Paris from the air. In 1918, after a remarkable escape from a German prison, Garros was shot down and killed. A proof copy of Cocteau's long poem dedicated to Garros was found in his cockpit. In the book, the airplane symbolizes the modern era: It frees humankind from earthly considerations, putting the pilot or passenger into a realm of new visions and solitude, where he can find his soul. At the same time, he faces death.

The poems in *Le Cap de Bonne-Espérance* are extremely sensual, despite the abstract element, and attempt to re-create the physical sensations of flying with fragmented lines and onomatopoeic vowels. These techniques were not original to Cocteau; the typographical effects had been used by Stéphane Mallarmé, Apollinaire, and Pierre Reverdy, and the *lettriste* effects by Pierre Albert-Birot. However, as Adrienne Monnier points out, it was daring of Cocteau to employ these still-radical devices. André Breton, among others, considered the collection not radical enough and had a sour expression the whole time Cocteau was reading it in Valentine Gross's apartment. Cocteau is said to have called his work old-fashioned, in an effort to charm Breton, but many see the reading as the beginning of Cocteau's long battle with the Surrealists. The book also provoked a letter from Proust, who gently asked whether it did not display a certain indiscriminate use of images.

DISCOURS DU GRAND SOMMEIL

Discours du grand sommeil (discourse of the great sleep) consists of eleven poems written between 1916 and 1918 and was inspired by Cocteau's experiences with the Fusiliers Marins, among whom he lived, illegally wearing the Marine uniform until discovered by an officer. A day after Cocteau was ejected from the front, most of the Fusiliers Marins were killed. Cocteau attempted in these poems to end once and for all his role as the "prince of frivolity." Though flippancy was always part of Cocteau's demeanor, he once asserted that it was the bourgeois way of dealing with catastrophe—that what appeared to be frivolity to others was actually Cocteau's way of dealing with his profound sadness. *Discours du grand sommeil*, writes Wallace Fowlie, is "a plunge downward," "a contact with the grim presence of death." The poems are quite effective in conveying the horror of war, of the exhausting marches, the screams of the dying, and the endless suffering. There is also an awakening sense of the soldier as symbolic of the tragedy of human existence and a movement toward a more classical style and attitude. The volume clearly points toward Cocteau's later aesthetic.

VOCABULAIRE

Vocabulaire also reveals a cleaner, purer style than that of Cocteau's youthful works yet still betrays the inordinate influence of the artistic movements of the war years, such as Dadaism, Futurism, Imagism, and cubism. Cocteau's fixation on certain images (such as snow turning to marble) is notable throughout his career. In this collection, the rose appears often, with obvious allusions to Pierre de Ronsard, in clear homage to French classicism. One finds Cocteau in search of himself, struggling as he had since the Ghéon review to achieve originality. The poems consist largely of philosophical speculations on the nature of change and the poet's role in metamorphosis. The endless flow of change is represented by the changes in clouds, aging, swans, the dissolution of salt statues, death, and snow. Cocteau's private mythology is fully developed here; several poems, such as "Tombeaux" (tombs) and "Oiseaux sont en neige" (birds are in snow), connect homosexuality to the themes of change and death. In these poems, Cocteau seems to be taking stock of his life, trying to find a direction and meaning to it.

Poésies, 1917-1920

Under Radiguet's influence, Cocteau was moving toward the tradition of French literature that employs the brief, clear, precise sentence. Cocteau renewed himself with this classicism and rediscovered the themes of classical antiquity. In *Poésies, 1917-1920*, Cocteau introduced a new set of topics, themes, and motifs, such as the clown, circus, angel, sailor, and athlete. Perhaps the most significant poem in the collection is "L'Ode à Picasso" (ode to Picasso), an attempt to grasp the complexity of the painter and artist whom Cocteau often watched at work for hours on end. The poem reveals Picasso as a man possessed by an inner fire, an embodiment of the concept, expressed by Socrates in Plato's *Iōn* (fourth century B.C.E.; *Ion*, 1804), of the madness of the poet. Painting, sculpture, film, and any other expression of art are therefore merely facets of the same thing: *poésie*. Cocteau sees in Picasso a man in constant contact with the Muses, free of mundane considerations. The poem expresses much of what Cocteau would attempt to be, would have the courage to be, after being inspired by Radiguet. The final poem of *Poésies, 1917-1920*, "Mouchoir" (handkerchief), bids farewell to influences of the past and sets the poet out on a voyage into the unknown. To be a poet is thus to move ahead relentlessly, to be uncertain of the results, to follow no one.

Plain-Chant

Plain-Chant reveals in its title a further move toward simplification and, in Fowlie's view, is central to the work of Cocteau. It is classically metered and uses the imagery of Angel, Muse, and Death, symbolism that recurs in much of the rest of Cocteau's oeuvre. The Angel in this lyric poem is clearly Radiguet, and the poem expresses Cocteau's great love for him and also his fear of the death that will inevitably separate them. The Angel is his guide through the mysteries of poetic art and also his protector when the Muse leaves him or Death presses in on him. As Bettina Knapp has observed, however, Death becomes a restorative power, a bridge to another world: "He burrowed within and reached new depths of cognition, with beauty of form and classical restraint." The poem was also strangely prescient, as Radiguet died in 1923, emotionally shattering Cocteau.

Opéra

Cocteau's discovery of his identity as a poet under the guidance of Radiguet was not lost in his plummet into despair brought about by the young man's death. The collection *Opéra* mixes Cocteau's visions induced by opium with lucid language and precise control. Even in his agony, he rigorously adheres to a classical detachment, a coolness that enhances the feelings and mythological dimensions of the works. A blending of Christian and pagan mythology points toward Cocteau's extensive revising and adapting of works of classical mythology for the stage and film. "L'Ange heurtebise" in *Opéra* is usually thought to be one of Cocteau's most significant poems. It explores the question of angels, which he had discussed in an essay, *Le Secret professionnel* (1922). The poet is stuck on an earthly plane, struggling to understand a larger reality, while the Angel stands above. The Angel reappears in work after work of Cocteau, inspiring poets and urging them to look on the human predicament with detachment.

LATER YEARS

Cocteau did not cease writing poetry until his death, but most critics seem indifferent to the large number of his works after *Opéra*. Perhaps his work in film and prose detracted from his development in poetry, though Cocteau himself saw all his artistic works as facets of the same creative impulse: It was all poetry to him. His influence on the literary scene waned, perhaps because he had finally found his own unique path, and artists and critics found it difficult to categorize and thus assess the measure of Cocteau's achievement. His variety contributes to the difficulty of an overall assessment: He began each mature collection of poems as if he had only recently become a poet.

At the very least, Cocteau's poetry exhibits many of the primary traits of twentieth century poetry in its clean, precise form, its development of personal mythology, and its exploitation through adaptation of traditional mythological and literary themes. These traits are significant elements of the mainstream of modern poetry, and Cocteau is clearly in the middle of it.

OTHER MAJOR WORKS

LONG FICTION: *Le Potomak*, 1919; *Le Grand Écart*, 1923 (*The Grand Écart*, 1925); *Thomas l'imposteur*, 1923 (*Thomas the Impostor*, 1925); *Le Livre blanc*, 1928 (*The White Paper*, 1957); *Les Enfants terribles*, 1929 (*Enfants Terribles*, 1930; also known as *Children of the Game*); *Le Fantôme de Marseille*, 1933; *La Fin du Potomak*, 1939.

PLAYS: *Le Dieu bleu*, pr. 1912 (ballet scenario; with Frédéric de Madrazo); *Parade*, pr. 1917 (ballet scenario; music by Erik Satie, scenery by Pablo Picasso); *Le Boeuf sur le toit*, pr. 1920 (ballet scenario; music by Darius Milhaud, scenery by Raoul Dufy); *Le Gendarme incompris*, pr. 1921 (ballet scenario; with Raymond Radiguet; music by Francis Poulenc); *Les Mariés de la tour Eiffel*, pr. 1921 (ballet scenario; music by Les Six; *The Wedding on the Eiffel Tower*, 1937); *Antigone*, pr. 1922 (libretto; English translation, 1961); *Les Biches*, pr. 1924 (ballet scenario; music by Poulenc); *Les Fâcheux*, pr. 1924 (ballet scenario; music by George Auric); *Orphée*, pr. 1926 (*Orpheus*, 1933); *Oedipus-Rex*, pr. 1927, pb. 1928 (libretto; English translation, 1961); *La Voix humaine*, pr., pb. 1930 (*The Human Voice*, 1951); *La Machine infernale*, pr., pb. 1934 (*The Infernal Machine*, 1936); *L'École des veuves*, pr., pb. 1936; *Les Chevaliers de la table ronde*, pr., pb. 1937 (*The Knights of the Round Table*, 1955); *Les Parents terribles*, pr., pb. 1938 (*Intimate Relations*, 1952); *Les Monstres sacrés*, pr., pb. 1940 (*The Holy Terrors*, 1953); *La Machine à écrire*, pr., pb. 1941 (*The Typewriter*, 1948); *Renaud et Armide*, pr., pb. 1943; *L'Aigle à deux têtes*, pr., pb. 1946 (*The Eagle Has Two Heads*, 1946); *Le Jeune Homme et la mort*, pr. 1946 (ballet scenario; music by Johann Sebastian Bach); *Phèdre*, pr. 1950 (ballet scenario; music by Auric); *Bacchus*, pr. 1951 (English translation, 1955); *Théâtre complet*, 1957 (2 volumes); *Five Plays*, 1961; *L'Impromptu du Palais-Royal*, pr., pb. 1962; *The Infernal Machine, and Other Plays*, 1964.

SCREENPLAYS: *Le Sang d'un poète*, 1930 (*The Blood of a Poet*, 1949); *Le Baron fantôme*, 1943; *L'Éternel Retour*, 1943 (*The Eternal Return*, 1948); *L'Aigle à deux têtes*, 1946; *La Belle et la bête*, 1946 (*Beauty and the Beast*, 1947); *Ruy Blas*, 1947; *Les Parents terribles*, 1948 (*Intimate Relations*, 1952); *Les Enfants terribles*, 1950; *Orphée*, 1950 (*Orpheus*, 1950); *Le Testament d'Orphée*, 1959 (*The Testament of Orpheus*, 1968); *Thomas l'Imposteur*, 1965.

NONFICTION: *Le Coq et l'Arlequin*, 1918 (*Cock and Harlequin*, 1921); *Le Secret professionnel*, 1922; *Lettre à Jacques Maritain*, 1926 (*Art and Faith*, 1948); *Le Rappel à l'ordre*, 1926 (*A Call to Order*, 1926); *Opium: Journal d'une désintoxication*, 1930 (*Opium: Diary of a Cure*, 1932); *Essai de la critique indirecte*, 1932 (*The Lais Mystery: An Essay of Indirect Criticism*, 1936); *Portraits-souvenir, 1900-1914*, 1935 (*Paris Album*, 1956); *"La Belle et la bête": Journal d'un film*, 1946 (*"Beauty and the Beast": Journal of a Film*, 1950); *La Difficulté d'être*, 1947 (*The Difficulty of Being*, 1966); *Journal d'un inconnu*, 1952 (*The Hand of a Stranger*, 1956; also known as *Diary of an Unknown*, 1988); *The Journals of Jean Cocteau*, 1956; *Poésie critique*, 1960.

TRANSLATION: *Roméo et Juliette*, 1926 (of William Shakespeare's play).

BIBLIOGRAPHY

Crowson, Lydia. *The Esthetic of Jean Cocteau*. Hanover: University of New Hampshire Press, 1978. Chapters on Cocteau's milieu, the nature of the real, and the roles of myth, consciousness, and power. Includes introduction and bibliography. This work is for advanced students who have already consulted more introductory works.

Griffith, Alison Guest. *Jean Cocteau and the Performing Arts*. Irvine, Calif.: Severin Wunderman Museum, 1992. This museum catalog includes critical analysis of Cocteau's work as well as information on his contribution to the performing arts. Bibliography.

Knapp, Bettina L. *Jean Cocteau: Updated Edition*. Boston: Twayne, 1989. A thorough revision of Knapp's 1970 volume, which begins with her memory of her introduction to the writing. Knapp pursues both psychological and literary views of Cocteau's work, with chapters following a chronological approach. Includes separate chronology, notes, bibliography, and index.

Lowe, Romana N. *The Fictional Female: Sacrificial Rituals and Spectacles of Writing in Baudelaire, Zola, and Cocteau*. New York: Peter Lang, 1997. Highlights the sacrificial victim common in nineteenth and twentieth century French texts: women. Lowe traces structures and images of female sacrifice in the genres of poetry, novel, and theater with close readings of Baudelaire, Zola, and Cocteau.

Mauriès, Patrick. *Jean Cocteau*. Translated by Jane Brenton. London: Thames & Hudson, 1998. A brief but excellent biography of Cocteau illustrated with many photographs.

Peters, Arthur King, et al. *Jean Cocteau and the French Scene*. New York: Abbeville, 1984. Essays on Cocteau's biography, his life in Paris, his intellectual background, his view of realism, and his work in the theater and movies. Also contains a chronology, an index, and many illustrations and photographs.

Saul, Julie, ed. *Jean Cocteau: The Mirror and the Mask—A Photo-Biography*. Boston: D. R. Godine, 1992. This compilation from an exhibit celebrating the one-hundred-year anniversary of his birth, with an essay by Francis Steegmuller, provides insights into the life of Cocteau.

Selous, Trista. *Cocteau*. Paris: Centre Pompidou, 2003. A retrospective catalog compiled by the Centre Pompidou and the Montreal Museum that offers an illustrated review of Cocteau's creative output. It also includes seventeen essays on Cocteau's life and work.

Steegmuller, Francis. *Cocteau*. Boston: D. R. Godine, 1986. A major biography of Cocteau. Discusses his childhood, the influence of his mother, and fellow poets. Defines him as a "quick-change" artist with a propensity for constant self-invention, discarding old views and activities and assuming new roles or guises with remarkable facility. Twelve appendixes plus numerous illustrations. Includes bibliography, index.

Tsakiridou, Cornelia A., ed. *Reviewing Orpheus: Essays on the Cinema and Art of Jean Cocteau*. Lewisburg, Pa.: Bucknell University Press, 1997. Focuses on Cocteau's film work but is valuable for insight into his general artistry.

J. Madison Davis

E. E. CUMMINGS

Born: Cambridge, Massachusetts; October 14, 1894
Died: North Conway, New Hampshire; September 3, 1962
Also known as: e. e. cummings

PRINCIPAL POETRY
Tulips and Chimneys, 1923
&, 1925
XLI Poems, 1925
Is 5, 1926
W: Seventy New Poems, 1931
No Thanks, 1935
1/20 Poems, 1936
Collected Poems, 1938
Fifty Poems, 1940
1 × 1, 1944
Xiape, 1950
Poems, 1923-1954, 1954
Ninety-five Poems, 1958
One Hundred Selected Poems, 1959
Selected Poems, 1960
Seventy-three Poems, 1963
E. E. Cummings: A Selection of Poems, 1965
Complete Poems, 1913-1962, 1968
Etcetera: The Unpublished Poems of E. E. Cummings, 1983, 2000; George James Firmage and Richard S. Kennedy, editors)

OTHER LITERARY FORMS

In addition to poetry, E. E. Cummings also published two long prose narratives, *The Enormous Room* (1922) and *Eimi* (1933); a translation from the French of *The Red Front*, by Louis Aragon (1933); a long play, *Him* (pb. 1927); two short plays, *Anthropos: The Future of Art* (pb. 1944) and *Santa Claus: A Morality* (pb. 1946); *Tom: A Ballet* (pb. 1935); a collection of his own drawings in charcoal, ink, oil, pastels, and watercolor, *CIOPW* (1931); his autobiographical Harvard lectures, *i: six nonlectures* (1953); and a collection of his wife's photographs with captions by Cummings, *Adventures in Value* (1962).

Of these, *The Enormous Room* and *Eimi* are of particular interest because of their contributions to Cummings's critical reputation and to his development as an artist. The former is the poet's account of his three-month confinement in a French concentration

E. E. Cummings
(Library of Congress)

camp in 1917. It was hailed on its appearance as a significant firsthand account of the war and has become one of the classic records of World War I. It is also significant in that it is Cummings's first book, and, although prose, it reflects the same kinds of linguistic experimentation and innovation apparent in his poetry. Also reflecting his stylistic innovations is *Eimi*, Cummings's account of a trip to Russia, which has a topical vitality similar to the war experiences. The major themes of the critical response to Cummings's poetry, which developed in the 1920's, were implicit in the responses to *The Enormous Room*. Those themes, explicit by 1933, also helped to shape the criticism of *Eimi*.

Similar to the two prose narratives, *Him*, a long, expressionistic drama, is also representative of Cummings's development and of his critical reputation. Experimental and distinctive, the drama was produced in 1928 by the Provincetown Players. In the program notes, Cummings cautioned the audience against trying to understand the play. Instead, he advised the audience to "let it try to understand you." As with the poetry and the prose, there were outraged cries claiming that the play was unintelligible, although there was also an affirmation of the lyrical originality and intensity of the play. The recognition of Cummings's lyrical talents was gradually to replace the often angry rejections of his work because of its eccentricity.

Stylistically distinctive and important in any full assessment of his achievement is the collection of Cummings's presentations as the annual Charles Eliot Norton Lecturer in Poetry at Harvard, *i: six nonlectures*. Of immediate interest, however, is the autobiographical content of the lectures. The first lecture is titled "i & my parents" and contains poetic and affectionate sketches of his mother and father; the second is titled "i & their son." The final four, less pointedly autobiographical in the usual sense of the word, are an exploration of the relationship between the poet's values and his sense of personal identity, between what he believes and what he is.

Achievements

E. E. Cummings is not usually included in the first rank of modernist poets, which always begins with T. S. Eliot, William Butler Yeats, and Ezra Pound and is, more often than not, rounded out with Wallace Stevens and William Carlos Williams. Two aspects of his career, however, give his achievement a great deal of significance. First, he was on the cutting edge of the modernist, experimental movement in verse. Pound, at the center of that movement, was dedicated to restoring value and integrity to the word by breaking the mold of the past, and in that cause, he evangelically admonished the poets of his generation to "make it new." Although a disciple of no one, Cummings led the assault on conventional verse, pushing experimentation to extremes and beyond with his peculiarly distinctive typography and his unconventional syntax, grammar, and punctuation. Although he paid the price of such experimentation, which brought charges of superficiality and unintelligibility, he served the modernist movement well by helping to educate an audience for the innovations in verse and prose of the second and third decades of the twentieth century.

Second, Cummings was not only a leading experimenter in an age of experimentation but also an intense lyric poet and an effective satirist. As a lyricist, he celebrated those experiences, values, and attitudes that lyric poets of all times have celebrated, and high on his list was love—sexual, romantic, and ideal or transcendental. His love poetry often reminds readers of Renaissance poets because of its subject matter, diction, and imagery. He is often bawdy, often sentimental, sometimes concrete, sometimes abstract, but almost always intense. Many of his lyrics express a childlike joy before nature and the natural state; he also celebrated personal relationships, particularly in his well-known tributes to his father and mother.

As a satirist, Cummings's principal target is man en masse. This thrust is the opposite of the celebration of individuality, a principal subject of his lyricism. In poems with a military setting, he satirically attacks not the military but the submergence of the individual into the mass that the military often brings about. He attacks the same submergence in poems that seem to be attacking modern advertising or salespeople. Neither, however, is the real object of his scorn; it is not modern advertising but the mass mind of the mass market that it engenders that he lashes out at in several of his most effective satiric pieces.

Cummings celebrates love, spontaneity, individuality, and a childlike wonder before nature. He attacks conformity, the mass mind, progress, and hypocrisy. His greatest achievement is that in an age of experimentation in verse, and in an age defensive and self-conscious about feeling, he fashioned a personal, highly idiosyncratic style that at its best provided him with effective vehicles for some of the finest lyric and satiric poetry of the modernist period.

Among the honors and awards he received were the *Dial* Award in 1925, Guggenheim Fellowships in 1933 and 1951, the Levinson Prize from *Poetry* magazine in 1939, the Shelley Memorial Award in 1945, the Academy of American Poets Fellowship in 1950, and a special citation by National Book Awards in 1955 for *Poems, 1923-1954*. He was awarded the Boston Arts Festival Award in 1957 and the Bollingen Prize for Poetry in 1958.

BIOGRAPHY

Edward Estlin Cummings was born in Cambridge, Massachusetts, on October 14, 1894, the first of two children born to Edward Cummings and Rebecca Haswell Clarke. His father was a Harvard graduate and lecturer, an ordained Unitarian minister, and pastor of the South Congregational Church from 1909 to 1925. Cummings received his degree magna cum laude from Harvard in 1915 and a Harvard M.A. the following year. A landmark in his career came in 1952 when he returned to Harvard to deliver the Charles Eliot Norton Lectures. Subsequently published as *i: six nonlectures*, all of which are highly personal and autobiographical, the first is of particular interest because of its affectionate, idealized portraits of his parents.

Cummings went to France in 1917 to join Norton Harje's Ambulance Corps. A combination of unfortunate and nearly ludicrous events led to his incarceration by the French authorities on suspicion of disloyalty. He and a friend were confined in a concentration camp at La Ferté Macé from late September through December, 1917. That experience is the subject matter of Cummings's first book, *The Enormous Room*, which has come to be regarded as a classic account of personal experience in World War I. Although prose, it launched the poet's career and, because of its style, set the tone and, implicitly, some of the basic themes that were to characterize the responses to his poetry for the next two decades. Before 1922, Cummings had published poems in the *Harvard Monthly*, in *The Dial*, and six poems in *Eight Harvard Poets*, but it was *The Enormous Room* that began his critical reputation. His first book of poems, *Tulips and Chimneys*, was published in 1923.

In 1923, Cummings moved to Patchin Place in New York City and lived there, spending the summers at his family's place in New Hampshire, until his death in 1962. Cummings traveled to Russia in 1931 and converted that experience into the second of his two major prose works, *Eimi*. In 1932, he married Marion Morehouse, a model, actress, and photographer. It was his third marriage and it survived. She died in 1969. The three decades Cummings spent with Marion and the nearly four decades at Patchin Place deserve emphasis in a biographical sketch because they provide a perspective that brings some balance to the poet's reputation as a bohemian enfant terrible. Although he never lost the cutting edge of his capacity to shock, he lived a relatively settled life devoted to painting and writing poetry.

Analysis

Since E. E. Cummings rarely used titles, all those poems without titles will be identified by reference to the Index of First Lines in *Complete Poems, 1913-1962*. An analysis of Cummings's poetry turns, for the most part, on judgments about his innovative, highly idiosyncratic versification. Some of Cummings's critics have thought his techniques to be not only cheap and shallow tricks but also ultimately nonpoetic. There was, from the early stages of his career, general agreement about his potential as a lyric and satiric poet. As that career developed through his middle and late periods, negative criticism of his verse diminished as affirmation grew. Although there always will be dissenting voices, the consensus for some time has been that his innovative verse techniques and his lyric and satiric talents were successfully blended in the best of his work.

"R-P-O-P-H-E-S-S-A-G-R"

Cummings wrote both free verse and conventional verse, particularly in the form of quatrains and sonnets. He also imposed on conventional verse the combination of typographical eccentricities and grammatical and syntactical permutations that constitute his distinctive hallmark. There is a considerable range between his most extreme free-verse poems, where the hallmark is superimposed, and his most conventional sonnets, where the hallmark is barely discernible. An example of the extreme is his "grasshopper" poem, "r-p-o-p-h-e-s-s-a-g-r," which is at the same time a masterpiece and a failure. The poem is a masterful blending of form and content, an achievement that might be described as pure technique becoming pure form. It fails as a poem, however, to move the reader or to matter very much except as a witty display of pyrotechnics. Its achievement, nevertheless, is a considerable one, and it serves as a useful model of one kind of poem for which Cummings is best known.

The poem "r-p-o-p-h-e-s-s-a-g-r" is structurally a free-verse poem in which Cummings employs many of his distinctive typographical devices. The word "grasshopper" occurs four times in the poem, its letters jumbled beyond recognition the first three times. The grasshopper's leap, capturing the essence of grasshoppers, brings its name into proper arrangement. Cummings also uses parentheses to break up words and to signal recombinations of letters and syllables resulting in conventional spelling, syntax, and meaning. At the literal and figurative center of the poem is the word "leaps," which links the first two versions of the word "grasshopper" to the final two, culminating in the resolution of the proper arrangement of letters. Cummings's diagonal typography for the word "leaps" is intended to render spatially, in the visual terms of a painter, the conceptual meaning of the word.

VISUAL EFFECTS

A poem of even less substance than "r-p-o-p-h-e-s-s-a-g-r," and therefore illustratively useful in the same way, is the "leaf-falling" poem "l(a." The four words of the poem, "a," "leaf," "falls," and "loneliness," are arranged along a vertical line with two or three letters or characters on each horizontal line, except for the final five of "iness." Thus, the poem begins with "l(a," with the rest of the poem directly below, two or three letters at a time, spaced out to suggest two triplets, set off by an opening, an intervening, and a closing single line. The use of the two parentheses, setting off "a leaf falls," actually helps in the reading of the poem. To the extent that the slender column of letters on the relatively vast whiteness of the page visually complements the theme of the poem, human loneliness engendered by the cyclical dying of the natural world in the fall of the year, Cummings has again succeeded in an effective union of form and content.

Other examples of this kind of verse are poems depicting a black, ragtime piano player ("ta"), a sunset ("stinging"), and a thunderstorm ("n(o)w/the"). The arrangement on the page of the portrait of the piano player is very much like that of "loneliness," as is the second half of the poem depicting a sunset by the sea. Cummings attempts in the thunderstorm poem to create visual effects to complement the conceptual meaning of the words "lightning" and "thunder." In one line, he states that the world "iS Slapped:with;liGhtninG"; thunder in the poems appears as "THuNdeR." These five poems represent some of Cummings's more effective uses of several of his most representative devices, particularly eccentric typography and spatial arrangement intended to create special visual effects. Often successful, these same devices at times fail completely, merely producing involved semantic puzzles hardly worth the effort necessary to solve them. More important, however, is the fact that the same features of versification exemplified by these poems of relatively little substance are to be found in his very best lyric and satiric poetry, the best of which stands between the highly eccentric versification of "r-p-o-p-h-e-s-s-a-g-r" and his relatively conventional uses of the sonnet form.

SONNETS

Cummings wrote many sonnets. A convenient sampling of his uses of the form is to be found in *Is 5*, which begins with five sonnets and closes with five. The first five are portraits or sketches of prostitutes and are among the few Cummings poems with titles—in this example, the respective names of each of the women. The subject matter of the final five sonnets of the collection, in sharp contrast to the portraits, is romantic love, and this set is more conventional than the portraits of the prostitutes. Cummings's best lyric poetry tends to be his more conventional verse: A comparative reading of the second and the tenth sonnets of *Is 5* will illustrate Cummings's mastery of conventional lyric forms.

Three observations can be made about the second sonnet of *Is 5*, the portrait of Mame ("Mame") and the tenth ("if I have made,my lady,intricate"). First, the former is a portrait of a prostitute, while the latter is addressed to "my lady." Second, Mame speaks in a Brooklyn dialect, such as "duh woild," "some noive," and "dat baby." What little quoted speech there is in "if I have made,my lady,intricate" is not dialect and would not be obtrusive in a Renaissance sonnet. Third, Mame's sonnet is relatively loose structurally, while my lady's is one of Cummings's most conventional. The loose structure of the former results largely from the dramatic presentation, particularly as it calls for the use of fragmented speech in dialect. Both sonnets are conventional syntactically, grammatically, and typographically. Formally and thematically, "if I have made,my lady,intricate" stands in dramatic contrast to "r-p-o-p-h-e-s-s-a-g-r." The sonnet is one of Cummings's better lyric poems, the best of which make use of the formal eccentricities of "r-p-o-p-h-e-s-s-a-g-r" in the poet's successful blending of traditional subject matter with his personally distinctive, modern verse forms.

LYRIC POETRY

Cummings's principal lyric subject matter is his celebration of romantic, sexual, and transcendental love and of the beauty, physical and spiritual, of lovers. A good example of a successful blend of his distinctive versification with a traditional lyric subject is "(ponder,darling,these busted statues." Formally, the poem might be thought of as standing near the middle of the range defined by the extremes of "r-p-o-p-h-e-s-s-a-g-r" and "if I have made,my lady,intricate." As such, it represents well the characteristics of Cummings's poetry. The blend of versification with a traditional subject is effective because of the appropriateness of the fragmented verse to the imagery of broken statuary and architectural ruins and of both to the poem's carpe diem theme.

The most obvious aspect of Cummings's distinctive verse is typographical, his sparse and erratic use of capitals and of parentheses. These particular details function in this poem of lyric substance to further understanding. Two sets of parentheses clearly delineate the three sections of the poem, the first and last being enclosed by them. The capitalization gives emphasis to the "Greediest Paws" of time and to the all-important "Horizontal" business. In addition to the typography, two examples of Cummings's manipulation of syntax also contribute to understanding his style: verse paragraphs 3 and 6. As with the typography, the unconventional syntax contributes to the unmistakable distinctiveness of Cummings's verse without in any way impeding the reader's comprehension and hence appreciation of the poem.

The poem "(ponder,darling,these busted statues" is the modern poet's address to the perennially coy mistress. As in Andrew Marvell's poem "To His Coy Mistress" (1650), the woman is asked to consider the mutability of all things and urged, since time passes irrevocably, to get on with meaningful "horizontal" business. Marvell's plea turns on his images of the grave and the desert of eternity. Cummings, the quintessential modern, stands with the woman among the architectural ruins of a past that must be not so much denied as ignored, or, at least, turned away from. Although it is a lesser poem than T. S. Eliot's *The Waste Land* (1922), it shares with that landmark of the modernist period the fragmented artifacts of the past. More important, Cummings, like Eliot, is addressing the fundamental question of their time: What does one do in the midst of such ruins? Cummings's answer, "make love," is direct, obvious, and highly ironic; it is not simply flippant and clever. The poet's urgent request to get on with the important horizontal business is one of the most traditional lyric responses to the overt awareness of mortality, one of humankind's principal talismans down through the centuries against the certainty of death.

The poems "somewhere i have never travelled,gladly beyond" and "you shall above all things be glad and young" provide good examples of Cummings's celebration of transcendental love. It should be noted that the categories, physical or sexual love and transcendental love, are not mutually exclusive. That is, nothing in "(ponder,darling,these busted statues" precludes the possibility that the lovers see something in each other deeper and more enduring than sex. However, it would be foolish to deny the sexual suggestiveness of the imagery of "somewhere i have never travelled,gladly beyond."

The poem "since feeling is first" is an explicit celebration of feeling, the wellspring of all lyricism. Examples of his affirmation of spontaneity, of nature, and of the natural and the childlike selves can be found in "when god lets my body be," "i thank You God for most this amazing," "in Just-," and "O sweet spontaneous." Cummings's intense tribute to his father, "my father moved through dooms of love," and his slight but moving poem for his mother, "if there are any heavens my mother will(all by herself)have," extend the range of lyric subject matter to include filial affection. The poem "anyone lived in a pretty how town" is Cummings's allegorical "everyman" which has a poignancy similar to that of Thornton Wilder's *Our Town* (1938).

These poems provide examples of Cummings's principal lyric subject matter. They also constitute a group useful for studying the formal variety found in some of his best poetry. Two of them, the poem on his father and "anyone lived in a pretty how town," are fairly conventional quatrains given a twist by Cummings's characteristic grammatical distortion: The parts of speech exchange roles. For example, the father moves "through griefs of joy" and sings "desire into begin." Everyman of "anyone lived in a pretty how town" "sang his didn't" and "danced his did." In general, the key to this special vocabulary, here and in other poems, is that the present, immediate, concrete, and spontaneous are being affirmed, while their opposites are being rejected. "Is" is superior to "was." The "dooms of feel" are to be celebrated; the "pomp of must and shall" scorned. In addition to these examples of Cummings's quatrains, this group also contains another of his fairly conventional sonnets, "i thank You God for most this amazing," and several free-verse poems, including "in Just-," and "O sweet spontaneous." As a group, they illustrate and support the generalization stated earlier that Cummings makes the most effective use of his distinctive devices in his more substantive lyric poetry.

SATIRIC POETRY

Because satirists use lyricism to intensify their satirical thrusts, there is often no hard line between satiric and lyric poetry. The distinction for Cummings in particular is more a matter of emphasis than a clear-cut distinction. Because so much of his poetry is primarily satirical, however, it is profitable to consider several appropriate examples. It is also instructive to note that, as with his best lyric poetry, his best satiric pieces are those characterized by an effective blending of his distinctive devices with the resources of traditional verse. An excellent example of such blending and of the use of lyric intensity for satiric purposes is "i sing of Olaf glad and big."

The poem looks and even sounds like free verse. It is, however, an intricately constructed set of interlocking quatrains and couplets in four-stress lines. The loosening of what sounds like very regular verse is effected by the spacing on the page and by the counterpoint of sentence or sense structure against the verse structure. That tension between verse and sense is intensified by the characteristic use of parentheses and syntactical inversions. As in "(ponder,darling,these busted statues," the parentheses are used conventionally for humorous asides, as when readers are told that colonel left the scene "hurriedly to shave," and for emphasis, as in the passages on Olaf's knees and Christ's mercy. The syntactical inversions effectively provide emphasis and hardly impede understanding. The hyphenating of the word "object-or" catches the genius of Cummings's style at its best. The poem is about a conscientious objector who becomes an "object" in the hands of his fellow soldiers.

The satire is directed not at the military or against war, but at the lockstep, group mentality that, although fostered particularly by the military, may be found in the highly organized structures of all institutions: corporate, religious, academic. For Cummings, affirmation of the bravery of the individual places heavy emphasis on "individual," and it is the group, crowd, or gang that is being indicated. The irony of the closing lines strongly suggests that the military is but the protective arm of the nation or culture locked into value systems symbolized by abstractions such as the nation's "blueeyed pride." Olaf, blond and blue-eyed, fits the abstraction, and hence his culpability is compounded. He was "blonder," however (that is, nearer the ideal of bravery and of manhood), than most and willing to pay lip service to the ideal, while others lose themselves in the false security of the crowd.

Two other satires set in the context of war but directed at more fundamental targets are "my sweet old etcetera" and "plato told." The first satirizes, in a light vein, attitudes very close to those of the soldiers of "i sing of Olaf glad and big." Aunts, sister, mother, and father all think war is glorious, while the soldier, who describes them, lies in the muddy trenches, thereby refuting the grandiose notions of those safe and comfortable at home. The satire "plato told" comes closest to being an indictment of war, but its focus is really on the obtuseness of "him," on his failure to understand what everyone has been telling him, which is that war is hell. All three of these "war" poems satirize a failure to see reality.

"Poem: Or, Beauty Hurts Mr. Vinal," one of Cummings's few titled poems, is a harsh but clever indictment of modern advertising and, implicitly, of the culture from which it derives. Cummings piles up actual lines from advertisements for garters, gum, shirt collars, drawers, Kodaks, and laxatives juxtaposed with fragments of lines from "America the Beautiful" and fragmented allusions to Robert Browning in the sixth verse paragraph. The poem makes fun of the glibness and excessive claims of advertising but then takes a turn toward the end to focus on Cummings's primary satiric target: men and women, "gelded" or "spaded," who have allowed themselves to be manipulated into anonymous units of the "market." Cummings makes the same point in one of his harshest sonnets, "a salesman is an it that stinks Excuse." Almost savage in tone, the poem once again links various seemingly incongruous activities in terms of the marketplace: the selling of "hate condoms education . . . democracy." The focus of Cummings's attack shifts from its ostensible targets—the military, advertising, and a salesman—to processes that rob people of their individuality and freedom of choice.

Cummings's innovative genius as a versifier, excessive in many of the lesser poems, is modified and restrained in his poems of substance, effecting in many of them happy unions of form and content. He is, as a result, a modernist poet of consequence.

OTHER MAJOR WORKS

PLAYS: *Him*, pb. 1927; *Tom: A Ballet*, pb. 1935; *Anthropos: The Future of Art*, pb. 1944; *Santa Claus: A Morality*, pb. 1946.

NONFICTION: *The Enormous Room*, 1922; *CIOPW*, 1931 (drawings); *Eimi*, 1933; *i: six nonlectures*, 1953; *Adventures in Value*, 1962 (photographs by Marion Morehouse).

TRANSLATION: *The Red Front*, 1933 (a selection of poems by Louis Aragon).

BIBLIOGRAPHY

Ahearn, Barry, ed. *Pound/Cummings: The Correspondence of Ezra Pound and E. E. Cummings*. Ann Arbor: University of Michigan Press, 1996. These interchanges cast light on both the poets and their times. Includes bibliographic references.

Bloom, Harold, ed. *E. E. Cummings*. Philadelphia: Chelsea House, 2003. A collection of essays on various aspects of the work and life of the poet Cummings.

Cowley, Malcolm. *A Second Flowering: Works and Days of the Lost Generation*. New York: Viking, 1973. Contains a chapter on Cummings that focuses on his life in the

1920's and 1930's. Discusses his philosophy and evaluates his poetry.

Dumas, Bethany K. *E. E. Cummings: A Remembrance of Miracles*. London: Vision Press, 1974. Contains a chapter on Cummings's life and several chapters analyzing his poetry, prose, and dramatic works. Includes a bibliography and indexes.

Flajšar, Jiří, and Zénó Vernyik, eds. *Words into Pictures: E. E. Cummings' Art Across Borders*. Newcastle, England: Cambridge Scholars, 2007. Contains essays examining Cummings's poetry and drama, particularly with respect to the limits of the linguistic, political, visual, and spatial vision of the poet.

Kennedy, Richard S. *Dreams in the Mirror: A Biography of E. E. Cummings*. New York: Liveright, 1980. A detailed, scholarly study of Cummings's life that discusses his poems and his philosophical views. Includes a chronological list of Cummings's works, a bibliographical essay on secondary works, an index, and illustrations.

_____. *E. E. Cummings Revisited*. New York: Twayne, 1994. Primarily an analysis of Cummings's major writings, it also provides a condensed version of his life interspersed with the analysis. Includes a chronology of the poet's life, a bibliography of works by and about him, an index, and numerous illustrations.

Kidder, Rushworth M. *E. E. Cummings: An Introduction to the Poetry*. New York: Columbia University Press, 1979. Kidder focuses on enduring values in Cummings's poetry. His commentaries are fresh and insightful, often correcting existing misconceptions. Includes a bibliography and indexes.

Lane, Gary. *I Am: A Study of E. E. Cummings' Poems*. Lawrence: University Press of Kansas, 1976. A good reference for new readers. Reprints selected poems, appending detailed discussions designed to make the obscure and complicated devices transparent. The critical apparatus features complete notes, an index, and a bibliographical note.

Sawyer-Lauçanno, Christopher. *E.E. Cummings: A Biography*. Naperville, Ill.: Sourcebooks, 2004. Massive in scope and in number of pages, this biography and literary study of Cummings is readable, comprehensive, and highly recommended.

Lloyd N. Dendinger

SERGEI ESENIN

Born: Konstantinovo (now Esenino), Ryazan province, Russia; October 3, 1895
Died: Leningrad, Soviet Union (now St. Petersburg, Russia); December 28, 1925

PRINCIPAL POETRY
Radunitsa, 1915 (*All Soul's Day*, 1991)
Goluben', 1918 (*Azure*, 1991; includes "Preobrazhenie," "Transfiguration"; "Prishestvie," "The Coming"; and "Inonia")
Ispoved' khuligana, 1921 (*Confessions of a Hooligan*, 1973)
Pugachov, 1922
Stikhi skandalista, 1923
Moskva kabatskaia, 1924
Anna Snegina, 1925
"Cherni chelovek," 1925
Persidskie motivi, 1925
Rus' sovetskaia, 1925
Strana sovetskaia, 1925
Sobranie sochinenii, 1961-1962 (5 volumes)
Selected Poetry, 1982
Complete Poetical Works in English, 2008

OTHER LITERARY FORMS

Sergei Esenin (yihs-YAYN-yihn) wrote little besides poetry. Some autobiographical introductions and a few revealing letters are helpful in analyzing his poetry. The short story "Bobyl i druzhok" and the tale "Yar" are rarely mentioned in critical discussion of Esenin's work, but his theoretical treatise "Kliuchi Marii" (1918; the keys of Mary) helps to explain his early revolutionary lyrics. This economically written, perceptive study traces the religious origins of various aspects of ancient Russian culture and art.

ACHIEVEMENTS

Perhaps the most controversial of all Soviet poets, Sergei Esenin is certainly also one of the most popular, among both Russian émigrés and citizens. The popularity of his poetry never diminished in Russia, despite a period of twenty-five years during which his work was suppressed and his character defamed. Officially, Esenin was labeled the Father of Hooliganism, and his works were removed from public libraries and reading rooms. In the early 1950's, however, his reputation was fully rehabilitated, and his poems have become widely available in Russia. In the twenty-first century, Esenin rivals

Aleksandr Blok, Vladimir Mayakovsky, and even Alexander Pushkin as the most popular of all Russian poets.

Although Esenin welcomed and supported the 1917 October Revolution, he soon began to have second thoughts. He did not like the transformation that was taking place in the rural areas, and he longed for the traditional simple peasant life and the old "wooden Russia." His flamboyant lifestyle, his alcoholism, and his dramatic suicide eventually brought him the scorn of the Soviet authorities.

The most important representative of the Imaginist movement in Russian poetry, Esenin at his best achieved a distinctive blend of deep lyricism, sincerity, melancholy, and nostalgia. Calling himself "the last poet of the village," Esenin used folk and religious motifs, images of nature, and colorful scenes from everyday village life, which he painted with a natural freshness and beauty. His disappointment with his own life, his unhappy marriages, and his apprehensions concerning the changes he saw at every hand—all are reflected in the mood of unfulfilled hope and sadness that pervades his poetry.

Biography

Sergei Aleksandrovich Esenin was born in the small village of Konstantinovo, since renamed Esenino in the poet's honor, in the fertile Ryazan province. His parents were poor farmers, and because his mother had married against the will of her parents, the Titovs, the couple received no support from their families. Esenin's father had to go to Moscow, where he worked in a butcher shop, in order to send home some money. When he stopped sending the money, his wife had no other choice but to find work as a live-in servant. Her parents at last decided to help and took the young boy to live with them.

Esenin's grandfather, Feodor Andreevich Titov, belonged to a religious sect known as the Old Believers; he frequently recited religious poems and folk songs, and he approached life with an optimistic vigor. Esenin's grandmother sang folk songs and told her grandson many folktales. Both grandparents adored the young Esenin, who lived a happy and relatively carefree life. They made a great impression on the young boy.

From 1904 to 1909, Esenin attended the village school, where, with little effort, he graduated with excellent marks. His grandfather Titov decided that Esenin should become a teacher and sent him to the church-run Spas-Klepiki pedagogical school from 1909 to 1912. At first, Esenin was extremely unhappy in the new surroundings; he even ran away once and walked forty miles back to his grandparents' home. Eventually, however, he became reconciled to his fate, and he was noticed by his teachers and peers for the unusual ease with which he wrote poetry. The boy with the blond, curly hair became self-confident and even boastful, which made him unpopular with some of his fellow students.

At the age of sixteen, after his graduation in 1912, Esenin decided not to continue his studies at a teacher's institute in Moscow. Instead, he returned to his grandparents' home and devoted his life to poetry. He was happy to be free to roam aimlessly through the fields and the forests, and his early poems reflect his love for animals and for the rural landscape. Although he also used religious themes in his early poems, Esenin was probably not very religious, certainly not as devoted as his grandfather. He was, however, very familiar with the religious traditions of the Old Believers and with the patriarchal way of life.

Esenin realized that to become known as a poet, he had to move to a big city. In 1912, he moved to Moscow, taking a job in the butcher's shop where his father worked. He disliked the job but soon found work as a bookstore clerk, where he was happier. Esenin also joined the Surikov circle, a large group of proletarian and peasant writers.

Esenin lost his job in the bookstore, but in May of 1913, he became a proofreader in a printing shop. The work strengthened his interest in the labor movement, and though he never completely accepted the ideology of the Social Revolutionary Party, he distributed illegal literature and supported other revolutionary activities. To learn more about history and world literature, Esenin took evening courses at the Shaniavski People's University in Moscow. With his goal of becoming a great poet, he recognized the need to broaden his education.

The foremost Russian writers of the time, however, lived in St. Petersburg rather than in Moscow, and in March of 1915, Esenin moved to Petrograd (as St. Petersburg was known between 1914, when Russia went to war against Germany, and 1924, when it became Leningrad). Upon his arrival, Esenin went to see Blok, who helped the young "peasant" and introduced him to well-known poets such as Zinaida Gippius, Feodor Sologub, and Vyacheslav Ivanov and to novelists such as Ivan Bunin, Aleksandr Kuprin, and Dmitry Merezhkovsky. The young poet Anatoly Mariengof became Esenin's intimate friend. Esenin was appointed as an editor of the political and literary journal *Severnie Zapiski*, an appointment that brought him in contact with other writers and intellectuals. Through the help of a fellow peasant poet, Nikolai Klyuyev, Esenin met the publisher M. V. Averyanov, who published Esenin's first volume of poems, *All Soul's Day*, in 1915.

In the autumn of 1915, Esenin was drafted into the army, which for him was a tragedy. He agonized in the dirty barracks and under the commands of the drill sergeant. Eventually, he succeeded in being transferred to the Commission of Trophies, a special unit for artists, but he neglected his duties so flagrantly that he was ordered to a medical unit stationed near the czar's residence in Tsarskoe Selo. The czarina discovered that the young poet was stationed nearby and invited him to the court to read his poetry. Esenin was flattered, but he also carried in his heart a deep hatred for the monarchy. Under some still unclear circumstances, Esenin left Tsarskoe Selo before February of 1917, and in 1918 he published his second volume of poetry, *Azure*.

In August of 1917, Esenin married Zinaida Raikh, who was then working as a typist for a newspaper published by the Socialist Revolutionary Party. The marriage ended in divorce in October, 1921, following the birth of two children. Raikh, who subsequently became a famous actress, married the great theatrical director Vsevolod Meyerhold. Esenin maintained ties with Raikh until the end of his life, and the dissolution of his first marriage established the pattern that was to mark his last years.

In 1918, however, Esenin was hopeful and ambitious, on the verge of fame. In March of 1918, he again moved to Moscow and continued to write optimistic, mythical poetry about the future of Russia. He tried to understand the revolution, although he abhorred the suffering it brought. In late 1918, during a visit to his native Konstantinovo, Esenin observed the passivity of the peasants. With the poem "Inonia," he tried to incite them to positive action.

During this period, Esenin, with several minor poets such as Mariengof, formed a literary movement known as Imaginism. The Imaginists (*imazhinisty*) had been inspired by an article about the Imagist movement in English and American poetry, founded by Ezra Pound. Except for the name, however, and—more important—the doctrine that the image is the crucial component of poetry, there was little connection between Pound's Imagism and the Russian Imaginism. For Esenin, the movement encouraged liberation from the peasant themes and mythical religiosity of his early verse. In addition, as is evident in the Imaginist manifesto of 1919, the movement was useful in attracting publicity, of which Esenin was very conscious.

In the fall of 1921, at a studio party, Esenin met the well-known American dancer Isadora Duncan, who was giving a series of dance recitals in Russia. Although Esenin spoke no English and Duncan knew only a few phrases in Russian, they found enough attraction in each other for Esenin to move immediately into Duncan's apartment. The turbulence of the relationship became notorious. In 1922, Duncan needed to raise money for her new dancing school in Moscow. She wanted to give a series of dance recitals in Western Europe and in the United States, but she also realized the difficulties she and Esenin would face in the United States if they were not legally married. On May 2, 1922, they were married, and Esenin became the first (and the only legal) husband of Duncan.

The United States disappointed Esenin. He could not communicate, and even Prohibition did not slow down his acute alcoholism. In the United States, he was seen merely as the husband of Duncan, not as a famous Russian poet. The skyscrapers could not replace the gray sky over the Russian landscape. After a nervous breakdown, Esenin returned alone to Russia, and when Duncan returned some time later, he refused to live with her again.

After his return to the Soviet Union, Esenin became increasingly critical of the new order. He was never able to accept the atmosphere of cruelty and destruction during the civil war, and the ruthless law of vengeance carried out by many fanatics, even after the war, was criminal in his eyes. It was difficult for Esenin both as an individual and as a poet to conform to Lenin's new economic policy period. To some extent, he regarded this difficulty as a personal failure and reacted to it with spells of depression alternating with outbursts of wild revelry. He styled himself a "hooligan," and he excused his heavy drinking, drug taking, barroom brawls, blasphemous verse, and all-night orgies as fundamentally revolutionary acts.

At the same time, Esenin saw himself as a prodigal son. He yearned for motherly love, the healing touch of nature, and the peaceful countryside. In 1924, he returned to his native village, but he could not find the "wooden Russia" that he had once glorified in his poems. *Rus' sovetskaia* (Soviet Russia), his famous poem of 1925, expresses his isolation in his own country. The revolution had not fulfilled Esenin's dreams of a rural utopia, and he, "the last poet of the village," was among its victims.

From September, 1924, until February, 1925, Esenin visited Baku and the Crimea, a trip that resulted in the publication of the collection *Persidskie motivi* (Persian motifs). In 1925, he married Sofya Tolstaya, one of Leo Tolstoy's granddaughters. The marriage was predictably unhappy; Esenin's deteriorating health caused him to be admitted repeatedly to hospitals. He managed to write the somewhat autobiographical long poem *Anna Snegina*, which describes the fate of the prerevolutionary people in the new Soviet society. The poor reception of the poem and the harsh criticism it provoked devastated Esenin.

The poet began to mention suicide more frequently. Even though his physical health improved, Esenin remained very depressed. In December of 1925, he left his wife in Moscow and went to Leningrad, where he stayed at the Hotel Angleterre. He was there for several days and was frequently visited by friends. On December 27, Esenin cut his arm and in his own blood wrote his last poem, "Do svidan'ia, drug moi, do svidan'ia..." ("Good-bye, My Friend, Good-bye"); later that day, Esenin gave the poem to friends (who neglected to read it) and showed the cut to them, complaining that there was no ink in his room. In the early hours of December 28, the poet hanged himself on a radiator pipe.

Esenin's widow arrived the next day and took her husband's body in a decorated railroad car to Moscow. In Moscow, thousands of people waited for the arrival of the train. Fellow writers and artists carried the coffin from the train station to its temporary resting place in a public building, where thousands more paid their last respects. Esenin was buried on the last day of 1925.

Analysis

Sergei Esenin's poetry can be divided into two parts: first the poetry of the countryside, the village, and the animals and, second, the primarily postrevolutionary poetry of *Moskva kabatskaia* (Moscow the tavern city) and of *Rus' sovetskaia*. Generally, the village poetry is natural and simple, while many of the later poems are more pretentious and affected. The mood of country landscapes, the joys of village life, and the love for animals is created with powerful melodiousness. The poet's sincere nostalgia for "wooden Russia" is portrayed so strongly that it becomes infectious. Esenin creates idylls of the simple Russian village and of country life with the freshness of a skilled painter, yet the musicality of his verse is the most characteristic quality of his poetry. His simple, sweet, and touching early lyrics are easy to understand and are still loved by millions of readers in Russia.

As a "peasant poet," Esenin differed from some other Russian peasant poets of the time, such as Nikolai Klyuyev and Pyotr Oreshin. Esenin stressed primarily the inner life of the peasant, while the others paid more attention to the peasants' environment. His peasants are free of material things, even though they are part of their environment, while in the work of other peasant poets, things are preeminent.

Esenin's early poems chiefly employ the vocabulary of the village; they reveal the influence of the *chastushki*, the popular folk songs widely heard in any Russian village. When he arrived in Petrograd, Esenin presented himself as "the poet of the people"; dressed in a peasant blouse adorned with a brightly colored silk cord, he chanted his poems about harvests, rivers, and meadows.

When Esenin moved to Petrograd, he began to learn the sophisticated techniques of the Symbolists, particularly from the poet Blok. Esenin was able to create a complete picture of a landscape or a village with a single image. He continued, however, to maintain the melancholy mood and the sadness that would always be typical of his poetry.

At the time of his suicide, Esenin was still quite popular, both in the Soviet Union and among Russian émigrés. Beginning in 1926, the State Publishing House published Esenin's collected works in four volumes, but many poems were missing from this edition. By that time, the "morally weak Eseninism" had been officially denounced. In 1948, a one-volume selection of Esenin's poetry was published, and it sold out immediately. By the early 1950's, Esenin was fully rehabilitated, and in 1961, a five-volume edition appeared, which has since been reprinted several times. According to Russian critics, Esenin's tremendous popularity can be explained by the fact that his poetry was consonant with the feelings of the Russian people during the most difficult days in their history.

All Soul's Day

Esenin's first collection, *All Soul's Day*, radiates happiness, although it is not free of the melancholy typical of his works. These early poems express the joy of village life, the poet's love for his homeland, and the pleasures of youth; even the colors are light and gay: blue, white, green, red. Esenin employs religious themes and Christian terminology, but the poems are more pantheistic, even pagan, than Christian. *All Soul's Day* was well received by the critical Petrograd audience, and this response immeasurably boosted Esenin's confidence. The poet was only twenty years old when he proved his mastery of the Russian language.

AZURE

Esenin's second collection, *Azure*, appeared after the revolution, in 1918, but the majority of the poems were written during World War I. These poems reflect Esenin's uncertainty concerning the future, although he did accept and praise the October Revolution. He visualized the revolution as a glorious cosmic upheaval leading to a resurrection of Russia and its rural roots. The style, mood, and vocabulary of *Azure* reveal the influence of Blok and Klyuyev.

Although Esenin undoubtedly was initially on the side of the Bolsheviks, his vision of the revolution was a highly individual one. He saw a return to peasant communities and to a primitive democratic simplicity. The threatening industrialization and the technological development of the mysterious electricity, the hidden source of power, which he witnessed later, horrified him. Three long poems with religiously symbolic titles, which were part of the *Azure* cycle, reflect this attitude: "Preobrazhenie" ("Transfiguration") "Prishestvie" ("The Coming"), and "Inonia."

The well-known poem "Inonia" reflects with particular clarity Esenin's wish for a peasant utopia, an anticapitalist, agricultural republic that could resist the industrial giants. Esenin saw himself as the prophet of a new religion that had to overcome the peasants' traditional Christianity to bring about a happy, rural, socialist paradise. By 1920, however, Esenin realized that the results of the revolution were slowly destroying his "rural Russia," and he saw himself as "the last poet of the village."

PUGACHOV

During this period of growing disillusionment, Esenin began to forsake the simplicity and the rural spirit of his early verse, although folk elements never disappeared from his work. Among the most significant of his more experimental Imaginist poems was the long dramatic poem *Pugachov*, published in 1922. This unfinished verse drama exhibits the unusual metaphors and verbal eccentricities that were characteristic of the Imaginists. The hero of Esenin's poem, the Cossack leader of a peasant rebellion in the 1770's, is highly idealized and bears little resemblance to the historical Pugachev. In contrast to Pushkin, who treated the same subject in his novella *Kapitanskaya dochka* (1836; *The Captain's Daughter*, 1846), Esenin sympathized with Pugachev and his peasants. He also drew parallels between Pugachev's revolt and the October Revolution: In his view, both had failed because of human egotism and people's unwillingness to sacrifice for the common good.

"STRANA NEGODIAEV"

In 1922 and 1923, partially during his trip to the United States and Western Europe and partially after his return, Esenin wrote another dramatic poem. "Strana negodiaev" (the country of scoundrels), influenced by Western cinema, marked a departure from the Imaginist style of *Pugachov*. In it, Esenin abandoned striking imagery in favor of a rather crude realistic style. He never completed the poem, however, realizing that it was a failure. In the poem, Esenin refers to America as a greedy trap in which deceit is the key to survival; at the same time, he acknowledges the industrial achievement of the West. In sympathizing with the anti-Soviet hero of this dramatic poem, Esenin confirmed that he had lost much of his enthusiasm for the revolution.

Moskva kabatskaia

Indeed, by 1923, Esenin saw himself as lost in his own country. He did not reject the revolution itself but the results of the revolution. He was already notorious for his alcoholism, his orgiastic lifestyle, and his escapades around Moscow. His most decadent poems were included in the collection *Moskva kabatskaia*. In these poems, he confessed that he would have become a thief if he had not been a poet, and he exposed all his vices. These poems reflect Esenin's disappointment with himself, with love, and with religion.

The poet of the village and the countryside became overshadowed in the 1920's by the alcoholic of *Moskva kabatskaia*. Esenin's manner became harsher, reflecting the worsening crisis of his life. Gentle laments for the passing of the idealized countryside were replaced by nostalgia for lost youth and the search for a home. Esenin largely abandoned the devices cultivated by the Imaginists, returning to the materials of his early verse yet handling them in a new manner—stark, assured, despairing.

With the poems of *Moskva kabatskaia*, Esenin sought to reconcile himself with the new Russia. In the celebrated poem "Rus' sovetskaia," he admits that he is too old to change, and he fears that he will be left behind by younger generations. In a mixture of resignation and defiance, he accepts the new order and resolves to continue writing poetry not by society's standards but by his own.

Persidskie motivi

During his visit to Baku and the Caucasus in 1925, Esenin wrote a cycle of short poems entitled *Persidskie motivi*. Technically, the poems are well written, but Esenin's love lyrics addressed to different girls, in which genuine nostalgia mingles with superficiality and a lack of conviction, suggest that the poet was nearing a dead end.

Anna Snegina

In 1925, Esenin also published the long autobiographical poem *Anna Snegina*, written during his stay in Batum. The poem describes a love affair set in a Russian village during the civil war. Soviet critics, however, were not interested in decadent love affairs; they expected poetry promoting the revolutionary spirit. Esenin was not able to produce this; he remained the anachronistic dreamer of a rural utopia. In his eyes, Soviet society had no need of him nor of his poetry.

Other major work

NONFICTION: "Kliuchi Marii," 1918.

Bibliography

Brengauz, Gregory. *Yesenin: Lyrics and Life—Introduction to Russian Poetry*. 2d ed. Tallahassee: Floridian Publisher, 2006. This biography, in Russian and English, looks at Esenin's life and works.

Davis, J. *Esenin: A Biography in Memoirs, Letters, and Documents*. Ann Arbor, Mich.: Ardis, 1982. Davis culls the autobiographical material from the poet's work and complements it with biographical commentaries, shedding light on various aspects of Esenin's life. These materials, in turn, shed light on his poetry.

De Graaff, Frances. *Sergei Esenin: A Biographical Sketch*. The Hague, the Netherlands: Mouton, 1966. In his valuable study of Esenin's life and poetry, De Graaff combines biography with the poet's works, bolstering his observations with citations from many poems, in Russian and English. Includes an extensive bibliography.

Esenin, Sergei. *Complete Poetical Works in English*. Translated by Victoria Bul. Tallahassee: Floridian Publisher, 2008. Contains an introduction and biography by the translator, poems by poets who influenced or were influenced by Esenin, and a section of Isadora Duncan's autobiography.

McVay, Gordon. *Esenin: A Life*. Ann Arbor, Mich.: Ardis, 1976. In this definitive biography of Esenin in English, the author encompasses the poet's entire life, including his tragic death by suicide. The book offers brief analyses of Esenin's works along with copious illustrations.

Mariengof, Anatoli. *A Novel Without Lies*. Translated by Jose Alaniz. Chicago: Ivan R. Dee, 2000. A detailed memoir of Mariengof's association with Esenin and the literary avant-garde of the 1920's.

Prokushev, Yuri. *Sergei Esenin: The Man, the Verse, the Age*. Moscow: Progress, 1979. In this biography of Esenin by a Russian scholar, Prokushev offers the Russian point of view of the poet and his poetry. The emphasis is on the biographical details. It is somewhat tinted ideologically, stressing Esenin's often failed efforts to adapt to the Soviet reality, his love for Russia, and the realistic aspects of his poetry. Despite its politically motivated slant, the book is full of interesting observations.

Thurley, Geoffrey. Introduction to *Confessions of a Hooligan*, by Sergei Esenin. Cheadle, England: Hulme, 1973. A book of translations of Esenin's poems about his struggle against alcoholism. In the introduction, Thurley examines circumstances that led to the writing of these poems.

Visson, Lynn. *Sergei Esenin: Poet of the Crossroads*. Würzburg, Germany: Jal, 1980. Visson undertakes a thorough, expert analysis of the stylistic features of Esenin's poetry, with extensive quotations from the poems, in Russian and in English, offering penetrating insights into the artistic merits of Esenin's poetry and gauging the scope of his contribution to Russian poetry.

Rado Pribic

BARBARA GUEST

Born: Wilmington, North Carolina; September 6, 1920
Died: Berkeley, California; February 15, 2006

PRINCIPAL POETRY
The Location of Things, 1960
Poems: The Location of Things, Archaics, The Open Skies, 1963
The Blue Stairs, 1968
I Ching: Poems and Lithographs, 1969
Moscow Mansions, 1973
The Countess from Minneapolis, 1976
The Türler Losses, 1979
Biography, 1980
Quilts, 1980
The Nude, 1986
Fair Realism, 1989
The Altos, 1991
Defensive Rapture, 1993
Selected Poems, 1995
Stripped Tales, 1995
Rocks on a Platter: Notes on Literature, 2000
Symbiosis, 2000
Miniatures, and Other Poems, 2002
The Red Gaze, 2005
The Collected Poems of Barbara Guest, 2008 (Hadley Haden Guest, editor)

OTHER LITERARY FORMS

Barbara Guest wrote mainly poetry, but she did publish in other genres. She wrote a number of plays, three of which were produced: *The Ladies Choice* (pr. 1953), *The Office* (pr. 1961), and *Port* (pr. 1965). Her only novel, *Seeking Air*, was published in 1978. She wrote a biography of poet H. D., *Herself Defined: The Poet H. D. and Her World* (1984). Guest also wrote articles and reviews for art magazines. She had a lifelong interest in visual art, which often served as the inspiration for her poems.

ACHIEVEMENTS

Barbara Guest was the best known of the female members of the New York School of poets. She earned many honors for her poetry, including a Yaddo Fellowship (1958), the Longwood Award (1968) for *The Location of Things*, a Poetry Foundation Prize

(1973) for *Moscow Mansions*, a grant from the National Endowment for the Arts (1978), three Fund for Poetry Awards (1978, 1994, 1996), the Lawrence J. Lipton Prize (1990) for *Fair Realism*, two Jerome J. Shestack Poetry Prizes (1991, 1994), two San Francisco State Poetry Center Book Awards (1993) for *Defensive Rapture* and 2008 for *The Collected Poems of Barbara Guest*, two American Awards for Literature in the best poetry category (1995, 1996), the Josephine Miles Award (1996), and the Frost Medal (1999). Guest was hailed by critics and fellow poets as producing works that masterfully blended the illusion of landscape paintings, classical literature, historical context, and a sort of mysticism that incorporated yet transcended all those influential subjects. Guest also collaborated with artists to create books of poetry that included watercolors or other artwork.

Biography

Barbara Guest was born Barbara Ann Pinson on September 6, 1920, in Wilmington, North Carolina, to James Harvey Pinson and Anna Mae Pinson. Her parents were in Wilmington a very brief time while her father looked for work. Guest had two brothers and two sisters. The family moved around a great deal, and the young Guest bounced between Charleston, West Virginia, where her grandparents lived, and small towns near Miami, Florida, where her parents were staying. The lack of a stable, consistent home and a secure place within her family created an anxiety-based tension in Guest that revealed itself later in her writings. Her work often reflected an undercurrent of impermanence and a sense of timelessness and lack of definitive parameters. Guest's early education was completed in small, rural rustic schools, where she outdistanced her classmates, having learned to read at age three.

Because the young Guest showed high aptitude at a very early age, her West Virginia grandmother thought it wise to encourage her talent by exposing her to a good liberal education. She was therefore sent to live with an aunt and uncle who lived in Los Angeles. Guest graduated from Beverly Hills High School in 1938. She then attended the University of California, Los Angeles, majoring in English literature. She met her future husband, painter and sculptor John Dudley, during her freshman year. Dissatisfied with the poetry classes, she transferred to the University of California, Berkeley, earning a B.A. in English literature in 1943. After returning to Los Angeles, Guest obtained a social work job and married Dudley. The couple moved to New York City in 1946 and were divorced later that year. Guest married Englishman Stephen Haden Guest and began writing poetry under the pen name of Barbara Guest. She gave birth to a daughter, Hadley Haden Guest, in 1949. Guest was divorced from her husband in 1954, and she soon married war historian Trumbull Higgins. The couple had a son, Jonathan Higgins, in 1955.

In the 1950's, Guest became a pivotal member of the New York School of poets and shortly thereafter began writing for *Art News*. Her play *The Ladies Choice* was staged in

New York City in 1953. Her first major volume of poetry, *The Location of Things*, was published in 1960.

Guest continued to write more highly acclaimed poems and poetry collections, and two more of her plays, *The Office* and *Port*, were staged. She wrote several other plays during this time, but they were not staged. Her one novel, *Seeking Air*, was published in 1978. For this effort, Guest received a National Endowment for the Arts grant and the Fund for Poetry Award.

Guest spent five years writing *Herself Defined*, a biography of the poet H. D. After its publication in 1984, it became one of her most noted prose efforts. Her choice of subject was inspired by the impact that H. D.'s works had on her; H. D. was famed throughout Europe as the poet who popularized a tightly constructed free-verse type of writing that became known as Imagism. That H. D. was a childhood sweetheart of renowned writer Ezra Pound only added to the appeal and widespread interest in her life and poetic works.

Guest continued to write poems, prose, and plays throughout the 1980's, 1990's, and up to her death in 2006. Her last publication was the poetry collection *The Red Gaze*, which appeared in 2005. After her death, her daughter, Hadley Haden Guest, published *The Collected Poems of Barbara Guest*, which contains all her published poems and some previously unpublished poems.

Analysis

Barbara Guest adamantly believed that poems should be elusive, mysterious, and obscure, yet at the same time concise and clear. She felt that poems should touch the reader in a self-identifying way, yet leave room for metaphorical ellipses of thought—words and thoughts left unsaid. Guest's use of white space and a pervading sense of erased thoughts and actions blurred the lines between subject, object, and intent, leaving the reader with both a sense of identity and mystery—life without boundaries. Guest also relied heavily on visual arts, infusing her works repeatedly with painterly aspects and nuance.

Symbiosis

Symbiosis, a poem fusing the written word and a painting, is a successful collaboration between Guest and artist Laurie Reid. Poet and artist join together to create a visually and emotionally harmonious yet elusive use of space, color, and texture. Within the poem is an unusual sense of time and space, created by Guest's reliance on actual white, or blank, space on the page. The artist and poet seem to use and feed each other in the process of creating the sense of imagery so often present in Guest's work. Many elements make up this imagery: separations and rejoinings of artist and writer; references to syntax, image, and literati to conjure up the work of a poet; and objects such as wood, paper, and wild berries that might be included in a still life by painters. Reid and Guest create a "symbiosis" of talent by expressing both their differences and their similarities.

Miniatures, and Other Poems

Miniatures, and Other Poems again fuses the gifts of poets and writers with cultural elements from the visual arts, music, theater, and dance. It contains poems that seem both sparse and all-encompassing. Incorporated within the poetry is concise syntax used to carry the reader to infinite conclusions. The collection is divided into three sections: "Miniatures," "Pathos," and "Blurred Edged." The poems in "Miniatures" include references to writers such as Anton Chekhov and John Keats, historical periods of visual art such as Romanticism, musical artists such as Franz Liszt and Richard Wagner, and a host of other artistic elements. Guest incorporates her own voice into this varied palette of artistic genres, with her usual and perfected sense of blurred time and space, imagination and reality.

The Red Gaze

The Red Gaze was published shortly before Guest's death. The seemingly obvious interpretation of *The Red Gaze* is to look, or gaze, on subjects of bright color, or to look through a brightly colored personal lens. Following Guest's belief that poetry should reflect art forms, especially painting, the poetry in this collection details those nuances usually found in paintings: color, texture, dimensions (real or distorted), light and dark, depth, and the intuitive reaction by the reader (or viewer) of the works.

The opening poem, "Nostalgia," is an elliptical tale that is initially suggestive of modern America failing to free itself from the traditions of ancestral Europe. The poem almost imperceptibly fades into the futility of focusing on the past and shifts its forward "gaze" into the modern world. The European traditions become so far distant that they disintegrate, a process that Guest symbolizes visually with fragmented lines within the poem. "Nostalgia" for the old ways, then, looks more and more like a rejection of those same ways. Ambiguity and its opposite, certainty, both play significant roles in this poem.

In the title poem, "The Red Gaze," color is the predominant impression. The poem's few lines also contain an evolution of sorts. The reader can easily see the painterly illusions within the poem, which takes a simple tree and its leaves through vibrancy and strength to starkness and death—although as might be expected of Guest, there is a hopeful hint of serenity and rebirth at the end of the poem. The very last line, though seemingly succinctly heralding the end of the poem, actually suggests a new beginning. This poem, therefore, could serve as a synopsis for Guest's artistic theories and style: fading in and out of hope and despair, looking on not only the solidity of material objects but also the suggestion of what has come before and may again return.

In "Hans Hoffman," the famous painter and teacher conducts a class in nature. Though the colors are vivid and warm, they soon mesh into dark and cold, returning again to the vibrant color of red to which Hans is so attached. Again in this poem, Guest invokes patterns of nature, color, perception, and nuances that reflect the world of art and her painterly poetic style.

OTHER MAJOR WORKS

LONG FICTION: *Seeking Air*, 1978.

PLAYS: *The Ladies Choice*, pr. 1953; *The Office*, pr. 1961; *Port*, pr. 1965.

NONFICTION: *Herself Defined: The Poet H. D. and Her World*, 1984; *Dürer in the Window: Reflections on Art*, 2003 (with Africa Wayne); *Forces of Imagination: Writing on Writing*, 2003.

BIBLIOGRAPHY

Caples, Garrett. "Barbara Guest in the Shadow of Surrealism." *Chicago Review* 53/54 (Summer, 2008): 153-161. Views Guest's later poetry in terms of its relation to Surrealism. Examines "Hotel Comfort," the last poem she wrote, and "The Shadow of Surrealism," an essay collected in *Forces of Imagination*. Half of this issue of the *Chicago Review* was devoted to a tribute to Guest.

Fox, Margalit. "Barbara Guest, Eighty-five: Pioneering Poet of the New York School." *The New York Times*, March 4, 2006, p. A11. Obituary of Guest examines her life and works, noting her inclusion in the New York School and her use of the visual in her poet.

Guest, Barbara. *The Collected Poems of Barbara Guest*. Edited by Hadley Haden Guest. Middletown, Conn.: Wesleyan University Press, 2008. This collection, edited by Guest's daughter, brings together Guest's works and adds a few new poems. Includes an introduction by Peter Gizzi, brief sections of analysis, and a time line that details personal milestones and career accomplishments.

Knight, Brenda. *Women of the Beat Generation: The Writers, Artists, and Muses at the Heart of a Revolution*. Berkeley, Calif.: Conari Press, 1996. Contains a chapter dealing with Guest and Elise Cowen.

Nelson, Maggie. *Women, the New York School, and Other True Abstractions*. Iowa City: University of Iowa Press, 2007. This discussion of the New York School examines Guest's role.

Rankine, Claudia, and Juliana Spahr, eds. *American Women Poets in the Twenty-first Century: Where Lyric Meets Language*. Middletown, Conn.: Wesleyan University Press, 2002. An anthology of women poets of the twenty-first century, including Guest, with analysis by the authors of the anthology.

Ronk, Martha. "A Foreign Substance." *Chicago Review* 53/54 (Summer, 2008): 109-114. Examines Guest's use of imagery, focusing on the poem "Wild Gardens Overlooked by Night Lights" and the essay "H. D. and the Conflict of Imagism." Ronk likens Guest's images to foreign substances.

Twyla R. Wells

ZBIGNIEW HERBERT

Born: Lvov, Poland (now Lvov, Ukraine); October 29, 1924
Died: Warsaw, Poland; July 28, 1998

PRINCIPAL POETRY
Struna światła, 1956
Hermes, pies i gwiazda, 1957
Studium przedmiotu, 1961
Selected Poems, 1968
Napis, 1969
Poezje wybrane, 1970
Wiersze zebrane, 1971
Pan Cogito, 1974 (*Mr. Cogito*, 1993)
Selected Poems, 1977
Raport z oblezonego miasta i inne wiersze, 1983 (*Report from the Besieged City, and Other Poems*, 1985)
Elegia na odejście, 1990 (translation in *Elegy for the Departure, and Other Poems*, 1999)
Elegy for the Departure, and Other Poems, 1999
The Collected Poems, 1956-1998, 2007 (Robert Hass, editor)

OTHER LITERARY FORMS

Zbigniew Herbert (KEHR-behrt) was primarily a poet, but he was also a prose writer of considerable originality and distinction. A collection of essays titled *Barbarzyńca w ogrodzie* (*Barbarian in the Garden*, 1985) appeared in Poland in 1962; these essays are a unique combination of personal, richly poetic, firsthand description with analytical, scholarly research. Herbert also wrote several plays, including radio plays as well as works for the stage; a collection of his dramatic works was published in 1970 under the title *Dramaty* (plays).

In addition, Herbert published works in a genre of his own invention, his "apocryphas." These prose pieces are a synthesis of the short story and the essay; they contest traditional accounts or interpretations of major historical events and present the very different ("apocryphal") interpretations of the author. Although most of Herbert's apocryphas take their subjects from Western European history, some go farther afield—to Chinese history, for example.

ACHIEVEMENTS

Zbigniew Herbert exerted great influence as a poet and as a moral force both in Poland and Western Europe. He was above all the spokesperson of the individual conscience. He excited interest as a political poet, but although his poems addressed major political issues, they went far beyond immediate issues and encompassed a broad range of problems that are both philosophical and personal. Herbert resisted categorization and never represented a group or school of any kind. He gave the impression of being entirely alone, answerable only to his conscience—yet he managed at the same time to pitch his voice in such a way that he was one of the most authentically public poets of the age. This was the paradox of Herbert that gives his poetry its particular stamp.

Although Herbert was an antirhetorical poet, it is difficult to separate the content of his writing from his style. His poetic forms and rhythms exerted a powerful influence on other poets. One of the two greatest living Polish poets (the other, Czesław Miłosz, has translated a number of Herbert's poems into English), his influence has been acknowledged not only by younger Polish poets such as Ryszard Krynicki, Stanisław Barańczak, and Jacek Bierezin but also by a wide range of poets in the United States and throughout the West.

Herbert's influence was recognized with several awards throughout his career. In 1958, he won the Polish Radio Competition Prize, and in 1964, he received the Millennium Prize from the Polish Institute of Arts and Sciences (United States). For his contribution to European literature, he was awarded the Nickolas Lenau Prize (Austria) in 1965. In 1973, he received both the Alfred Jurzykowski Prize and the Herder Prize. He also won the Petrarch Prize in 1979, the Bruno Schulz Prize in 1988, the Jerusalem Literature Prize in 1991, and a Jurzykowski Foundation Award.

Biography

Zbigniew Herbert grew up in the Polish city of Lvov; in 1939, when he was fifteen years old, this part of Poland was invaded by the Soviet Union. Herbert began to write poetry during World War II, and the war permanently shaped his outlook. The face of postwar Poland was permanently changed, socially, physically, and politically: Herbert's native city became part of the Soviet Union.

In 1944, Herbert studied at the Academy of Fine Arts in Kraków—he was always interested in painting, sculpture, and architecture—and a year later, he entered the Academy of Commerce, also in Kraków. In 1947, he received a master's degree in economics and moved to Toruń, where he studied law at the Nicolas Copernicus University. He received the degree of master of laws in 1950. Herbert stayed on in Toruń to study philosophy and was influenced by the philosopher Henryk Eizenberg. In 1950, he lived briefly in Gdańsk and worked there for the *Merchant's Review* before moving to Warsaw, where for the next six years, he held a variety of jobs: in the management office of the peat industry, in the department for retired pensioners of the Teachers' Cooperative, in a bank, in a store, and in the legal department of the Composers' Association.

Herbert's poems began to appear in periodicals in 1950, but no collection was published in book form; during the increasing social and cultural repression of the Stalinist years, several of the magazines publishing Herbert's work were closed by the government. It was only after the "thaw" of 1956 that his first two collections of poems were published, almost simultaneously. The event of publication after enforced silence is poignantly described in Herbert's poem "Drawer."

In the late 1950's, Herbert made his first trip to Western Europe. His collection of essays, *Barbarian in the Garden*, reveals the impact of this experience. Herbert spent 1965 to 1971 abroad, based in West Berlin but traveling to many countries, among them Greece, Italy, France, and the United States. He spent the 1970-1971 academic year teaching at California State University, Los Angeles. After returning to Poland to live in 1971, Herbert moved to West Berlin again in 1974, staying there intermittently until 1980, when he returned to Warsaw. He again left Poland in 1986 in protest of Communist policies but returned to Warsaw once communism was ended around 1990. Around this time, his health began to deteriorate and when, in 1996, the Nobel Prize was awarded to Wisława Szymborska (only seventeen years after another Pole and adopted Californian, Czesław Miłosz), the joy of this deserved distinction was mixed with a touch of regret for Herbert. For many, Herbert's achievements equaled those of his two honored compatriots, and there were those who considered him superior to both. He died in Warsaw on July 28, 1998.

Analysis

Zbigniew Herbert was a member of the generation of poets who came to maturity during World War II. They are known as the War Generation, but they are also referred to in Polish literary criticism as *Kolumbowie* (Columbuses), because it was they who first "explored" the new postwar reality. This generation proved to be one of the most talented in twentieth century Polish literature, including, in addition to Herbert, such varied figures as Tadeusz Różewicz, Miron Bialoszewski, Tymoteusz Karpowicz, Szymborska, and Anna Swir. The war left an indelible imprint on all of them; as late as 1969, in the poem "Prologue," which introduced Herbert's fourth collection of poems, he wrote about those who took part in the war: "I must carry them to a dry place/ and make a large mound of sand/ before spring strews flowers for them/ and a great green dream stupefies them."

Lessons from the War

Few assumptions about the world and about civilization—what it is and what it is not—survived the war unscathed. The sense of continuity was broken, and many shared the vantage point of what might be called the "rubbish heap" of the present. Herbert's poem "Przebudzenie" ("Awakening"), from *Wiersze zebrane*, is a fine description of this attitude. It begins:

> When the horror subsided the floodlights went out
> we discovered that we were on a rubbish-heap in very
>   strange poses
>
> . . . .
>
> We had nowhere to go we stayed on the rubbish-heap
> we tidied things up
> the bones and sheet iron we deposited in an archive
> We listened to the chirping of streetcars to a
>   swallow-like voice of factories
> and a new life was unrolling at our feet.

The common experience of wartime destruction and of starting a "new life" united Herbert and the other members of his generation and gave them their unique temporal perspective. They drew very different conclusions from their experiences, however, and there is no consensus of attitude or ideology among them. Herbert is sometimes linked to Różewicz, another poet who lived through the war, because they were close in age and were both moralists. Their values, however, were in fundamental conflict. Różewicz's poetry after the war denied all previous values and emphasized purely personal experience, whereas Herbert arrived at entirely different conclusions. He wrote:

> Something makes me different from the "War Generation." It seems to me that I came away from the war without accepting the failure of the earlier morality. It is still attractive to me most of all because I painfully feel the lack of tablets of values in the contemporary world.

Herbert was a more positive poet than many other members of the War Generation, although rarely have positive values been won against greater opposition and with greater struggle.

USE OF THE PAST

One of the most striking features of Herbert's poetry was the manner in which he used the past. It was remarkably alive for him; historical figures frequently appeared in his poems with the vividness of contemporaries. In Western Europe and the United States, poetry that invokes the great traditions of Western culture is often associated with reactionary values. In Poland during the decade after World War II, however, a paradoxical situation arose in which some of the writers who had most completely rejected the prewar culture found that they had little basis for rebelling against the Stalinist present; on the other hand, a poet such as Herbert, who strived to repossess the culture of the past, was able to express revolt in one of its most intense and radical forms.

It is a mistake, however, to call Herbert a classicist, as he was sometimes labeled. For him, the past was not a static source of value; he is not an antiquarian, as his poem "Classic" made clear. For Herbert, the past represented living experience rather than lifeless forms. He did not adhere to the past at the expense of the present; instead, the past is the ally of the present. The distinction is a useful one and even crucial, for Herbert's use of the past was the opposite of that of a genuine classicist such as the contemporary Polish poet Jaroslaw Rymkiewicz. Herbert felt the dead are alive, made of flesh and blood. If there was a division between the past and the present, it was often spatial rather than temporal. In Herbert's famous poem "Elegy of Fortinbras," he assumed the persona of Fortinbras, who addresses Hamlet as his immediate contemporary; the poem ends by translating death into terms of spatial distance: "It is not for us to greet each other or bid farewell we live on archipelagos/ and that water these words what can they do what can they do prince." The ever-present tension and dialogue between past and present did not restrict Herbert's poetry; in fact, the reverse is true: He confronted the world in all its breadth, and his experience is placed in a seamless historical continuum.

AVANT-GARDE INFLUENCE

Herbert was influenced both by the Catastrophists, such as Miłosz, who stressed philosophical and historical themes in their poetry, and by the avant-garde poets of the 1920's and the 1930's, such as Józéf Czechowicz, who eschewed punctuation. Several other poets of Herbert's generation who lived through the war also turned to the avant-garde in their search for poetic forms that were capable of rendering their experience. Many of Herbert's early poems shared the phenomenological preoccupations of the avant-garde; at the most fundamental level, poets were asking: How can one describe the world? How can one describe one's experience? Herbert's poems "I Would Like to Describe," "Attempt at a Description," "Voice," "Episode in a Library," "Wooden Bird," "Nothing Special," and the later "Mr. Cogito Thinks About the Voice of Nature and the Human Voice" all approached this concern from different angles.

Herbert's phenomenological preoccupations are particularly apparent in his handling of punctuation. Conventional punctuation was not automatically accepted by serious poets in Poland after the war, and Herbert was by no means alone in questioning its use. Prewar avant-garde poetry still enjoyed a high esteem among poets, and punctuation also had a political coloring: Lack of conventional punctuation became associated with revolt and with individualism. Herbert's first collection of poems, *Struna światła* (chord of light), which represented work done during the first postwar decade, eschewed conventional punctuation, particularly the use of periods. In a prose poem written somewhat later, "Period," he placed punctuation in a very broad historical and social context; the poem ends: "In fact the period, which we attempt to tame at any price, is a bone protruding from the sand, a snapping shut, a sign of a catastrophe. It is a punctuation of the elements. People should employ it modestly and with proper consideration, as is customary when one replaces fate." In other words, for Herbert, the "period" marked a hiatus in the texture of the world and of reality. Its thoughtless use is presumptuous and even destructive, violating the living tissue and the continuities of the real world.

In England and America, the traditional use of punctuation was—with notable exceptions—maintained after the war; accepted practice had not been put into doubt by new experience. In Central and Eastern Europe, however, especially in those countries that had experienced the worst destruction during the war and that had suffered under Nazi occupation, conventional punctuation was sharply questioned, along with other inherited poetic practices. Indeed, punctuation became one of the major topoi, or themes, of postwar Eastern European literature.

THE PROSE POEM

Parallel to Herbert's radical reduction of punctuation (he frequently employed dashes, as well as occasional parentheses and question marks) was his development of the prose poem; much of the prose poetry written in Poland since 1957 was influenced by Herbert's explorations in the genre. While his first collection of poems was restricted to largely punctuation-free verse, his second, *Hermes, pies i gwiazda* (Hermes, dog and star), had a separate section of prose poems, comprising sixty of the book's ninety-five poems. Originally, Herbert intended these prose poems to constitute a separate volume, and he called them *bajeczki* (little fairy tales). His project was thwarted by an editor, however, and they were included in his second volume of poems. In subsequent volumes, Herbert intentionally interspersed prose poems among his punctuation-free verse poems, and this became his regular practice.

In his third collection, *Studium przedmiotu* (study of the object), the ratio of prose to verse poems is eighteen to twenty-eight; in his fourth collection, *Napis* (inscription), fourteen to twenty-six; and in his fifth, *Mr. Cogito,* five to thirty-five. The choice to use one form or the other was always highly deliberate with Herbert, depending on his attitude toward the subject of the poem, his distance from it, and his tone, as well as the rhythms he used. The more reflective poems, especially those that assume considerable distance from the subject and those that use strong irony, were frequently written in prose. The various modulations of these two basic forms were always carefully worked out. This is only one of the ways, but an important one, in which the form of Herbert's poetry is related to its content, and the resulting range of forms is astonishingly broad.

INANIMATE OBJECTS

Herbert's many poems about inanimate objects should be seen in the context of his attempt to explore the relationship between experience and reality. Herbert wrote fine poems (and again, his practice has been imitated by many younger Polish poets) about a pebble, a stool, a watch, armchairs, a clothes wringer; indeed, the title of one of Herbert's collections of poems means "study of the objects." Some readers have wondered why a poet such as Herbert, who was so consistently concerned with life and human experience, should write about lifeless objects. The poems were part of Herbert's attempt to separate what is subjective from what is objective and to see clearly. In "I Would Like to Describe," Herbert wrote: ". . . so is blurred/ in me/ what white-haired gentlemen/ separated once and for all/ and said/ this is the subject/ and this is the object." Herbert was always interested in inanimate objects but not because they are inhuman. On the contrary, he tended to find human traits in objects (rather than vice versa) and to discover a community of interest between humans and objects. In a conversation in 1969, Herbert said that he was fascinated by objects because

> they are so completely different from us, and enigmatic. They come from a totally different world from ours. We are never sure that we understand them; sometimes we think so, other times we don't, depending on how much of ourselves we project on them. What I like about them is their ability to *resist* us, to be silent. We can never really conquer them or tame them, and that is good.

Thus, while Herbert humanized objects, he also respected their fundamental opacity. At the same time, there was no abyss between humans and inanimate objects—on the contrary, there is a sense of identity with them, based on the realization of human fallibility and imperfection. Herbert was engaged in breaking down the barrier between the human and the inanimate and in extending the limits of the human.

ENDURING THEMES

Herbert's first volumes contain most of the themes that interested him throughout his career; certainly, his enforced silence during the Stalinist decade in Poland, from 1946 to 1956, contributed to the ultimate strength of these poems. Others of his generation, such as Różewicz and Szymborska, adapted to the Stalinist demands and were permitted to publish; as a result, their books that appeared during this period are inferior to their later work. Herbert wrote for a long time without a public audience, but his poems assumed a firm core of consistency and strength as he developed his themes. First among them was the imperative to resist, to listen to the individual conscience; he was willing to suffer for his ideals. The moral demand to direct one's gaze at reality itself is present in Herbert's first volume, as is his gift for infusing the past with life. Some of these early poems are about the difficulty of writing after the war, about the loss of ideals; at a profound level, they reflected Herbert's formal training in philosophy—not because the poems are explicitly "philosophical" but because they are informed by an intense, overriding concern for truth and clarity. Herbert consistently directed his attention outward, at the world as it exists. It was this stance that also makes it possible to consider Herbert as a "public" poet. The lines in these early poems are relatively short; they often seem to follow the rapidity of thought, and they already display the great agility that is typical of Herbert's style.

HERMES, PIES I GWIAZDA

Herbert's second volume, *Hermes, pies i gwiazda*, is marked by the sudden infusion of prose poems in the second section. Irony becomes more prominent, and the poet's tone is increasingly mordant. The individual lines of poems are sometimes longer in this volume, although there is the same agility and rapid spontaneity of association that marked the first volume.

STUDIUM PRZEDMIOTU

Herbert's third volume, *Studium przedmiotu*, carried his dialogue with objects to its furthest point. The volume is also among his most critical, taking aim at contemporary social and political reality. As he did this, however, Herbert evidently felt the need to assume a greater distance—critical distance—from the reality he sought to describe, and thus he adopted a variety of personas in this volume, giving his critique greater depth and historical reverberation.

NAPIS

Herbert's fourth book, *Napis*, shows a greater concern for textures, and the lines have become somewhat longer. This volume has been called Herbert's "expressionist" volume; in it, he gave full rein to his delight in dramatic metaphor. He developed further many of his previous themes, but the reader senses that there is a shift in the target of Herbert's sense of revolt. Focusing less on immediate social and political realities, the poet was increasingly concerned with the universal and the archetypal, extending back into the past and into the subconscious.

MR. COGITO

In Herbert's fifth collection of original poems, *Mr. Cogito*, the dominant theme is the identity of the self, explored through the title figure. Sometimes the persona of Mr. Cogito is entirely playful; at other times, he allows the poet to confront painful personal matters without obtrusive emotion. The volume contains a number of poems of striking philosophical depth, among them "Georg Heym—the Almost Metaphysical Adventure" and "Mr. Cogito Tells About the Temptation of Spinoza." Many poems in this book have longer lines than those of earlier volumes and are more meditative. They require a longer, deeper breath to read aloud, and some are very close to prose. A few are quite long and have a highly developed logical structure.

REPORT FROM THE BESIEGED CITY, AND OTHER POEMS

Report from the Besieged City, and Other Poems marks a sharp return to topicality and contemporary events—in this case, the coup d'état of General Wojciech Jaruzelski and the imposition of martial law. Again, events are seen in the context of a broad historical framework, but they are observed in the present, taking place under one's very eyes, as the title indicates. There are two major themes in this new collection. The first is the necessity to "bear witness" to the truth. Herbert assumed the role of chronicler of the "siege," and although he said this role is secondary to that of the people who are fighting, it is really of the utmost importance. Knowledge of the true nature of the war, the reality of the lives of those who take part in it, and even their very identity depend on the chronicler, the poet. The second major theme is suffering and the need for suffering, never presented fatalistically but rather combined with the imperative to revolt no matter how hopeless the situation. Rarely in contemporary literature has the need for resistance been stated so clearly, so forcefully, and with so few illusions.

The collection begins where "The Envoy of Mr. Cogito," the last poem in Herbert's previous volume, ended. In that poem, Herbert wrote that even if "the informers executioners cowards . . . will win," the individual must still revolt:

> go upright among those who are on their knees
> among those with their backs turned and those
>   toppled in the dust
> you were saved not in order to live
> you have little time you must give testimony
> . . . .
> go because only in this way will you be admitted to
>   the company of cold skulls
> to the company of your ancestors: Gilgamesh Hector Roland
> the defenders of the kingdom without limit and the city of ashes
> Be faithful Go

ELEGY FOR THE DEPARTURE, AND OTHER POEMS

Elegy for the Departure, and Other Poems is made up of a translation of poems from *Elegia na odejście* (1990) as well as translations of works uncollected in English from throughout Herbert's career. Its four sections draw chronologically from his writing, and a less politicized Herbert is evident in the selected poems. Darkness was certainly pouring into Herbert's poetry and possibly into his life around the time when most of the poems from the 1990 collection were composed, but it was present in his verse from the beginning, especially in his early poems, in which he bid farewell to the ghosts of his friends fallen during the war.

The English volume opens with one such poem, called "Three Poems by Heart," which originally appeared in *Struna światła*. The first of its three movements is a search for a person, or rather for a language, in which the memory of that person can be extracted from among horrifying images of wartime destruction:

> I can't find the title
> of a memory about you
> with a hand torn from darkness
> I step on fragments of faces
> soft friendly profiles
> frozen into a hard contour.

Readers will discern that here Herbert's voice is growing more personal, his irony more astringent. His stoicism seems to falter in the face of very human and basic fear, as in "Prayer of the Old Men," that ends on a mournful, pleading note:

> but don't allow us
> to be devoured
> by the insatiable darkness of your altars
> say just one thing
> that we will return later

The book's last section, focused on Herbert's late poetry, contains some of his most spacious work, a groundspring of vitality and variety. There is a tarantella of a poem about Leo Tolstoy fleeing family and keepers at the end "with great bounds/ his beard streaming behind." There is a somber, perfectly tuned image of Emperor Hirohito, history's wildness departed, laboring over a *tanka* (a genre of Japanese poem) about the state railroad. There is the unsparingly registered loss of "Prayer of the Old Men":

> when the children women patient animals have left
> because they can't bear wax hands
> we listen to sand pouring in our veins
> and in our dark interior grows a white church
> of salt memories calcium and unspeakable weakness.

The book ends with the expansive "Elegy for the Departure of Pen Ink and Lamp," in which Herbert laments the three objects presented in the poem both as companions of studious childhood and as symbols of the three ideas most often associated with "the Herbertian" vision: the critical mind, a "gentle volcano" of imagination, and "a spirit stubbornly battling" the darker demons of the soul. The tone of the poem is cryptic, and readers are unable to discern the nature of the personal catastrophe that seems to lie at its center. One learns only that the departure of the objects was caused by an unspecified "betrayal" on the part of the speaker and that it leaves him feeling guilty and powerless. The book ends with last words of the poem: "and that it will be/ dark." With that, the door closed on the work of Herbert.

OTHER MAJOR WORKS

PLAYS: *Jaskina filozofów*, pb. 1970 (wr. 1950's; *The Philosophers' Den*, 1958); *Dramaty*, 1970 (collection of four plays).

NONFICTION: *Barbarzyńca w ogrodzie*, 1962 (*Barbarian in the Garden*, 1985); *Martwa natura z wedzidlem*, 1993 (*Still Life with a Bridle: Essays and Apocryphas*, 1991); *The King of the Ants: Mythological Essays*, 1999.

Bibliography

Anders, Jaroslaw. *Between Fire and Sleep: Essays on Modern Polish Poetry and Prose.* New Haven, Conn.: Yale University Press, 2009. Contains a chapter on Herbert that provides extensive analysis and notes the exploration of darkness in his poetry.

Barańczak, Stanisław. *A Fugitive from Utopia: The Poetry of Zbigniew Herbert.* Cambridge, Mass.: Harvard University Press, 1987. A useful introduction, one of the first book-length studies published in English.

Carpenter, Bogdana. "*The Barbarian in the Garden*: Zbigniew Herbert's Reevaluations." *World Literature Today* 57, no. 3 (Summer, 1983): 388-393. Excellent coverage in English by Herbert's translator.

Carpenter, Bogdana, and John Carpenter. Afterword to *Selected Poems*, by Zbigniew Herbert. 1977. Reprint. Kraków: Wydawnictwo Literackie, 2007. The translators' afterword to a reprint of *Selected Poems* provides a biography and some analysis of the works.

Hacht, Anne Marie, and David Kelly, eds. *Poetry for Students.* Vol. 22. Detroit: Thomson/Gale, 2005. Analyzes Herbert's "Why the Classics." Contains the poem, summary, themes, style, historical context, critical overview, and criticism. Includes bibliography and index.

Kraszewski, Charles. *Essays on the Dramatic Works of the Polish Poet Zbigniew Herbert.* Lewiston, N.Y.: E. Mellen Press, 2002. Five essays on Herbert as playwright, comparing his drama with his poetry.

Nizynska, Joanna. "Marsyas's Howl: The Myth of Marsyas in Ovid's *Metamorphoses* and Zbigniew Herbert's 'Apollo and Marsyas.'" *Comparative Literature* 53, no. 2 (2001): 151-170. Compares the Roman and Polish uses of the myth, emphasizing Herbert's "translation" of the story.

Shallcross, Bozena. *Through the Poet's Eye: The Travels of Zagajewski, Herbert, and Bridsky.* Evanston, Ill.: Northwestern University Press, 2002. Analyzes Herbert's *The Barbarian in the Garden*, focusing on the poet as traveler and observer.

Wood, Sharon. "The Reflections of Mr. Palomar and Mr. Cogito: Italo Calvino and Zbigniew Herbert." *Modern Language Notes* 109, no. 1 (1994): 128-142. Compares the two writers' creations of alter egos.

Zagajewski, Adam. Introduction to *The Collected Poems, 1956-1998*, Zbigniew Herbert. Translated and edited by Alissa Valles. New York: Ecco, 2007. Informative introduction that provides background and critical analysis.

John Carpenter
Updated by Sarah Hilbert

KENNETH KOCH

Born: Cincinnati, Ohio; February 27, 1925
Died: New York, New York; July 6, 2002

PRINCIPAL POETRY
Poems, 1953
Ko: Or, A Season on Earth, 1960
Permanently, 1960
Thank You, and Other Poems, 1962
The Pleasures of Peace, and Other Poems, 1969
Sleeping with Women, 1969
When the Sun Tries to Go On, 1969
The Art of Love, 1975
The Duplications, 1977
The Burning Mystery of Anna in 1951, 1979
From the Air, 1979
Days and Nights, 1982
Selected Poems, 1950-1982, 1985
On the Edge, 1986
Selected Poems, 1991
On the Great Atlantic Rainway: Selected Poems, 1950-1988, 1994
One Train, 1994
Straits, 1998
New Addresses, 2000
A Possible World, 2002
The Collected Poems of Kenneth Koch, 2005

OTHER LITERARY FORMS

In addition to poetry, Kenneth Koch published one novel, *The Red Robins* (1975), and books of dramatic pieces, including *Bertha, and Other Plays* (1966) and *A Change of Hearts: Plays, Films, and Other Dramatic Works, 1951-1971* (1973). Both Koch's novel and his works for the stage are imaginative and improvisatory in their consistent portrayal of the comic drama of life.

The plays achieve their comic repercussions primarily through the juxtaposition of incongruous situations, and by means of rapid, often unpredictable changes of language, character, and scene. The plays echo and imitate older dramatic forms such as the Elizabethan chronicle and the court masque, frequently appropriating the earlier dramatic conventions for comic purposes. *E. Kology* (pb. 1973), for example, a five-act play in rhymed verse, is as much masque as play. In it, the main character, E. Kology, persuades various polluters of air and water to abandon their destructive habits. An additional masque element is provided by a troupe of young men and women who assist E. Kology, performing a series of celebratory dances as part of the play's action. An even more masquelike play is *The Moon Balloon*, performed in New York's Central Park on New Year's Eve, 1969. *The Moon Balloon* is an entertainment in rhymed verse that makes use of spectacle, celebration, and metamorphosis.

History forms the basis for humor and metamorphosis in Koch's two historical plays, *Bertha* (pr. 1959), a historical pageant, and *George Washington Crossing the Delaware* (pr. 1962), a chronicle play. Bertha is a Norwegian queen who saves her people from the barbarian menace. She performs this feat regularly, whenever she becomes bored with routine rule. The humor of the play resides in the use of formal Elizabethan language to describe Bertha's idiosyncratic behavior, and in strangely concatenated literary allusions such as the linked references to William Shakespeare's *Antony and Cleopatra* (pr. 1606-1607) and Lewis Carroll's *Alice's Adventures in Wonderland* (1865), Bertha being related to both the tragic queen of Egypt and the mad queen of Wonderland.

George Washington Crossing the Delaware, perhaps Koch's best play, is part myth, part chronicle, and part comedy. Its comic incongruities, its colloquial deflation of a more stately heroic language, and its juxtaposition of low comedy and high seriousness serve to make it a surprising and inventive theatrical entertainment.

Achievements

Kenneth Koch's achievements are notable and varied. He received numerous fellowships, including several from the Fulbright Foundation (1950-1951, 1978, and 1982), the Guggenheim Foundation (1960-1961), and the Ingram Merrill Foundation (1969). His literary awards are impressive: the Ohioana Book Award for Poetry (1974), an Academy Award in Literature (1976) and an Award of Merit for Poetry from the American Academy and Institute of Arts and Letters (1986), the Shelley Memorial Award (1994), the Bollingen Prize (1995), the Bobbitt National Prize for Poetry (1996) for *One Train*, a Chevalier de l'ordre des arts et des lettres, France (1999), and the Levinson Prize from *Poetry* magazine (2000). He was twice nominated for a National Book Award, in 1963 for *Thank You, and Other Poems* and in 2000 for *New Addresses*. In 1995, he was elected to the American Academy of Arts and Letters.

Biography

Kenneth Koch was born in Cincinnati, Ohio, on February 27, 1925. Although he wrote his first poem when he was five, he did not begin writing seriously until he was seventeen, when he read the novels of John Dos Passos and was thereby stimulated to imitate their particular style of stream of consciousness. Koch served as a rifleman in the

U.S. Army during World War II. After the war, he earned a B.A. degree from Harvard University in 1948 and a doctorate from Columbia in 1959. At Harvard, Koch was a friend of John Ashbery and Frank O'Hara, poets who held similar views about the nature of poetry. Later, when they had settled in New York, Ashbery, O'Hara, and Koch came to be thought of as principal poets of the New York School.

Koch spent three important years in Europe, mostly in Italy and France. During that time, he was influenced by the humorous, surrealistic verse of Jacques Prévert. In a brief autobiographical account that appeared in *The New American Poetry, 1945-1960* (1960; Donald Allen, editor), Koch noted that French poetry "had a huge effect" on his own work. Moreover, he acknowledged that he tried to get into his own writing "the same incomprehensible excitement" that he found in French poetry.

During the late 1960's and early 1970's, Koch began teaching poetry writing at P.S. 61, a grammar school in New York City, and at a neighborhood museum in Brooklyn. A few years later, he taught similar classes at a New York nursing home. Out of these experiences came a series of books about the teaching of poetry to children and the aged. The first of these, *Wishes, Lies, and Dreams: Teaching Young Children to Write Poetry* (1970), is perhaps the best known. A companion volume, *Rose Where Did You Get That Red?*, followed in 1973. Both are noteworthy for their inventive approach to teaching poetry, especially for the imaginative ways they keep reading and writing poetry together. An additional value of the books and of two later volumes (*I Never Told Anybody: Teaching Poetry in a Nursing Home*, 1977, and *Sleeping on the Wing: An Anthology of Modern Poetry with Essays on Reading and Writing*, 1981), is that all reveal something about Koch's poetic temperament and inclinations. The qualities that Koch encourages in his students' writing animate his own poems. Open forms, loose meter, memory and feeling, joy and humor, colloquial language, imaginative freedom—these reflect Koch's view that "there is no insurmountable barrier between ordinary speech and poetry."

Koch taught at Brooklyn College (now of the City University of New York), Rutgers University, and the New School for Social Research. In 1971, he began his long tenure at Columbia University as a professor of English and comparative literature. Exhibitions of Koch's collaborative work have been held at the Ipswich Museum, England, in 1993; at the Tibor De Nagy Gallery, New York City, in 1994; and at Guild Hall, East Hampton, New York, in 2000. He lived in New York City until his death on July 6, 2002.

Analysis

At his best, Kenneth Koch was a good comic poet and a fine parodist. A poet of limited tonal range yet of a wide and resourceful imagination, Koch used random structures, open forms, and loose meters to give his poetry freedom and surprise that occasionally astonish and often delight. Just as often, however, the formlessness of Koch's poems results in slackness and self-indulgence. The tension that one expects in good poetry, deriving largely from exigencies of form, is missing in Koch's poems.

In *The King of the Cats* (1965), F. W. Dupee compared Koch to Marianne Moore. Dupee notes that while both Koch and Moore make poetry out of "poetry-resistant stuff," Koch lacks Moore's patient scrutiny and careful, sustained observation. Preferring to participate imaginatively rather than to observe carefully, Koch often seems more interested in where he can go with an observation, with what his imagination can make of it, than in what it is in itself. At his best, Koch's imaginative facility translates into poetic felicity; at his worst, Koch's freedom of imagination obscures the clarity and lucidity of the poems, frequently testing the reader's patience.

Perhaps the most trenchant and perceptive criticism of Koch's work has been that of Richard Howard in his book on contemporary poetry, *Alone with America: Essays on the Art of Poetry in the United States Since 1950* (1969). Howard suggests that the central poetic problem for Koch is to sustain the interest of the instant, to hold onto the momentary imaginative phrase or the surprising conjunction of dichotomous ideas, experiences, and details. Koch frequently hurries beyond moments of imaginative vitality and verbal splendor; rather than sustaining or developing them, he abandons them. At his best, however, such abandonments lead to other moments that are equally splendid, culminating in convincingly coherent poems.

Some of Koch's most distinctive and successful poems are parodies. His parody of Robert Frost, "Mending Sump," in which he alludes to and satirizes the style and situation of both "Mending Wall" and "The Death of the Hired Man," is one of his most famous. A modestly successful parody, "Mending Sump" does not compare with Koch's brilliant and witty parody of William Carlos Williams's brief conversational poem "This Is Just to Say." Koch entitles his parody "Variations on a Theme by William Carlos Williams." In four brief stanzas, Koch parodies the occasion, structure, rhythm, and tone of a poet whose work has powerfully influenced his own.

Although in his nonparodistic poetry Koch did not often attempt to imitate Williams, he did try to accomplish what Williams achieved in his best work: the astonishment of the moment; the astonishment of something seen, heard, felt, or understood; the magic and the beauty of the commonplace. Koch, too, could astonish—but not by acts of attention like those of Williams nor by his power of feeling. Koch astonished by his outrageous dislocations of sense and logic, his exuberant and risk-taking amalgamation of utterly disparate experiences. His achievement, finally, consists of small surprises, delights of image and allusion, phrase and idea; his poems rarely possess the power to move or instruct, but they do entertain.

Among Kenneth Koch's long poems are *Ko: Or, A Season on Earth*, a mock-heroic epic in ottava rima about a Japanese baseball player, a poem with a variety of story lines; *The Duplications*, a comic epic about sex that employs trappings of Greek mythology and that in its second part becomes a self-reflexive poem concerned with the poetic vocation; and *When the Sun Tries to Go On*, a poem that goes on for one hundred twenty-four-line stanzas, in large part because Koch wanted to see how long he could go on with what was originally a seventy-two-line poem. All three poems are characterized by Koch's infectious humor, his far-fetched analogies, and his digressive impulse.

More interesting and more consistently successful are Koch's shorter poems, ranging in length from a dozen lines to a dozen pages. In the poems included in Koch's best collections, *The Art of Love* and *The Pleasures of Peace, and Other Poems*, one encounters Koch at his most graceful and disarming. In the best poems from these volumes (and there are many engaging ones), Koch exhibits his characteristic playfulness, deliberate formlessness, and almost surrealistic allusiveness. The poems are humorous yet serious in both their invitations and their admonitions.

THE PLEASURES OF PEACE, AND OTHER POEMS

Koch's major poetic preoccupations find abundant exemplifications in his volume *The Pleasures of Peace, and Other Poems*. The title poem is divided loosely into fourteen sections, each section describing different kinds of pleasures: of writing, of peace, of pain, of pleasure itself, of fantasy, of reality, of memory, of autonomy, of poetry, and of living. The poem is both a catalog and a celebration of the rich pleasures of simply being alive. Its self-reflexiveness coexists with its Whitmanesque embrace of the range, diversity, and variability of life's pleasures. Another stylistic hallmark evident in this poem is a playful use of literary allusion. In addition to evoking Walt Whitman, Koch alludes directly to William Butler Yeats ("The Lake Isle of Innisfree"), Andrew Marvell ("To His Coy Mistress"), Robert Herrick, Percy Bysshe Shelley, and William Wordsworth. The allusions are surprising: Koch's lines modify and alter the words of the earlier poets as they situate them in the context of a radically different poem.

These observations about "The Pleasures of Peace" fail to account for what is perhaps its most distinctive identifying quality: a wild, surrealistic concatenation of details (pink mint chewing gum with "the whole rude gallery of war"; Dutch-speaking cowboys; the pleasures of agoraphobia with the pleasures of blasphemy; the pleasures of breasts, bread, and poodles; the pleasures of stars and of plaster). Moreover, amid the litany of the poem's pleasures occur several notes of desperation—for the horrors of war and suffering. Koch seems to find it necessary to remind his readers of the peaceful pleasures of life largely because the horrors of war and the futility of modern life allow them to be forgotten.

Although Sigmund Freud is an obvious influence on Koch's "The Interpretation of Dreams," a zany poem that imitates the syntax of dream in its associative structure, in its dislocations and disruptions of continuity, and in its oddly mismatched characters, Whitman is the dominant voice and force behind most of the other poems in the volume. Whitman's influence is discernible in "Hearing," a rambling play on sounds in which Koch makes music out of the disparate noises of waterfalls and trumpets, throbbing hearts and falling leaves, rain and thunder, bluebirds singing and dresses ripping. The poem, concluding with the words "the song is finished," owes something also to the other American poets it invokes: Ezra Pound, William Carlos Williams, and Wallace Stevens.

It is Whitman, however, who stands behind Koch's "Poem of the Forty-eight States," especially the Whitman of "On Journeys Through the States"; and it is Whitman who hovers over the incantatory litany of Koch's "Sleeping with Women," especially the Whitman of "The Sleepers" and "Beautiful Women." Perhaps the most successful of Koch's Whitmanesque poems is "Faces," which, while less uniform in tone than "Sleeping with Women," with its hypnotic, anaphoric incantation, and not as close to Whitman's own tone, nevertheless carries something of Whitman's power of suggestion in its implication that the variety of faces called up in the poem (Popeye and Agamemnon, Herbert Hoover and the poor of the Depression) reflect the life of the speaker of the poem. By implication, Koch seems to suggest that each reader could create a similar yet highly individual and personal collage of faces that, taken together, reflect the range and variety of his or her experience and that, in a concentrated yet variegated image, sum up his or her life.

THE ART OF LOVE

Koch's other important volume, *The Art of Love*, while retaining something of the humorous tone of *The Pleasures of Peace, and Other Poems* as well as something of its imaginative wit, reaches more deeply in feeling and ranges more widely in thought. Many of the poems are cast in an admonitory mode; others are ironic, while still others include both irony and admonition. "The Art of Poetry" alternates between ironic posture and serious gesture in its descriptions of poetic attitudes, ideals, and practices. The speaker advises poets to stay young even while growing and developing, something that Koch has consistently tried to do. He suggests that a poet should imitate other poets, try on other styles, and try out other voices in an effort to form, paradoxically, his or her own style. After addressing the problems of beginning a poem, sustaining and ending it (and also revising it), the speaker reminds the poet to be absorbed totally in poetry, for only such a total immersion will enable the poet to see poetry as "the mediation of life." Such is Koch's poetic credo.

This poetic creed notwithstanding, perhaps the most unusual and the most useful advice in "The Art of Poetry" is given in a set of questions and answers that further reveal the direction and impulse of Koch's own poetry: Is the poem astonishing? Is it wise? Is it original? Does it employ cheap effects, tricks, or gimmicks? Does it engage heart and mind? Would the poet envy another's having written it? If the answer is "yes" to all but the fourth question, the poem qualifies, if not for greatness, at least for honesty and integrity, qualities and standards certainly deserving of respect and admiration. In his "The Art of Poetry," Koch seems to have achieved them.

Although not overtly about the art of poetry, "Some General Instructions" can be taken as describing Koch's poems even as it gives more explicit advice about living. One statement in particular suggests the connection between poetry and life: "Things have a way of working out/ Which is nonsensical, and one should try to see/ How the process works." This implies that nonsense ultimately makes sense, that beneath the apparent confusion lies order, purpose, and meaning. The statement provides a helpful gloss on the best of Koch's poems, which often go by way of nonsense to make a final and useful kind of sense.

"Some General Instructions" alternates between aphorism and meditative commentary. Like any set of aphorisms, it bristles with contradictions. Even so, it shines with joy and radiates humor. Koch seems to enjoy juxtaposing serious moral and ethical advice with comic yet practical admonition. He advises, for example, that his readers be glad; that they savor life, love, pleasure, and virtue; and that they not eat too many bananas.

Although a similar tone mixing playful humor with thoughtful advice permeates Koch's lovely and beautiful "On Beauty," a rather different note is struck by two other poems in the volume. In "The Circus," a nostalgic reminiscence about the time he wrote an earlier poem with the same title, Koch wonders about the value of the earlier poem, and then, by extension, about the value of any of his poems and the value of his poetic vocation. Moving out of a concern with poetry, "The Circus" becomes more somber, turning into a meditation on time, death, and loss, especially the loss of friends. In "The Art of Love," a how-to manual of eroticism, the speaker describes a set of outrageous sadomasochistic procedures. The practical nature of the advice ranges from how to meet and greet a girl, to how to get her to do the things described in the poem. "The Art of Love" ends with a catalog of questions about love, some serious, some humorous. Ludicrous answers are provided to each question. Full of high spirits, erotic fantasies, hyperbole, and insult, the poem needs to be taken ironically if it is not to be considered an offense against decency. Even then, its specificity of reference and particularity of detail make it seem less an ironic poem about the art of love than a degrading if witty description of perverse fantasies.

ON THE EDGE

Koch's 1986 volume, *On the Edge*, consists of two long poems, the title poem and "Impressions of Africa." The former is a strongly autobiographical work; the latter, as its title suggests, presents images and impressions gathered while the poet was in Africa. Although both present difficulties, with their fragmentations and free associations that attempt to represent experience and memory in Koch's unique way, the structure is not entirely haphazard. "Impressions of Africa," more than the usual Koch work, gives the reader a sense of how a place objectively appears, in lines that sometimes remind one of diary entries transformed into verse. "On the Edge" is harder to grasp. In the poem, events involving Koch and his friends circle an apparently fictional character named

Dan. Moments of clarity are scattered among thoughts that interrupt themselves, such as "Our modern—fragmentary—Dan stands up—it's about time—reason." Koch's charm and sense of humor appear throughout, but the landscape of the work frequently exists so deep within the poet's consciousness that it seems indecipherable.

Koch's talent is perhaps best manifested in *The Pleasures of Peace, and Other Poems* and *The Art of Love*. Although the poems do not range widely in style, theme, and technique, they do offer a distinctive set of pleasures for the accepting and patient reader, the pleasures of engaging an unusual and unpredictable poetic imagination as it reveals itself in a colloquially inflected idiom that is, by turns, earnest and ironic. The deliberate dislocations of logical organization, the profusion of incongruities in image and idea, the exaggeration and far-fetched analogies are all part of Koch's effort to avoid the predictable, the stodgy, and the dull. They are all part of his effort to create a poetry full of fun and surprise that even though it only infrequently ends in wisdom, nevertheless very often sustains the delight with which it begins.

STRAITS

In *Straits*, persons searching and journeying appear in the volume's title poem, a dazzling array of sentences of failure, success, discovery, and change, with everything happening at once. The "straits" of this collection represent a possibility, and they grant access to ecstasy, unity, freedom, and completeness. Running through *Straits* is Koch's preoccupation with time and making time run, not after him but in circles. Thus the seventeen quatrains of "Ballade," each titled for a year of the poet's life, undo chronology, beginning with the seventy-first and ending with the thirtieth year, and ranging in age from five to seventy-three, in no particular order. Themes of aging, seasonal change, and "the loss of the sacred in everyday life" are amply evident (on being seventy-three, Koch comments, "I have lots of years and decades in me/ And they divide me like Sunday ads./ It's the Big Sale of the Week, when I can speak in song").

The volume spans a wide range of form and content, of experiences culled from Koch's life ("Currency") and those that are formed merely in an exuberant imagination. The sequence "The Seasons," dedicated to the eighteenth century poet James Thomson, maker of *The Seasons* (1730, 1744), is perhaps Koch's best contribution in this volume. Here linear time is supplanted by Koch's cyclic interpretations, the rhythms of day and night and of "The seasons' lazy susan." It calls forth New York urban pastoralism—hotdog stands, the World Series, opera, and snowplows—and finds renewal even in autumn: "harbinger of rebirth/ Of school and love and work."

NEW ADDRESSES

In Koch's *New Addresses*, he presents fifty free-verse poems, each an ode to a different subject ("To Psychoanalysis," "To My Father's Business," "To 'Yes'"), making the "addresses" in his title quite literal. It is perhaps his most autobiographical collection, a volume that recalls, for the first time in his poetry, a pivotal moment in his life: his military service during World War II. Putting such an experience into verse proved a challenge he could not resist: "I'd never really been able to write [about the war] because it's like being psychotic to be in a war. You're walking around with a gun . . . and they shoot you!" However, the poet found that treating the war as a character, like any other person, "enabled me to get some of the feelings back, like the crazy idea that I couldn't be killed because I had to write." His encounter with a faulty explosive in "To Carelessness" is unnerving with its understated lesson in the dumb luck of staying alive in battle. "To World War Two," a much longer poem, captures the combatant's sense of his sheer insignificance: "If you could use me/ You'd use me, and then forget. How else/ Did I think you'd behave?/ I'm glad you ended. I'm glad I didn't die."

Other bits of Koch's life are also revealed throughout the addresses (for example, childhood is probed in "To Piano Lessons"; later periods in Koch's life in "To My Fifties"), where readers find the speaker accusing, praising, or querying abstract concepts, emotions, his character, and his past. Some are overtly emotional ("To My Father's Business" or "To Jewishness"), while some favor his characteristic playfulness ("To Testosterone" or "To Some Abstract Paintings").

OTHER MAJOR WORKS
LONG FICTION: *The Red Robins*, 1975.
PLAYS: *Bertha*, pr. 1959; *George Washington Crossing the Delaware*, pr. 1962; *Bertha, and Other Plays*, 1966; *The Moon Balloon*, pr. 1969; *A Change of Hearts: Plays, Films, and Other Dramatic Works, 1951-1971*, 1973; *E. Kology*, pb. 1973; *The New Diana*, pr. 1984; *The Gold Standard: A Book of Plays*, 1996.
NONFICTION: *Wishes, Lies, and Dreams: Teaching Young Children to Write Poetry*, 1970; *Rose Where Did You Get That Red?*, 1973; *I Never Told Anybody: Teaching Poetry in a Nursing Home*, 1977; *Sleeping on the Wing: An Anthology of Modern Poetry with Essays on Reading and Writing*, 1981 (with Kate Farrell); *The Art of Poetry: Poems, Parodies, Interviews, Essays, and Other Work*, 1996; *Making Your Own Days: The Pleasures of Reading and Writing Poetry*, 1998.
MISCELLANEOUS: *The Collected Fiction of Kenneth Koch*, 2005.

BIBLIOGRAPHY
Auslander, Philip. *The New York School Poets as Playwrights: O'Hara, Ashbery, Koch, Schuyler, and the Visual Arts*. New York: Peter Lang, 1989. Auslander discusses the plays written by these poets who attended the New York School of Art. Their life in New York affects their artistic endeavors, regardless of their form: poetry, experimental drama, short story, or visual art. This survey is useful as it gives an idea of Koch's competency in varied artistic media.
Carruth, Hayden. "Kenneth Koch." In *Contemporary Poets*, edited by James Vinson

and D. L. Kirkpatrick. 4th ed. New York: St. Martin's Press, 1985. Carruth, an outstanding poet in his own right, outlines Koch's background and work. Carruth first covers Koch's apprenticeship with the New York School of poets in the 1950's, then discusses Koch's current poetry, which is simpler and more effective than his earlier work. A good introduction for all students.

Howard, Richard. *Alone with America: Essays on the Art of Poetry in the United States Since 1950.* New York: Atheneum, 1969. In his chapter on Koch, Howard discusses his emphasis on the individual moment and (paradoxically) its movement. Howard also notes Koch's ability to be funny, calling him a master parodist, and mentions devices that Koch uses in his "improvisational plays."

Koch, Kenneth. Interview by Anselm Berrigan. *Publishers Weekly* 247, no. 13 (March, 2000): 72. An interview with Koch and a discussion of *New Addresses*.

_____. "An Interview with Kenneth Koch." Interview by John Tranter. *Scripsi* 4 (November, 1986): 177-185. In this interview, Koch discusses the evolution of his work from his rebellious New York School days to his 1980's poetic style. He also talks about his work in the theater, which is experimental and plentiful. For all students.

_____. "Kenneth Koch." Interview by Daniel Kane. In *What Is Poetry: Conversations with the American Avant-Garde*, edited by Kane. New York: Teachers & Writers Books, 2003. Koch describes his life, works, and influences.

Lang, Nancy. "Comic Fantasy in Two Postmodern Verse Novels: *Slinger* and *Ko*." In *The Poetic Fantastic: Studies in an Evolving Genre*, edited by Patrick D. Murphy and Vernon Ross Hyles. Westport, Conn.: Greenwood Press, 1989. This article compares the use of fantasy for fun in Koch's *Ko: Or, A Season on Earth* and Edward Dorn's *Slinger*.

Merrin, Jeredith. "The Poetry Man." *Southern Review* 35, no. 2 (Spring, 1999): 403-409. Merrin discusses Koch's poetry and nonfiction writing.

Robert DiYanni
Updated by Sarah Hilbert

AMY LOWELL

Born: Brookline, Massachusetts; February 9, 1874
Died: Brookline, Massachusetts; May 12, 1925

PRINCIPAL POETRY
 A Dome of Many-Coloured Glass, 1912
 Sword Blades and Poppy Seed, 1914
 Men, Women, and Ghosts, 1916
 Can Grande's Castle, 1918
 Pictures of the Floating World, 1919
 Legends, 1921
 A Critical Fable, 1922
 What's O'Clock, 1925
 East Wind, 1926
 Ballads for Sale, 1927
 Selected Poems of Amy Lowell, 1928 (John Livingston Lowes, editor)
 The Complete Poetical Works of Amy Lowell, 1955 (Louis Untermeyer, editor)
 A Shard of Silence: Selected Poems of Amy Lowell, 1957 (G. R. Ruihley, editor)
 Selected Poems, 2004 (Honor Moore, editor)

OTHER LITERARY FORMS

In addition to collections of poetry, Amy Lowell published translations, criticism, and a literary biography. Her output was prodigious, fourteen of her books being published within a thirteen-year span. In addition, she wrote numerous essays and reviews and kept up an active correspondence, much of it concerning literature. Lowell edited a three-volume anthology of Imagist poetry: *Some Imagist Poets* (1915, 1916, 1917). Her three critical works were *Six French Poets: Studies in Contemporary Literature* (1915), essays drawn from her lectures on the post-Symbolist poets; *Tendencies in Modern American Poetry* (1917), essays also drawn from lectures on contemporary poetry and six poets in particular, including two Imagists; and *Poetry and Poets* (1930), essays compiled from her lectures and published posthumously. Although she did other translations (of operettas and verse dramas), Lowell's only published translations, with the exception of those in the appendix to *Six French Poets*, were those in *Fir-Flower Tablets* (1921), a collection of ancient Chinese poetry done in collaboration with Florence Ayscough. Lowell's monumental two-volume biography, *John Keats*, appeared in 1925, shortly before her death. A sampling of Lowell's letters can be found in *Florence Ayscough and Amy Lowell: Correspondence of a Friendship* (1945).

Amy Lowell
(Library of Congress)

Achievements

During her lifetime, Amy Lowell was one of the best-known modern American poets. This reputation had as much to do with Lowell the person and literary spokesperson as with Lowell the poet, though her work was certainly esteemed. In 1926, *What's O'Clock* won the Pulitzer Prize in poetry. In the twenty-first century, her place in literary history as a whole is still to be determined, but her importance in the limited field of early twentieth century American letters is undisputed.

In her day, as F. Cudworth Flint has said, both Lowell and poetry were "news." Between 1914 and 1925, she spoke out for Imagism, free verse, and the "New Poetry" more frequently, energetically, and combatively than any of its other promoters or practitioners. She took on all comers in Boston, New York, Chicago, and any other city where she was invited to speak. "Poetry Society" meetings were often the best show in town when Lowell was on the platform. In 1924, she was awarded the Levinson Prize from *Poetry* magazine.

Lowell's art probably suffered as a result of her taking on the role of promoter as well as producer of the new poetry, but she unquestionably helped to open the way for younger poets among her contemporaries and for free expression and experimentation in poetic form and theme. T. S. Eliot's *The Waste Land* (1922), which Lowell did not admire, might not have had such an immediate impact on the development of modern poetry had Lowell not helped to prepare for its reception.

Critical opinion on Lowell's own poetry is divided. Her detractors argue that she lacks passion and feeling; that she is concerned only with the surfaces of things; that she is imitative, an assimilator without any original creative force. Some even say that she never really understood the new poetry she so tirelessly advocated, that she was temperamentally grounded in the conservatism and sentimentality of the nineteenth century.

Her supporters, on the other hand, cite the enormous variety of her subject matter; the breadth of forms she employed and the extent to which she developed rhythmical variation in her polyphonic prose; the freshness and vitality of many of her lyrics, particularly her poetry dealing with love; her brilliant and vivid sensory perceptions; the intelligence that complemented emotion in her poetry; and the range of emotions that her verse expressed. Contemporary feminist critics, in particular, in their revisionist readings of Lowell, have found her worthy of greater prominence than literary criticism has generally accorded her.

What most critics would probably agree on is that Lowell wrote at least a handful of excellent poems worthy of inclusion in any anthology of American poetry. There would also be general agreement that she played a paramount role in the poetic renaissance of the early twentieth century.

Biography

Amy Lawrence Lowell was born in the family home (named Sevenels after her birth because there were then seven Lowells) in Brookline, Massachusetts, just outside Boston. Both of her parents were from distinguished and wealthy Massachusetts families. Her father, Augustus Lowell, was a member of the wealthiest branch of the Lowells, the prominent family who had come to America in 1639 and later had become a major force in the intellectual and industrial history of Massachusetts. The mill town of Lowell, Massachusetts, was named for the family. Lowell's mother, Katherine Bigelow Lawrence, was the daughter of Abbot Lawrence. The Lawrences were also an old American family, and another Massachusetts mill town was named for them.

Although the Lowells also owned a townhouse for the winter months, most of Lowell's childhood was spent at Sevenels, and she continued to live there, with the exception of summers in New Hampshire and abroad, until her death. After her parents' deaths, her mother's in 1895 and her father's in 1899, Lowell settled into Sevenels and made it her own, remodeling and refurnishing it extensively. The gardens there were the source of much of Lowell's imagery.

Lowell had two brothers and two sisters. Both brothers distinguished themselves, each in a different area. The elder, Percival, after ten years in Asia and the publication of two books on the Far East, went to Flagstaff, Arizona, where he founded the Lowell Observatory and made discoveries concerning Mars. The younger brother, Abbott Lawrence, became president of Harvard University in 1909.

Lowell's formal education was limited. She was a mischievous pupil who was easily bored and a challenge to her teachers. Although she received a private school education, she did not attend college. Her own comment on her formal education was that "it really did not amount to a hill of beans." Most of her real education came from her avid reading in her father's library and in the Boston Athenaeum, a building she later wrote about and saved from razing. Her future profession was foreshadowed when she discovered Leigh Hunt's *Imagination and Fancy* and read it through and through. She was particularly taken with John Keats, about whom she later wrote a biography. Hunt's ideas about poetry were those of an earlier time, however, and were responsible, in part, for Lowell's unsuccessful first volume of rather old-fashioned poetry.

Because of a glandular condition, the five-foot-tall Lowell became obese in her adolescence and remained so, eventually weighing about 250 pounds. In spite of such corpulence, she was a successful debutante, having some sixty dinners given for her. Suitors, however, were few. Those who did appear were interested chiefly in her family connections. Lowell rejected two proposals of marriage and then accepted a third, only to be rejected later by her fiancé.

Eventually reconciled to spinsterhood, though not without much suffering, including a nervous breakdown requiring several years of convalescence, Lowell finally turned to poetry as a focus for her life. It also seemed to serve as a substitute for the orthodox Christian faith of her childhood, which she had rejected. Lowell had always been fascinated by the theater and was a creditable performer. Many thought that had she not been heavy, she would have become a professional actress. Her interest in theater, and indeed in all the arts, continued throughout her life. Perhaps not so coincidentally, then, it was an actress, the great Eleanor Duse, who inspired Lowell to become a poet. It was 1902, the third time that she had seen Duse perform. Lowell later said that watching her "loosed a bolt in my brain and I knew where my true function lay." Having little training in poetry, Lowell began a long period of study and writing, with Hunt as her primary tutor. It was eight years before she published her first poems and ten before her first book appeared. During those years, she gradually withdrew from her many civic activities to concentrate on poetry. She received much support and encouragement throughout this period from Carl Engel, a young composer who also introduced her to new music.

On March 12, 1912, she met the person who was later to become her companion, critic, supporter, and confidante for life, Ada Dwyer Russell, an actress whom Lowell eventually coaxed into retirement. Many of Lowell's poems were inspired by, or written for, Mrs. Russell.

On October 12, 1912, her first collection of poems, *A Dome of Many-Coloured*

Glass, was published to uniformly bad reviews, including one by Louis Untermeyer, who was later to become her friend and eventually to edit her collected poems. The year 1912 was an important one in American poetry. Harriet Monroe launched her new magazine *Poetry* in that year, a journal to which Lowell contributed both money and poems. The early issues of *Poetry* alerted Lowell to a group of poets in England who called themselves Les Imagistes and who were led by Ezra Pound and T. E. Hulme. Recognizing her own poetic tendencies in what she read, Lowell sailed for England, in the summer of 1913, to meet with Pound and the other poets and learn more about Imagism. She returned enthusiastic about what she had learned and about her own future. Within a year, Pound was in the center of a new movement, Vorticism, though he had recently edited a small anthology called *Des Imagistes*. Lowell traveled to England again in 1914, meeting, among others, D. H. Lawrence, who was to become a close friend and whose talent Lowell immediately recognized. During that summer, Lowell and Pound parted in disagreement over the editorial policy of the next edition of *Des Imagistes*, and Lowell, with many of the poets on her side, took over the editorship of the anthology. She also took over the leadership of the Imagist movement and of the battle in the United States for the new poetic forms. Pound later dubbed the American movement "Amygism."

Lowell had learned much in two years, and *Sword Blades and Poppy Seed* was published in 1914 to great success, although only about one-fourth of the poems were actually written in free verse. Lowell herself, in a short preface to the volume, used the term "unrhymed cadence." Three of the poems were written in what she called "polyphonic prose," a technique that she explained in the preface to a later book, *Can Grande's Castle*.

In 1915, 1916, and 1917, Lowell published the three volumes called *Some Imagist Poets*, picking up where Pound's *Des Imagistes* had left off and presenting seven to ten poems by each poet. Also in 1915, she published the successful *Six French Poets*, a book that brought her numerous speaking and reading engagements. From 1915 to 1918, Lowell was indefatigable. She gave countless lectures and readings, often traveling long distances on behalf of her own verse and of the New Poetry. She also wrote essays and reviews and produced several books. Always she was a friend to good writing and good writers, crusading tirelessly for others as well as for herself.

Men, Women, and Ghosts, her next collection of poems, followed her French study. Next came another critical work, *Tendencies in Modern American Poetry*, followed by another volume of verse, *Can Grande's Castle*, her virtuoso production in polyphonic prose. In 1916, Lowell injured herself lifting a carriage out of a ditch, causing the hernia that would eventually necessitate four operations and contribute to her death.

Her next publications were *Pictures of the Floating World*, reflecting her long study of Asia, *Legends*, and *Fir-Flower Tablets*, translations of Chinese poetry done in collaboration with Florence Ayscough. *A Critical Fable* followed, and then Lowell began work on the book that was to be the culmination of a lifetime devotion to a single poet, John Keats. *John Keats* appeared in 1925; Lowell, driving herself to accomplish the task, became physically weaker and weaker during the course of its writing. On May 12, 1925, she saw the side of her face droop while looking in a mirror, and in that moment, according to Damon, she "recognized her death." She died less than two hours later. On August 25, *What's O'Clock* was published, and the following spring, it won the Pulitzer Prize in poetry.

Analysis

In its entirety, Amy Lowell's work is, as F. Cudworth Flint has observed, a history of the poetry of her time. Born in the 1870's, she died just three years after the publication of *The Waste Land*.

Although her first published work owed much, in both theme and form, to the Romantics and the Victorians, by her second book, Lowell was planted more firmly in the twentieth century and, more specifically, in what has come to be known as the Poetic Renaissance. She herself used this term in her critical work, *Tendencies in Modern American Poetry*. It was a time of experimentation in all the arts, in the United States as well as abroad. Lowell took control in America of the movement to revolutionize and modernize poetic forms, and by the end of her life at fifty-one, she was largely responsible for the acceptance in America of the "New Poetry." Poetry was popular in Lowell's day, and Lowell made it even more so. Though both her poetry and her ideas about it often enraged her audience, they never failed to elicit responses, and Lowell was such a dynamic saleswoman that she usually had the final word. Not a highly original thinker or writer, Lowell was able, nevertheless, to absorb the best of what was going on around her and build on it.

Lowell's work, though often faulted for being focused on externalities and devoid of emotion, is psychologically revealing, both of her own emotional states and, in some poems, of the ideas of Sigmund Freud and modern psychology. Many of her poems reveal her own experiences and emotions, and much of her imagery derives from her own life. Lowell's childhood at Sevenels, at least into adolescence, when she became very heavy, was largely a happy one, and one of her greatest joys was her father's garden, later to become hers. Her knowledge and love of flowers, gardens, and birds permeates her work. The imagery is not all joyful, however, for Lowell lived out her life at Sevenels and her life also had its great disappointments and pain. Her obesity was probably responsible for her failure to marry and have a family, and in disillusionment, she embraced poetry, almost as a spouse. Disillusionment about her work also occurs in the poems. In all, there is a tremendous amount of psychological as well as intellectual energy in her poems, partly a result of Lowell's driving need to achieve and compensate for what she had lost or never had. There is also peace in many of the poems, inspired by the security and contentment she found during the last eleven years of her life with Mrs.

Russell. Many of the poems centering on love and devotion were inspired by Mrs. Russell.

Lowell's poetic subjects were wide-ranging. She wrote narratives on subjects as disparate as the frustration of a violinist's wife and the attempted rape of the moon by a fox. She wrote lyrics on such traditional subjects as love, disillusionment, artistic inspiration, and gardens, but she also wrote poems on buildings, cities, and wars. She wrote quasi epics that encompassed different centuries and countries, and dialect tales set in rural New England.

Glenn Richard Ruihley finds these diverse subjects unified by Lowell's transcendentalism, her search for the "Numinous or Divine" residing in all people and things. It was, according to Ruihley, the possibility of transcendence that she recognized that night while watching Duse act.

Her technical virtuosity was as great as her thematic range. Her use of metaphors and symbols was extensive. According to Ruihley, the only way to understand much of Lowell's work is through a study of "her chosen symbols." Though an outspoken advocate of poetic experimentation, she wrote in traditional forms as well as in free verse and polyphonic prose, often ranging through several forms in a single poem. Her virtuosity was unquestioned, but like most virtuosity, it was exhausting as well as dazzling. She exhausted not through sheer variety of poetic forms but through a prolixity, particularly in much of her polyphonic prose, that left the reader drugged with sheer sensation and unable to absorb more.

Though she professed to be an Imagist, at least in her early work, and was the movement's leader in the United States, Lowell was never contained or restrained enough in her work to be truly Imagistic in the sense that the movement is usually defined. She was too expansive. In many of her poems, however, sometimes only in individual groups of lines, she did achieve what is usually thought of as Imagistic expression.

"On Looking at a Copy of Alice Meynell's Poems"

One of the recurring themes in Lowell's poetry is her disillusionment, self-doubt, and even despair. A representative poem in this vein is "On Looking at a Copy of Alice Meynell's Poems: Given Me Years Ago by a Friend" (*Ballads for Sale*). When Lowell learned of Meynell's death in November, 1922, she turned again to the volume of Meynell's poems given to her twenty-five years earlier by Frances Dabney. In that year, 1897, Lowell had had her marriage engagement broken off by her young Bostonian suitor. Hoping to alleviate her grief, Dabney had given her the poems. In rereading the poems on Meynell's death, Lowell found little to admire, but the poems did renew her feelings of despair and bitterness.

Written in a rhyming, metered, and regular stanzaic form, the poem records Lowell's present and past reflections on Meynell's book. She evaluates it both as a gift and as a work of art. As she reads again the "whispered greeting" inscribed by Dabney, the memories surface, "dim as pictures on a winking wall," but vivid enough in the illumination of the moment to revive her emotions. Dabney's gift, intended "to ease the smart," was instead a painful "mirror," reflecting Lowell's own tragic lack of fulfillment, yet Lowell remembers how she once "loved to quote" these lines.

From her present perspective, Lowell wonders at both her own and Dabney's judgment. She distances herself from her memories as she contemplates the changes brought by time. Both Dabney and Meynell are dead, and the verses that once seemed so brilliant now seem merely "well-made." Lowell has "lived the almanac" since that time and still has "so much to do." Though Meynell's and Lowell's old griefs seem insignificant now and Lowell refuses to linger any longer with them, she is still sympathetic to the pain, a sympathy tempered, however, by her awareness of old age and death and the ultimate futility of fame and happiness. These feelings are briefly captured in the magnificent and poignant third-from-the-last stanza: "So cried her heart, a feverish thing./ But clay is still, and clay is cold,/ And I was young, and I am old,/ And in December what birds sing!" Lowell cannot allow herself to remain in this mood, and in the final two stanzas, she returns the book to its shelf where "dust" will again cover the pain. For Ruihley, "Lowell's incompleteness" and "longing for wider satisfactions" are shared in some measure by everyone, albeit for varying reasons and in varying degrees. Her poem, then, transcends her own experience in its applicability and appeal.

RELATIONSHIPS BETWEEN PEOPLE AND THINGS

A second theme running throughout Lowell's work, and one that is suggested rather than directly stated, is the relationship between human beings and material forms. Lowell's pictorialism is brilliant and abundant, but rather than representing only surface effects as it was often unfairly accused of doing, it has its origin in sympathetic feeling and reveals a passionate heart. A beautiful example of this theme (and the poem that was most often requested at Lowell's frequent readings) is "Lilacs" (*What's O'Clock*).

"Lilacs" expresses clearly the relationship between things or places and people, a relationship indivisible and full of emotion. The poem expansively chronicles the spatial and temporal domain of the lilac. It is a list that finally incorporates the poet herself until she and New England and history and time and the lilac are one. Throughout the poem, the lilac is an active participant in its settings, playing many roles—conversing, watching, settling, staggering, tapping, running, standing, persuading, flaunting, charging, and calling. Having originated in the East, the lilac beckons to those who sail in from China, but it has become most fully itself in the soil of New England. The flower is both in its settings and of its settings, and finally it becomes its settings as it mingles with places and lives and takes on a significance far beyond that of any of its individual manifestations:

> You are the great flood of our souls
> Bursting above the leaf-shapes of our hearts,
> You are the smell of all Summers,
> The love of wives and children,
> The recollection of the gardens of little children,
> You are State Houses and Charters. . . .

In the last stanza, Lowell identifies herself directly with the lilac as it embodies her own soil, New England ("Lilac in me because I am New England"). Her litany of reasons for such a union, underscored by repetitive structures, serves to emphasize the force and passion of her feelings.

Another example of the emotional import of material forms in Lowell's work is the popular "Meeting-House Hill." The scene portrayed is a simple one. The poet, from the eminence of "a squalid hill-top," observes a quiet scene: "the curve of a blue bay beyond a railroad track" and "a white church above thin trees in a city square." The scene itself is unremarkable except as it affects the poet, who suggests that she must be "mad, or very tired." The bay seems to sing to her and the church "amazes . . . as though it were the Parthenon." The imagination and emotion of the poet give movement to the scene until it is transformed into the final arresting image, which occupies ten of the poem's twenty-five lines. The spire of the church becomes the mast of a ship just returned from Canton. As the ship enters the bay carrying "green and blue porcelain," the poet sees a "Chinese coolie leaning over the rail/ Gazing at the white spire." It is a vivid scene and the reader too feels the emotion of the moment and sees the transformation.

The "coolie" is both of the spire (the mast of his ship) and gazing at it, both passive object of contemplation and active contemplator, so that the two worlds of reality and imagination merge fully. This is far from a mere portrayal of the surfaces of things. Objects, landscapes, flowers, and birds are emblems in Lowell's work and are always portrayed with feeling.

LOVE AND DEVOTION

A third dominant theme in Lowell's poetry is that of love and devotion. It is "love in its combined physical and spiritual totality," as Jean Gould points out, that is celebrated in Lowell's work. Poems on this theme take many forms and honor many subjects, but the greatest are those inspired by Eleanor Duse and Mrs. Russell. Among those written for Russell are several of Lowell's most popular and enduring lyrics: "Madonna of the Evening Flowers," "Venus Transiens," "A Sprig of Rosemary," and "A Decade," all from *Pictures of the Floating World*; "In Excelsis" (*What's O'Clock*); and "The Taxi" (*Sword Blades and Poppy Seed*).

The scene in "Madonna of the Evening Flowers" is again simple. Lowell, tired from her day's work, calls for Russell. She is answered only by the wind and the sun shining on the remnants of her companion's recent activity—her books and her sewing implements. Though Lowell impatiently continues the search for her friend, the scene above has foreshadowed for the reader the simple domestic setting in which Russell will eventually be found. When finally spotted, Russell is "Standing under a spire of pale blue larkspur,/ With a basket of roses on [her] arm." The rest of the poem records Russell's practical responses to Lowell and Lowell's concomitant reflections. Lowell's attitude is worshipful, in contrast with the secular nature of Russell's concerns, and the natural and human scene merges with the divine as Lowell hears the imagined "*Te Deums* of the Canterbury Bells."

"In Excelsis" again strikes a worshipful note and one full of rapture. In it, Lowell sees Russell as both the creator of the natural world and the embodiment of it. It is Russell whose movements control the processes of nature and Russell who is herself the "air—earth—heaven" of Lowell's universe. As in "Madonna of the Evening Flowers," the poet's impulse is to kneel before such glory, but she restrains herself from excesses: "Heaven" is not a "boon deserving thanks." She will accept the life that Russell brings to her; her poems will be her thanks, "rubies" set in "stone."

"The Taxi" has a different tone. Probably written during one of Lowell's separations from Russell, the poem speaks of the pain of separation. The images are vivid and startling, hauntingly modern in their metaphors. In the loved one's absence, the world turns hostile to the poet. The streets "wedge" Russell away from Lowell, and the city lights "prick" Lowell's eyes. The night has "sharp edges" that "wound."

Other love poems are more tranquil, projecting neither the rapturous adoration of "Madonna of the Evening Flowers" and "In Excelsis" nor the fearful tension of "The Taxi." The poet is often at peace in her love, admiring the beauty of her friend as if she were Botticelli's Venus ("Venus Transiens"), reflecting on the restfulness of her hands and voice ("A Sprig of Rosemary"), and savoring the simple nourishment of her presence ("A Decade").

Lowell's importance as a force in American literary history is undisputed. Her crusading efforts on behalf of modern poetry and poets had a formative influence on the development of American poetry in the twentieth century. The place of her own poetry is not as solidly determined. An untiring experimenter in verse forms, she was not a great poet, but she did write a few enduring poems that, it seems likely, will find a permanent place in the literary canon of her time.

OTHER MAJOR WORKS

NONFICTION: *Six French Poets: Studies in Contemporary Literature*, 1915; *Tendencies in Modern American Poetry*, 1917; *John Keats*, 1925; *Poetry and Poets*, 1930; *Florence Ayscough and Amy Lowell: Correspondence of a Friendship*, 1946; *The Letters of D. H. Lawrence and Amy Lowell, 1914-1925*, 1985.

TRANSLATION: *Fir-Flower Tablets*, 1921 (with Florence Ayscough).

EDITED TEXT: *Some Imagist Poets*, 1915-1917 (3 volumes).

BIBLIOGRAPHY

Benvenuto, Richard. *Amy Lowell*. Boston: Twayne, 1985. Aims to give a fair and detailed reading of Lowell's poetry to suggest the strengths and limitations of her art as well as to acquaint the reader with poems that, in Benvenuto's opinion, should not be neglected. Besides being an uneven writer, Lowell was, Benvenuto argues, one of the most important literary figures of her time. Includes an annotated bibliography.

Flint, F. Cudworth. *Amy Lowell*. Minneapolis: University of Minnesota Press, 1969. This brief pamphlet devoted to Lowell's life and work contains useful information about her participation in the Imagist movement. Addresses the question of how Lowell was able to achieve what Flint calls a "para-literary" eminence so quickly. Contains a bibliography.

Galvin, Mary E. *Queer Poetics: Five Modernist Women Writers*. Westport, Conn.: Greenwood Press, 1999. In an exploration of the relationship between poetics and queer theory, Galvin presents a theoretical framework that can illuminate the reading of the specific poetic innovations of the writers in this study by placing them in a different social and epistemological context—that of "queer" existence.

Gould, Jean. *Amy: The World of Amy Lowell and the Imagist Movement*. New York: Dodd, Mead, 1975. Gould asserts that Lowell was one of the outstanding influences in the literary art of her time and focuses his discussion on her role in creating the Imagist movement. In her campaign for modern freedom of expression in poetry, Gould portrays Lowell as a vociferous advocate of revolutionary rhythms and free verse. Includes a bibliography.

Hughes, Glenn. "Amy Lowell: 'The Success.'" In *Imagism and the Imagists: A Study in Modern Poetry*. Stanford, Calif.: Stanford University Press, 1931. In this dated but excellent study of Lowell's life and work, Hughes, interested in the new effects of Lowell's work, discusses the polyphonic aspects of her poetry. Examines both her contribution to American poetry and her influence on it. Passages from individual poems are analyzed.

Munich, Adrienne, and Melissa Bradshaw, eds. *Amy Lowell, American Modern*. New Brunswick, N.J.: Rutgers University Press, 2004. This scholarly collection of essays by various critics and scholars is an invaluable complement to the study of Lowell's work.

Ruihley, Glenn R. *The Thorn of a Rose: Amy Lowell Reconsidered*. Hamden, Conn.: Archon Books, 1975. One of the most useful critical studies on Lowell, this book assesses Lowell's rightful place in American literature. In attempting to redress the balance of critical opinion in her favor, the author argues that it is necessary to understand the inner character of Lowell's life and work—for example, the philosophical framework of her poetry. Focuses on the art of Lowell's middle and late periods. Contains a bibliography.

Elaine Gardiner

STÉPHANE MALLARMÉ

Born: Paris, France; March 18, 1842
Died: Valvins, France; September 9, 1898

PRINCIPAL POETRY
L'Après-midi d'un faune, 1876 (*The Afternoon of a Faun*, 1936)
Les Poésies de Stéphane Mallarmé, 1887
Un Coup de dés jamais n'abolira le hasard, 1897 (*A Dice-Throw*, 1958; also as *Dice Thrown Never Will Annul Chance*, 1965)
Igitur, 1925 (English translation, 1974)
Poems by Mallarmé, 1936 (Roger Fry, translator)
Herodias, 1940 (Clark Mills, translator)
Selected Poems, 1957
Les Noces d'Hérodiade, 1959
Pour un "Tombeau d'Anatole," 1961 (*A Tomb for Anatole*, 1983)
Poésies, 1970 (*The Poems*, 1977)
Collected Poems, 1994

OTHER LITERARY FORMS

Stéphane Mallarmé (mah-lahr-MAY) is known chiefly for his poetry. A selection from his numerous critical essays and reviews, including some important theoretical statements, was published in *Divagations* (1897; English translation, 2007). Following the example of Charles Baudelaire, Mallarmé translated Edgar Allan Poe. He also published an idiosyncratic introduction to English philology, *Petite Philologie à l'usage des classes et du monde: Les Mots anglais* (1878; little philology for classroom use and for society: English words). It should be noted that Mallarmé wrote a number of prose poems, treated by some critics as prose works. The best edition of Mallarmé's poetry and essays is the Pléiade *Œuvres complètes de Stéphane Mallarmé* (1945), prepared by Henri Mondor and G. Jean-Aubry, although it is not a complete collection.

ACHIEVEMENTS

Stéphane Mallarmé's work is both the culmination of French Romanticism and the harbinger of the more hermetic poetry of the twentieth century. His vision of poetry as a sacred art, created with considerable sacrifice by an elite, derives from the Romantic image of the poet as prophet, typical of Victor Hugo. Mallarmé's "pure poetry," without reference to history or to social reality and characterized by a dense and elliptical style, however, deliberately abandons the attempt of many Romantics to bring poetry closer to life and to make it a social force. Very early in his career, Mallarmé said that it was heresy to try to make poetry understandable to a large audience. He sought instead to give expression to a higher form of intellectual experience in a language that is suggestive and indirect. Mallarmé's disciples, notably Paul Valéry, used the term "symbolism" to describe the new poetry. Mallarmé exerted a great personal influence on the theories developed in modernist artistic circles through his Tuesday receptions in his apartment on the rue de Rome in Paris.

Biography

Stéphane Mallarmé was born Etienne Mallarmé into a middle-class Parisian family of government administrators. His mother died when he was five. He was taken in by his maternal grandparents, who placed him in a series of boarding schools from the time he was ten. This forcible separation from a family environment was particularly painful because it deprived him of the company of his only sibling, his sister, Maria, who was younger by two years. He continued to write to her until her death at the age of thirteen. This disappearance of mother and sister, both idealized figures strongly linked in Mallarmé's mind to the religious life, seems to have caused Mallarmé to abandon conventional religious beliefs and to seek in his adolescent poetry a way of preserving the memory of these beloved presences. At the same time, Mallarmé's active sexual life seems to have left him disappointed and perhaps guilty about physical pleasure.

In 1860, Mallarmé took a position with the French administration, then went to London in 1862 with a young German woman, Maria Gerhard, whom he married in 1863. At the end of that year, he took his first position as a teacher of English. His entire professional career consisted of a series of appointments in secondary schools, first in the provinces and then, after 1871, in Paris. He retired in 1894. During the 1870's, Mallarmé published translations, textbooks, a women's fashion magazine, and his own poetry.

His period of great celebrity began around 1884, when Paul Verlaine and Joris-Karl Huysmans acclaimed him in their own works. During the last fifteen years of his life, Mallarmé exercised enormous influence on the younger poets, who hailed him as the prophetic exemplar of Symbolism. Mallarmé himself did not seek honor or public attention. He left the publication of manifestos to his followers and preferred to devote his time to research for his oeuvre, his great "work," which he never finished. His poetic works, considerable as they are, did not live up to his ambition, although his manuscripts give evidence of intense labor.

Analysis

"Everything in the world exists to end up in a book," wrote Stéphane Mallarmé in 1895. It is this attitude toward reality and toward the importance of the book that makes Mallarmé the preeminent Symbolist poet. For him, reality exists only in the symbol, which, in poetry, is constructed out of language. This position, apparently influenced by Hegelian idealism, does not mean that poetry is necessarily about language—although a number of Mallarmé's poems are about language and poetry themselves—but rather that language provides the only systematic and rational framework, the only escape from randomness, in a world in which there is no sign of a personal God. Mallarmé's poetry is a kind of metaphysical poetry, in that it aspires to go beyond the physical reality of everyday life to uncover the mysterious world of a pure ideal that can exist nowhere except in the mind and in language.

Even though many of Mallarmé's poems seem at first to be completely obscure, in most cases careful reading will reveal that a kernel drawn from everyday life has been transformed into a spare, unsentimental, timeless formal variation (in the way that a composer makes a variation on a musical theme). The effect is neither an enshrinement of a particular moment, place, or picturesque character nor an appeal to emotional sympathy. It is still less a moral or political message. Instead, such poems invite the reader to experience the power of the mind and of language.

For Mallarmé, the most important experience is the experience of the poem itself, and if such a statement seems commonplace and even trite, it is because Mallarmé's influence has been so pervasive. For him, however, the experience of the poem was particularly concrete and precise, and he frequently wrote about acts and objects connected with writing and reading with a kind of religious awe. The word *livre* (book) and such kindred terms as *grimoire* (book of magic incantations) and *bouquin* (old book) have in his vocabulary an importance rarely found in other bodies of poetry except in religious texts, where "the book" is the sacred scripture explaining and justifying the world. Mallarmé attempted during his life to create a nonreligious scripture.

Most of his poems, however, are playful occasional pieces such as "Eventail de Madame Mallarmé" ("Madam Mallarmé's Fan"); brief poems written in honor of other artists, such as the "Hommage" to Richard Wagner and "Le Tombeau d'Edgar Poe" ("The Tomb of Edgar Poe"); erotic poetry based on elliptical sexual fantasy, such as *The Afternoon of a Faun* and "Victorieusement fui le suicide beau" ("The Beautiful Suicide Victoriously Escaped"); or the long series of poems lamenting the difficulty of escaping from the base material world and of writing the higher kind of poetry. The last category includes the well-known "L'Azur," sometimes called the "Swan Sonnet," "Les Fenêtres" ("The Windows"), and "Le Pître châtié" ("The Clown's Punishment"). Only the three longer poems, *Herodias, Igitur* (read to friends in unfinished form and published posthumously), and *Dice Thrown Never Will Annul Chance* (published in the magazine *Cosmopolis* in May, 1897, but not published in book form until 1914) give some idea of the form of Mallarmé's more ambitious projects.

There is nevertheless a stylistic and thematic coherence in Mallarmé's work, which proceeds by a kind of condensation and subtraction. The extremely difficult but logical grammar absorbs the reader in the enigmatic possibilities of meaning, thus fixing attention on the poem's language. Objects and persons named in the poems are described as absent or "abolished."

"All the Soul Indrawn..."

A good way to begin with Mallarmé's poetry is to look at his brief poem "Toute l'âme résumée..." ("All the Soul Indrawn..."), which is a witty response to a survey on free verse. Mallarmé compares making poetry to smoking a cigar. The successive rings of smoke are "abolished" by those that follow, and the ash keeps falling away from the "bright kiss of fire." Poetry is not what is left behind, Mallarmé implies; it is rather the process itself, momentary but renewed. Because the word *âme* can mean both "soul" and, with some etymological delving, "breath," and *résumée* means both "summed up" and "drawn in," Mallarmé has put into play a metaphor for the content of poetry that eludes the traditional distinction between form and content, vehicle and tenor. The breath is what permits the cigar to keep burning; it is also the proof that one is alive. Yet this thing, which is so essential to smoking and to life, is empty. Similarly, the burning tip of the cigar, the thing showing that the cigar is "alive," is the fire that can survive only by emptying itself of the ash. Like smoking, Mallarmé suggests, poetry should be regarded as pure activity, without product and without connection with any external reality. After making this comparison explicit in the third quatrain, which advises writers to exclude vile reality, Mallarmé concludes with a distich that pointedly inverts the usual literary and rhetorical values of his day: "A too precise meaning scratches out/ Your vague literature." The more definite and specific the reference a poem makes to reality, the less it can be considered precisely literary.

"My Old Books Closed at the Name of Paphos"

Another celebrated poem centered on the powers of literature, considered this time from the point of view of the reader, is "Mes bouquins refermés sur le nom de Paphos" ("My Old Books Closed at the Name of Paphos"). The speaker of the poem tells of closing his book and looking out on a snowy landscape where he imagines a Mediterranean scene. There is a parallel between the foam of the sea splashing against a ruin in the first quatrain and the white snow presented as part of the reader's material reality in the second quatrain. The speaker makes clear, however, that he will not wail a funeral lament (*nénie*) if the snowy reality does not coincide with his imagined seascape. The tercets make clear why the speaker so calmly accepts the divorce of dream from reality. The absence of things, which one notices because literature draws one's attention to such lacunae, is presented as a superior value. Mallarmé's negative approach, his preference for hollowing out a dream world by "abolishing" elements of the everyday world, appears in the speaker's claim: "My hunger, which is satisfied here by no fruits/ Finds in their learned lack an equal savor." To be satisfied by "no fruits" is not the same as being unsatisfied. It is a state in which the learned vision imposes a preference for the dream.

The second tercet goes even further, recalling that absence is not merely in the speaker's present world but in the scene imagined as well. Apparently addressing a lover, he confesses: "I think longer, perhaps desperately,/ Of the other, with the seared breast of an ancient Amazon." The scene is not only absent but also organized around an absence, the missing breast of one of the legendary warrior-women who founded the city of Paphos. Even these two absences are not all one can find here. The adverb translated as "desperately" or "distractedly" to describe the speaker's preoccupation with the Amazon is *éperdument*, which contains the word *perdu* (lost). The speaker, as reader, is thus also in some way lost to the everyday world and to ordinary love.

"HER PURE FINGERNAILS ON HIGH OFFERING THEIR ONYX"

The procedure of creating a scene by "abolishing" is taken closer to Mallarmé's project of a great magical work in the sonnet "Ses purs ongles trés haut dédiant leur onyx" ("Her Pure Fingernails on High Offering Their Onyx"), known as the "Sonnet in yx" because of its unusual rhymes. This sonnet apparently describes a deserted parlor belonging to a magician, the "Master," who has gone to get tears in the underworld from the river Styx. The vessel the Master will use is a *ptyx*. This is a word that has a meaning in Greek but none in French. Mallarmé may have meant it to remain meaningless, for the *ptyx* is called "this unique object of which Nothingness is proud." Furthermore, the *ptyx* is designated in the poem only as an absence: "in the empty parlor: no ptyx,/ Abolished trinket of sonorous inanity."

Scholars have studied the problem of the *ptyx* at length with reference to its ancient meanings, ranging from "book" to "seashell." As one scholar has noted, however, the more meanings that are proposed for the word, the less it actually signifies. It has become an empty form that traps the reader into deep and repeated investigations of semantic, phonetic, and etymological networks in the sonnet in the hope of finding some meaning. This sonnet certainly follows the precepts of "All the Soul Indrawn . . ." in avoiding a "too precise sense." It also exemplifies the kind of dream to which Mallarmé wanted to lead his readers. Although psychoanalytic readings of Mallarmé have been among the most interesting, Mallarmé himself did not use the word *rêve* (dream) to designate a person's unconscious. For Mallarmé, "dream" suggested both the aspiration to a world of pure thought without material limitation (this is particularly clear in "The Windows") and the realm in which language unfolds in all its ambiguity. The Master's absence from this parlor could be interpreted as the author's desire to absent himself from the scene within which the reader can experience the possibilities of language, including the possibility that the most important words exist anagrammatically within the evident ones.

HERODIAS

Of Mallarmé's longer poems, those that seem to be part of his "great work," only *Herodias* and *Dice Thrown Never Will Annul Chance* gave the public some idea of the synthesis of poetic research of which he often spoke. Those works and the posthumous publications are all extremely difficult to interpret, but they seem to have at their core a struggle between the magic of the poetic symbol and the Nothingness (*le Néant*) that, for Mallarmé, constituted the universe. Because he rejected the physically present world for an ideal one and yet did not believe in religious spirituality, the magic of the great work would be to create a place where the ideal could exist. The language of the great work would have to be a special one, not the "unrefined and immediate" but the "essential" word free from the "chance" of usage, as he wrote in a preface to a work by René Ghil.

Herodias, a verse drama with little of the apparatus of a theater script, unites the themes of incantation, abolition, cerebral eroticism, and the preservation of the memory of the beloved dead. In most editions of Mallarmé, *Herodias* is divided into an "overture," in which the nurse of Princess Herodias describes the imaginary setting; a "scene," consisting of a dialogue between Herodias and her nurse; and a "canticle," in which the voice of John the Baptist sings at the moment of his decapitation. In the overture, the palace is evoked as empty and abandoned, like the parlor of the "Sonnet in yx." The king is long absent, the basin deserted by its swan, the sun rising red for the last time.

Even if one could create such a setting on the stage, the words of the overture make it clear that the real stage for these words is in the mind. The nurse, for example, speaks of a voice that evokes the past and then asks, "Is it my voice ready for the incantation?" If the speaker responsible for the exposition is not sure whether she has spoken, this suggests that she has merely thought the words. Moreover, the words that her voice may be ready to pronounce are an evocation of the past. Future and past thus join to create a situation in which imminent doom, nostalgia, and uncertainty about time coexist in a paradoxical equilibrium. The abstract quality of this setting is further emphasized by such metaphors as "the bed with pages of velum." The princess's bed is thus characterized as entirely chaste, while the whole drama takes on the aura of something entirely within a book.

In "Scene," the nurse tries to persuade Herodias to satisfy her awakening sexuality, while the princess insists that she loves the "horror" of being a virgin and that she cannot tolerate any touch. In place of touch, sight becomes the only sense through which Herodias can open herself to sexuality or even to consciousness. The scene is full of mirrors, described as cold and distant like "water frozen from boredom." All the mirrors serve to reflect the princess's image, excluding the menacing outside world. In the last lines, Herodias, at the departure of the nurse, announces that she is waiting for an unknown thing and that she has lied to her nurse about her voluntary solitude.

The connection between "Scene" and "Canticle," which follows it, is not clear, although the fragments edited by Gardner Davies in *Les Noces d'Hérodiade* permit some conjectures. Several critics have advanced the idea that John the Baptist has seen Heriodas, who then feels that only his death can restore her sense of intactness. The saint is what the fragment calls the "somber pretext" for the princess's full achievement of self-consciousness. His crime is to be different from a mirror, which offers a neutral image without judgment. According to "Canticle," there is a tension between the ideal and the physical in John as well, and this tension is released by the decapitation, in which the saint sees salvation. Mallarmé, however, avoids religious statement by concluding with the word *salut*, which can mean both "salvation" and "salute." The word describes both the movement of the head as it follows its trajectory up and then down and the hope expressed by baptism. In the unfinished version of this drama, Herodias seems to have captured the dying glance of John and to consider herself united to the prophet in a wedding that is both sexual and ideal. She addresses the head, saying "I reason for you, head, not about you."

Herodias's hope to snatch consciousness from death was apparently the long-term result of Mal larmé's adolescent poetic meditations on death. It is also a hope that appears in the fragmentary *A Tomb for Anatole* (edited by Jean-Pierre Richard), in which the poet tried to re-create the life of his dead son through imagination. In a passage similar to that in which Herodias declares that she will think for John, Mallarmé tells his dead son that the poet will *be* the son hereafter. The question of the apparent futility of such a project is addressed by two other long poems by Mallarmé, *Igitur* and *Dice Thrown Never Will Annul Chance*.

IGITUR

Igitur, a prose poem written between 1867 and 1870 and left unfinished at Mallarmé's death, was edited by the scholar Edmond Bonniot, the poet's son-in-law, who discovered the manuscript in 1900. The poem relates the adventures of Igitur, a prince haunted by a supreme "Idea" and by the destiny imposed by his race, which has somehow projected Igitur outside time. The next-to-last section is titled "A Roll of Dice" and takes place in the family tomb. There, Igitur confronts the problem of the relationship among personal action, necessity, and chance. Understanding that action is absurd except as a return to infinity, which is a form of the pure absolute, he throws the dice before laying himself on the ashes of his ancestors. This metaphysical hero, described by critics as a Hamlet stripped of psychology, confronts the problems of individual time-bound existence (versus a timeless ideal) and of the tradition of a nation or race. This can be considered as Mallarmé's own problem, for the poet is both haunted by the literary and scriptural tradition and faced with the apparent randomness of his own efforts. Mallarmé's flight from a psychological and emotional poetry toward an intellectual and apparently impersonal one corresponds to the desire to escape from chance into a pure rationality in which everything would be determined and necessary, although not foreseeable to the human mind.

DICE THROWN NEVER WILL ANNUL CHANCE

Dice Thrown Never Will Annul Chance follows from *Igitur* and seems to be the work that most closely approaches Mallarmé's ambition for "pure poetry." This work has had a wide influence on such twentieth century movements as Dada, Surrealism, and Lettrism, not because of its theme but because of its innovative typographical form. Mallarmé had the text set in type of various sizes and specified the exact location of each word on the double-page layouts. Some pages have as few as four words, while others have nearly a hundred. The poet can control more than the verbal aspect of the poem by dealing directly with the visual domain usually left to the printer. Mallarmé here manifests his obsessive concern for the concrete aspects of the book, for the obliteration of the distinction between form and content, and for the reduction of chance in the production of a literary work. The title of the poem runs in the largest type through the poem in such a way that the last word, "Chance," appears only on the ninth double-page unit (out of a total of eleven). Interrupting the title sentence are qualifications expressed in subordinate clauses and in various forms of apposition in various smaller type sizes. The effect is one of suspense, like that which attends a throw of the dice. The last small line of the poem reveals an application of the metaphor of the dice: "Every thought makes a roll of the dice."

Even though Mallarmé eschewed appeals to a broad public, and despite the fact that, aside from a half-dozen shorter poems frequently taught in *lycées* and colleges, his work does not have a wide readership, he has had an enormous influence on twentieth century poets, artists, and critics.

Other major works

NONFICTION: *Petite Philologie à l'usage des classes et du monde: Les Mots anglais*, 1878; *Les Dieux antiques*, 1880; *Divagations*, 1897 (English translation, 2007); *Correspondance*, 1959-1984 (10 volumes); *Documents Mallarmé*, 1968-1971 (3 volumes); *Mallarmé in Prose*, 2001 (Mary Ann Caws, editor).

TRANSLATION: *Les Poémes d'Edgar Poe*, 1888.

MISCELLANEOUS: *Album de vers et de prose*, 1887; *Pages*, 1891; *Vers et prose*, 1893; *Œuvres complètes de Stéphane Mallarmé*, 1945; *Selected Prose Poems, Essays, and Letters*, 1956; *Mallarmé*, 1965; *Selected Poetry and Prose*, 1982; *Divagations: The Author's 1897 Arrangement, Together with "Autobiography" and "Music and Letters,"* 2007.

Bibliography

Cohn, Robert Greer, ed. *Mallarmé in the Twentieth Century*. London: Associated University Presses, 1998. A collection of essays by many of the most eminent figures in the study of Mallarmé, including Julia Kristeva, Mary Ann Caws, Albert Cook, Anna Balakian, and Robert Cohn. An important summary of the state of scholarship on the poet.

Lloyd, Rosemary. *Mallarmé: The Poet and His Circle*. Ithaca, N.Y.: Cornell University Press, 1999. A literary biography of the poet and his period. Mallarmé hosted gatherings attended by writers, artists, thinkers, and musicians in France, England, and Belgium. Through these gatherings and voluminous correspondence Mallarmé developed and recorded his friendships with Paul Valéry, André Gide, Berthe Morisot, and many others. Includes bibliographical references and index.

Millan, Gordan. *A Throw of the Dice: The Life of Stéphane Mallarmé*. New York: Farrar, Straus and Giroux, 1994. This biography of Mallarmé, who has a reputation for difficulty and obscurity, proves equally valuable to students and specialists. The narrative is aimed at the general reader while the ample footnotes provide material for the specialist. The text draws on previously unpublished correspondence and new documentation and includes bibliographical references and an index.

Pearson, Roger. *Unfolding Mallarmé: The Development of a Poetic Art*. New York: Oxford University Press, 1996. An account of the development of Mallarmé's poetry from his earliest verse to his final masterpiece. Close readings demonstrate the intricate linguistic and formal play to be found in many of his major poems.

Sartre, Jean Paul. *Mallarmé: Or, The Poet of Nothingness*. Translated by Ernest Sturm. University Park: State University of Pennsylvania Press, 1988. A leading existentialist's view of Mallarmé.

Sugano, Marian Zwerling. *The Poetics of the Occasion: Mallarmé and the Poetry of Circumstance*. Stanford, Calif.: Stanford University Press, 1992. Focuses on Mallarmé's occasional poems.

Takeda, Noriko. *The Modernist Human: The Configuration of Humanness in Stéphane Mallarmé's "Hérodiade," T. S. Eliot's "Cats," and Modernist Lyrical Poetry*. New York: Peter Lang, 2008. Takeda examines modernist humanity as evidence in the poetry of Mallarmé and Eliot. Contains a general discussion of Mallarmé's poetry.

Temple, Michael. *The Name of the Poet: Onomastics and Anonymity in the Works of Stéphane Mallarmé*. Exeter, England: University of Exeter Press, 1995. Study of the use of place-names versus personal anonymity in Mallarmé's work.

———, ed. *Meetings with Mallarmé*. Exeter, England: University of Exeter Press, 1998. Critical interpretation of Mallarmé's major works. Includes bibliographical references and index.

John D. Lyons

ALICE NOTLEY

Born: Bisbee, Arizona; November 8, 1945

PRINCIPAL POETRY
165 Meeting House Lane, 1971
Incidentals in the Day World, 1973
Phoebe Light, 1973
Alice Ordered Me to Be Made: Poems 1975, 1976
For Frank O'Hara's Birthday, 1976
A Diamond Necklace, 1977
Songs for the Unborn Second Baby, 1979
When I Was Alive, 1980
How Spring Comes, 1981
Waltzing Matilda, 1981
Sorrento, 1984
Margaret and Dusty, 1985
Parts of a Wedding, 1986
At Night the States, 1987
From a Work in Progress, 1988
Homer's Art, 1990
The Scarlet Cabinet: A Compendium of Books, 1992 (with Douglas Oliver)
Selected Poems of Alice Notley, 1993
To Say You, 1994
Close to Me and Closer . . . (The Language of Heaven) and *Désamère*, 1995
The Descent of Alette, 1996
Etruscan Reader VII, 1997 (with Wendy Mulford and Brian Coffey)
Byzantine Parables, 1998
Mysteries of Small Houses, 1998
Disobedience, 2001
Iphigenia, 2002
Alma: Or, the Dead Women, 2006
Grave of Light: New and Selected Poems, 1970-2005, 2006
In the Pines, 2007
Above the Leaders, 2008
Reason and Other Women, 2010

OTHER LITERARY FORMS

Although Alice Notley (NAHT-lee) has dedicated her life to poetry, her writing of nonfiction has allowed for further exploration of her literary ideas. She has written introductions, memoirs, and essays, some of them collected in *Coming After: Essays on Poetry* (2005). She has also included short nonfiction pieces within her poetry volumes.

Notley's work as editor has had a particularly significant impact, in that she has been instrumental in keeping the works of her late husband, Ted Berrigan, before the public. With Douglas Oliver, Notley edited the Paris-based journal *Gare du Nord*. After Oliver's death, she edited his prose and poetry reflections on Paris, which were published as *Arrondissements* (2003). Notley has worked in the visual arts, sometimes presenting collages, sketches, and watercolors alongside her written pieces. In the 1980's, she also wrote for the theater.

Achievements

Alice Notley has received numerous awards and honors, including the 1981 San Francisco Poetry Center Book Award for *How Spring Comes*. *Mysteries of Small Houses* was nominated for the Pulitzer Prize and was awarded the Los Angeles Times Book Prize for poetry. In 2001, she received an Academy Award in Literature from the American Academy of Arts and Letters and the Shelley Memorial Award from the Poetry Society of America. For *Disobedience*, she was named international winner of the 2002 Griffin Poetry Prize. In 2005, Notley won the Lenore Marshall Poetry Prize for *Grave of Light*.

Biography

Born in Arizona, Alice Notley spent her childhood in Needles, California. She earned her bachelor's degree from Barnard College (1967) and an M.F.A. (1969) from the University of Iowa. After a period of wandering, which took her from San Francisco to London, she settled in New York City's lower East Side, there becoming prominent in the eclectic group considered to be the second generation of the New York School of poetry. In 1972, she married poet Berrigan, with whom she had two sons. After Berrigan's death in 1983, she married British poet Oliver. The couple moved to Paris in 1992. Although Oliver died in 2000, Notley remained in Paris.

Analysis

Alice Notley early established herself as a poet able to express with unabashed candor both her disaffection with the larger world and her sensitive appreciation of the microcosm of family life. Her early poem "Dear Dark Continent" (from *Phoebe Light*) reveals her recognition of how much of herself derived from her family: "I'm wife I'm mother I'm/ myself and him and I'm myself and him and him." Rather than finding this domestic necessity disagreeable, she seems to accept it as an element in the "whole long universe," an element that helps lift her out of a solipsistic or narcissistic point of view. In many early poems, Notley's embrace of the realm of the home and of child rearing is notable. Poems such as "January," published in *How Spring Comes*, reflect her interest in capturing the freshness of a child's perception.

However important this domestic focus in her poetry may be, Notley consistently displays a fully alert and outwardly turned consciousness, at times by expressing a strong sense of disillusioned realism. Showing the influence of models including William Carlos Williams and Frank O'Hara, as well as such contemporaries as Berrigan, Anselm Hollo, and Anne Waldman, Notley's poems illuminate the fleeting moment and frame her perceptions of the world in terms of common objects. The bold, often sharply incisive quality in many of her works seems to reflect a secure faith in the value of acting as witness to this daily life. Although a political attitude can be found within the poems, Notley's elevation of the personal above the political gives them an exploratory immediacy.

Early in her writing career, Notley demonstrated her comfort with writing longer poems. As she moved toward the writing of poem sequences instead of individual, unrelated poems and then toward the composition of book-length narrative poems, Notley was able to unify her previously divergent approaches to poetry through the exploration of a set of images that had deeply personal meaning to her and that she was able to infuse with the quality of myth. The strength of this approach found its most powerful expression in her ambitious and highly imaginative feminist epic, *The Descent of Alette*.

In her chapbook *Homer's Art*, the title work is a short essay on Homer. After arguing that the depictions of women by men are depictions of men, she ponders the possibility that poetry might reclaim the Homeric epic. She contrasts the twentieth century poem that "uses language to generate more language" with the Homeric epic, in which "language hurries to keep up." It would be a service to poetry, Notley states, to take narrative back from the novel and return it to poetry. "Another service," she concludes, "would be to write a long poem, a story poem, with a female narrator/hero."

THE DESCENT OF ALETTE

Notley's long story poem with a female narrator/hero, *The Descent of Alette*, may come to be regarded as her most important single work. Certainly it ranks high among the notable achievements of American poetry in the 1990's. Among its unusual aspects is its mode of presentation. In one way, it is unusually traditional in its presentation of individual poems broken into quatrains. Consistently throughout the book, however, each line is broken down into smaller units by the use of quotation marks, as for example in these opening lines:

> "One day, I awoke" "& found myself on" "a
> subway, endlessly"
> "I didn't know" "how I'd arrived there or" "who
> I was" "exactly"

Notley offers a prefatory note about this approach, which she developed while writing earlier poems. She notes that although the poem's appearance initially puts off readers, it quickly becomes part of the reader's experience. The quotation marks are "there, mostly, to measure the poem. The phrases they enclose are poetic feet." They break these longer lines into shorter units of usually two or three stresses. Such small units are often referred to as dipodic or tripodic, although those terms refer to the number of feet per line, as, for example, in describing the short lines in a nursery rhyme. Notley is offering quotation-enclosed phrases as the rhythmic units of *The Descent of Alette*. The effect for the reader is akin to that achieved by Walt Whitman in "Song of Myself," in which the short, loose groupings of phrases impart a rhythmic vitality that is not based on the repetitions of traditional measures. The quotation marks also affect how the poem might be recited. This may well have influenced Notley, given her stated interest in reviving a form that arose out of oral tradition.

Although the reader quickly realizes that the quatrains are less structural than conventional ones, the quatrains seem to reflect Notley's effort to make this poem as accessible as possible to the reader. Notley is far from the most obscurantist of twentieth century American poets, but her work at times does offer difficulties. In *The Descent of Alette*, in contrast, the evocation of tradition graphically through the use of quatrains seems allied to her intention to communicate with the utmost clarity to her audience, with that clarity itself being a part of traditional epic practice. Each poem within *The Descent of Alette* individually offers a story, or a scene, often with a strongly fantastical or visionary element, and the entirety offers the overarching narrative of Alette's journey. In the first part of the poem, Alette is riding the endless subway in the company of women and men whose words, actions, and transformations introduce her to the new reality in which she finds herself. In the second part, she goes through a series of new experiences inside deeper caverns, which transform Alette, giving her presence and power within this subterranean region. Her search takes on a twofold definition, for she has been placed in opposition to a figure named the Tyrant while she undertakes a search for someone she regards as the original Mother. In the third and last part of the poem, Alette succeeds in meeting the original Mother and confronting the Tyrant. The individual verses in which a creation myth unfolds underline the feminist-epic aspect of this unusual work.

The Descent of Alette stands alone as a powerful narrative poem. It can also be viewed as a part of a continuum of longer poems by Notley, beginning with "White Phosphorus," which appeared in *Homer's Art*, and which introduced some of the techniques and preoccupations found in *The Descent of Alette*. Later volumes continued Notley's exploration of her personal mythology.

MYSTERY OF SMALL HOUSES

Although other books before and after *Mystery of Small Houses* offer a remarkable re-imagining of personal experience in narrative and mythic terms, in this volume, Notley returns to her earlier mode of directly invoking personal experience, often to critique the world in which she finds herself. Several poems express cynicism about the contemporary poetry scene, such as "As Good as Anything," addressing the Iowa City poetry crowd, and "1992," addressing the larger scene of poets, prizes, and publishing. Throughout the volume, Notley is obviously grappling with the past, at times engaging in imaginary and perhaps remembered discourse with Berrigan.

DISOBEDIENCE

Disobedience offers a partial return to the personal mythmaking of *The Descent of Alette*; the poem include some of Notley's most unrestrained expressions of her thoughts and ideas.

Notley's poems are empowered by a consistent concern with being a witness to the world. Although this act of witness brings her to incorporate mundane elements of daily life and even to discuss figures from the news or popular media, Notley's type of witnessing is not that of either the social commentator or the activist. Even when confronting and critiquing such an event as the Vietnam War, Notley's view of the universe includes not only consciously perceived elements but also unconsciously perceived ones, with her concern for the latter leading her to draw heavily on poetic elements provided by her dreams.

This embrace of the subconscious, however, is not an abdication of Notley's responsibility as poet. In "Change the Forms in Dreams," she observes with some envy a fellow traveler: "Man on métro speaks to himself/ and so he can say anything he wants./ I wish I were him." She is not him, however. Her ability, or compulsion, to express what she needs to express rather than what she wants to express makes her one of the most compelling of American poets.

OTHER MAJOR WORKS

PLAY: *Anne's White Glove*, pr., pb. 1985.

NONFICTION: *Doctor Williams' Heiresses: A Lecture*, 1980; *Tell Me Again*, 1982 (autobiography); *Coming After: Essays on Poetry*, 2005.

EDITED TEXTS: *A Certain Slant of Sunlight*, 1988 (by Ted Berrigan); *The Sonnets*, 2000 (by Berrigan); *Arrondissements*, 2003 (by Douglas Oliver); *The Collected Poems of Ted Berrigan*, 2005 (with Anselm Berrigan and Edmund Berrigan).

BIBLIOGRAPHY

Bendall, Molly. Review of *The Descent of Alette*. *Antioch Review* 55, no. 2 (March, 1997): 247-248. Provides valuable insights into one of Notley's most significant works.

Falconer, Rachel. "Dante Upside-Down: Alice Notley's *The Descent of Alette*." In *Hell in Contemporary Literature: Western Descent Narratives Since 1945*. Edinburgh: Edinburgh University Press, 2005. Falconer examines Notley's story of Alette's descent as part of the literature on hell.

Kane, Daniel. *All Poets Welcome: The Lower East Side Poetry Scene in the 1960's*. Berkeley: University of California Press, 2003. A pioneering study of the second-generation New York School, discussing the poets (including Notley) as individuals and as part of a closely knit community.

⎯⎯⎯, ed. *Don't Ever Get Famous: Essays on New York Writing After the New York School*. Urbana-Champaign, Ill.: Dalkey Archive Press, 2006. A collection of essays focusing on the years Berrigan and Notley were leading lights in Lower East Side poetry, emphasizing cultural, sociological, and historical aspects of the community, with special focus on small-press publications and workshops.

McCabe, Susan. "Alice Notley's Epic Entry: 'An Ecstasy of Finding Another Way of Being.'" *Antioch Review* 56, no. 3 (June, 1998): 273-280. An in-depth exploration of the epic ambition evident in *The Descent of Alette*.

Nelson, Maggie. "Dear Dark Continent: Alice Notley's *Disobedience*." In *Women, the New York School, and Other True Abstractions*. Iowa City: University of Iowa Press, 2007. Discusses, among many topics, Notley's involvement with the New York School and her later distancing herself from the movement by writing epics.

Notley, Alice. "Alice Notley." Interview by Edward Halsey Foster. In *Postmodern Poetry: The Talisman Interviews*. Hoboken, N.J.: Talisman House, 1994. Notley describes her experiences and literary background.

⎯⎯⎯. "An Interview with Alice Notley by Claudia Keelan." Interview by Claudia Keelan. In *Innovative Women Poets: An Anthology of Contemporary Poetry and Interviews*, edited by Elisabeth A. Frost and Cynthia Hogue. Iowa City: University of Iowa Press, 2006. Notley discusses her poetry and life in an interview. The book also contains a short essay on Notley and some of her poetry.

Waldman, Anne. *Nice to See You: Homage to Ted Berrigan*. Minneapolis, Minn.: Coffee House Press, 1991. This literary collage offers insight into New York's Lower East Side poetry community of the 1960's and 1970's, through the words of its members.

Mark Rich

FRANK O'HARA

Born: Baltimore, Maryland; June 27, 1926
Died: Mastic Beach, New York; July 25, 1966

PRINCIPAL POETRY
A City Winter, and Other Poems, 1952
Oranges, 1953
Meditations in an Emergency, 1957
Odes, 1960
Lunch Poems, 1964
Love Poems (Tentative Title), 1965
In Memory of My Feelings: A Selection of Poems, 1967 (Bill Berkson, editor)
The Collected Poems of Frank O'Hara, 1971, 1995 (Donald Allen, editor)
Selected Poems, 1974 (Allen, editor)
Early Poems, 1946-1951, 1976
Poems Retrieved, 1951-1966, 1977, 1996
Selected Poems, 2008 (Mark Ford, editor)

OTHER LITERARY FORMS

Frank O'Hara was always a poet, no matter what he wrote. His plays (published in *Selected Plays*, 1978), only a few of which are actually capable of being produced with any degree of dramatic effectiveness, are more often plays with words and visual effects than exploration of character or idea through dramatic conflict. Some juxtapose a vast variety of characters (from O'Hara's own friends to Benjamin Franklin, Marlene Dietrich, William Blake, and Generalissimo Franco), most with only a single short speech, with connections nonexistent outside O'Hara's fertile imagination. Others of these short plays offer sustained characters speaking in non sequiturs or in monologues unheard by other characters. In one play, *Try! Try!* (pr., pb. 1951), the monologues work in an interesting way, since there is a plot with a recognizable triangle of characters and actual dialogue, besides some poetic and psychologically suggestive monologues. Another produced play, *The General Returns from One Place to Another* (pr. 1964), uses verbal, visual, and dramatic means to satirize the American military abroad, particularly in the person of Douglas MacArthur.

O'Hara's prose has been collected in *Standing Still and Walking in New York* (1975, Donald Allen, editor). The volume consists chiefly of miscellaneous pieces on modern art and contains a small quantity of literary criticism as well.

Besides writing for *Art News*, O'Hara worked on the catalogs for various exhibits at the Museum of Modern Art, including those on contemporary American painters Jack-

Frank O'Hara

son Pollock and Robert Motherwell. His art criticism tends to be impressionistic rather than technical, but it effectively conveys the essence of contemporary painting.

ACHIEVEMENTS

Other than the advent of the Beat movement, probably the most exciting thing to happen to American poetry in the mid-twentieth century is the ascendance of vital and natural voices, with all the immediacy of actual human talk, through the work of the New York School of poets. Heading them were Frank O'Hara, John Ashbery, and Kenneth Koch, with O'Hara's voice being the dominant one. Drawing elements from Walt Whitman, William Carlos Williams, Gertrude Stein, French Surrealists such as Guillaume Apollinaire and Pierre Reverdy, and the Russian poets Vladimir Mayakovsky and Boris Pasternak, O'Hara shattered the prevailing poetic standards regarding language, form, and content and forged his own verse with tremendous vigor and fire. He did not want to produce the sort of pristine, shapely work that could be found in scores of other volumes, admired by the literary establishment of New Critics for their traditional forms, metaphoric complexities, and mythic overtones. O'Hara rejected all these familiar ingredients, writing in unfettered free verse, shifting images and metaphors wildly throughout a poem, and dealing with earthy subject matter or very personal experiences without any effort to make them seem universally significant. He received the Avery Hopwood Major Award in Poetry in 1951 and the National Book Award in Poetry in 1972 for *The Collected Poems of Frank O'Hara.*

Most of O'Hara's poems flow, without any attempt to structure them formally, through the free association of his surrealistic poems, where one image or word leads to another, however logically unrelated, or through the simple recording of his actual activities, thoughts, and feelings on special occasion (or not-so-special ones). Because he was so keenly in tune with his feelings, such poems work splendidly in conveying the moods that generated them, especially through the marvelously vivid vocabulary that dances across his pages.

Not least among his achievements is his lively sense of humor, sometimes just a light tone that flavors much of his work as he playfully recounts his activities or observations, sometimes satiric views of various cultural and political icons (including the movies), sometimes raucous comedy full of delightful surprises, such as the sun appearing to chat with the poet abed or a vision of bugs walking through the apartment "carrying a little banner/ which says 'in search of lanolin.'" Delight in words and experience, surprise at the variety of existence: These are the keynotes of O'Hara's poetry, which retains its freshness and appeal far beyond the attempts of so many others to imitate it.

Biography

Although born in Baltimore and reared in rural Massachusetts, Francis Russell O'Hara discovered a more appropriate milieu first among fellow poets and aficionados of the other arts at Harvard (where he received his B.A. degree in English literature in 1950) and subsequently in New York City. In the meantime, he had spent two years in the U.S. Navy in the South Pacific and a year at the University of Michigan, where he received his M.A. in 1951 and the Avery Hopwood Major Award in Poetry for a manuscript collection of poetry (his master's thesis). Once in New York, he rejoined fellow Harvard graduates Ashbery and Koch and involved himself in various arts in assorted capacities, while remaining, with the others, quite apart from the literary establishment of the day. He worked for the Museum of Modern Art, advancing from a staff position working on circulating exhibitions to an associate curatorship, selecting numerous exhibitions of contemporary American and Spanish artists and being responsible for the catalogs published in conjunction with the exhibits. He also wrote occasional articles and reviews for *Art News* and had several plays performed. He adopted a very casual attitude toward his poetry, sending poems off to friends without keeping a copy, stuffing them in drawers, gathering material only under pressure from eager editors such as John Bernard Myers. He was intensely involved (whether as friend or lover) with many different and interesting women and men throughout these New York years until his death after a freak accident on Fire Island.

Analysis

To enter the world of Frank O'Hara is to abandon all familiar road maps, to give up hope for a straight and clear way through, for recognizable landmarks that indicate where one is going, where one has been. With "no revolver pointing the roadmarks," the reader is free to travel without preconceptions and without insistent points made by the poet. O'Hara's world is closer to Lewis Carroll's than to Robert Frost's, being full of surprises, twists in the road, byways, cul-de-sacs, a grotesquerie of roadside attractions, and few places to stop or rest, so that one ends up nowhere near one's anticipated goal, perhaps not even at an ending at all but simply at a halt, like running out of gas. For that is how many O'Hara poems conclude—with neither a bang nor a whimper, but only a sudden cessation of the impetuous, rapid drive of words and images and feelings that has made up the poem. His poetry is exciting, startling, dizzying, frightening, overwhelming, demanding, involving, crude, elaborate, stark, disorderly, sexy, and sometimes very funny. As a poet crafting his art, O'Hara had as much gleeful fun—even when dealing with feelings considerably less than euphoric—as the liveliest child or the most daredevil racer.

O'Hara was the epitome of the New York poet: fast, frenzied, jazzy, upbeat, smart-aleck, shrewd, unzipped, down-to-earth, open, and full of action. Like his fellow New York poets (friends, some contemporaries, some followers or students from a workshop he offered), he thrived on the bustle of the city and participated in its multitude of activities. Far from being a poetic hermit in an ivory tower, he actively involved himself with people and with the other arts—notably with painters, but also with dancers and musicians. The kind of painting he favored was action painting, a style indigenous to New York and led by Jackson Pollock. Its random quality, abstractness, and emphasis on the process of painting rather than the static permanence demonstrated in a still life or a portrait all have their correspondences in O'Hara's poetry.

This poetry pulses with action of all sorts—sexual, mental, emotional, physical, natural, industrial, transportational—all the types of action, in fact, that make up the United States. Action itself is the subject of some of his poems, such as his self-styled "I do this I do that" poems. The action of the poem may be expressed in vocabulary (colorful concrete nouns and vivid active verbs expressing dynamic movement); in syntax (whether conventional—using such devices as piled-up participial phrases, short sentences, and parataxis, though quite grammatically—or unconventional—omitting parts of a sentence or letting a single word or phrase serve two different but simultaneous functions in two adjacent syntactical units); in interjections ("Hey!," "Yeah!"); or in rapid shifts of subject, place, or time—from stanza to stanza, sentence to sentence, line to line, and even from one word or phrase to the next.

"My Heat"

"My Heat" provides evidence of all these. The opening stanza is filled with verbs denoting vigorous action: four finite verbs ("committed," "fell off the balcony," "I'd force the port!/ Violate the piers"), one infinitive ("to refountain myself"), and two present participles ("jetting," "turning in air"). Unconventional syntax and punctuation give a sensation of dizziness fitting this turning and falling: The "if" clause seems to have two main verbs unseparated by a conjunction or comma, both with "I" as subject; then O'Hara does not set off what is presumably his main clause by a comma after the subordinate clause, so that the infinitive could be regarded as part of either the subordinate or the main clause. The verb's unfamiliarity ("refountain") also sharpens the reader's attention, as does the unclearness of its connection with the rest of the sentence. This main clause seems to end with the exclamation point after "port," yet the next word is another verb, presumably another main verb for the subject "I"—unless it is an imperative for the two vocatives ending the stanza ("you bores! you asses!"). Keeping readers alert, the very next word, "geology," at the beginning of the next stanza, not only has nothing to do with "the balcony," "the port," or "the piers," but also is punctuated by a question mark.

The punctuation is certainly not completely unorthodox, though it is surprising. What would give the traditional poetry reader more trouble are the rapid shifts in imagery, but this is part of O'Hara's point: the pleasure he takes in "jetting" from one image to whatever it suggests, the pleasure he takes in "jetting" such words and phrases from his typewriter—all as opposed to the "you" in this poem, who always seems a few steps behind poet "Frank," who proclaims, with another surprising but apt and active verb choice, "I've kayoed your popular cant/ I'd rather jet!"

A New Critic such as John Crowe Ransom would probably throw up his hands at the untidiness of O'Hara's metaphorical maneuverings. There is no clear one-to-one correspondence between tenors and vehicles here; there is certainly no single picture provided out of which the meaning derives, no identifiable incident that gives rise to the poetic expression. The meaning, rather, resides in the exuberant movement of the poem and its words, images that—in themselves and in their transformations throughout the poem—suggest the force of creativity as well as that of sexuality.

This poem is, in fact, only one of the most compressed treatments of sexuality among O'Hara's work, from the ejaculatory "jetting" of its opening line on to the final line: "'That's no furnace, that's my heart!'" The heat of passion is inflated to the power of a furnace. The diffuse jetting rampant throughout the poem amply reflects the exuberant sexuality—not a sexual desire directed at a single person and thus capable of being satisfied, but rather directed at no one in particular, an all-pervasive urge, reveling in the fact of sexuality and the pleasure of the sexual feeling itself. O'Hara's images are used not as specific metaphors—he mixes them too outrageously for that—but rather as evocations of the many flavors and feelings of sexuality (or, in other poems, whatever has motivated that poetic outburst): its sweetness and beauty in roses, its violence (in violating the piers), its power (as a volcano "to melt everyone into syrup"), its self-containment, its richness, even its humor ("laughing like an old bedspring," a simile that makes a believable aural comparison as well as fitting the sexual subject matter).

JOYFUL SEXUALITY, IMAGISTIC FERTILITY

O'Hara's eroticism is far from fin de siècle decadence, which hints at more than it tells; nor does it explicitly depict sexual acts, as in pornography. Rather, it revels in a joyous sexuality that fellow gay poet Whitman would certainly recognize and appreciate. Only rarely does O'Hara depict an actual sexual act, as in "Twin spheres full of fur and noise/ rolling softly up my belly" for an act of fellatio. A lively choice of images ("my mouth is full of suns") and abstractions ("that softness seems so anterior to that hardness"), with a climactic hint of Apollo's chariot of the sun, raises the experience to a mythic level, but not for long. O'Hara's poetry must constantly move, never rest, and of course the moment of sexual ecstasy dissolves, even as it is achieved: "It must be discovered soon and disappear."

Sex is not, however much it may appear so from these examples, O'Hara's only concern; like Whitman, he felt intense pleasure simply in living, and since sex represents the most intense form of physical pleasure, he naturally perceived a sexual quality in his relationship with living—in all its aspects—and hence with the rest of the world. He could penetrate the world—make an impact on it, enter its multifarious experiences—just as he could penetrate a lover; he could also be penetrated by experience, by the myriad sensory impressions all around him—just as a lover might penetrate him. This openness to both roles parallels his sexual orientation; his homosexuality, indicating openness to nonstandard sexual practices, may have a share in O'Hara's imagistic fertility, as he presents (in "Easter," for example) nonhuman and inanimate nature surging with sexuality ("it's the night like a love it all cruisy and nelly"). Such images, which cannot be deciphered into metaphorical correspondences of tenor and vehicle with an "underlying" subject behind the metaphorical development, serve to suggest sexuality in O'Hara's more public poems (as contrasted with private poems such as "Twin Spheres," written for his lover Vincent Warren) without having to be gender-specific.

In most of his poems, the images shift constantly; the reader is meant to flow with the stream of O'Hara's free associations, which is often remarkably easy to do because of his vivid and emotionally evocative choice of nouns, verbs, and adjectives, even when the precise meaning of a passage remains indecipherable. "Savoy" shifts ground even more rapidly than "My Heat," yet it conveys a rich sequence of moods.

"SAVOY"

"Savoy" opens with a feeling of terror, although its cause is unclear. Like other O'Hara poems, it begins with an image that he proceeds to join to a simile—a logical enough poetic device—but the simile proceeds to take over as the poem's main concern. However, O'Hara writes elsewhere, "How I hate subject matter!," and the reader realizes that actually neither simile nor its tenor is the subject of the poem. Looking at the extended so-called simile ("like a bespectacled carapaceous witch doctor of Rimini/ beautifying an adolescent tubbed in entrails of blue cement . . .") reveals that it is hardly to be apprehended in the manner of a metaphysical conceit. What is a witch doctor doing in Rimini, on the Italian seacoast? How can anyone be beautified in a bath of "blue cement"? A few lines down, who is the "you" suddenly addressed? The rapid changes mirror those of a dream or nightmare, in which identities shift inexplicably. This is the method of Surrealist poetry, which O'Hara brought into American poetry with a new force after it had flourished in Europe several decades earlier. O'Hara clearly indicates a romance with the word and whatever lively images it evokes rather than with its specific literal denotation. Even in describing terrors and dangers in "Savoy," O'Hara is having fun; the pleasure is in the movement of the poem, not in discerning its "meaning."

"I DO THIS I DO THAT" POEMS

O'Hara's less surrealistic poems, however, which record his actions, are not hard to understand at all. Simple in form and structure, the "I do this I do that" poems, as he calls them in "Getting Up Ahead of Someone (Sun)," are, at their best, more than a mere transcription of the day's activities; they convey the quality of the poet's conscious mind and the shifting moods stirred by his activities. The most famous—and most moving—example of this sort of poem is "The Day Lady Died," which pays tribute to singer Billie Holiday upon her death but is hardly a standard elegy with explicit presentation of grief and concentration on praise for the deceased. Instead, O'Hara begins the poem—and carries on for the bulk of it—with an account of his movements, fairly random, around New York on a Friday afternoon. Suddenly he is caught short by "a NEW YORK POST with her face on it," and he is reminded of hearing Holiday ("Lady Day") sing "in the 5 SPOT," when "everyone and I stopped breathing." This last action (or rather lack of it) stunningly conveys the whole impact not only of Holiday's art but also of her death and is especially effective in stopping movement and thought after such a bustling buildup. The rest of the poem does not prepare the reader for such a conclusion at all.

Most of his "I do this I do that" poems are much less serious, and often poke fun at himself or take a delightfully lighthearted approach to the addressee, a friend or a lover, and the particular relationship they share. In fact, O'Hara's humor is one of his most characteristic traits; however, his work is quite different from light verse because it rarely satirizes and certainly does not use rhyme and rhythm. Rather, it is based on surprise, giving his readers the unexpected, as his Surrealist pieces do. Those, however, are rarely comic because they so constantly shift ground that the reader has no solid base to stand on, a necessity if comic surprise is to hit with true effectiveness.

"POEM (LANA TURNER HAS COLLAPSED!)"

A true comic gem is "Poem (Lana Turner has collapsed!)," a delightful little poem that O'Hara wrote on the spur of the moment on a ferryboat to a poetry reading. Written in the conversational tone at which he was so adept, it enters the world of comedy with the very first line, with its hysterical exclamation point like a sensationalistic headline (as the poem later reveals it in fact to be). The reader knows not to take this as seriously as Lady Day's death, first because of the exclamation point, then because this announcement appears at the beginning of the poem rather than at its climax.

The second line continues the humorous tone with O'Hara's verb choice—"I was trotting along." The speaker is obviously not a horse, nor does this verb have the intensity of suggestion of those in "My Heat"; it merely gives the reader a funny sense of the light, frolicsome quality of the poet's movements. The humor continues—and builds—stylistically with the paratactic structure of short clauses joined by coordinating conjunctions, then in content with the poet's slight disagreement with his friend about the weather (whether it was raining and snowing or hailing), and further, with the surprising apparent shift in position of the "you," who at first appears to be with the speaker and then is seen as the goal he is walking toward. The poet notes the traffic "acting exactly like the sky," using the humorous idiom of very mild outrage ("isn't that exactly like so-and-so?"). Then comes the appearance of the headline—to complete what now appears to be a flashback after the poem's opening line. The poet proceeds to assure the motion-picture star that she has no reason to collapse, there being no snow or rain in Hollywood; moreover, he refers to his own behavior at parties, where he himself has never collapsed. He concludes with an actual address to the actress—comically unpunctuated, although it encompasses an interjection, a vocative, and two short clauses not joined by conjunctions: "oh Lana Turner we love you get up." This last line suggests that all the motion-picture star needs here is reassurance of her fans' love and an affectionately authoritative encouragement. O'Hara is implying that he cannot take this inflated problem seriously, nor should anyone else; he is gently mocking the superhuman status accorded celebrities. Of course this is a poem simply to be enjoyed, hardly to be pondered seriously. Although O'Hara certainly took poetry seriously, he also believed in enjoying it, as he did life.

Living in a throbbing city, he had countless experiences to enjoy, from attending films and ballet to walking the streets (as in the poems just discussed) to meeting with a wide range of acquaintances, for a Coke, a trip to a museum, a party, or even sex. All these experiences are celebrated in his vital poetry, through which he has vividly conveyed not only a sense of the excitement of life but also a rich sense of himself as a living person: As with Whitman, it is not a mere book one encounters when reading O'Hara: "Who touches this touches a man."

OTHER MAJOR WORKS

PLAYS: *Try! Try!*, pr., pb. 1951; *The General Returns from One Place to Another*, pr. 1964; *Selected Plays*, 1978.

NONFICTION: *Jackson Pollock*, 1959; *New Spanish Painting and Sculpture*, 1960; *Robert Motherwell, with Selections from the Artist's Writings*, 1965; *Standing Still and Walking in New York*, 1975 (Donald Allen, editor).

MISCELLANEOUS: *Early Writing*, 1977.

Bibliography

Cappucci, Paul R. *William Carlos Williams, Frank O'Hara, and the New York Art Scene*. Madison, N.J.: Fairleigh Dickinson University Press, 2010. Examines the New York School of poets and O'Hara, as well as Williams and his influence on the poet.

Feldman, Alan. *Frank O'Hara*. Boston: Twayne, 1979. This book introduces O'Hara as a New York poet. His language, style, and degrees of coherence are analyzed. Themes of "the self," varieties of feelings, and humor are examined in succeeding chapters. Includes chronology, select bibliography, and index.

Gooch, Brad. *City Poet: The Life and Times of Frank O'Hara*. New York: HarperPerennial, 1994. This biography of O'Hara details his life from his Massachusetts Catholic boyhood to Harvard University and to New York, where his art criticism became seminal to the abstract expressionist painters and sculptors.

Perloff, Marjorie. *Frank O'Hara: Poet Among Painters*. Rev. ed. Chicago: University of Chicago Press, 1998. This revised edition of a 1977 work adds a new introduction. Perloff analyzes O'Hara's "aesthetic of attention" and surveys the early poems. Her central chapter looks at his "poem-paintings," and then his "great period" is presented. Includes illustrations, notes, a bibliographical note, and an index.

Shaw, Lytle. *Frank O'Hara: The Poetics of Coterie*. Iowa City: University of Iowa Press, 2003. Argues that O'Hara is a coterie poet in that he valued relationships and linkages between people, including the mock family that consisted of his friends, and that being a coterie poet is not a negative thing in the case of O'Hara.

Ward, Geoff. *Statutes of Liberty: The New York School of Poets*. New York: Palgrave, 2001. An acclaimed account of the New York School and its key figures, John Ashbery, O'Hara, and James Schuyler, and their growing influence on postmodern poetics.

Scott Giantvalley

PIERRE REVERDY

Born: Narbonne, France; September 13, 1889
Died: Solesmes, France; June 17, 1960

PRINCIPAL POETRY
Poèmes en prose, 1915 (*Prose Poems*, 2007)
La Lucarne ovale, 1916
Quelques poèmes, 1916
Les Ardoises du toit, 1918 (*Roof Slates*, 1981)
Les Jockeys camouflés, 1918
La Guitare endormie, 1919
Cœur de chêne, 1921
Étoiles peintes, 1921
Cravates de chanvre, 1922
Grande Nature, 1925
La Balle au bond, 1928
Sources du vent, 1929
Pierres blanches, 1930
Ferraille, 1937
Plein verre, 1940
Plupart du temps, 1945 (collected volume, 1913-1922)
Le Chant des morts, 1948
Main d'œuvre: Poèmes, 1913-1949, 1949
Pierre Reverdy: Selected Poems, 1969
Roof Slates, and Other Poems of Pierre Reverdy, 1981
Selected Poems, 1991

OTHER LITERARY FORMS

Pierre Reverdy (ruh-VEHR-dee) worked extensively in other forms besides poetry. He wrote two novels and many stories and published collections of prose poems. Most of these are in a Surrealist vein, mixing experimentation in language with personal and unconscious reflection. As an editor of an avant-garde review, Reverdy also contributed important theoretical statements on cubism and avant-garde literary practice. Later in his career, he published several volumes of reminiscences, including sensitive reevaluations of the work of his near contemporaries, including Guillaume Apollinaire.

ACHIEVEMENTS

Pierre Reverdy is one of the most central and influential writers in the tradition of twentieth century avant-garde poetry. Already well established in terms of both his

Pierre Reverdy

work and his theoretical stance by the mid-1910's, Reverdy exerted considerable influence over the Dada and Surrealist movements, with which he was both officially and informally affiliated.

Reverdy's firm conviction was in a nonmimetic, nontraditional form of artistic expression. The art he championed and practiced would create a reality of its own rather than mirror a preexisting reality. In this way, the language of poetry would be cut loose from restraining conventions of meter, syntax, and punctuation in order to be able to explore the emotion generated by the poetic image.

In connection with the avant-garde artists of cubism, Dada, and Surrealism, Reverdy's formulations helped to break down the traditional models of artistic creation that then held firm sway in France. Reverdy's firm conviction was that artistic creation precedes aesthetic theory. All the concrete means at an artist's disposal constitute his aesthetic formation.

Along with Apollinaire, his slightly older contemporary, Reverdy became a central figure and example for a whole generation of French poets generally grouped under the Surrealist heading. His having been translated into English by a range of American poets from Kenneth Rexroth to John Ashbery shows the importance of his work to the modern American tradition as well.

Biography

Pierre Reverdy was born on September 13, 1889, in Narbonne, France, a city in the Languedoc region. The son and grandson of sculptors and artisans in wood carving, he grew up with this practical skill in addition to his formal studies. The Languedoc region at the turn of the century was an especially volatile region, witnessing the last major peasant uprising in modern French history.

After completing his schooling in Narbonne and nearby Toulouse, Reverdy moved to Paris in 1910, where he lived on and off for the rest of his life. Although exempted from military service, he volunteered at the outbreak of World War I, saw combat service, and was discharged in 1916. By profession a typesetter, Reverdy also worked as the director of the review *Nord-Sud*, which he founded in 1917.

From 1910 to 1926, Reverdy worked in close contact with almost all the important artists of his time. He had especially close relationships with Pablo Picasso and Juan Gris, both of whom contributed illustrations to collections of his verse. As the editor of an influential review, he had close contact with and strong influence on the writers who were to form the Dada and Surrealist movements. Already an avant-garde poet and theorist of some prominence by the late 1910's, Reverdy was often invoked along with Apollinaire as one of the precursors of Surrealism. He collaborated with the early Surrealist efforts and continued his loose affiliation even after a formal break in 1926.

That year saw Reverdy's conversion to a mystic Catholicism. From then until his death in 1960, his life became more detached from the quotidian, and he spent much of his time at the Abbey of Solesmes, where he died.

Analysis

In an early statement on cubism, Pierre Reverdy declaimed that a new epoch was beginning, one in which "one creates works that, by detaching themselves from life, enter back into it because they have an existence of their own." In addition to attacking mimetic standards of reproduction, or representation of reality, he also called for a renunciation of punctuation and a freeing of syntax in the writing of poetry. Rather than being something fixed according to rules, for Reverdy, syntax was "a medium of literary creation." Changing the rules of literary expression carried with it a change in ideas of representation. For Reverdy, the poetic image was solely responsible to the discovery of emotional truth.

From 1915 to 1922, Reverdy produced many volumes of poetry. The avant-garde called for an overturning of literary conventions, and Reverdy contributed with his own explosion of creative activity. In addition to editing the influential review *Nord-Sud*, he used his experience as an engraver and typesetter to publish books, including his own. The list of artists who contributed the illustrations to these volumes of poetry by Reverdy reads like a Who's Who of the art world of the time: Gris, Picasso, André Derain, Henri Matisse, Georges Braque, among others. Reverdy's work, along with that of Apollinaire, was cited as the guiding force for Surrealism by André Breton in his *Manifestes du surréalisme* (1962; *Manifestoes of Surrealism*, 1969).

Reverdy's early work achieves an extreme detachment from mimetic standards and literary conventions that allows for the images to stand forth as though seen shockingly for the first time. The last two lines from "Sur le Talus" (on the talus), published in 1918, show this extreme detachment: "L'eau monte comme une poussière/ Le silence ferme la nuit" (The water rises like dust/ Silence shuts the night). There can be no question here of establishing a realistic context for these images. Rather, one is cast back on the weight of emotion that they carry and that must thus guide their interpretation. Reflections off water may appear to rise in various settings, though perhaps particularly at twilight. The dust points to a particular kind of aridity that may be primarily an emotional state. The sudden transition from an (implied) twilight to an abrupt nightfall undercuts any kind of conventional emotional presentation. The quick cut is a measure perhaps of the individual's lack of control over external phenomena and, by extension, inner feelings as well.

"Carrefour"

Much of Reverdy's early work is based on just such an imagistic depiction of interior states, with a strong element of detachment from reality and a certain resulting confusion or overlapping. The force of emotion is clearly there, but to pin it down to a particular situation or persona proves difficult because any such certainty is constantly being undercut by the quick transitions between images. The complete suppression of punctuation as well as a certain freedom of syntax as one moves from line to line are clearly tools that Reverdy developed to increase the level of logical disjunction in his poetry. At times, however, this disjunction in the logical progression of word and image gives way to a resolution. The short poem "Carrefour" (crossroad) sets up a surreal image sequence:

> De l'air
> De la lumière
> Un rayon sur le bord du verre
> Ma main déçue n'attrape rien
>
> Air
> Light
> A ray on the edge of the glass
> My disappointed hand holds nothing

Here the elements are invoked, and then two images, one of an inanimate object and one the hand of the speaker. From this atmosphere of mystery and disjunction, the poem's conclusion moves to a fairly well-defined emotional statement:

> Enfin tout seul j'aurai vécu
> Jusqu'au dernier matin
> Sans qu'un mot m'indiquât quel fut le bon chemin
>
> After all I will have lived all alone
> Until the last morning
> Without a single word that might have shown me
> which was the right way

Here, as in many of Reverdy's poems, the emotion evoked is a kind of diffused sadness. The solitary individual is probably meant to stand for an aspect of the human condition, alone in a confrontation with an unknown destiny.

"Guerre"

Reverdy saw military duty during World War I, and it may well be that this experience muted the youthful enthusiasm that pervades his earliest works. It may also be the case that Reverdy, while espousing radical measures in literary practice, still was caught in the kind of bittersweet ethos that characterizes fin de siècle writers generally. Whatever the case may be, there is no question that Reverdy wrote some of the most affecting war poems in the French language. One of the most direct is titled simply "Guerre" (war). Running through a series of disjointed, if coherent, images, Reverdy toward the end of the poem approaches direct statement, when the speaker says:

> Et la figure attristée
> Visage des visages
> La mort passe sur le chemin
>
> And the saddened figure
> Visage of visages
> Death passes along the road

Close to a medieval allegorizing of death, this figure also incorporates a fascination with the effect of the gaze. One's face is revealing of one's emotion because of the way one looks—the distillation of the phenomenon into a general characteristic is a strong term to describe death. If this image is strong, the poem's ending is more forceful still:

> Mais quel autre poids que celui de ton corps
> as-tu jeté dans la balance
> Tout froid dans le fossé
> Il dort sans plus rêver
>
> But what other weight than that of your body
> have you thrown in the balance
> All cold in the ditch
> He sleeps no longer to dream

Philosophers have questioned whether the idea of death is properly an idea, since strictly speaking, it has no content. Caught between viewing another's death from the outside and facing one's own death, which one can never know, death is a supreme mystery of human existence. Reverdy in these lines seems to cross the line between the exterior, objective view of another's death and the unknowable, subjective experience of the individual. This is what he means by the emotion communicated through the poetic image.

Despite a continued tendency toward the surreal image in Reverdy's work, these poems in *Sources du vent* (sources of the wind) also represent the first major collection of poems after Reverdy's conversion to a mystic Catholicism in 1926. Increasingly, his poetry of the postconversion period tends toward an introjection of the conflicts raised through the poetic image. While a tone of lingering sadness had always been present from the earliest work, in these poems, the atmosphere of sadness and loss moves to the center of the poet's concerns. Unlike the conservative Christian poets Charles-Pierre Péguy and Paul Claudel, the content of the poems is never directly religious. Rather, a mood of quietism seems to become more prominent in the collections of poems after the conversion. A concurrent falling off in the level of production also takes place. After 1930, Reverdy publishes only two more individual collections of verse, along with two collected volumes and works in other forms. After 1949, for the last twelve years of his life, the heretofore prolific Reverdy apparently ceased to write altogether.

"MÉMOIRE"

The poem "Mémoire" (memory) from *Pierres blanches* (white stones), shows this mood of increasing resignation in the face of worldly events. The poem invokes a "she," someone who has left or is going to leave, but then, in apparent reference to the title, says there will still be someone:

> Quand nous serons partis là-bas derrière
> Il y aura encore ici quelqu'un
> Pour nous attendre
> Et nous entendre
>
> When we will have gone over there behind
> There will still be someone
> To wait for us
> And to understand us

The positive mood of these lines, however, is undercut by the poem's ending: "Un seul ami/ L'ombre que nous avons laissée sous l'arbre et qui s'ennuie" ("A single friend/ The shadow we have left beneath a tree and who's getting bored"). The impersonality tending toward a universal statement that was present in Reverdy's early work here seems to work toward an effacement of the individual personality. If memory can be imaged as a bored shadow left beneath a tree, the significance of the individual seems tenuous at best. The emotion generated through the poetic image here seems to be one of sadness and extreme resignation.

The interpretation of a poet's work through biography must always be a hazy enterprise, all the more so in a poet such as Reverdy, whose life directly enters into his work not at all. In a general sense, then, the course of his poetic life and production might be said to mirror the course of French literary life generally. The enthusiasm of the avant-garde literary and artistic movements in Europe generally in the early years of the twentieth century saw a reaction in the post-World War I years toward an art that questioned societal assumptions. Dada and Surrealism can be seen in terms of this large movement, and Reverdy's work as an example. The coherence of the Surrealist movement in turn breaks down in the late 1920's and early 1930's with the split coming over what political allegiance the Surrealist artists should take, according to its leaders. Reverdy's personal religious convictions cause him to cease active involvement with the movement altogether. It is a measure of his status as a strong precursor to the movement that he is not attacked directly by the more politically motivated leaders of Surrealism.

"MAIN-MORTE"

With the extreme politicization of the Surrealist movement in the late 1930's, even some of the most dedicated younger adherents to Surrealism cut their formal ties with the movement. René Char is an example. The young Yves Bonnefoy is an example of a poet with early leanings toward Surrealism who in the late 1940's moved more in the direction of a poetry expressive of essential philosophical and human truths. It might be possible, in like manner, to trace Reverdy's increasing distance from Surrealism as a movement to some kind of similar feelings that have been more openly expressed by his younger contemporaries. His collection *Plein Verre* (full glass) does indeed move more toward the mode of longer, contemplative poems, still in the atmosphere of sadness and resignation to life. The end of "Main-Morte" (dead-hand) shows this well:

> Entre l'aveu confus et le lien du mystère
> Les mots silencieux qui tendent leur filet
> Dans tous les coins de cette chambre noire
> Où ton ombre ni moi n'aurons jamais dormi
>
> Between the confused vow and the tie of mystery
> The silent words which offer their net
> In every corner of this black room
> Where your shadow nor I will have ever slept

Even the highly suggestive early lyrics do not contain quite the level of hovering mystery and intricate emotional states offered in these lines. One may well wonder if the "you" invoked here even refers to a person or whether it might be a quasi-human interior presence such as that invoked in the later poems of Wallace Stevens (such as "Final Soliloquy of the Interior Paramour"). The weight of the images in the direction of silence lends to this whole utterance an aura of high seriousness.

"ENFIN"

The last poem in *Plein Verre*, titled "Enfin" (at last), also ends with a statement hinting at a highly serious attitude. The speaker states:

> À travers la poitrine nue
> Là
> Ma clarière
> Avec tout ce qui descend du ciel
> Devenir un autre
> À ras de terre

> By means of the naked breast
> There
> My clearing
> Along with all that descends from the sky
> To become an other
> At earth level

More and more in the later poems, a level of ethical statement seems to emerge. Whereas the early poems introduce strange and startling images in an apparently almost random fashion, the images here seem to be coordinated by an overall hierarchy of values, personal and religious. The naked breast at the beginning of this passage thus could refer to the lone individual, perhaps alone with his or her conscience. This is in contrast to something which descends from the sky, an almost unavoidably religious image. The wish "To become an other/ At earth level" might then be interpreted as the fervent desire of an extremely devoted individual to attain a higher level of piety here on earth.

LE CHANT DES MORTS

The extended sequence, *Le Chant des morts* (the song of the dead), composed in 1944-1948 and published in 1948 as part of the collected volume *Main d'œuvre* (work made by hand), presents an extended meditation on the emotional inner scene of war-devastated France. In this sequence, as in his earlier poems on World War I that drew on his direct experience of the horrors of war, Reverdy uses a diction stripped bare of rhetoric, preferring instead the direct, poignant images of death and suffering. Death in these poems is both inescapable and horrible, or as he calls it: "la mort entêtée/ La mort vorace" ("stubborn death/ Voracious death"). As a strong countermovement to the implacable march of death, there is also a tenacious clinging to life. As the poet says: "C'est la faim/ C'est l'ardeur de vivre qui dirigent/ La peur de perdre" ("It is hunger/ It is the ardor to live that guide/ The fear of losing"). The poet of the inner conscience in these poems confronts the essential subject of his deepest meditations: the conscious adoption of his authentic attitude toward death.

The ultimate renunciation of poetry that characterizes the last years of Reverdy's life is preceded by an exploration of the subject most suited to representing death (remembering Sigmund Freud)—that is, silence.

"ET MAINTENANT"

The poem that Reverdy seems to have chosen to come at the end of his collected poems, titled "Et Maintenant" (and now), ends with a poignant image of silence: "Tous les fils dénoués au delà des saisons reprennent leur tour et leur ton sur le fond sombre du silence" ("All the unknotted threads beyond the seasons regain their trace and their tone against the somber background of silence"). Reverdy here seems to hint at what lies beyond poetic expression in several senses. His entire ethos of poetic creation has been consistently based on an act of communication with the reader. Thus, the threads he refers to here could well represent the threads of intention and emotion that his readers follow in his poetry to achieve an experience of that emotion themselves, or to discover an analogous emotional experience in their own memory or personal background. He might also be hinting at those threads of intention and emotion that led beyond the limitations of individual life in a reunification with a divine creator. In the former interpretation, the background of silence would be that silence which precedes the poetic utterance or act of communication, as well as the silence after the act of communication or once the poet has ceased to write. In the religious interpretation, the background of silence would be that nothingness or nonbeing out of which the divine creation takes place and which, in turn, has the capability of incorporating silence or nonbeing into self, a religious attitude of a return to the creator even in the face of one's own personal death.

LEGACY

Reverdy is a complex and fascinating figure in the history of French poetry in the first half of the twentieth century. He was a committed avant-garde artist in the years directly preceding, during, and following World War I; his outpouring of poetry and aesthetic statements made him one of the most significant precursors to the movements of Dada and Surrealism. Though his formal affiliation with the Surrealist movement was of brief duration, his example of using the poetic image to communicate emotion is central to everything for which Surrealism stood. The extreme respect shown to his work by other poets and artists confirms his importance as a creative innovator. Reverdy, in turn, paid respectful homage to his poet and artist contemporaries a stance that shows his ongoing intellectual commitment to the importance of art and literature in human terms, despite his personal isolation and quietism toward the end of his life. The poems from the end of his career that bear the weight of a continued meditation on death are a moving commentary on that from which language emerges and into which it returns: silence.

OTHER MAJOR WORKS
LONG FICTION: *Le Voleur de Talan*, 1917; *La Peau de l'homme*, 1926.
SHORT FICTION: *Risques et périls*, 1930.
NONFICTION: *Self Defence*, 1919; *Le Gant de crin*, 1927; *Le Livre de mon bord*, 1948; *Cette émotion appellée poésie: Écrits sur la poésie, 1932-1960*, 1975; *Nord-Sud, Self Defence, et autres écrits sur l'art et la poésie*, 1975; *Note éternelle du présent*, 1975.

BIBLIOGRAPHY
Greene, Robert W. *The Poetic Theory of Pierre Reverdy*. 1967. Reprint. San Bernardino, Calif.: Borgo Press, 1990. An analysis of Reverdy's work in poetic theory.
Pap, Jennifer. "Transforming the Horizon: Reverdy's World War I." *Modern Language Review* 101, no. 4 (October, 2006): 966-978. Pap examines the theme of war in Reverdy's works, noting that although he favored an art that followed its own aims, he did treat the war in his poetry.
Rizzuto, Anthony. *Style and Theme in Reverdy's "Les Ardoises du toit."* Tuscaloosa: University of Alabama Press, 1971. Rizzuto's critical study of one of Reverdy's poetic works. Includes bibliographic references.
Rothwell, Andrew. *Textual Spaces: The Poetry of Pierre Reverdy*. Atlanta: Rodopi, 1989. A critical analysis of Reverdy's works. Includes bibliographic references.
Schroeder, Jean. *Pierre Reverdy*. Boston: Twayne, 1981. An introductory biography and critical study of selected works by Reverdy. Includes an index and bibliographic references.
Sweet, David LeHardy. *Savage Sight/Constructed Noise: Poetic Adaptations of Painterly Techniques in the French and American Avant-gardes*. Chapel Hill: Department of Romance Languages, University of North Carolina, 2003. The poetry of experimental poets Reverdy, Guillaume Apollinaire, André Breton, Frank O'Hara, and John Ashbery is examined for the poets' use of painterly techniques.

Peter Baker

JAMES SCHUYLER

Born: Chicago, Illinois; November 9, 1923
Died: New York, New York; April 12, 1991

PRINCIPAL POETRY
Salute, 1960
May 24th or So, 1966
Freely Espousing, 1969
The Crystal Lithium, 1972
A Sun Cab, 1972
Hymn to Life, 1974
The Fireproof Floors of Witley Court: English Songs and Dances, 1976
Song, 1976
The Home Book: Prose and Poems, 1951-1970, 1977 (Trevor Winkfield, editor)
The Morning of the Poem, 1980
Early in '71, 1981
A Few Days, 1985
Selected Poems, 1988
Collected Poems, 1993
Last Poems, 1999
Selected Poems, 2007
Other Flowers: Uncollected Poems, 2010

OTHER LITERARY FORMS

James Schuyler (SKI-lur) wrote (or cowrote) three novels. Beginning with *Alfred and Guinevere* (1958), the novels deal with the upper middle class and show a good ear for the comic trivialities of ordinary conversation, whether of children and adolescents, sophisticated young adults, or middle-aged couples. They also demonstrate, with their precision in naming, Schuyler's connoisseur's eye for furniture, design, and objects used or displayed in the household. The satiric *A Nest of Ninnies* (1969), cowritten with John Ashbery, lacks the plot and fully developed characters of *What's for Dinner?* (1978), his most substantial novel, giving rich evidence of true command of the form as it traces an alcoholic's recovery in a mental hospital, her husband's simultaneous affair with a widowed friend, and the progress of several other patients on short-term stays in the hospital.

Three of Schuyler's plays have been produced: the one-act pieces *Presenting Jane* (pr. 1952) and *Shopping and Waiting* (pb. 1953), and *Unpacking the Black Trunk*, another collaboration with a fellow poet (Kenward Elmslie), produced off-Broadway in

1965. He wrote the libretto ("mostly collage from newspapers," he says) for *A Picnic Cantata: For Four Women's Voices, Two Pianos, and Percussion* (pr. 1953), for which the writer Paul Bowles composed the music; it was recorded by Columbia Records.

Like fellow New York poets Ashbery and Frank O'Hara, Schuyler also wrote art criticism—particularly for *Art News*, where he served for a time as associate editor.

Achievements

James Schuyler won the Pulitzer Prize in poetry in 1981 for *The Morning of the Poem*. His other awards include the Frank O'Hara Prize from *Poetry* in 1969, the Bernard F. Connors Prize for Poetry from the *Paris Review* in 1985, a Whiting Writers' Award in 1985, and a Lambda Literary Award in 1993. He received grants and fellowships, including a National Endowment for the Arts grant and an Academy of American Poets Fellowship.

Biography

Born in Chicago to a family with extensive roots in the United States, James Marcus Schuyler grew up in Washington, D.C., and Buffalo and East Aurora, New York, the family seat to which he returned. He attended Bethany College in West Virginia, served in the U.S. Navy in World War II, and worked for Voice of America in New York City before traveling to Italy, where he attended the University of Florence and lived in W. H. Auden's house in Ischia, typing some of the elder poet's manuscripts (as he notes in his obituary poem, "Wystan Auden"). After he returned to New York in the early 1950's, he became involved in art and poetry circles and took a curatorial position in the Department of Circulating Exhibitions at the Museum of Modern Art, organizing a number of shows. He also served as associate editor of *Art News*, for which O'Hara and Ashbery also worked. Together, and with a number of other young poets, they changed the poetry scene in New York and became a major force in contemporary American poetry. Close friends as well as colleagues, they often have referred to one another in their books and poems and sometimes collaborated. Painters and musicians are included in this group; various artist friends of Schuyler not only are mentioned in his poems but also have contributed cover illustrations for several of his books. Schuyler suffered personal traumas in the 1970's, and his recovery from a nervous breakdown is recorded in *The Morning of the Poem*; he also sustained severe burns after falling asleep while smoking in bed. Nevertheless, in the late 1970's, he began reading publicly for the first time. Schuyler died in New York City in 1991 after suffering a stroke.

Analysis

James Schuyler was a keen observer of the most intimate details of the world around him and of the sensations they evoked in him. His poetry captures those detailed impressions and sensations, however ephemeral they may be. This very ephemerality is the singular distinction of his world, particularly in his presentation of nature. The individual poem lives not so much as a perfected piece of art, frozen under glass; rather, it shimmers with movement and conveys a sense of being nearly as ephemeral as the impressions it records. Sometimes, of course, the impressions and mood are so fleeting as to leave the reader with virtually nothing but random actions and details—or even only words. This is the danger of Schuyler's method—one which its great advocate, O'Hara, did not always steer clear of himself. Thus, some poems read as little more than notebook jottings.

However, the method is also responsible for the brilliance of his two long poems, "Hymn to Life" and "The Morning of the Poem" (the title poem of the volume for which he was awarded the Pulitzer Prize). These poems ramble, it is true, down the streams of Schuyler's consciousness, across several weeks' time, from place to place, subject to subject, and mood to mood. However, each attains a remarkable unity through the skill and exactness with which Schuyler has captured his own voice, developed over the course of a rather short career (barely two decades of serious publishing), to penetrate and reveal his own mental and emotional states. His highly individual, warmly personal, and frankly intimate voice is characterized by unforced humor, gentle self-deprecation, eagerness, equivocation, wonder, doubt, and fascination. This is the voice, as well, of a series of simple and tender love poems, joyful and physical without being actually erotic, addressing another man with the greatest ease and naturalness imaginable. Schuyler's achievements in evoking the processes of nature, love, and mind are praiseworthy, for producing not only such thought-provoking and appealing major works as the two long poems but also many shorter ones that are sure to enchant readers over the years.

Schuyler was a master of subtle changes—in growing things, in weather, in time of day or year, and in moods and thoughts. These he conveyed appropriately, without big effects, sudden bursts of insight, or harsh contrasts. Rather, his poems have the shimmering magical quality of familiar scenes and objects rendered in watercolor landscapes or still lifes, but they are anything but still: Even his most quiet and peaceful scenes contain movement, even if nearly imperceptible. Such constant, inevitable movement is the manifestation of life for Schuyler, and through his poetry, the reader too gains a more intense appreciation for the many wonders and delights of even the smallest details in this life, once a moment is taken to observe them.

In an interview, Schuyler once said, "Much of my poetry is as concerned with looking at things and trying to transcribe them as painting is. This is not generally true of poetry." Evidence of Schuyler's affinities to painting (which doubtless stem largely from his friendship with many painters as well as his own work in the art world) is abundant throughout his work, in his attention to color, light, texture, and other visual effects.

Besides being "very visual," his work also "seems to be especially musical," he went on to say. Indeed, he counted important composers such as Virgil Thomson and Ned

Rorem among his friends and wrote about music from Johannes Brahms and Sergei Rachmaninoff to Janis Joplin and Carly Simon. His is not the music of the conventional sonneteer, however, although he made an obligatory gesture or two in that direction. Rather, his poetry, almost without exception, ignores regular rhyme and meter in favor of free verse, appropriate for his emphasis on endless change. His styles of free verse change radically too, from lines of only two or three syllables in his self-styled "skinny poems," providing a slow, even, almost hesitant, occasionally fragmented pace appropriate for the meditative stance of some of these poems, to lines as long as each individual sentence unit requires (in "The Cenotaph"), to lines a page wide or more in the long poems. Line breaks are often capricious, but this very unpredictability allows him some splendid effects. For example, the minimally punctuated "Buttered Greens" has lines which make sense in one way, until the next line indicates that the last part of the preceding line is meant not as a completion of the preceding thought but as the beginning of a new statement: "inside all/ is not con-/ tent, yet/ the chance/ of it is/ there, free." A reader automatically assumes that "free" modifies "chance," but the next line suggests that it modifies the botanical noun: "there, free/ leaves fall." Often he abandons punctuation altogether, and a whole series of sensory impressions flows down or across the page as unmediated sensory input ("A Sun Cab"). Sentence fragments, composed of nouns, adjectives, and prepositional phrases, are frequent in many of these shorter poems, reminiscent of William Carlos Williams, whom Schuyler acknowledged as an early influence.

However, musical aspects are present in occasional devices of structure and sound. Words or images are repeated, like leitmotifs; recurring themes and images are particularly important in the long poems, where depiction of rain or of sites in Washington, D.C., acts both as a cohesive device and as a counterpoint to other concerns in the poem. His free-verse lines often emulate the startling and open structures of much modern music. Finally, Schuyler does not neglect the traditional musical devices of sound; pleasing patterns of alliteration, assonance, consonance, and even exact rhyme (though usually internal and never long-sustained) appear casually in occasional poems such as "Song" and "Just Before Fall."

Most of his poems purport to do no more than map the stream of his consciousness, whether it consists chiefly of external impressions which engage his full attention or of thoughts and feelings and whatever sensory recollections they invoke. Sometimes it is a combination of the two—external impressions giving rise to memories, which are in turn interrupted by more sensory input from the present moment. Schuyler's is very much a poetry of the present. Nearly every poem begins directly in the present tense, often indicating the setting of place, time, and weather; recollections of the past may intrude, described in the past tense as appropriate, but their appearance is strongly grounded in the immediacy of the present moment, rather than being a meditation on "remembrance of things past" or "emotion recollected in tranquillity" undertaken as an end in itself.

Time is certainly a central theme for Schuyler, but with an emphasis quite unlike that of most other poets. It passes as quickly (or slowly) for him as for another, but he does not bemoan its passing. He is not without regrets, but these are for friends who have died, lovers who have left: He accepts his move ahead into age, not with resignation but as merely another stage of life, for "Life will change and/ I am part of it and/ will change too."

Such an attitude informs his two longest poems, "Hymn to Life" and "The Morning of the Poem." Each embraces and celebrates change, the prevailing force in his work, the dominant characteristic of all life itself. In the earlier poem, Schuyler takes the reader with him along the paths of his mind and experiences, recording his various thoughts and sensory impressions as time moves on. It begins the day before spring (that is, in March), then moves imperceptibly into April and May. These shifts occur not with an abrupt, secretarial ripping-off of the old month's calendar page but with the gradualism of nature itself: This seventeen-page poem is not broken into sections as the time passes but reveals each new month's presence only in mid-line, appropriately for the subtle recognition of something new in the air, a change that has occurred while one was watching but was perhaps momentarily distracted, watching the many wonderful details all around, so exquisitely conveyed in this poem.

"SONG"

Such unremarked changes, so lovingly dwelt on, are Schuyler's stock-in-trade, for the times between (parts of the year or the day) are his favorite poetic subjects. "Song," for example, concentrates on the hour of sunset. It begins: "The light lies layered in the trees" (with melodious alliteration and use of long vowel sounds). Then the sun sets, "not sharply or at once," but in "a stately progress down the sky." Other details around him, however, attract his attention: "Traffic sounds and/ bells resound . . . the grass is violent green." Several color sensations then yield to the sound of a car starting up, as the visual sense surrenders to darkness. Two short lines ("A horsefly vanishes./ A smoking cigarette.") capture the sense of increasing darkness: The normally quite visible insect is lost to sight while the glowing of the cigarette, normally not noticeable in daylight, appears, contrasting with the lack of light around it. Finally, the leaves merge, "discriminated barely/ in light no longer layered," because of the departure of the sun's light.

This poem, like so many others by Schuyler, simply presents a sequence of sensory images, vividly capturing the various components of a particular moment as it is experienced. Schuyler does not pretend to deal with the earth-shattering problems of humanity: That becomes editorial writing, he has said. Consequently, his poetry has often been regarded as trivial. Indeed, many of his poems do fail to register any significant impression. The comic criticism of himself that he quotes in "The Morning of the Poem"— "All he cares about are leaves and/ flowers and weather"—has validity, but not at all as a criticism. These subjects serve as indicators of his own understanding of life—its beauty, its transience, and its variability, qualities that every human being must understand and accept to come fully to terms with existence as well as with such major human concerns as love and death.

These important concerns are not in the least absent from Schuyler's work. He often confronts death as he recalls or writes elegies for friend and fellow poet Frank O'Hara, other friends and lovers (Bill Aalto, his first lover, who died of leukemia after they had broken up), and musicians as diverse as Libby Holman, Janis Joplin, and Bruno Walter. Their deaths may be violent or gentle, but Schuyler accepts them with deepest serenity. He portrays love as "quiet/ ecstasy and sweet content." A lovely series in *Hymn to Life* records with utmost simplicity such joys as lying on the beach beside his lover or eagerly awaiting his return from a trip; later poems reveal with welcome understatement the pain of being without him, once the relationship has ended.

"THE MORNING OF THE POEM"

Love (and sex) and death, in addition to time and change (indeed, in conjunction with them, for the latter are ineluctably implicated with the former) form the major strands of the intricate but not at all impenetrable tapestry of Schuyler's longest poem, "The Morning of the Poem," which reads almost like a run-on, candid, and charmingly intimate conversational journal. Because it proceeds through sixty-one pages with no break other than a dot in the exact middle of the poem (separating an elegy from a grocery list), it would seem to be all of one piece. Schuyler maintains unity of place—that is, the East Aurora room where he sits at his typewriter—although his thoughts may range to New York City, New Brunswick, England, and Paris, and among similarly diverse subjects. Yet the reader discovers, moving through the poem, that these meditations occur not on a single morning or afternoon but over a nearly two-month span.

"The Morning of the Poem" takes Schuyler from the beginning of July to late August, when he leaves his rural family home in western New York to return to Manhattan. As he sits at his typewriter, thinking of his friend painting in New York (and addressing him, as if in a letter, throughout much of the poem), the weather, assorted deliveries, his aged mother's nagging, and many memories from various stages of the past (last night's dream, cruising another middle-aged man in the grocery store, boyhood and adolescent incidents, lovers and friends and a beloved dog now gone) impinge on his consciousness and accordingly enter the poem. Amid the many surrenders to thought and recollection, the recurring descriptions of the rainy weather, several lawn mowings, and a few passing references to the time of month give readers their bearings as to the progression of time—always to their surprise at its speed.

Schuyler has a vested interest in moving time rapidly—he is looking forward to rejoining his painter friend in New York. His recollections of the past enable time to pass more quickly for him, while the present-tense descriptions of the weather and activities around the house slow it down, reminding him only of the stretch of time still facing him. However, this does not deny his ability to find pleasure even in the moments that drag on.

Schuyler keeps imagining his friend painting on his rooftop in New York and praises "the dedication of the artist" which characterizes him. Schuyler's question, "Whoever knows what a painter is thinking?" is echoed near the end of the poem, upon receipt of a postcard from composer Ned Rorem: "I wonder what it's like, being a composer?" He finds these other arts mysterious: painting involves colors whose names he cannot remember; music demands "so much time" to write down "the little notes," whereas his own writing "goes by so fast:/ a couple of hours of concentration, then you're/ spent." Presented in counterpoint to these other artists, one introduced at the very beginning of the poem, the other at the end, Schuyler as poet, seated at his typewriter, is seen by the reader to be every bit as dedicated, even when drinking limeade, or just lost in reverie—dedicated to the pursuit of self-knowledge, of an empathy with the life around him, natural and human. It has certainly demanded great effort to make this poem, composed presumably in countless sittings over two months, flow so smoothly and achieve a unity among the many subjects of its meanderings.

A poetry of sheer stream of consciousness, of simple recording of sensory and mental experiences, would seem to be an easy achievement; many lesser poets have attempted it, but without the aura of mystery, celebration, wonder, and joy that Schuyler brings to such moments. He has no poetic program, no ambition to make his poems "more open," as "a clunkhead" suggests; rather, he wants "merely to say, to see and say, things/ as they are." It thus seems important to name things exactly, and he displays a splendidly precise vocabulary of nouns and verbs when describing his environment (climate, plant life, sea life, forest life, furnishings, and art works). It is understandably frustrating, therefore, when he fails to remember certain names for things, as throughout "The Morning of the Poem." Yet specific names may not be so important when considered against appreciation for the things themselves and the experiences they create, as he tells his "dead best friend" in "The Morning of the Poem":

> this is not
> your poem, your poem I may
> Never write, too much, though it is there and
> needs only to be written down
> And one day will and if it isn't it doesn't matter:
> the truth, the absolute
> Of feeling, of knowing what you know, that is
> the poem . . .

To capture such "truth," such an "absolute of feeling" in words is, of course, far from easy. In "Hudson Ferry," Schuyler writes, with a kind of comic disgust, "You can't talk about the weather"—it is so easily susceptible to clichés. However, Schuyler has paradoxically persisted, as "The Morning of the Poem" makes clear. How? He continues to remark that "You can't get at a sunset naming colors," so he uses other means: For example, noting the effects of the sunset in "Song," he is not afraid to use metaphors and similes—but characteristically with freshness and aptness: "An almost autumn sky, a swimming pool awash/ with cinnamon and gentian." However, he also often mocks the poet's metaphorical and personifying tendencies and can undercut such poeticisms with a deft phrase, like the parenthesis that immediately follows the lines just quoted: "(The sky's the swimming pool, that is)," or the deflation of the grandiose apostrophe "O Day!" with the no less and possibly more appreciative "literal/ and unsymbolic/ day." As he writes in "The Cenotaph": "The hawkweed flowers are an idea about the color of fire./ The hawkweed are one thing and the fire is another." Thus he reminds the reader that the objects compared retain their own identities; it is the human mind that draws such parallels. For that very reason—that the human mind perceives things by making such comparisons—these poetic figures which indicate similarities must not be omitted from the writing of poetry; they are indispensable to the mind's process of perception. What he does seek to avoid poetically are the familiar standard associations: "fall/ equals melancholy, spring,/ get laid." "An Almanac" succeeds in this splendidly, tracing the passage of the seasons in an utterly fresh way—through nothing but discrete details of action, predominantly human, which indicate clearly the particular changes accompanying each new season, from fall to spring: "Shops take down their awnings . . . In cedar chests sheers and seersuckers displace flannels and wools."

Schuyler's poetry revels in the experience of any sort of weather, season, time of day, or environment. He seems equally at home in city and country (though favoring the latter) and can paint a Manhattan street scene as luminously as a Long Island beach or a woodland walk in Vermont. The variety of the scenes he can enjoy and his ability to capture accurately the feel of such a range of experience richly display his appreciation for the fact of change—even in the breakup of love affairs, even in the losses of death. Toward the end of "The Morning of the Poem," he realizes "how this poem seems mostly about what I've lost," yet none of these losses has broken him. He does not elegize them with the typical "life must go on" resolution, for he knows very well that, *sub specie temporis*, there is nothing else life can do: "Life will change and/ I am part of it and/ will change too. So/ will you, and you. . . ." Death is merely another form of this change. The process of life contains "in repetition, change:/ a continuity, the what/ of which you are a part." There is no stability, as each season fades into the next, yet in each season is the promise of the future ones; as Schuyler writes in "Buttered Greens," our life means "leavings and/ the permanence/ of return."

When Schuyler in "The Morning of the Poem" receives a letter from a friend telling of her brother's dying while "the grandchildren and the dogs ran in and out as usual," Schuyler responds quoting the familiar litany, which is no less true: "'In the midst of life we are in death, in the/ Midst of death we are in life.'" This is the essence of Schuyler's attitude toward both life and death, including a healthy recognition of the passage of time and the inevitability of change ("This beauty that I see . . . it goes, it goes."). After he hears about a hurricane on Long Island, Schuyler asks himself in "The Morning of the Poem," "Why so much pleasure in wrack and/ ruin?" It may be the proof it gives of the ephemeral nature of all security and permanence. After all, "the scattered wrack" contains "(always) some cut-up surprise." Change gives no cause for fear or regret, Schuyler suggests through his wonderfully serene poetry; change in nature creates endless sequences of beauty, like the changing days in "Hymn to Life": "each so unique, each so alike." The seasons are predictable, yet full of unexpected variations: a cold, rainy July, a balmy November.

During the course of the marvelous abundance of "The Morning of the Poem," Schuyler, indulging in a favorite pastime, eating ("grapes, oysters/ And champagne"), remarks that "bliss is such a simple thing." So is most of Schuyler's poetry, yet it conveys a rich sense of the world around him and a healthy, joyous approach to existence.

OTHER MAJOR WORKS

LONG FICTION: *Alfred and Guinevere*, 1958; *A Nest of Ninnies*, 1969 (with John Ashbery); *What's for Dinner?*, 1978.

PLAYS: *Presenting Jane*, pr. 1952 (one act); *A Picnic Cantata: For Four Women's Voices, Two Pianos, and Percussion*, pr. 1953 (music by Paul Bowles); *Shopping and Waiting*, pb. 1953; *Unpacking the Black Trunk*, pr. 1965 (one act, with Kenward Elmslie).

NONFICTION: *Two Journals: James Schuyler, Darragh Park*, 1995; *The Diary of James Schuyler*, 1996; *Selected Art Writings*, 1998 (Simon Pettet, editor); *Just the Thing: The Selected Letters of James Schuyler*, 2004 (William Corbett, editor); *The Letters of James Schuyler to Frank O'Hara*, 2006 (Corbett, editor).

EDITED TEXTS: *Broadway: A Poet's and Painter's Anthology*, 1979; *Broadway 2: A Poet's and Painter's Anthology*, 1989.

BIBLIOGRAPHY

Auslander, Philip. *The New York School Poets as Playwrights*. New York: Peter Lang, 1989. Although the focus of this volume is on plays, the chapter on Schuyler also examines his poetry, including his link to the New York School.

Corbett, William, and Geoffrey Young, eds. *That Various Field for James Schuyler*. Great Barrington, Mass.: The Figures, 1991. A good overview.

Schuyler, James. *The Diary of James Schuyler*. Edited by Nathan Kernan. Santa Rosa, Calif.: Black Sparrow Press, 1997. Schuyler's diary is a devastating account of his decline into mental illness and a narrative of his achievements. Includes bibliographical references.

Vinson, James, ed. *Contemporary Poets*. 3d ed. New York: St. Martin's Press, 1980.

The entry on Schuyler, by Michael Andre, identifies his artistic leanings and his prolific writings. Calls *Salute* representative of his poems, which are "sensitive and perceptive." Notes that much of Schuyler's poetry describes what he sees and what he loves—and that is not New York.

Ward, Geoff. *Statues of Liberty: The New York School of Poets*. 2d ed. New York: Palgrave, 2001. An account of the key figures of the New York School including Schuyler. Ward provides updated material on the group and its influence on postmodern poetics. Includes bibliographical references and index.

Scott Giantvalley

DELMORE SCHWARTZ

Born: Brooklyn, New York; December 8, 1913
Died: New York, New York; July 11, 1966

PRINCIPAL POETRY
In Dreams Begin Responsibilities, 1938 (includes poetry and prose)
Genesis, Book I, 1943
Vaudeville for a Princess, and Other Poems, 1950
Summer Knowledge, 1959
Last and Lost Poems of Delmore Schwartz, 1979 (Robert Phillips, editor)

OTHER LITERARY FORMS

Although Delmore Schwartz thought of himself primarily as a poet, he wrote short stories, plays, and literary and film criticism as well. His masterful 1937 story, "In Dreams Begin Responsibilities," prefigures the major concerns of his later work and provides the title for his first collection of poetry in the following year. *The World Is a Wedding* (1948) contains this and most of the remainder of Schwartz's best stories. The later stories collected in *Successful Love, and Other Stories* (1961) are generally less noteworthy. Schwartz's retooling of William Shakespeare in *Coriolanus and His Mother*, which occupies a large part of *In Dreams Begin Responsibilities*, and the autobiographical *Shenandoah* (pb. 1941) are interesting, if not particularly stageworthy, contributions to verse drama. A good sampling of his essays on modern literature and its critics—T. S. Eliot, Ezra Pound, Edmund Wilson, Lionel Trilling—as well as occasional pieces on films such as *The Seven Year Itch* and *The Blackboard Jungle* reveals the characteristic interplay of his mind between high and popular culture, and may be found in the posthumous *Selected Essays of Delmore Schwartz* (1970). Schwartz's papers, recovered and presented to Yale University by his literary executor, Dwight Macdonald, mainly record the abandoned projects that littered Schwartz's career.

ACHIEVEMENTS

Delmore Schwartz burst onto the New York literary scene when his best-known story, "In Dreams Begin Responsibilities," was published in the front of the first issue of the revised *Partisan Review* in Autumn, 1937. Not yet twenty-four, Schwartz had passionately dramatized the adolescent trauma of the Jewish urban intellectual edging nervously into manhood in the 1930's. Vladimir Nabokov ranked "In Dreams Begin Responsibilities" among his half-dozen favorite modern stories. With the appearance of his first collection of poetry in 1938, Schwartz's reputation was firmly established. This volume, again titled *In Dreams Begin Responsibilities*, was praised by such luminaries as Allen Tate, John Crowe Ransom, W. H. Auden, and Wallace Stevens as the work of the ablest of the younger American poets. Schwartz's passionate rhetoric and unrelieved pessimism seemed to evoke perfectly the bleakness of the 1930's in poems that explored the tragic gap between human aspiration and fulfillment. Before the age of twenty-five, Schwartz was bemoaning lost innocence and passing time and had fastened on his obsessive theme: the failure of life's hopes. Schwartz would embody his own poignant illustration of the life of shattered dreams; only rarely would his poetry approach the brilliance of his first collection.

Schwartz pinned his hopes for enduring fame on *Genesis*, an epic poem that expressed the "Spirit of America" through the life of Hershey Green, the poet's surrogate. Schwartz believed that the poem would confirm him as heir apparent to the modernist mantle of Eliot, one of his literary heroes. Despite some isolated passages of great brilliance, *Genesis*, too long, too diffuse, too remorselessly narcissistic, failed to embody its grandiose design. For some time, Schwartz continued the saga of Hershey Green, but with a mounting sense of futility; the proposed books 2 and 3 of *Genesis* never appeared.

Vaudeville for a Princess, and Other Poems, a grab bag of poems, comic prose, and literary burlesque, represents a further decline from Schwartz's earlier work. He received a National Institute of Arts and Letters Award in 1953, the Levinson Prize from *Poetry* magazine in 1959, and the Shelley Memorial Award in 1960. Often his own harshest critic, Schwartz admitted the collection's failure by including only three of its poems in *Summer Knowledge*. The first half of this volume consists of poems, many in revised versions, that appeared originally in 1938; the remainder is made up of new poems, the three from *Vaudeville for a Princess, and Other Poems*, and a selection from *Genesis*. Nearly all Schwartz's enduring poetry is contained in this collection, for which he became the youngest poet ever to win the prestigious Bollingen Prize (1960). Ironically, it marked the end of his poetic career. The remaining seven years of his life completed the paradigm of the tragic fate of the sensitive artist whose precipitous decline parallels his meteoric rise. Once the most precocious voice of his generation, Schwartz ended as the symbol of dazzling promise only sporadically fulfilled.

Biography

Delmore David Schwartz, who once confessed that his only subject was himself, owed his birth to a fluke, a fact that he never tired of recounting. To conceive, Rose Schwartz needed an operation, which she financed by selling a French war bond, the gift of an overseas uncle. Since Harry Schwartz was unaware of Rose's ploy, Delmore's birth was the result of a deception that fascinated and repelled the poet for the rest of his life. Life with argumentative and histrionic parents is translated into the art of "In Dreams Begin Responsibilities," where the boy-narrator watches his parents' courtship unfold on the screen of an imaginary theater. When they decide, despite lingering doubts, to marry, the boy leaps from his seat screaming at them to reconsider. Perhaps the most traumatic episode of Schwartz's childhood occurred one summer day in 1921 when Rose dragged him into a roadside café and found her husband with another woman, whom she denounced as a whore. Young Hershey Green in *Genesis* learns that this incident will critically influence his later life. Schwartz's father left home permanently in 1923 when Delmore was nine. Like his parents, Schwartz was to doubt the wisdom of marriage; both of his own marriages were conceived in uncertainty and terminated in divorce.

Brilliant but erratic, Schwartz decided early to become a poet, although he majored in philosophy, earning a B.A. degree from New York University in 1935. He started graduate study at Harvard but left in March, 1937, without taking a degree, and returned to New York, where his criticism, poetry, and fiction soon began appearing in magazines. By the early 1940's, Schwartz's life had assumed the sort of pattern it would maintain thereafter, eddying between Cambridge, where he taught composition and advanced writing from 1940 to 1947, and New York, where he served as poetry editor of the *Partisan Review* from 1943 to 1955.

During his adolescence, Schwartz, the child of Jewish immigrants from Eastern Europe who could barely speak English, had lived simultaneously in Irving Howe's "world of our fathers" and the gleaming promised land of the aspiring New York literati. In one of Schwartz's finest stories, "America! America!," a promising young writer, Shenandoah Fish, listens to his mother's poignant tale of immigrant neighbors and gains a new appreciation of their lives that belies his initial contempt. Indeed the first and last names of Schwartz's hero reflect the odd mixture of the grandiose and mundane in his own. The tragedy of Schwartz's life was that the dialectical opposites so beautifully resolved in the fiction of "America! America!" and another fine story, "The Child Is the Meaning of This Life," could not be mediated in the real world. His inherent nobility and high purpose gave way to suspicions about wives, friends, and colleagues, resulting finally in paranoia. At Harvard, he envisioned a faculty cabal convened for the sole purpose of denying him tenure; his jealousy and insults finally alienated his most supportive colleague, Harry Levin. Back in New York, he reviled ancient enemies and steadfast friends alike, and the gloom of his last days was lightened only by friends such as Dwight Macdonald, Meyer Schapiro, and Saul Bellow, whose loyalty he could not destroy.

By then, however, Schwartz no longer cared. A boy wonder in 1938, he never surpassed and only rarely equaled his early achievements. By 1945, the failure of his first marriage, the lukewarm reception of *Genesis*, on which he had staked everything, and his heavy drinking had made him a "changed man" in the opinion of William Barrett, an old friend who renewed acquaintance with Schwartz on returning from the war. Ironically, the onset of Schwartz's long decline coincided with his solidifying reputation as an American man of letters; by 1947, he was the most widely anthologized poet of his generation (which included Robert Lowell and John Berryman), one of the ablest critics of modern poetry and writing, and an editor of *Partisan Review*, the most respected intellectual journal of its day. However, the only poetry he published during the remainder of his life was the slight *Vaudeville for a Princess, and Other Poems* and *Summer Knowledge*, the bulk of which was selected from his work prior to 1938.

By the 1950's, heavy drinking, sleeping pills, and massive doses of amphetamine had, according to James Atlas, Schwartz's biographer, exacerbated his chronic insomnia, confirmed his manic-depressive mood cycles, and led to the "notorious paranoia that dominated his last years." After a painful three-year stint at Syracuse University in the mid-1960's, arranged by Schapiro with the help of recommendations from Lowell and Bellow, whose novel *Humboldt's Gift* (1975) brilliantly evokes Schwartz's last days, the poet returned to New York to die. Sporadically incarcerated in Bellevue, Schwartz finally succumbed to a heart attack in the seedy Manhattan hotel that was his last home, on July 11, 1966.

Analysis

Coming of age in the intellectual climate of New York in the 1930's, Delmore Schwartz could hardly have avoided the twin influences of Sigmund Freud and Karl Marx, whose ghosts meet to analyze the hero's motives in *Coriolanus and His Mother*. Freud argues for Volumnia's primacy in the formation of Coriolanus's psyche, Marx for Rome's. Finally, mother and city merge into a symbol of the past which neither Coriolanus nor the poet can escape. The model is elaborated in one of his best essays, "The Two Audens," which appeared in the first issue of *Kenyon Review* in 1939. In the essay, Schwartz defined the Marxist Auden, the poet of contemporary social concerns, and the Freudian Auden, who reported the "intuitions of psychic life." While Schwartz preferred Auden's latter persona, it is clearly the interplay between public (ego) and private (id) selves that fascinated him.

However, it was Eliot who was Schwartz's "culture hero," the seer who discovered new forms and a new idiom for the modern world. Schwartz's ambition was to provide for the 1930's and 1940's the image of the times that Eliot had etched for an earlier generation. So long as Schwartz maintained a degree of Eliot's intellectual objectivity, his poetry, especially that of *In Dreams Begin Responsibilities*, brilliantly fulfilled his program, but he was compelled to treat the history of his times as inseparable from the history of himself. Thus *Genesis* is largely vitiated by Schwartz's obsession with the minutiae of Hershey Green's life, which is still bogged down in adolescence after two hundred pages of verse. James Atlas argues that Schwartz's background militated against the adoption of Eliot's poetic manner—authoritarian, aloof, detached—and that Arthur Rimbaud (whose *Une Saison en enfer*, 1873; *A Season in Hell*, 1932; he quirkily translated) and especially Charles Baudelaire provoked his rhetorical flights of grief and rage.

Baudelaire, Eliot, and another of his literary heroes, James Joyce, embody Schwartz's obsession with the social alienation of the poet, although Eliot was firmly ensconced in the literary establishment by the 1930's. The titles of such essays as "The Isolation of Modern Poetry," "The Vocation of the Poet in the Modern World," and "The Present State of Poetry" hint at the poet's marginality. Schwartz's alienation as a poet, deepened by his Jewishness, often took the form of a paranoia that he found increasingly difficult to suppress in his poetry.

Most of Schwartz's poetry is based on a varied but traditional iambic pentameter line that tends to lengthen and loosen in his later work. Images of snow—pacifying, concealing, obliterating—and light—dazzling, clarifying, transcending—permeate his poetry. No matter how they are structured and whatever imagery they employ, Schwartz's poems relentlessly explore his intertwined themes: the nature of the self, the alienation of the poet and Jew, the burden of the past, and the defeat of human aspirations. A discussion of his best poems most conveniently follows the order of their appearance in *Summer Knowledge*.

"The Ballad of the Children of the Czar"

"The Ballad of the Children of the Czar" imagines two events occurring simultaneously in 1916: The czar's children play with an erratically bouncing ball in their father's garden; six thousand miles away the two-year-old Schwartz eats a baked potato in his high chair. Simultaneity is reinforced by the mention of the poet's grandfather, who, after suffering in the czar's army, hid in a "wine-stinking barrel" for three days in Bucharest, and escaped to America where he "became a king himself." However, the poem is no parable of freedom—quite the opposite. The czar's children cannot control the ball which rolls beyond the garden's iron gate; their frustrated howls are echoed by the infant Schwartz whose buttered potato slips from his hands. Next year, the Russian Revolution will seal the fate of the czar's children, prefigured in the loss of their ball. A lost ball, a dropped potato: Humans can neither arbitrate their happiness nor control their fate. Children of czars and immigrants alike are victims of inherited history, which is at once irrecoverable and inescapable. Ironically, the very ubiquity of the past underlines humanity's fatal inability to change it. The poem recalls Aeneas bearing old Anchises on his back as they flee burning Troy; so must all children bear their fathers' weight, the burden of which they can never unload.

"In the Naked Bed, in Plato's Cave"

"In the Naked Bed, in Plato's Cave" expands Schwartz's discussion of the limits of human knowledge. Underlying the poem is Plato's parable of the cave, where chained prisoners face a wall on which they can see only shadows cast by firelight. So are all men chained, argues Plato, by their limited knowledge; they are doomed to take shadows for the reality that lies in the sunlight outside their cave. Schwartz, lying awake in bed, sees reflected headlights sliding along his wall and hears the hammering of carpenters, the grinding of truck traffic, and finally the milkman striving up the stairs, his bottles chinking. Perplexed, still woozy from sleep, he greets the morning, which heralds the mystery of beginning again and again.

Schwartz takes over Plato's distinction between appearance and reality, but reverses the conclusions of the parable. An actual bedroom replaces the symbolic cave, and the intensity and immediacy of the narrator's impressions contrast with the shadowy and fragmentary perceptions of Plato's chained prisoners. Moreover, the narrator sidles between bed and window, between sleep and wakefulness; Plato's men are perpetual sleepers, condemned to watch an eternal shadow play. The poem's conclusion points equally to human limitations, although in a different manner. The world in time—that is, the world apprehended by the speaker—is the real world. Schwartz has met Plato's dilemma, not by resolving its dualism but by denying its existence. "In the Naked Bed, in Plato's Cave" thus confirms the validity of human perception even as it fixes its boundaries.

"FAR ROCKAWAY"

"Far Rockaway" takes its title from the public beach where New Yorkers cast aside the "rigor of the weekday" with their shoes. The radiant seashore, the swaying light, the "passionate sun," and the glittering sea are positive images which, in the poem's first four stanzas, propose freedom not only from weekday care but also perhaps from time itself. The fifth stanza, however, introduces "the novelist," a detached observer, an introspective man whose concern is "the cure of souls" first cited in the epigraph of the poem, where it is attributed to Henry James. In a series of rhetorical questions, the intruder reduces weekend joy to trivial escapism: a "cure" for the body but no surcease for the soul. Day's radiance yields to a "haunting, haunted moon." The lesson of the master, suitably opaque, may be that sensual abandonment, the summum bonum of the masses, is a delusion and is, in any case, impossible for the detached artist, forever on the boardwalk, never on the beach.

"TIRED AND UNHAPPY, YOU THINK OF HOUSES"

A variation on this theme occurs in "Tired and Unhappy, You Think of Houses," wherein another outsider imagines a cozy family scene, which, for him, must remain a "banal dream." Turning away to the anonymity of the subway rush, he is "Caught in an anger exact as a machine!" Still another instance of the artist's social alienation is expressed dramatically in "Parlez-Vous Francais?" This time the scene is a barbershop, which, like the beach of "Far Rockaway" and the home of "Tired and Unhappy, You Think of Houses," embodies the communal values of everyday life. On the radio, the voice of a demagogue Caesar, probably Adolf Hitler, seduces the recumbent men with extravagant promises calculated to appeal to their basest instincts. Enter the writer, "shy, pale, and quite abstracted," whose three-day beard and lack of tie define his separateness. He cries out—in French—that Caesar knows that most men lead lives of quiet desperation and can be deceived by dreams and lies that will inevitably lead them to war and death. Naturally the writer's rage is incomprehensible to the men, none of whom understands this "foreigner"; just as naturally his use of French deliberately underscores his estrangement. Whether the unheeded seer of "Parlez-Vous Francais?," the unnoticed observer of "Far Rockaway," or the wistful dreamer of "Tired and Unhappy, You Think of Houses," the artist remains divorced from quotidian life.

"PROTHALAMION"

"Prothalamion" announces Schwartz's forthcoming marriage. Its opening sections treat the subject with Spenserian reverence and dignity: "The feast of bondage and unity" is approached with "great piety"; the poet affirms his need for love and remembrance; the bride's beauty will engender the self-forgetfulness necessary for married life. There follows a catalog of events best forgotten: his mother's rage before her seven-year-old son when she trapped her husband "At dinner with his whore"; his terror at thirteen when "a little girl died," and he first confronted death.

Freud and Marx are invited to the wedding to "mark out the masks that face us there," since "No form is cruel as self-deception." Wolfgang Amadeus Mozart shows up to reveal the "irreducible incorruptible good," presumably that arising from a life dedicated to high art. Then come jewelers, acrobats, florists, and finally Robinson Crusoe and Charlie Chaplin, as the poem explodes into joyous celebration.

These last two names, however, invoke the loneliness intrinsic to the human condition. The sublime vision of the wedding feast dissolves into something "fantastic and pitiful," as hopes and wishes yield to the "fear" that closes four of the stanza's eight lines. Even as he pledges to live with and care for his bride, the poet alludes to the heavy burden of his own mortality and of hers, which he must henceforth bear on his back. Moreover, the poet's unstable personality poses a threat to the marriage "because my circus self/ Divides its love a million times." Only a God conceived in the gathering darkness of the poet's fears can give the bride the understanding of the husband he wishes to be. The ending is ambiguous. Is the poet making a last desperate plea for the human understanding which will make life with another possible? Or, is he eschewing the lesson of Freud and Marx in embracing a final self-deception, one not so cruel as necessary for the survival of his marriage? The magic of the Spenserian moment is, in either case, long gone.

"THE HEAVY BEAR WHO GOES WITH ME"

Burdened with his past in "The Ballad of the Children of the Czar," with his affections in "Prothalamion," Schwartz is finally burdened with his very body in "The Heavy Bear Who Goes with Me." One of his finest and most anthologized pieces, this poem employs a beast fable to examine traditional philosophical dichotomies. Concerning the relationship between mind and body, "The Heavy Bear Who Goes with Me" immediately establishes its context by its epigraph—"The withness of the body"—originally attributed to the distinguished philosopher, Alfred North Whitehead, one of Schwartz's favorite Harvard professors. The bear—"clumsy," "lumbering," "brutish"—represents the grossness of the human body above which the aspiring spirit cannot ascend. "That inescapable animal" has accompanied the speaker from birth, distorting his gestures, thwarting his better impulses, and reducing his existence to a "scrimmage of appetite." The poem's brilliance results from Schwartz's manipulation of the bear metaphor: its honey-smeared face, its frenzied howling in the night, and its clownish showing-off evoke a primordial force as terrifying as it is grotesque.

"A DOG NAMED EGO, THE SNOWFLAKES AS KISSES"

An equally brilliant companion piece immediately follows "The Heavy Bear Who Goes with Me" in *Summer Knowledge*. "A Dog Named Ego, the Snowflakes as Kisses" again explores the gulf between body and soul by means of an animal metaphor. This time the duality is expressed in Freudian rather than Platonic terms; the dog, unlike the bear, is inseparable from the self. Perhaps it is best to consider the dog as an aspect of the self, as its name suggests. The narrator, the central ego of the poem, is the dog's master, at least in the sense that his walking the dog constitutes the poem's dramatic movement. Still another complication in the man-dog relationship is introduced by the speaker's description of the dog's actions. By observing the dog, he observes himself, and thereby dramatizes the human ego in the act of self-scrutiny.

Accompanying his master one chilly December evening, the dog Ego is distracted by falling snowflakes. While the man placidly accepts "the snowflakes as kisses," the dog, growing more and more excited, tries to swallow the snow, which continues "falling from some place half believed and unknown." The snow's kisses recall Schwartz's most haunting scene: waking to "the bleak winter morning of my 21st birthday, the windowsill shining with its lip of snow," which concludes "In Dreams Begin Responsibilities." In both contexts the snow—pure, beautiful, evanescent—promises a momentary vision of transcendence in its fleeting life between falling and melting.

Accompanied by such a dog, however, the hungering self destroys the object of its quest. Prey to his appetites embodied in the barking dog frantically devouring the snowflakes, the narrator helplessly witnesses the reversal of the master-dog relationship and his consequent enslavement by Ego. The drama of the lost self is played out in the dog's pursuit of the snowflakes, which now signify only illusion and obliteration. As night collapses around him, the speaker's double isolation—from self and heart's desire—is expressed in the repeated ending, "And left me no recourse, far from home."

"A Dog Named Ego, the Snowflakes as Kisses" contains Schwartz's most profound treatment of the self-alienation that results from thwarted aspiration. The poem implies, additionally, that this alienation lies at the root of the social estrangement portrayed in so many of his other poems. Whereas "The Heavy Bear Who Goes with Me" dramatizes

Schwartz's dualism no less forcefully, "A Dog Named Ego, the Snowflakes as Kisses" is a subtler evocation of the interplay between the physical and spiritual. Taken together, the poems constitute Schwartz's most powerful essay on the endlessly fascinating topic of the divided self.

SUMMER KNOWLEDGE

The later poems in *Summer Knowledge* reveal a mellower Schwartz. On the surface, they represent an acceptance of the here and now heralded by an intensified use of light imagery and a new reliance on images drawn from nature. Schwartz describes his newly acquired "summer knowledge" as "supple recognition of the fullness and the fatness and the roundness of ripeness"; it might as easily be recognized as a surrender of the possibility of knowing. This shift from retrospective analysis to intuitive acceptance undermines the dialectical tension that rippled through Schwartz's youthful poems. More and more often his late poetry collapses into prosaic statement as its lines lengthen, its syntax relaxes, and its imagery diffuses. The quintessential poet of urban life and its discontents, Schwartz seems vaguely uncomfortable in his new role as celebrant of nature and its satisfactions. While the later work is more positive in its reconciliation of the self and the world and in its insistence on the primacy of the love equated with "summer knowledge," its forced earnestness and flaccid execution indicate the decline of Schwartz's power.

"SEURAT'S SUNDAY AFTERNOON ALONG THE SEINE"

Among the few later poems that bear comparison with Schwartz's early work, none is finer than "Seurat's Sunday Afternoon Along the Seine." This long poem, consisting of a meticulous description of Seurat's famous pointillist paiting *Un Dimanche d'été à la Grande Jatte* (called *A Sunday Afternoon on the Island of La Grand Jatte* in English), interspersed with narrative commentary, employs dazzling visual imagery to re-create the luminosity of George Seurat's greatest painting. Perhaps Schwartz was drawn to the painting by the intensity of its light, or he may have identified with Seurat, whose finest achievement came at twenty-five, when he hardly suspected—in the words of Schwartz's poem—"that in six years he will no longer be alive!" In any event, the poem's depiction of the communal enjoyment of the crowd recalls the weekend revelry of "Far Rockaway" but with a crucial difference. The radiant images of "Far Rockaway" were ironically conceived to expose carefree enjoyment as illusory escapism; reality was the province of the critically observant "novelist" strolling the boardwalk above the beach. In "Seurat's Sunday Afternoon Along the Seine," the shining sun fixes the Sunday people, "In glowing solidity, changeless, a gift, lifted to immortality." The warm leisure of their holiday has been transmuted by Seurat into the transcendent reality that eluded the narrators of Schwartz's earlier poems. Invoking John Keats—"O happy, happy throng,/ It is forever Sunday, summer, free"—whose urn depicted figures immortalized by the painter's art, Schwartz affirms the primacy of immediate sensory experience. The world evoked on Seurat's canvas is ultimate reality; but does reality consist of life's everyday actions, or the formal expression of those actions in works of enduring art?

"Seurat's Sunday Afternoon Along the Seine" may owe something to Stevens's idea, most poignantly expressed in the similarly titled "Sunday Morning," that the poet must rediscover the earth. He does so by creating a "supreme fiction" that endows life with the value once conferred by religion. Stevens, who ranked with Yeats and Eliot among Schwartz's heroes of modern poetry, treated reality as an extension of the artist's imagination and thereby bridged the gulf between the self and the world. In the penultimate stanza of his poem, Schwartz seems in like manner to have resolved the dualism that provided the imaginative framework for so much of his previous poetry. It only remains for the last stanza of "Seurat's Sunday Afternoon Along the Seine" to reestablish the unity of Schwartz's best work and, in the haunting tragedy of its conclusion, provide a fitting coda to his achievement.

The last stanza begins with a final affirmation of the immutability of art, which defies time and change. Although the nineteenth century has yielded to the twentieth and Seurat's painting has been transplanted to Chicago, his art endures: "All of his flowers shine in monumental stillness fulfilled." Abruptly, Gustave Flaubert's voice cries, "Ils sont dans le vrai," referring to people such as those in Seurat's painting, who have apparently discovered the truth—"The kingdom of heaven on earth on Sunday summer day"—and incidentally confirming the ultimate reality of the visible world. Franz Kafka repeats Flaubert's phrase, but in a voice "forever sad, in despair's sickness," fatally poisoning the poem's context. The everyday pleasures of forebears, marriages, and heirs, he suggests, are unavailable to the likes of Flaubert, Kafka, and, of course, Schwartz. As in "Prothalamion," when the invocation of Crusoe and Chaplin shattered the Spenserian moment, the voices of Flaubert and Kafka confirm Schwartz's eternal alienation. The closing lines of "Seurat's Sunday Afternoon Along the Seine" ironically redefine "summer knowledge" as a devastating epiphany of human defeat.

OTHER MAJOR WORKS

SHORT FICTION: *The World Is a Wedding*, 1948; *Successful Love, and Other Stories*, 1961.

PLAY: *Shenandoah*, pb. 1941.

NONFICTION: *Selected Essays of Delmore Schwartz*, 1970; *Letters of Delmore Schwartz*, 1984; *The Ego Is Always at the Wheel: Bagatelles*, 1986; *Portrait of Delmore: Journals and Notes of Delmore Schwartz, 1939-1959*, 1986.

CHILDREN'S LITERATURE: *"I Am Cherry Alive," the Little Girl Sang*, 1958.

MISCELLANEOUS: *Screeno: Stories and Poems*, 2001.

Bibliography

Atlas, James. *Delmore Schwartz: The Life of an American Poet*. 1977. Reprint. San Diego, Calif.: Harcourt Brace Jovanovich, 2000. A full-length, comprehensive biography that attempts to cut through the poses and personae of Schwartz. Contains enriching details of Schwartz's life and extracts of his poems illustrating his development as a poet.

Bawer, Bruce. *The Middle Generation: The Lives and Poetry of Delmore Schwartz, Randall Jarrell, John Berryman, Robert Lowell*. Hamden, Conn.: Archon Books, 1986. Bawer persuasively argues that these poets "shared an affliction." His particularly useful study, integrating biographical detail with literary analysis, teases out the important thematic threads connecting these late modern writers: rocky childhoods, quests for love and faith, and disillusionment in maturity.

Deutsch, Robert H. *The Poetry of Delmore Schwartz*. Edited by John N. Serio. Potsdam, N.Y.: Wallace Stevens Society Press, 2007. Presents critical analysis of the poetry of Schwartz, from the early to late works.

Ford, Edward. *A Reevaluation of the Works of American Writer Delmore Schwartz, 1913-1966*. Lewiston, N.Y.: Edwin Mellen Press, 2005. While at the time of his death Schwartz had been largely forgotten, later scholars have come to recognize his importance, as in this volume.

Keller, Jim. "Delmore Schwartz's Strange Times." In *Reading the Middle Generation Anew: Culture, Community, and Form in Twentieth-Century American Poetry*, edited by Eric Haralson. Iowa City: University of Iowa Press, 2006. Examines how Schwartz was a poet who wrote during a time of transition and discusses how this affected him. Begins by describing how Schwartz's body lay in the morgue for several days before a relative claimed it.

Kirsch, Adam. *The Wounded Surgeon: Confession and Transformation in Six American Poets—Robert Lowell, Elizabeth Bishop, John Berryman, Randall Jarrell, Delmore Schwartz, and Sylvia Plath*. New York: W. W. Norton, 2005. Chapter on Schwartz describes him as having set the course that Lowell and the other confessional poets would follow by incorporating the personal into his poetry.

McDougall, Richard. *Delmore Schwartz*. New York: Twayne, 1974. Provides an overview of Schwartz's writing career, placing emphasis on the theme of alienation and relating it to Schwartz's status as poet and Jew in modern times.

New, Elisa. "Reconsidering Delmore Schwartz." *Prooftexts: A Journal of Jewish Literary History* 5, no. 3 (September, 1985): 245-262. In this fine essay, New suggests that the Jewish American heroes in Schwartz's stories "map out danger zones of intergenerational paralysis where we languish in the throes of a cultural adolescence that will not let us stop selling ourselves as Americans, hawking our goods, both material and intellectual."

Lawrence S. Friedman

JAROSLAV SEIFERT

Born: Prague, Bohemia, Austro-Hungarian Empire (now Czech Republic); September 23, 1901
Died: Prague, Czechoslovakia (now in Czech Republic); January 10, 1986

PRINCIPAL POETRY
Město v slzách, 1921 (*City of Tears*, 1998)
Samá láska, 1923 (*Only Love*, 1990; revised as *Svatební cesta*, 1938; translated as *Honeymoon Ride*, 1990)
Na vlnách TSF, 1925 (*Over the Waves of TSF*, 1990)
Slavík zpívá špatně, 1926 (*The Nightingale Sings Out of Tune*, 1990; also known as *The Nightingale Sings Badly*, 1998)
Poštovní holub, 1929 (*Carrier Pigeon*, 1998)
Jablko z klína, 1933 (*An Apple from Your Lap*, 1998)
Ruce Venušiny, 1936 (*The Hands of Venus*, 1998)
Zpíváno do rotačky, 1936 (*Songs for the Rotary*, 1998)
Jaro, sbohem, 1937, 1942 (*Good-bye, Spring*, 1998)
Osm dní, 1937
Zhasněte světla, 1938
Vějíř Boženy Němcové, 1939 (*Božena Němcová's Fan*, 1990)
Světlem oděná, 1940 (*Robed in Light*, 1998)
Kamenný most, 1944
Přilba hlíny, 1945 (*A Helmetful of Earth*, 1998)
Prsten Třeboóské Madoně, 1946, 1966
Ruka a plamen, 1948
Píseó o Viktorce, 1950 (*Song About Viktorka*, 1990)
Koncert na ostrově, 1965 (*Concert on the Island*, 1998)
Halleyova kometta, 1967 (*Halley's Comet*, 1987)
Odlévání zvonů, 1967 (*The Casting of the Bells*, 1983)
Nejkrásnější býacute;vá šílená, 1968
Morový sloup, 1977 (*The Plague Column*, 1979; also known as *The Plague Monument*, 1980)
Deštník z Piccadilly, 1979 (*An Umbrella from Piccadilly*, 1983)
Býti Básníkem, 1983 (*To Be a Poet*, 1990)
The Selected Poetry of Jaroslav Seifert, 1986
Dressed in Light, 1990
The Early Poetry of Jaroslav Seifert, 1997

A Sbohem, 1999
The Poetry of Jaroslav Seifert, 1998
Treba vám nesu ruze, 1999
The Vrtba Garden, 2006 (photographs by Lada Panchartkova)

OTHER LITERARY FORMS

For much of his life, Jaroslav Seifert (ZI-furt) worked as a journalist, and he wrote countless newspaper articles. During the decade after World War II, Seifert was under attack, vilified by the adherents of Socialist Realism, and withdrew from public life. His publications were limited to editing the works of various Czech authors, to translating—his translation of the biblical Song of Songs is outstanding—and to writing poetry for children.

Seifert's memoirs, *Všecky krásy světa* (1981; *Autobiography*, 1985), were first published in Czech in Toronto; a parallel edition under the same title, with minor deletions and alterations, was published shortly afterward in Prague. Seifert also produced children's literature in *Maminka: Yybor básni* (1954; *Maminka*, 1991).

ACHIEVEMENTS

The critic René Wellek once observed, "Lyrical poetry was always the center of Czech literature." One reason for this is that poets have probably expressed the concerns and aspirations of the Czech people better than writers in other genres. Jaroslav Seifert was the author of nearly thirty volumes of poetry, and he won the Nobel Prize in Literature for 1984. He was a member of one of the most remarkable groups of poets in the history of Czech literature, along with Vítězlav Nezval, Konstantin Biebl, František Halas, and Vladimír Holan. They were all born around the turn of the century, began to write when Czechoslovakia gained its independence after World War I, and took part in the numerous literary movements that flourished during the next two decades. They also lived through World War II, which their work records in depth, as well as the imposition of communism on Czechoslovakia. Seifert survived the period of Stalinism, participating in the Prague Spring of 1968. He was honored by the government in 1966 and was named a National Artist; he served as acting chairman of the Union of Czechoslovak writers in 1968; and he was its chairman in 1969-1970. In addition, he received state prizes for his verse in 1936, 1955, and 1968. Holan, Halas, Biebl, and Nezval all died before Seifert; he was the last surviving member of this extremely talented group of poets, dying at the age of eighty-four.

Seifert was remarkably popular in Czechoslovakia, both as a poet and as a symbol of freedom of expression for writers under an oppressive regime. In 1968, he condemned the Soviet invasion of his country and was one of the original signers of the Charter 77 Civil Rights movement.

Biography

Jaroslav Seifert was born in 1901 in Prague, in a working-class neighborhood called Žižkov. Throughout his life, Seifert liked to recall his childhood in this part of Prague with its strong proletarian flavor, many tenements, railroad tracks, taverns, and its own dialect. Seifert's mother was Catholic, his father an atheist and socialist. Although his parents were poor, Seifert was able to attend a *gymnasium* (academic secondary school), from which, however, he was not graduated; he left the *gymnasium* early and started working as a journalist.

Seifert wrote his first poems during World War I, when the future Czechoslovakia was still a province of the Austro-Hungarian Empire. Czechoslovakia became independent in October, 1918; Seifert was associated with the left wing of the Social Democratic Party and became one of the first members of the Communist Party when it was organized in 1921. Although "workers' poetry" was fashionable at the time, Seifert was one of the few practitioners who actually came from a working-class background.

The evolution of Seifert's poetry in the 1920's and 1930's is almost identical to the general evolution of Czech poetry during the period, proceeding from one major movement to the next. Seifert's friends, especially Karel Teige and Stanislav Neumann, weaned him from his earlier "proletarian poetry" and brought him closer to avant-garde artistic circles. Seifert joined them in founding a group called Devětsil; the name comes from a medicinal herb and flower that means, literally, "nine strengths." The group was inspired both by the Russian Revolution and by the heady atmosphere of freedom and national independence at the end of World War I. Its aim was nothing short of the rebuilding of the world.

Seifert also took part in the important Poetism movement that left its imprint on almost all the arts in Czechoslovakia after 1924. Poetism was influenced both by Franco-Swiss Dadaism and by Surrealism. It was an avant-garde movement oriented toward the future, considering all aspects of life as art forms—in the future, art would become life, and life would become art. For the Poetists, poetry became an imaginative game of chance associations of ideas, images, and words, often illogical and paradoxical. Sound effects were strongly emphasized in poetry, as well as fresh, startling rhymes; logical connections were loosened. The subject matter of poetry was broadened to include areas previously considered to be nonpoetic, such as science, technology, and exotic information. The poets drew on all the arts for their inspiration: film, music, the ballet, pantomime, the circus, and the music hall. The movement represented a sharp break with proletarian poetry. In morality, the poets tended to be skeptical; they were indulgent in sensual aspects of life and art, and often generalized their enthusiasms. They are sometimes accused of artistic insincerity, but they performed the great service of expanding the frontiers and technical devices of poetry.

In the early 1920's, Seifert wrote for a variety of newspapers and reviews. He was a reporter for a Communist newspaper in Prague, then in Brno, the Moravian capital;

Jaroslav Seifert
(©The Nobel Foundation)

later, he worked for a Communist bookstore and publishing house in Prague and edited a Communist illustrated magazine. During this time, Seifert also traveled; he went to northern Italy and France. He also went to the Soviet Union in 1925 and 1928.

By 1929, Seifert believed that the closely knit circle of Devětsil had outlived its purpose, and he became disenchanted with the new leadership of the Communist Party. With eight other Czech Communist writers, he signed a letter protesting the new party line and cultural program. He was expelled from Devětsil and the Communist Party, which he never rejoined.

The 1930's saw a great shift of taste in Czech literature. The previous decade had sought liberation from tradition in theme, form, and style. The pendulum began to swing back, and there was a decline in free verse and a return to punctuation in poetry. Formerly avant-garde writers began to use classical forms such as the sonnet and ron-del. Seifert, too, used regular, compact, stanzaic verse forms during the 1930's, with ingenious rhymes and frequent refrains. He showed an unsuspected gift for pure lyrical poetry, especially the poetry of love, with a new sense of spiritual or moral values. It was during this beleaguered decade that Seifert found and developed the two major themes that were to mark his poetic output and were to become the basis of his reputation: the theme of love for women and his stance as a national poet. He wrote his cycle of elegies on T. G. Masaryk, *Osm dní* (eight days), in 1937. Masaryk, the president-liberator, symbolized the independence of Czechoslovakia, and his somber funeral was an occasion for both nationalistic pomp and an outburst of lyric verse. Seifert's volume was reprinted six times before it satisfied popular demand. Seifert's next collections turned to children's poetry and the writer Božena Němcová; during World War II, Seifert published three collections, and most of the poems were about Prague, which comes to symbolize the continuity of Czech history. *Přilba hlíny* (helmet of clay) celebrates the May, 1945, uprising in Prague and the subsequent liberation of the city.

After the liberation, Seifert again became active in journalism, but he was attacked by the new Communist regime; in an article titled "Not Our Voice," one minor critic accused him of being alien, bourgeois, and even anti-Communist. Seifert was forced to withdraw from public life. It was only after 1954, following the death of Joseph Stalin, that he was able to publish selections from his past works and some new poetry. In 1956, he spoke from the platform at the Second Congress of the Union of Czechoslovak writers, advocating that writers express ethical conscience, civic consciousness, and public commitment—in his words, "May we be truly the conscience of our people."

After a decade of serious illness, Seifert emerged with a surprising new poetic manner. In *Koncert na ostrově* (concert on the island), he gave up much of his songlike intonation, rhyme, and metaphor for the sake of simpler, declarative free verse. It was during the Prague Spring, the time of maximum liberalization, when Alexander Dubček became leader of the Czech Communist Party, that Seifert was named a National Artist of Czechoslovakia. In August, 1968, after the invasion of the country by the Soviet Union, Seifert rose from his sickbed, called a taxi, and went to the building of the Union of Writers. Those present elected him acting chairman of the independent Union of Writers. A year later, the union was dissolved. Isolated and sick, Seifert continued to write; his poems were typed and distributed in copies by individual readers. He lived in a suburb of Prague, Břevnov, helping anyone who called on him and writing reminiscences of his long life as a poet. Between 1968 and 1975, only sections from his old works were published in Czechoslovakia, but some new poems were published in Czech in periodicals abroad. He became an original signer of Charter 77. Illness required him to be frequently hospitalized; in 1984, he received the Nobel Prize in his hospital bed, where television crews and reporters descended on him, asking for interviews. His son-in-law and secretary, Daribor Plichta, was to go to Stockholm to receive the Nobel Prize on behalf of the ailing Seifert, but the Czechoslovak government refused to give Plichta an exit permit. In 1985, Seifert was well enough to leave the hospital and return home, where he continued to write poetry. He died a year later.

ANALYSIS

Jaroslav Seifert's life and poetry are closely interwoven, and it is a mistake to separate them. He took part in all the major poetic movements of his long life. During some of these phases, it is possible to say that he was surpassed by a friend and colleague. Perhaps Neumann wrote superior poems of political commitment during the 1920's, and in the 1930's perhaps Josef Hora expressed the sense of attachment to the native land better than anyone else in his monumental poem "Zpěv rodné zemi" ("Song of the Native Land"). Indignation at the violent excesses of Communism was the most powerfully rendered in Halas's superb "Potopa" ("The Deluge"). Holan's output of meditative lyrics, published during the decade after World War II, was especially impressive. However, it is futile to contrast Seifert to these poets as if they were competitors: They were often remarkably close and engaged in similar endeavors, and Seifert wrote poems addressed to most of these poets. Seifert's own poems are consistently interesting, of remarkably high quality, and unique.

Seifert's main themes were the love of woman and the celebration of what is most positive in life. His finest collections were probably written after World War II, when these themes were increasingly associated with his defense of the individual conscience. Before the war, in the words of Arne Novák, Seifert was "a poet readily inspired by contemporary events and an unusually fluent improviser; he was a master of intimate, emotional, and highly musical verse." It should be added that he was able to express the feelings and aspirations of a remarkably broad audience. After the war, unable to publish regularly, he was to increase the depth and resonance of his poems until the end of his life.

LOVE AS PROTEST

In Western European countries and the United States , there has been some confusion about Seifert's emphasis on women, on the sensual love for them and their beauty, which he consistently expressed in his poems from 1930 onward. Sensuality, sexuality, love: These are often thought to be asocial, purely private concerns. In Eastern Europe, however, they assume a much greater importance. They are central to that domain where the individual man or woman still has freedom, where the state is unable to intrude, and where a human being is able to wrest a small, habitable space from a hostile environment. There a person is able to express love, intimacy, and his or her most positive values. Love becomes a form of protest and of personal commitment, even of heroism. Seifert was able to express this theme in language that is not abstract but very concrete and specific, not moralistic or sanctimonious but frequently erotic. This is the unique synthesis of Seifert: The poems appear to be about specific experiences, but at the same time they are always more than this. He could define heaven and hell in these concrete terms, from "Jen jednou" ("Once Only"):

> Hell we all know, it's everywhere
> and walks upon two legs.
> 	But paradise?
> It may be that paradise is only
> a smile
> 	we have long waited for,
> and lips
> 	whispering our name.
> And then that brief vertiginous moment
> when we're allowed to forget
> that hell exists.

Although many of Seifert's poems about women may appear at first glance to be simply erotic, about his desire for an individual woman, he almost always manages to raise that desire to a higher degree of generality, simultaneously maintaining the utmost concreteness and specificity. He writes in his poem, titled "Vlastní životopis" ("Autobiography"), "But when I first saw/ the picture of a nude woman/ I began to believe in miracles." This notion of a "miracle" stayed with him as a measure of what was most positive, of the highest value. Toward the close of his life, in "Merry-Go-Round with White Swan," he wrote:

> Goodbye. In all my life I never committed
> any betrayal.
> That I am aware of,
> and you may believe me.
>
> But the most beautiful of all gods
> is love.

The notion of a principle, and fidelity to it, might be easily missed. The strength of Seifert's notion of love is that it is both a positive moral concept and concretely erotic (entirely un-Calvinistic) at the same time.

A skeptical reader might ask, Is this love singular or plural? Does Seifert write of one woman, or several, or many? Or all women? Seifert moves from the singular to the plural with great ease, and the answer is that love is both singular and plural, one woman and many, concrete and universal. In addition, the concept is expanded in Seifert's many poems about Prague, which becomes "her," a distinctly feminine presence.

LOVE DEFINED BY ITS OPPOSITE

The notion of love is often defined in terms of its opposite:

> Those who have left
> and hastily scattered to distant lands
> must realize it by now:
> The world is horrible!
>
> They don't love anyone and no one loves them.
> We at least love.
>
> So let her knees crush my head!

A passage such as this one might be misread by a Western reader, who lives in a democracy and assumes a sharp dividing line between private life and society; this dichotomy is upheld by democratic laws, rights, and institutions. In a totalitarian society, however, the division is abolished. The individual must create his freedom and positive values by his own efforts on a daily basis.

In another passage, love is again defined in terms of its opposite. Here it is opposed to war, presumably World War II; once again the love is not escapist, but raised to a higher level of generalization and affirmation:

> The many rondels and the songs I wrote!
> There was a war all over the world,
> and all over the world
> was grief.
> And yet I whispered into bejewelled ears
> verses of love.
> It makes me feel ashamed.
> But no, not really.

Although such a passage might seem, on a superficial level, to mock feats of armed resistance, it should be read carefully. The love here is raised to a principle, it is almost a weapon used against war. Seifert is modest and shies away from large claims or abstract words; usually he seems whimsical, his agile verse leaps from image to image, but the reader should not be fooled by the self-demeaning manner. The jeweled earrings belong not only to a soft, attractive body (here unseen, carefully removed from the picture) but also to an object of intense devotion, menaced by the war but momentarily beyond its reach.

THE CASTING OF THE BELLS

Love is also defined and contrasted to another opposite—death. Especially in *The Casting of the Bells*, Seifert looks forward to his own death, which serves as a foil for his theme of love. In "Dvořákovo requiem" ("A Requiem for Dvořák"), he describes a place on the Vltava River where two lovers killed themselves by drowning. Most of the poem describes the efforts to drag for the couple with hooked poles and the reactions of the men as they finally see the naked body of the girl. In the hands of another poet, this might easily degenerate into an exercise in necrophilia or voyeurism. However, Seifert maintains—surely, deliberately—the contrast between death and the beauty of life throughout:

> The men in the boat called to the shore:
> "Drag it out, boys!"
> Well, you know, there were many of them.
> As if stuck to the ground in iced terror,
> not one of them moved.

The ending of the poem occurs not with the conclusion of this scene but the next day, "a peaceful, normal day" when "The grass-pillows smelled hot/ and invited lovers again/ to the old game." The entire volume of *The Casting of the Bells* is a sustained meditation on imminent death and on life. The notion of the "casting" of a bell is a metaphor for the body, which is "cast" or formed by sexual desire. Paradoxically, some poems in the volume are among Seifert's most positive.

"THE BLOW"

Seifert creates a similar structure of contrasts in his cycle of poems on the bombing of the town of Kralupy during World War II. He was forced to take cover in a cemetery, behind a low grave in "Uder" ("The Blow"). When the dead girl buried there "gave me her hand," Seifert "held" it and was able to resist the explosions coming from the town nearby. The gesture became an affirmation of life, and of Seifert's strong ties to what is most positive in life: Even the dead, through the feeling of love they once felt—human, sexual, and erotic—are able to participate in these ties.

THE PLAGUE COLUMN

Seifert most explicitly contrasts love to totalitarian politics in *The Plague Column*. As in Albert Camus's novel *La Peste* (1947; *The Plague*, 1948), Seifert's concept of a plague is allegorical and refers to contemporary history. The plague goes on and on:

> Don't let them dupe you
> that the plague has come to an end:
> I've seen too many coffins hauled past.
>
> The plague still rages and it seems the doctors
> are giving different names to the disease
> to avoid panic.

The "plague" is the communism of the 1970's; it is also a grisly time of burning corpses and "cynical drinking songs." Like the young Seifert, the older poet again has an oppositional politics "in the name of love," though his politics is now anticommunist rather than procommunist. Love is given its maximal meaning not only as a foil to death, and to war, but also to the rampant "plague" of political terror.

LATE POEMS

This theme of love also has its special style. It closely resembles the alert and highly agile style that Seifert developed in his last three volumes. It is flexible and allusive, moves in unexpected directions, and is always surprising. Seifert is an extremely subtle poet. The translations of his work vary widely in quality; different translations of the same passage in Czech can give rise to totally different interpretations—what might seem whimsy to one reader may appear to be sharp irony to another, and the American or English reader relying on translations of Seifert should beware. The unique style of Seifert's last volumes is characterized above all by intimacy, also by freedom and sensuality. He harks back to his style during the period of Poetism, with its Surrealist and Dadaist overtones, but it has more depth and follows the contours of thought, the rhythms of intimate impulse and feeling, with far greater closeness and fidelity. As Seifert told a French interviewer near the end of his life:

> As one grows older, one discovers different values and different worlds. For me, this meant that I discovered sensuality.... All language can be thought of as an effort to achieve freedom, to feel the joy and the sensuality of freedom. What we seek in language is the freedom to be able to express one's most intimate thoughts. This is the basis of all freedom.

Style, too, can be a function of a principle of love, of those most positive values that Seifert opposes to political repression. Professor Eduard Goldstücker, chairman of the Czech Writers Union in 1968 and subsequently exiled, emphasized Seifert's consistent role as a poet of resistance when he wrote in 1985: "Seifert's poems were always in the front line of resistance. In those dark years [of occupation by the Germans] he became the poet of his people, and he has remained so until this day."

OTHER MAJOR WORKS

NONFICTION: *Hvězdy nad rajskou zahradou*, 1929; *Všecky krásy světa*, 1981 (*Autobiography*, 1985).

CHILDREN'S LITERATURE: *Maminka: Ybor básni*, 1954 (*Maminka*, 1991).

MISCELLANEOUS: *Dílo*, 1953-1970 (collected works).

BIBLIOGRAPHY

French, Alfred. *The Poets of Prague: Czech Poetry Between the Wars*. New York: Oxford University Press, 1969. Provides the larger context for Seifert's work in its formative phase, including poems by all the major poets of his generation in translation and the original Czech for comparison.

Gibian, George. Introduction to *The Poetry of Jaroslav Seifert*. North Haven, Conn.: Catbird Press, 1998. A brief biography that focuses primarily on Seifert's literary activities and explores his literary ancestry and evolution as a poet. In a country in which poetry is highly regarded, Seifert achieved the status of a national poet who was widely respected and loved.

_____. "The Lyrical Voice of Czechoslovakia." In *The Selected Poetry of Jaroslav Seifert*. New York: Macmillan, 1986. Concise, insightful essay on Seifert's life and work by the dedicated editor who created one of the best anthologies of Seifert in English. Includes vivid description of Gibian's face-to-face meetings with Seifert in Prague. Seifert's poetry translated by Ewald Osers, prose by Gibian.

Iggers, Wilma A. "The World of Jaroslav Seifert." *World Literature Today* 60 (Spring, 1985): 8-12. Scholarly interpretation of Seifert's career, filling in some of Seifert's lesser-known literary associations.

Loewy, Dana. Introduction to *The Early Poetry of Jaroslav Seifert*. Translated by Dana Loewy. 1997. Reprint. Evanston, Ill.: Northwestern University Press, 1999. In his introduction, Loewy disavows claims by Seifert critics that his early work is untranslatable. Although some aspects of his poetry will be lost, his "musicality, playfulness, and lyricism can be imitated in English with the help of internal rhymes, half-rhymes, and assonance."

Parrott, Sir Cecil. Introduction to *The Plague Column*, by Jaroslav Seifert. Translated by Ewald Osers. London: Terra Nova Editions, 1979. Appreciative essay on Seifert's career, by a journalist who was an eyewitness to much of it, with particular awareness of the political subtleties.

Sternstein, Malynne M. *The Will to Chance: Necessity and Arbitrariness in the Czech Avant-garde from Poetism to Surrealism*. Bloomington, Ind.: Slavica, 2007. Provides the context in which Seifert's poetry developed as well as his place in it.

John Carpenter

GERTRUDE STEIN

Born: Allegheny (now in Pittsburgh), Pennsylvania; February 3, 1874
Died: Neuilly-sur-Seine, France; July 27, 1946

PRINCIPAL POETRY
Tender Buttons: Objects, Food, Rooms, 1914
Before the Flowers of Friendship Faded Friendship Faded, 1931
Two (Hitherto Unpublished) Poems, 1948
Bee Time Vine, and Other Pieces, 1913-1927, 1953
Stanzas in Meditation, and Other Poems, 1929-1933, 1956

OTHER LITERARY FORMS

Most of Gertrude Stein's works did not appear until much later than the dates of their completion. Much of her writing, including novelettes, shorter poems, plays, prayers, novels, and several portraits, appeared posthumously in the Yale Edition of the Unpublished Writings of Gertrude Stein, in eight volumes edited by Carl Van Vechten. A few of her plays have been set to music, the operas have been performed, and the later children's books have been illustrated by various artists.

ACHIEVEMENTS

Gertrude Stein did not win tangible recognition for her literary achievements, though she did earn the Medal of French Recognition from the French government for services during World War II. Nevertheless, her contribution to art, and specifically to writing, is as great as that of Ezra Pound or James Joyce. It is, however, diametrically opposed to that of these figures in style, content, and underlying philosophy of literature. She advanced mimetic representation to its ultimate, doing away progressively with memory, narration, plot, the strictures of formalized language, and the distinction among styles and genres. Her view of life was founded on a sense of the living present that shunned all theorizing about meaning and purpose, making writing a supreme experience unto itself. For the first fifteen years of her artistic life, she worked at her craft with stubborn persistence while carrying on an active social life among the Parisian avant-garde. She became influential as a person of definite taste and idiosyncratic manners rather than as an artist in her own right. Her parlor became legend, and writers as diverse as Ernest Hemingway and Sherwood Anderson profited from her ideas. In the 1920's, she was the matron of the American expatriates, and her work, by then known to most writers, was either ferociously derided or enthusiastically applauded.

It was the poetry of *Tender Buttons* that first brought Gertrude Stein to the attention of the public. After 1926, however, her novels, critical essays, and prose portraits in-

Gertrude Stein
(Library of Congress)

creasingly circulated. She secured a place in American letters with the publication of *The Autobiography of Alice B. Toklas* (1933), which was also a commercial success. She did not receive any official recognition during her lifetime, except as a curiosity in the world of letters.

Literary criticism has traditionally simply skirted the "problem" of Gertrude Stein, limiting itself to broad generalizations. There exists a group of Stein devotees responsible for preserving the texts; this group includes Robert Bartlett Haas, Carl Van Vechten, Donald Gallup, and Leon Katz. Stein's work has been illuminated by two indispensable scholar-critics, Richard Bridgman and Donald Sutherland; and there are useful interpretive suggestions in studies by Rosalind Miller, Allegra Stewart, Norman Weinstein, and Michael J. Hoffman. Stein's major impact has been on writers of later generations, especially in the late 1950's, through the 1960's, and up to the present time; the poetry of Aram Saroyan, Robert Kelly, Clark Coolidge, Jerome Rothenberg, and Lewis Welch is especially indebted to Stein. New insights into this revolutionary writer in the wake of global revisions of the notion of writing and critical thinking have been offered in short pieces by S. C. Neuman, William H. Gass, and Neil Schmitz. Today, a place of eminence is accorded to Stein's fairy tales and children's stories, the theoretical writings, the major works *The Autobiography of Alice B. Toklas* and *The Making of Ameri-*

cans: *Being a History of a Family's Progress* (1925, 1934), the shorter works *Three Lives* (1909) and *Ida, a Novel* (1941), and finally *Tender Buttons*, considered by many to be a masterpiece of twentieth century literature.

BIOGRAPHY

Gertrude Stein was born in Allegheny, Pennsylvania, on February 3, 1874. Her grandfather, Michael Stein, came from Austria in 1841, married Hanna Seliger, and settled in Baltimore. One of his sons, Daniel, Gertrude's father, was in the wholesale wool and clothing industry. Daniel was mildly successful and very temperamental. He married Amelia Keyser in 1864 and had five children, Michael (born in 1865), Simon (1867), Bertha (1870), Leo (1872), and Gertrude (1874). In 1875, the family moved to Vienna, and three years later, Daniel returned to the United States, leaving his family for a one-year stay in Paris. In 1879, the family moved back to the United States and spent a year in Baltimore with Amelia Keyser's family. In 1880, Daniel found work in California, and the family relocated again, to Oakland. Memories of these early moves would dot Gertrude's mature works. Leo and Gertrude found that they had much in common, took drawing and music lessons together, frequented the Oakland and San Francisco public libraries, and had time to devote to their intellectual and aesthetic interests. When their mother died of cancer in 1888, Leo and Gertrude found themselves more and more detached from the rest of the family. In 1892, Daniel Stein died, and the eldest son, Michael, took the family back to Baltimore, but the Steins began to scatter. In 1892, Leo entered Harvard, while Gertrude and Bertha stayed with their aunt, Fannie Bachrach. Michael, always patriarchal and the image of stability, married Sarah Samuels and later moved to Paris, where he became a respected member of the intellectual elite, maintaining a Saturday night open house at their apartment in rue Madame. Matisse's portrait of Michael is now in San Francisco.

Gertrude was a coddled and protected child. At sixteen, she weighed 135 pounds, and later in college she hired a boy to box with her every day to help her lose weight. Her niece, Gertrude Stein Raffel, recalls that her heaviness "was not unbecoming. She was round, roly-poly, and angelic looking." During her adolescent years, she became very introspective and critical, and was often depressed and concerned with death. Already emotionally independent, owing to her mother's protracted invalidism and her father's neglect and false representation of authority, Gertrude saw in her brother Leo her only friend. Their bond would not be broken for another twenty years, and she would follow him everywhere, the two delving into matters of mutual interest.

In 1893, Gertrude Stein entered the Harvard Annex, renamed Radcliffe College the following year. She gravitated toward philosophy and psychology, and took courses with such luminaries as George Santayana, Josiah Royce, Herbert Palmer, and William James. In 1894, she worked in the Harvard Psychological Laboratory with Hugo Münsterberg. Her interest in psychology expanded, and in 1896, she published, together with Leon Solomons, a paper on "Normal Motor Automatism," which appeared in the *Psychological Review*. A second article, "Cultivated Motor Automatism," appeared two years later. In 1897, Stein followed her brother to The Johns Hopkins University and began the study of medicine. She specialized in brain research and was encouraged to continue, even though by 1901 her dedication had waned. She attempted four examinations, failed them, and withdrew without a degree.

In 1902, Stein began her travels, first to Italy and then to London, where she met philosopher Bertrand Russell. She spent much time in the British Museum Library studying the Elizabethans, especially William Shakespeare. In the meantime, Leo also abandoned his studies, reverting to an earlier passion for history. A specialist in Renaissance costume, he was drawn to contemporary art, and when, in 1904, he and his sister saw a Paul Cézanne exhibit in Florence, they started buying paintings; Leo would became a major collector of Henri Matisse. The two settled in the now-famous apartment at 27 rue de Fleurus, where Gertrude's literary career began, though her first sustained effort, *Q.E.D.*, written in 1903, remained unpublished until 1950 (as *Things as They Are*). In 1905, while working on a translation of Gustave Flaubert's *Trois contes*, she wrote *Three Lives*. During that period, she met Pablo Picasso, who would be very influential in her thinking about art and with whom she would remain friends for decades. The following year, he painted the famous portrait now at the Metropolitan Museum. These days of intense work and thinking saw Stein fast at work on her first major long novel, *The Making of Americans*, which she completed in 1910.

Gertrude's trips abroad and throughout France from her home base in Paris became an essential part of her existence. In 1907, her brother Michael introduced her to Alice B. Toklas, who soon became her secretary, going to work on the proofs of *Three Lives*. Toklas learned to use a typewriter, and the following year, in Fiesole, Italy, she began to copy parts of the manuscript of *The Making of Americans*. Leo, intellectually independent, was moving toward his own aesthetic, though he was still busy promoting new American and French talents. As a painter, Leo was not successful, and he came eventually to dislike all contemporary painters except the cubists. In 1913, he moved from the rue de Fleurus apartment, and with him went all the Renoirs and most of the Matisses and Cézannes, while Gertrude kept the Picassos. Leo's place had been taken by Toklas, who stayed with Gertrude until her death in 1946.

The writer first began to be noticed as a result of Alfred Stieglitz's publication of her "portraits" of Matisse and Picasso in *Camera Work* in 1912. She spent the summer of that year in Spain, capturing the sense of her idea of the relationship between object and space, with which she had been struggling. Here she began the prose poem *Tender Buttons*, which brought her to the attention of most of her contemporaries, eliciting varying reactions. She continued to write "portraits" while visiting Mabel Dodge in Florence, at the Villa Curonia. At the Armory Show in New York in 1913, Stein was responsible for the presentation of the Pablo Picasso exhibit. When the war broke out, she was in London, where she met the philosopher Alfred North Whitehead. She continued to work intensely, mostly on poetry and plays, and visited Barcelona and Palma de Majorca. In 1916, Stein and Toklas returned to France and the next year did voluntary war relief work in the south. In 1922, Stein was awarded a Medaille de la Reconnaissance Française.

With the appearance of her first collected volume, *Geography and Plays*, in 1922, Stein's fame among the cognoscenti was assured, together with a lively controversy over her truly original style. She was invariably visited by the younger expatriate artists from the United States, and her parlor became a focal point for the exchange of ideas. Sherwood Anderson introduced her to Hemingway in 1922, and the younger writer learned much from her about the craft of writing. Hemingway was influential in securing publication of parts of *The Making of Americans* in Ford Madox Ford's magazine, *Transatlantic Review*. (The nine-hundred-page work was later abridged to half its size by her translator into French, and the shorter version was published in 1925 by Contact Editions, Paris.) Her relationship with Hemingway, however, because of conflicting temperaments, was short-lived; their friendship soon degenerated into bickering.

Stein entered another phase of her life when she was asked to lecture in Oxford and Cambridge in 1926. The text of the conference, "Composition as Explanation," constituted her first critical statement on the art of writing; she subsequently returned to a personal exposition of her ideas in *How to Write* (1931), breaking new ground at the stylistic level. This period of major intellectual and thematic upheaval witnessed several transformations in her art. She began to devote more time to the theater and eventually tackled the difficult task of writing about ideas in the little known *Stanzas in Meditation, and Other Poems, 1929-1933* (not published until 1956). In 1929, she left Paris and moved to Bilignin. Her *Lucy Church Amiably* (1930) had not pleased her, but *Four Saints in Three Acts* (pr., pb. 1934), with music by Virgil Thomson, was successfully produced in New York. After publication of the well-received *The Autobiography of Alice B. Toklas* in 1933, she traveled to the United States for a lecture tour. Her *Lectures in America* (1935) dealt with her philosophy of composition.

Compelled to close her apartment at rue de Fleurus shortly after her return to France, Stein moved with Toklas to rue Christine; with the onset of the war in 1939, however, they returned to Bilignin. During the war, the two women lived for a time in Culoz, where they first witnessed the German occupation and then the arrival of the Americans, which would be recounted in *Wars I Have Seen* (1945). In December, 1944, she returned to Paris, only to leave soon afterward to entertain U.S. troops stationed in occupied Germany. Her views on the U.S. soldier and the society that produced him changed considerably during these two years. In October, 1945, she traveled to Brussels to lecture. Weary and tired, she decided to visit her friend Bernard Fay in the country. Her trip was abruptly interrupted by her illness, and she entered the American Hospital in Neuilly-sur-Seine, where, after an unsuccessful cancer operation, she died on July 27, 1946.

ANALYSIS

It is customary to refer to Gertrude Stein's poetry—and her work in general—with the qualifiers "abstract," "repetitive," and "nonsensical," terms that do little if any justice to a most remarkable literary achievement. The proper evaluation of Stein's work requires a willingness to rethink certain basic notions concerning art, discourse, and life, a task that is perhaps as difficult as the reading of Stein's voluminous production itself. Her work, however, is really not excessively abstract, especially when one considers that her poetic rests on the fundamental axiom of "immediate existing." Nothing could be more concrete than that. Whatever she may be describing, each unit is sure to be a complete, separate assertion, a reality immediately given—in the present, the only time there is.

Repetition is insistence: A rose is a rose is a rose is a rose. Each time it is new, different, unique, because the experience of the word is unique each time it is uttered. Stylistically, this entails the predominance of parataxis and asyndeton, words being "so nextily" in their unfolding. Repetition of the same is often supplanted by repetition of the different, where the juxtaposition is in kind and quality. An example of the latter is the following passage from *A Long Gay Book* (1932):

> All the pudding has the same flow and the sauce is painful, the tunes are played, the crinkling paper is burning, the pot has cover and the standard is excellence.

Whether operating at the syntagmatic or at the paradigmatic level, as above, the repetition serves the purpose of emphasizing and isolating a thing, not simply anything. The break with all previous associations forces one to consider this pudding and this sauce, allowing a concretization of the experience in this particular frame of the present. If the content appears to have no "logical" coherence, it is because it is not meant to, since the experience of the immediate does not warrant ratiocination or understanding of any sort. Art in Stein is perception of the immediate, a capturing of the instantaneity of the word as event, sense, or object. The notion is clearly nonreferential in that art does not need a world to know that it exists. Although it occasionally refers to it, it does not have to—in fact, the less it does, the better. What is of paramount importance is that this self-contained entity comes alive in the continuous present of one's experience of it, and only then. The influence of Stein's painter friends was unequivocal. Not all discourse that links the work of art to history and other realms of life is, properly speaking, a preoccupation of the artist: It does not constitute an aesthetic experience, remaining just that—criticism, sociology, and philosophy. Meaning is something that comes after the experience, thanks to reflection, the mediation of reason, and the standardization of logic and grammar; it is never given in the immediacy of the poetic expression. Stein's writings attempt to produce the feeling of something happening or being lived—in short, to give things (objects, emotions, ideas, words) a sense that is new and unique and momentary, independent and defiant of what an afterthought may claim to be the "true" meaning or sense of an experience or artistic event. From this perspective, can it still be honestly said that Stein's work is "nonsense," with all the negative implications usually associated with the epithet?

THINGS AS THEY ARE

Stein had from very early in her career a keen sense of the distance that naturally exists between objects and feelings as perceived, and their transposition into conventional formalized speech. Her first novel, *Q.E.D.* (for the Latin *quod erat demonstrandum*, meaning "which was to be proved"), written in 1903 and known after 1950 as *Things as They Are*, dealt with the then taboo topic of lesbianism in a ménage à trois of three women. However, the work is already shorn of such typical narrative features as symbolism, character development, climax, and descriptions of setting, though it is cast in an intelligible variation of standard prose. At the limits of the (Henry) Jamesian novel, what happens among the characters and the space of emotional relatedness is more important than the characters as characters. The focal point is the introspection of these human natures, and all elaborations and complications of feelings remain internal, intimate, within the consciousness of the individual being described or, most often, within the dialectic of the relationship. Doing away with all contingent background material meant zooming in on the poetic process itself; but for all practical purposes the author is still struggling within the precincts of the most sophisticated naturalism: She is still representing, in the tradition of Henry James and Gustave Flaubert, two authors whom she admired greatly. The characters are at odds with the author: They are white American college women constantly preoccupied with the propriety of their relationship and therefore demand of the author a polite, cultivated, and literary realization.

THREE LIVES

The problem of the language to employ in writing is dealt with in the next work, *Three Lives*, where the progressive abandonment of inherited expressive forms is much stronger and can be said to constitute a first milestone in Gertrude Stein's stylistic development, especially in "Melanchta," the last of the three stories. Here Stein describes a love story set among lower-class blacks, where she can explore the intensity of "uneducated" speech and where, as Donald Sutherland quite aptly points out, there exists "a direct relationship between feeling and word." Typical of her entire literary career, at the time of publication the printer inquired whether the author really knew English. In *Three Lives*, Stein was "groping for a continuous present and for using everything again and again." This continuous present is immediate and partakes of the human mind as it exists at any given moment when confronted with the object of writing. It is different from the prolonged present of duration, as in Henri Bergson, where aspects of human nature may enter. At the stylistic level, punctuation is rare and the present participle is employed as a substantive for its value in retaining the sense of process, of continuity in a present mode that knows no before and no after. This "subjective time" of writing is paralleled by similar developments in the visual and plastic arts, from which Stein drew copiously. Her admiration and appreciation of what Cézanne had done for painting was matched by the unrelenting support that she bestowed on the upcoming younger generation of artists, such as Picasso, Matisse, Juan Gris, and Francis Picabia. Cézanne had taught her that there are no less important areas on a canvas vis-à-vis the theme or figure that traditionally dominated representational painting, and he returned to "basics," such as color, tone, distribution, and the underlying abstractions, reaching out for those essentials in the welter of external detail to capture a sense without which there would be no painting. Picasso went even further, forsaking three-dimensional composition for the surface purity of plane geometry, ushering in cubism. For Stein, perception takes place against the tabula rasa of immediate consciousness, and cubism offered the flatness of an interior time that could be brought to absolute elementalism, simplicity, and finality.

TENDER BUTTONS

Things as They Are and *Three Lives*, for all their stylistic experimentation, are clearly works of prose. In *Tender Buttons*, however, Stein blurs the distinction between prose and poetry. She works with "meaningless" babble, puns, games, rhymes, and repetitions. Much as in Lewis Carroll and Tristam Tzara, the word itself is seen as magic. In a world of pure existence, dialogue disappears, replaced by word lists and one-word utterances. Interactions of characters are no longer tenable, and people give way to objects. The portrait is supplanted by the still life, and the technique of composition is reminiscent of Picasso's collages, not of automatic writing. The intention seems to be to give the work its autonomy independent of both writer and reader: One sees and reads what one sees and reads, the rest being reconstruction from memory or projections of the viewer's intellect. The effort is ambitious: to see language being born. Disparate critical ideas have been invoked to "interpret" *Tender Buttons*, and it is likely that Norman Weinstein (*Gertrude Stein and the Literature of Modern Consciousness*, 1970) comes closest when he summons the studies of Jean Piaget, the Sapir-Whorf language hypothesis, R. D. Laing, and the dimension of schizophrenia. On the opposite bank, Allegra Stewart (*Gertrude Stein and the Present*, 1967) reads the work as a Jungian mandala and relates the alchemical correspondences to all the literary movements of the epoch, such as Dada, Futurism, and so on.

"A jack in kill her, a jack in, makes a meadowed king, makes a to let." The plastic use of language permits the bypassing of the rule where, for example, a substantive is the object of a preposition. The infinitive "to let" appears as the object of a verb and is modified by the indefinite article "a." If analysis emphasizes the dislocation, the derangement, of standard usage, suggesting that alternative modes of expression are possible and even revealing, no matter how unwieldy, it should also note the foregrounding of "events" in an atemporal framework, where even nouns are objects that do not need the passing of ages to be what they are. Sense, if not altogether certain meanings, can be obtained only in the suspended perception of the reading, especially aloud.

This effort to see and write in the "continuous present" requires, Stein said, a passionate identification with the thing to be described: A steady, trance-like concentration on the object will first of all divest it of all its customary appellations and then permit the issuing forth of words and structures that alone can speak as *that* thing in front of the observer.

"Poetry and Grammar"

In "Poetry and Grammar" (1935), Stein says, "Poetry is concerned with using with abusing, with losing with wanting, with denying with avoiding with adoring with replacing the noun.... Poetry is doing nothing but using losing refusing and pleasing and betraying and caressing nouns." In this spirit of reevaluation of the nature and process of naming things she will then go all out in making sure that the things she looks at will by themselves elicit the way they are to be called, never being for a moment worried that such a process may be at odds with the limited range of possibilities offered by conventional reality; she wanted not only to rename things but also to "find out how to know that they were there by their names or by replacing their names." As Shakespeare had done in Arden, the goal was to create "a forest without mentioning the things that make a forest."

With this new discovery, for the ensuing twenty years Stein kept busy revisiting timeworn forms and models of poetic expression, charging them with fresh blood and impetus. The underlying magic would be constant: "looking at anything until something that was not the name of that thing but was in a way that actual thing would come to be written." This process was possible because Stein had arrived at a particular conception of the essence of language: It is not "imitation either of sounds or colors or emotions," but fundamentally an "intellectual recreation." The problem of mimesis and representation was forever behind her, and the idea of play became fundamental in her work.

1920's and 1930's

The third stage of Stein's poetry came in the late 1920's and early 1930's, when she was both very happy at receiving some recognition and much depressed about some new problems of her craft. Of the three materials that she felt art had to deal with—sight, sound, and sense, corresponding to the spatial, the temporal, and the conceptual dimensions of the mind—she had up to then worked intensely on the first two, relegating the third to the background by ignoring it or by simply rejecting it as a response to conventional grammatical and logical sense. At times, she handled the problem of sense by mediating it through her theoretical writings, especially after 1925.

With the ending of the Roaring Twenties, however, much of the spatiality in literature also disappeared. Painting became intellectual, poets became religious or political, and the newer waves did not seem to hold much promise. Stein had also reached a conclusion concerning works of art: that there are no masterpieces containing ideas; in philosophy, there are no masterpieces. Ideas and philosophy require almost by definition a mediated, sequential array of items over time and in history, ideas being about something or other. For a poetic of the unique, concrete thing—again, against all claims that Stein's is a poetic of the abstract—the task of dealing with ideas, which are by nature abstract, posed no small problem. Still, owing also to her attention to religious thought and the artistic implications of meditation, communion, trance, and revelation, she felt the need to come to terms with this hitherto untrodden ground.

STANZAS IN MEDITATION

Stein set about writing a poem of ideas without all the historical and philosophical underpinnings and referents that accompany works such as Ezra Pound's *The Cantos* (1925-1972) and T. S. Eliot's *The Waste Land* (1922). True to the credo that art is immanent and immediate, she wrote *Stanzas in Meditation*, a long poem made up of five parts and running to 163 stanzas, some a line long, others extending over several pages.

Remarkably little has been written about this forgotten but truly major composition, for the difficulty once again is the unpreparedness of criticism to deal with another of Stein's innovations: Instead of writing about ideas, she writes the ideas themselves: Thinking, in other words, does not occur in the mind after reading the words on the page, but the words themselves are the ideas, making ideas partake of the human mind instead of human nature. The old reliable technique of stopping the momentous thoughts on the page as consciousness becomes aware of them creates once again the typical situation with Stein's art: One experiences ideas as one reads; one cannot lean back and expect to put together a "coherent" whole. There are in fact no philosophical terms in the traditional sense and no organization as such. Norman Weinstein writes that "The poem is not *about* philosophy, but *is* philosophy set into motion by verbal action." The disembodied, fragmentary, and discontinuous vision of the cubists is here interwoven with the process-philosophy of William James and Whitehead.

Stylistically, each line tends to be objective and stable and corresponds to what in prose is the sentence. As the lines build up into a stanza, they swell with tension, and, like the paragraph, constitute a specific unit of attention. The poem will occasionally evidence images and allow symbols, but these are accidental, perhaps because the idea itself can best or only be expressed in that particular fashion. According to Sutherland, the poem can be entered in a tradition that lists Plato, Pindar, the English Metaphysicals, and Gerard Manley Hopkins. The poem can be read by simply beginning at random, which is perhaps the best way for the uninitiated to get a "sense" of it and familiarize themselves with the tone, lyricism, and surprisingly deceiving content. The technique of repetition is still present, revealing new contexts for given words, and Stein coins new expressions for ancient truisms. The text is a gold mine of brilliant aphorisms: "There is no hope or use in all," or "That which they like they knew."

THE AUTOBIOGRAPHY OF ALICE B. TOKLAS

Between the time of the appearance of *The Autobiography of Alice B. Toklas* and the publication, shortly before her death, of *The Gertrude Stein First Reader and Three Plays* (1946), thirteen other books came out, among which were the highly successful and important *The Geographical History of America* (1936) and *Everybody's Autobiography* (1937). During these years, Stein's major efforts were directed to the problem of self-presentation and the formal structure of autobiography. She put the writer on the same ground as the reader, ending the privileged position of both biographer and autobiographer. She continued to elaborate the poetic of impersonal, timeless, and spaceless writing, ensuring that experience, flow, and place remain within the confines of the continuous present of perception. Her poetry during this period was chiefly written for children, rhymed and chanted and playful, with no pretense at being anything more than a momentary flash in the continuum of life, a diversion, a game. Many of these works were published either as limited editions or posthumously in the Yale edition of her uncollected writings, where they can now be read in chronological sequence.

OTHER MAJOR WORKS

LONG FICTION: *Three Lives*, 1909; *The Making of Americans: Being a History of a Family's Progress*, 1925 (abridged, 1934); *Lucy Church Amiably*, 1930; *A Long Gay Book*, 1932; *Ida, a Novel*, 1941; *Brewsie and Willie*, 1946; *Blood on the Dining-Room Floor*, 1948; *Things as They Are*, 1950 (originally known as *Q.E.D.*); *Mrs. Reynolds and Five Earlier Novelettes, 1931-1942*, 1952; *A Novel of Thank You*, 1958.

SHORT FICTION: *As Fine as Melanctha*, 1954; *Painted Lace, and Other Pieces, 1914-1937*, 1955; *Alphabets and Birthdays*, 1957.

PLAYS: *Geography and Plays*, pb. 1922; *Operas and Plays*, pb. 1932; *Four Saints in Three Acts*, pr., pb. 1934; *In Savoy: Or, Yes Is for a Very Young Man (A Play of the Resistance in France)*, pr., pb. 1946; *The Mother of Us All*, pr. 1947; *Last Operas and Plays*, pb. 1949; *In a Garden: An Opera in One Act*, pb. 1951; *Lucretia Borgia*, pb. 1968; *Selected Operas and Plays*, 1970.

NONFICTION: *Composition as Explanation*, 1926; *How to Write*, 1931; *Matisse, Picasso, and Gertrude Stein, with Two Shorter Stories*, 1933; *The Autobiography of Alice B. Toklas*, 1933; *Portraits and Prayers*, 1934; *Lectures in America*, 1935; *Narration: Four Lectures*, 1935; *The Geographical History of America*, 1936; *Everybody's Autobiography*, 1937; *Picasso*, 1938; *Paris, France*, 1940; *What Are Masterpieces?*, 1940; *Wars I Have Seen*, 1945; *Four in America*, 1947; *Reflections on the Atomic Bomb*, 1973; *How Writing Is Written*, 1974; *The Letters of Gertrude Stein and Thornton Wilder*, 1996

(Edward Burns and Ulla E. Dydo, editors); *Baby Precious Always Shines: Selected Love Notes Between Gertrude Stein and Alice B. Toklas*, 1999 (Kay Turner, editor).
CHILDREN'S LITERATURE: *The World Is Round*, 1939.
MISCELLANEOUS: *The Gertrude Stein First Reader and Three Plays*, 1946; *The Yale Edition of the Unpublished Writings of Gertrude Stein*, 1951-1958 (8 volumes; Carl Van Vechten, editor); *Selected Writings of Gertrude Stein*, 1962; *The Yale Gertrude Stein*, 1980.

BIBLIOGRAPHY

Curnutt, Kirk, ed. *The Critical Response to Gertrude Stein*. Westport, Conn.: Greenwood Press, 2000. This guide includes quintessential pieces on Stein by Carl Van Vechten, William Carlos Williams, and Katherine Anne Porter, as well as previously obscure estimations from contemporaries such as H. L. Mencken, Mina Loy, and Conrad Aiken.

Dydo, Ulla E., with William Rice. *Gertrude Stein: The Language That Rises, 1923-1934*. Evanston, Ill.: Northwestern University Press, 2003. Dydo, a renowned Stein scholar, provides a comprehensive analysis of the letters, manuscripts, and notebooks Stein generated in a twenty-year period.

Kellner, Bruce, ed. *A Gertrude Stein Companion*. New York: Greenwood Press, 1988. Kellner supplies a helpful introduction on how to read Stein. The volume includes a study of Stein and literary tradition, her manuscripts, and her various styles; and biographical sketches of her friends and "enemies." Includes an annotated bibliography of criticism.

Knapp, Bettina. *Gertrude Stein*. New York: Continuum, 1990. A general introduction to Stein's life and art. Discusses her stylistic breakthrough in the stories in *Three Lives*, focusing on repetition and the use of the continuous present. Devotes a long chapter to *Tender Buttons* as one of Stein's most innovative and esoteric works; discusses the nonreferential nature of language in the fragments.

Malcolm, Janet. *Two Lives: Gertrude and Alice*. New Haven, Conn.: Yale University Press, 2007. Malcolm examines the good and the bad in the life shared by Stein and Alice B. Toklas.

Mitrano, G. F. *Gertrude Stein: Woman Without Qualities*. Burlington, Vt.: Ashgate, 2005. A study of Stein's writing and a look at why it remains relevant to twenty-first century readers.

Murphy, Marguerite S. *A Tradition of Subversion: The Prose Poem in English from Wilde to Ashbery*. Amherst: University of Massachusetts Press, 1992. Devotes a chapter to *Tender Buttons*. Argues that Stein borrowed her genre from painting. Discusses the experimental nature of Stein's prose poems in the collections.

Pierpont, Claudia Roth. *Passionate Minds: Women Rewriting the World*. New York: Alfred A. Knopf, 2000. Evocative, interpretive essays on the life paths and works of twelve women, including Stein, connecting the circumstances of their lives with the shapes, styles, subjects, and situations of their art.

Simon, Linda. *Gertrude Stein Remembered*. Lincoln: University of Nebraska Press, 1994. Consists of short memoirs of the modernist writer by her colleagues and contemporaries. Selections include pieces by Daniel-Henri Kahnweiler, Sylvia Beach, Sherwood Anderson, Cecil Beaton, and Eric Sevareid, each of whom offer intimate and often informal views of Stein.

Wineapple, Brenda. *Sister Brother: Gertrude and Leo Stein*. Lincoln: University of Nebraska Press, 2008. Wineapple looks at the long and close relationship between Stein and her brother, Leo, and the emergence of her writing voice, which may been in part responsible for the rift between the two siblings.

Peter Carravetta

TRISTAN TZARA
Sami Rosenstock

Born: Moineşti, Romania; April 4, 1896
Died: Paris, France; December 24, 1963

PRINCIPAL POETRY
  La Première Aventure céleste de Monsieur Antipyrine, 1916
  Vingt-cinq Poèmes, 1918
  Cinéma calendrier du coeur abstrait, 1920
  De nos oiseaux, 1923
  Indicateur des chemins de coeur, 1928
  L'Arbre des voyageurs, 1930
  L'Homme approximatif, 1931 (*Approximate Man, and Other Writings*, 1973)
  Où boivent les loups, 1932
  L'Antitête, 1933
  Primele Poème, 1934 (English translation, 1976)
  Grains et issues, 1935
  La Deuxième Aventure céleste de Monsieur Antipyrine, 1938 (wr. 1917)
  Midis gagnés, 1939
  Une Route seul soleil, 1944
  Entre-temps, 1946
  Le Signe de vie, 1946
  Terre sur terre, 1946
  Morceaux choisis, 1947
  Phases, 1949
  Sans coup férir, 1949
  De mémoire d'homme, 1950
  Parler seul, 1950
  Le Poids du monde, 1951
  La Première main, 1952
  La Face intérieure, 1953
  À haute flamme, 1955
  La Bonne heure, 1955
  Miennes, 1955
  Le Temps naissant, 1955
  Le Fruit permis, 1956 (wr. 1946)
  Frère bois, 1957
  La Rose et le chien, 1958

De la coupe aux lèvres, 1961
Juste présent, 1961
Selected Poems, 1975

OTHER LITERARY FORMS

Although the largest part of the work of Tristan Tzara (TSAH-rah) consists of a vast body of poetry—filling more than thirty volumes—he did experiment with drama, publishing three plays during his lifetime: *Le Coeur à gaz* (pb. 1946; *The Gas Heart*, 1964), *Mouchoir de nuages* (pb. 1924; *Handkerchief of Clouds*, 1972), and *La Fuite* (pb. 1947; the flight). His important polemical writings appeared in two collections: *Sept Manifestes Dada* (1924; *Seven Dada Manifestos*, 1977) and *Le Surréalisme et l'après-guerre* (1947; Surrealism and the postwar period). Much of Tzara's critical and occasional writing, which is substantial in volume, remains unpublished, including book-length works on François Rabelais and François Villon, while the published portion includes *Lampisteries* (1963; English translation, 1977), *Picasso et la poésie* (1953; Picasso and poetry), *L'Art Océanien* (1951; the art of Oceania), and *L'Égypte face à face* (1954).

ACHIEVEMENTS

Tristan Tzara's importance as a literary figure of international reputation rests primarily on his relationship to the Dada movement. Of all the avant-garde movements that challenged the traditional foundations of artistic value and judgment at the beginning of the present century, Dada was, by consensus, the most radical and disturbing. In retrospect, the Dada aesthetic, which was first formed and expressed in Zurich about 1916, seems to have been a fairly direct response to World War I; the Dadaists themselves suggest as much in many of their works during this period.

The harsh, confrontational nature of Dada is notorious, and Tzara was one of the most provocative of all the Dadaists. In his 1930 essay, "Memoirs of Dadaism," Tzara describes one of his own contributions to the first Dada soiree in Paris, on January 23, 1920, in which he read a newspaper while a bell rang. This attitude of deliberate confrontation with the conventional, rational expectations of the audience—to which the Dadaists juxtaposed their illogical, satirical productions—is defended by Tzara in his most famous polemical work, "Manifeste Dada 1918" ("Dada Manifesto 1918"), in which he asserts the meaninglessness of Dada and its refusal to offer a road to truth.

To escape the machinery of human rationality, the Dadaists substituted a faith in spontaneity, incorporating the incongruous and accidental into their works. Even the name by which the Dadaists called themselves was chosen rather arbitrarily. According to most accounts (although this report is subject to intense difference of opinion among Dadaists), it was Tzara himself who chose the word *dada*, in February of 1916, by opening a French dictionary to a randomly selected entry.

Tzara's achievements are not limited solely to his leadership in the Dada movement.

Until recently, Tzara's later work—which is more optimistic in tone and more controlled in technique—has been overshadowed by his more violent and sensational work from the Dada period. It is now becoming apparent to many readers and critics that the Surrealist phase of Tzara's work, the little-known work of his post-Surrealist phase, and his early pre-Dada work in Romanian, are equally important in considering his contribution to modern literature. In the 1970's and 1980's, largely through the work of editors and translators such as Mary Ann Caws, Henrí Behar, and Sasa Pană, this work became more readily available.

Biography

Tristan Tzara, whose real name was Sami Rosenstock, was born on April 4, 1896, in Moineşti, a small town in the province of Băcău, in northeastern Romania. His parents were Jewish, his father a prosperous merchant. Tzara first attended school in Moineşti, where Romanian was spoken, but later, when he was sent to Bucharest for his secondary education, he attended schools where instruction was also given in French. In addition to languages, Tzara studied mathematics and music. Following his graduation in 1913, he attended the University of Bucharest for a year, taking courses in mathematics and philosophy.

It was during this adolescent period, between 1911 and 1915, that all Tzara's Romanian poems were written. His first published poems appeared in 1912 in *Simbolul*, a short-lived Symbolist review that he helped to edit. These first four poems were signed with the pseudonym S. Samyro. The subsequent poems in Romanian that Tzara published during this period were often signed simply "Tristan" or "Tzara," and it was not until near the end of this period, in 1915, that the first Romanian poem signed "Tristan Tzara" appeared.

In the fall of 1915, Tzara went to Zurich, in neutral Switzerland, where he became involved with a group of writers and artists—including Hugo Ball, Richard Huelsenbeck, Marcel Janco, and Hans Arp—who were in the process of forming an artistic movement soon to be called Dada. This period, between Tzara's arrival in Zurich in the fall of 1915 and February of 1916, was the germinating period of the Dada movement. The Dadaists' first public announcement of the birth of a new movement in the arts took place at the Cabaret Voltaire on the evening of February 5, 1916—the occasion of the first of many such Dada soirees. These entertainments included presentations such as "simultaneous poems," which confronted the audience with a chaotic barrage of words made incomprehensible by the din; recitations of "pure sound-poems," often made up of African-sounding nonsense syllables and recited by a chorus of masked dancers; satirical plays that accused and insulted the audience; and, always, the ceaseless manifestos promoting the Dada revolt against conformity. Tzara's work during this period was written almost entirely in French, and from this time on he used that language exclusively for his literary productions.

As the activities of the Zurich Dadaists gradually attracted notice in other countries, especially Germany and France, Tzara's own fame as an artist spread to an increasingly larger audience. The spread of Dada's fame from Zurich to other centers of avant-garde activity in Europe was aided by the journal *Dada*, edited by Tzara and featuring many of his most provocative works. Although this journal lasted only through five issues, it did draw the attention of Guillaume Apollinaire in Paris, and through him the devoted admiration of André Breton, who was later to be one of the leaders of the Surrealist movement. At Breton's urging, Tzara left Zurich shortly after the Armistice was declared, arriving in Paris in December of 1919.

For a short period between January of 1920, when the first public Dada performance in Paris was held, and May of 1921, when Breton broke his association with Tzara to assume the leadership of the developing Surrealist movement, Breton and Tzara organized an increasingly outrageous series of activities that frequently resulted in public spectacles. Following Breton's break with the Dada group, Tzara continued to stage public performances in Paris for a time, collaborating with those who remained loyal to the Dada revolt. By July of 1923, however, when the performance of his play *The Gas Heart* was disrupted by a Surrealist counter demonstration, even Tzara regretfully admitted that Dada was effectively dead, a victim of its own destructive impulses. Tzara gave up the Dada ideal reluctantly and continued to oppose the Surrealists until 1929, when he joined the Paris Surrealist group, accepting Breton's leadership. Tzara's resumption of activities with Breton's group was also accompanied by an increasing move toward political engagement.

The same year that he joined the Surrealists, Tzara visited the Soviet Union, and the following year, in 1930, the Surrealists indicated their dedication to the Communist International by changing the name of their own journal, *La Révolution surréaliste*, to *Le Surréalisme au service de la révolution*. For Tzara, this political commitment seemed to be a natural outgrowth of his initial revolt, for, as he wrote later in *Le Surréalisme et l'après-guerre*: "Dada was born ... from the deep feeling that man ... must affirm his supremacy over notions emptied of all human substance, over dead objects and ill-gotten gains."

In 1935, Tzara broke with the Surrealists to devote himself entirely to the work of the Communist Party, which he officially joined at this time. From 1935 to 1937, he was involved in assisting the Republican forces in the Spanish Civil War, salvaging art treasures and serving on the Committee for the Defense of Culture. This political engagement continued during World War II, with Tzara serving in the French Resistance, all the time continuing to publish his work, despite widespread censorship, under the pseudonym T. Tristan. In 1946 and 1947, he delivered the lectures that make up *Le Surréalisme et l'après-guerre*, in which he made his controversial assessment of Surrealism's failure to influence Europe effectively between the wars. In 1955, Tzara published *À haute flamme* (at full flame), a long poetic reminiscence in which he reviewed the stages of his lifelong revolt and reaffirmed his revolutionary aesthetic. Tzara continued to affirm the authenticity of his position until his death in Paris at the age of sixty-seven, a victim of lung cancer.

Analysis

Whatever else Tristan Tzara was—Dada instigator and polemicist, marginal Surrealist, Communist activist, or Romanian expatriate—his great skill as a poet is abundantly apparent. At his death, Tzara left behind a vast body of poems, extremely diverse in style, content, and tone. Important features of his work are his innovations in poetic technique and his development of a highly unified system of symbolic imagery. The first of these features includes the use of pure sound elements, descriptive ideophones, expressive typography, enjambment that creates complex syntactic ambiguities, and multiple viewpoints resulting in a confusing confluence of speaking voices. The second important feature includes such elements as Tzara's use of recurring verbal motifs and refrains, ironic juxtapositions, and recurring image clusters.

Tzara's earliest period extends from 1911 to 1915 and includes all the poetry he wrote in his native Romanian. Until recently, little attention has been given to Tzara's Romanian poetry. Several Romanian critics have noted the decisive but unacknowledged influence on Tzara of the Romanian poet Urmuz (1883-1923), virtually unknown in the West, who anticipated the strategies of Dada and Surrealism. Much of Tzara's early work, however, is relatively traditional in technique, although it must be remembered that this period represents his poetic apprenticeship and that the poems were written when he was between the ages of fifteen and nineteen. The poetry of this period often displays a curiously ambivalent tone, mixing a detached ironic perspective—which is sometimes gently sarcastic and at other times bitterly resentful—with an uncritically sentimental nostalgia for the past. In some of the poems, one of these two moods dominates, as in Tzara's bitterly ironic treatment of war's destructive effect on the innocence of youth in "The Storm and the Deserter's Song" and "Song of War," or the romantic lyricism of such highly sentimental idylls on nature as "Elegy for the Coming of Winter" and "Evening Comes."

PRIMELE POÈME

The most successful poems of this period—later collected as *Primele Poème*—are those which mix nostalgia with irony, encompassing both attitudes within a single poem. The best example of this type of poem is "Sunday," whose conventional images of leisurely activities that occupy the inhabitants of a town on the Sabbath are contrasted with the bitter reflections of the alienated poet-speaker who observes the scene. The scene seems idyllic enough at first, presenting images of domestic tranquillity. Then the reflecting consciousness of the alienated speaker intrudes, introducing images that contrast darkly with and shatter the apparently false impression he himself has just created.

Into the scene of comfortable regularity, three new and disturbing elements appear: the inescapable presence of death in wartime, the helplessness of parents to protect their children from danger, and the futility of art stagnated by Decadence.

VINGT-CINQ POÈMES

This mixture of sentimental lyricism with ironic detachment is developed to an even greater degree in Tzara's first collection of poems in French, *Vingt-cinq Poèmes* (twenty-five poems), a collection that, although published after he had already arrived in Zurich, still resembles in technique and content the early Romanian poems. In "Petite Ville en Sibérie" ("Little Town in Siberia"), there are a number of new elements, the most important of which are Tzara's use of typography for expressive purposes, the complex syntactic ambiguity created by enjambment, the rich confluence of narrative voices, and the appearance of images employing illogical juxtapositions of objects and qualities:

> a blue light which flattens us together on the ceiling
> it's as always comrade
> like a label of infernal doors pasted on a medicine bottle
> it's the calm house tremble my friend

This disorienting confluence of voices is deliberate, and it evokes in the reader a futile desire to resolve the collage (based on the random conjunction of several separate discourses) into a meaningful and purposeful poetic statement.

DE NOS OISEAUX

In Tzara's second period—extending from 1916 until 1924—he produced the Dadaist works which brought him international fame. To the collage technique developed in *Vingt-cinq Poèmes*, the poems that make up *De nos oiseaux* (of our birds)—the major collection from this period—introduce several innovations, including pure sound elements such as African- sounding nonsense words, repeated phrases, descriptive ideophones, use of multiple typefaces, and catalogs of discrete, separable images piled one upon the other. Tzara's collage technique has become more radical in these poems, for instead of simply using the juxtaposition of speaking voices for creating ironic detachment, in the Dada poems the narrative itself breaks down entirely into a chaotic barrage of discontinuous fragments that often seem to lack any discursive sense. These features are readily apparent in "La Mort de Guillaume Apollinaire" ("The Death of Guillaume Apollinaire") and "Les Saltimbanques" ("The Circus Performers"), two of the best poems from *De nos oiseaux*.

"THE DEATH OF GUILLAUME APOLLINAIRE"

In his Dadaist elegy for Apollinaire, Tzara begins with a series of propositions that not only establish the resigned mood of the speaker but also express the feeling of disorder created in the reader by the poem itself. A simple admission of man's inability to comprehend his situation in the world is followed by a series of images that seem designed to convey the disparity the speaker senses between a world which is unresponsive to human needs (the unfortunate death of Apollinaire at such an early age is no doubt one aspect of this) and a world in which he could feel comfortable (and presumably learn to accept the death of his beloved friend):

> if snow fell upward
> if the sun rose in our houses in the middle of the night
> just to keep us warm
> and the trees hung upsidedown with their crowns . . .
> if birds came down to us to find reflections of
>   themselves
> in those peaceful lakes lying just above our heads
> THEN WE MIGHT UNDERSTAND
> that death could be a beautiful long voyage
> and a permanent vacation from flesh from structures
>   systems and skeletons

The images of this poem constitute a particularly good illustration of Tzara's developing symbolic system. Although the images of snow falling upward, the sun rising at night, trees hanging upside down, and birds coming to earth at first appear unrelated to one another, they are actually related in two ways. First, Tzara is describing processes within the totality of nature which give evidence that "nature is organized in its totality." Humanity's sorrow over the inescapable cycles of life and death, of joy and suffering, is caused by a failure to understand that humans, too, are a part of this totality. Second, Tzara's images suggest that if one's perspective could only be reversed, one would see the reality of things properly. This method of presenting arguments in nondiscursive, imagistic terms was one of Tzara's primary poetic accomplishments, and the uses to which he put it in this elegy for Apollinaire were later expanded and developed in the epic scope of his masterpiece, *Approximate Man, and Other Writings*.

"THE CIRCUS PERFORMERS"

"The Circus Performers" illustrates Tzara's increasing use of pure sound elements in his work. The images of this poem attempt to capture the exciting rhythms of the circus performance that Tzara is describing. In the opening vignette of the poem, in what seems at first an illogical sequence of statements, Tzara merges the expanding and contracting rhythm of the verses with his characteristic use of imagery to convey thought in analogical, nondiscursive terms. Describing a ventriloquist's act, Tzara uses an image that links "brains," "balloons," and "words." In this image, "brains" seems to be a metonymic substitution for ideas or thoughts—that which is expressed by "words."

Here the brains themselves are inflating and deflating, as are the balloons. What is the unstated analogical relation between the two? These words are treated like the words and thoughts of comic-strip characters—where words are enclosed in the "balloons" that represent mental space in newspaper cartoons. To help the reader more easily identify the analogy, Tzara has included an explanatory aside, enclosed in parentheses. A second example of Tzara's use of sound in this poem is the presence of "ideophones"— words that imitate the sounds of the actions they describe. Pure sound images devoid of abstract meaning are scattered throughout the poem.

APPROXIMATE MAN, AND OTHER WRITINGS

By all standards of judgment, *Approximate Man, and Other Writings*, a long epic in nineteen sections, is Tzara's greatest poem. It was Tzara's most sustained effort, its composition and extensive revisions occupying the poet between 1925 and 1931, the year that the final version appeared. Another important characteristic of the work is its epic scope, for *Approximate Man, and Other Writings* was Tzara's attempt to discover the causes of modern humanity's spiritual malaise, drawing on all the technical resources he had developed up to the time of its composition. The most important feature of the poem, however, is its systematic presentation of Tzara's revolutionary ideology, which had begun to reflect, in a guarded form, the utopian vision of Surrealism.

Approximate Man, and Other Writings is about the intrusion of disorder into modern life, and it focuses on the effects of this disorder on the individual. Throughout the poem, Tzara makes it clear that what he is describing is a general disorder or sickness, not a personal crisis. This is one of the key ideas that is constantly repeated in the form of a refrain: "approximate man like me like you reader and like the others/ heap of noisy flesh and echoes of conscience/ complete in the only element of choice your name." The most important aspect of the poem's theme is Tzara's diagnosis of the causes of this debilitating universal sickness, since this indicates in a striking way his newly found attitude of commitment.

The first cause of humanity's sickness is the very condition of being "approximate." Uncertain, changeable, or lacking commitment to any cause that might improve the world in which he lives, Approximate Man wanders aimlessly. For Tzara, the lost key for curing the sickness is commitment, as Tzara himself declared his commitment to the work of the Communist Party in 1935, shortly after the completion of this poem.

Humanity's sickness arises not only from inauthentic relationships with others but also from an exploitative attitude toward nature—an attitude encouraged by the development of modern technology. In Tzara's view, this modern belief in humanity's preeminent importance in the universe is a mistaken one, as is evident in "The Death of Guillaume Apollinaire," and such vanity contributes to the spiritual sickness of humankind.

Tzara finds a third cause of humanity's spiritual sickness in humans' increasing reliance on the products of their own alienated consciousness, especially reason and language. In *Approximate Man, and Other Writings*, Tzara's efforts to describe this solipsistic entrapment of humans by their own systems gives rise to many striking images, as in the following passages: "vapor on the cold glass you block your own image from your/ sight/ tall and insignificant among the glazed frost jewels/ of the landscape" and "I think of the warmth spun by the word/ around its center the dream called ourselves." These images argue that human reason is like a mirror in which the reflection is clouded by the observer's physical presence, and that human language is like a silken cocoon that insulates people from the external world of reality. Both reason and language, originally created to assist humans, have become debased, and to attain a more accurate picture of the world, humans must learn to rely on instinct and imagination. These three ideas, which find their fullest expression in *Approximate Man, and Other Writings*, form the basis of Tzara's mature poetic vision and constitute the most sustained expression of his critique of the modern sensibility.

OTHER MAJOR WORKS

PLAYS: *Mouchoir de nuages*, pb. 1924 (*Handkerchief of Clouds*, 1972); *Le Coeur à gaz*, pb. 1946 (wr. 1921; *The Gas Heart*, 1964); *La Fuite*, pb. 1947.

NONFICTION: *Sept Manifestes Dada*, 1924 (wr. 1917-1918; *Seven Dada Manifestos*, 1977); *Le Surréalisme et l'après-guerre*, 1947; *L'Art Océanien*, 1951; *Picasso et la poésie*, 1953; *L'Égypte face à face*, 1954; *Lampisteries*, 1963 (English translation, 1977).

MISCELLANEOUS: *Œuvres complètes*, 1975-1991 (6 volumes).

BIBLIOGRAPHY

Browning, Gordon Frederick. *Tristan Tzara: The Genesis of the Dada Poem: Or, From Dada to Aa*. Stuttgart, Germany: Akademischer Verlag Heinz, 1979. A critical study of Tzara's Dada poems. Includes bibliographical references.

Caws, Mary Ann. Introduction to *Approximate Man, and Other Writings*, by Tristan Tzara. Translated by Mary Ann Caws. Detroit: Wayne State University Press, 1973. This book is an excellent selection of English translations of Tzara's poetry, and the introduction provides a helpful guide to each phase of his work.

_____, ed. *Surrealist Painters and Poets: An Anthology*. Cambridge, Mass.: MIT Press, 2001. Contains translations of several prose pieces by Tzara as well as works by many of his contemporaries, providing an overview of the context in which he operated. Includes many illustrations.

Forcer, Stephen. *Modernist Song: The Poetry of Tristan Tzara*. Leeds, England: Legenda, 2006. Traces Tzara's development and changing poetry from his early works to publications in the 1950's.

Marcus, Greil. *Lipstick Traces: A Secret History of the Twentieth Century*. 1989. 20th anniversary ed. Cambridge, Mass.: Belknap Press, 2009. A highly original and accessible study of nihilistic movements in art, music, and literature, from Dada to punk rock. Tzara is only one of many figures discussed here, but this book deserves mention because of its broad historical scope and excellent analysis of the relationship between popular culture and the avant-garde.

Motherwell, Robert, and Jack D. Flam, eds. *The Dada Painters and Poets: An Anthology*. 2d ed. Cambridge, Mass.: Harvard University Press, 1989. A collection of Dada documents including journals, reviews, and manifestos that hold valuable biographical and historical details of the life and work of Tzara.

Peterson, Elmer. *Tristan Tzara: Dada and Surrational Theorist*. New Brunswick, N.J.: Rutgers University Press, 1971. A study of Tzara's aesthetics. Includes bibliographical references.

Richter, Hans. *Dada: Art and Anti-Art*. New York: Thames & Hudson, 1997. Through selections from key manifestos and other documents of the time, Richter records Dada's history, from its beginnings in wartime Zurich to its collapse in the Paris of the 1920's.

Sandqvist, Tom. *Dada East: The Romanians of Cabaret Voltaire*. Cambridge, Mass.: MIT Press, 2006. Looks at Dadaism in Romania, where Tzara was born.

Steven E. Colburn

CÉSAR VALLEJO

Born: Santiago de Chuco, Peru; March 16, 1892
Died: Paris, France; April 15, 1938

PRINCIPAL POETRY
Los heraldos negros, 1918 (*The Black Heralds*, 1990)
Trilce, 1922 (English translation, 1973)
España, aparta de mí este cáliz, 1939 (*Spain, Take This Cup from Me*, 1974)
Poemas en prosa, 1939 (*Prose Poems*, 1978)
Poemas humanos, 1939 (*Human Poems*, 1968)
Obra poética completa, 1968
César Vallejo: The Complete Posthumous Poetry, 1978
Poesía completa, 1978
Selected Poems, 1981
The Complete Poetry: A Bilingual Edition, 2007 (Clayton Eshleman, editor)

OTHER LITERARY FORMS

César Vallejo (vah-YAY-hoh) wrote fiction, plays, and essays, as well as lyric poetry, although his achievement as a poet far outstrips that in any other genre. His short stories—many of them extremely brief—may be found in *Escalas melografiadas* (1923; musical scales). A longer short story, "Fabla salvaje" (1923; primitive parlance), is a tragic idyll of two rustic lovers, and *Hacia el reino de los Sciris* (1967; toward the kingdom of the Sciris) is set in the time of the Incas. *El tungsteno* (1931; *Tungsten*, 1988), is a proletarian novel with an Andean setting that was written in 1931, the year Vallejo joined the Communist Party. Another story, *Paco Yunque* (1969), is about the mistreatment of a servant's son by a classmate who happens to be the master's son.

Vallejo became interested in the theater around 1930, but he destroyed his first play, "Mampar." Three others, *Entre las dos orillas corre el río* (pb. 1979; the river flows between two banks); *Lock-Out* (pb. 1979), and *Colacho hermanos: O, presidentes de América* (pb. 1979; Colacho brothers), never published during the poet's lifetime, are now available in *Teatro completo* (1979; complete theatrical work). His long essay, *Rusia en 1931: Reflexiones al pie del Kremlin* (1931; reissued in 1965), was followed by *Rusia ante el segundo plan quinquenal* (1965); *Contra el secreto profesional* (1973); and *El arte y la revolución* (1973). His master's thesis, *El romanticismo en la poesía castellana*, was published in 1954.

ACHIEVEMENTS

Finding an authentic language in which to write has always represented a fundamental problem for Latin American writers, since it became evident that the language inherited from the Spanish conquerors could not match Latin American reality. The problem of finding such a language goes hand in hand with that of forging a separate cultural identity. An important attempt at renovating poetic language was made by the Spanish American *Modernistas* around the turn of the century, but their verse forms, imagery, and often exotic subject matter were also becoming obsolete by the time César Vallejo reached maturity. It was thus up to him and his contemporaries to find a language that could deal with contemporary concerns involving war, depression, isolation, and alienation. Although hardly recognized in his lifetime, Vallejo did more than perhaps any other poet of his generation to provide an idiom that would at once reflect the Spanish tradition, his own Peruvian heritage, and the contemporary world. Aware of his heritage from Spain's great writers of the past, he blended traditional poetic vocabulary and tropes with homely Peruvian idioms and even the language of children. Where the result was still inadequate, he made up new words, changed the function of old ones, and incorporated a lexicon never before seen in poetry, often savaging poetic convention.

Vallejo's gradual conversion to Marxism and Communism is of great interest to those attempting to understand how collectivist ideals may shape poetry. The evolution of his ideology continues to be studied intensively by many individuals committed to bettering the conditions of poverty and alienation about which Vallejo wrote so eloquently—conditions that still exist in Latin America and other parts of the world. His unflinchingly honest search for both linguistic and moral solutions to the existential anguish of modern human beings gives his poems universal validity, while their density and complexity challenge critics of the most antithetical modes.

BIOGRAPHY

César Abraham Vallejo was born in Santiago de Chuco, a primitive "city" of some fourteen thousand inhabitants in Peru's northern mountains that could only be reached by a rail trip and then several days ride on mule or horseback. Both of his grandfathers had been Spanish priests and both of his grandmothers native Peruvians of Chimu Indian stock. His parents were literate and of modest means; his father was a notary who became a subprefect in the district. Francisco de Paula Vallejo and María de los Santos Mendoza were an upright and religious pair whose marriage produced twelve offspring and who were already middle-aged when their youngest child, César, was born. In his writings, Vallejo was often to remember the security and warmth of his childhood home—games with three of his older siblings, and particularly with his mother, who might have been especially indulgent with her sensitive youngest child.

At age thirteen, Vallejo left Santiago de Chuco to attend high school in Huamachuco, another mountain village, where he received an introduction to literature and began scribbling verses. Economic difficulties prevented him from continuing the university studies that he had begun in the larger coastal cities of Trujillo and Lima in 1911. The young man first went to work in a nearby tungsten mine—an experience that he would later draw upon for his Socialist Realist novel *Tungsten*—and then on a coastal sugar plantation. While there, he observed the tightly structured hierarchy that kept workers in misery while the middle class, to which he himself belonged, served the needs of the elite. In 1913, he returned to the University of Trujillo and graduated two years later, having written a master's thesis titled *El romanticismo en la poesía castellana*. For the next few years, he studied law in Trujillo, supporting himself by becoming a first-grade teacher. One of his pupils, Ciro Alegría, later to become an important novelist, described Vallejo in those days as lean, sallow, solemn, and dark skinned, with abundant straight black hair worn somewhat long, brilliant dark eyes, a gentle manner, and an air of sadness.

During these years, Vallejo became familiar with the writings of Ralph Waldo Emerson, José Rodó, Friedrich Nietzsche, Miguel de Unamuno y Jugo, Walt Whitman, and Juan Ramón Jiménez. Vallejo also read the poems of two of the leading Spanish American *Modernistas*, Rubén Darío and Julio Herrera y Reissig, as well as those of Peruvian poets of the day. Vallejo declaimed his own poems—mostly occasional verse—at various public ceremonies, and some of them appeared in Trujillo's newspapers. Critical reception of them ranged from the cool to the hostile, since they were considered to be exaggerated and strange in that highly traditional ambience. Vallejo fell in love with a young Trujillo girl, Zoila Rosa Cuadro, the subject of several poems included in *The Black Heralds*. The breakup of this relationship provided one motive for his departure, after he had obtained a law degree, for Lima in 1918. There he found a position teaching in one of the best elementary schools and began to put the finishing touches on his first volume of poems.

Vallejo was soon in love with the sister-in-law of one of his colleagues, a woman identified only as "Otilia." A number of the *Trilce* poems, which he was writing at the time, deal with this affair. It ended when the poet refused to marry the woman, resulting in the loss of his job. This crisis was compounded by the death of his mother, a symbol of stability whose loss made him feel like an orphan. For some time, Vallejo had thought of going to Paris, but he decided to return first to his childhood home in Santiago de Chuco. During a national holiday, he was falsely accused of having been the instigator of a civil disturbance and was later seized and imprisoned for 112 days despite the public protests of many Peruvian intellectuals. The experience affected him profoundly, and the poems that he wrote about it (later published in *Trilce*) testify to the feeling of solidarity with the oppressed that he voiced for the first time. While in prison, he also wrote a number of the sketches to appear in *Escalas melografiadas*. In 1923, he sailed for Europe, never again to return to Peru.

While Vallejo's days in Lima had often been marked by personal problems, in Paris, he experienced actual penury, sometimes being forced to sleep in the subway. Eventually, he found employment in a press agency but only after a serious illness. He began to contribute articles to Lima newspapers, made friends with a number of avant-garde artists, and journeyed several times to Spain, where he was awarded a grant for further study. Increasingly concerned with injustice in the world, he made his first trip to Russia in 1928 with the intention of staying. Instead, he returned within three weeks, living soon afterward with a Frenchwoman, Georgette de Philippart, who was later to become his wife. With some money that had come to her, the pair set out on a tour by train through Eastern Europe, spending two weeks in Moscow and returning by way of Rome. As Vallejo's enthusiasm for Marxism became increasingly apparent in his newspaper articles, he found them no longer welcome in Lima, and in 1930, he was ordered to leave France because of his political activity. Once again in Spain, he wrote several plays and the novel *Tungsten* and published *Rusia en 1931*, the only one of his books to sell well. No publisher could be found for several other works. After a third and final visit to Russia as a delegate to the International Congress of Writers, he wrote *Rusia ante el segundo plan quinquenal* (Russia facing the second five-year plan) and officially joined the Communist Party.

In 1932, Vallejo was permitted to return to Paris, where he tried unsuccessfully to publish some new poems. In 1936, the Spanish Civil War broke out, and Vallejo became an active supporter of the Republic, traveling to Barcelona and Madrid to attend the Second International Congress for the Defense of Culture. He visited the battlefront and learned at first hand of the horrors suffered by the Spanish people in the war. Returning to Paris for the last time, he poured his feelings into his last work, *Spain, Take This Cup from Me*. In March, 1938, he became ill. Doctors were unable to diagnose his illness, and Vallejo died a month later on Good Friday, the day before the troops of Francisco Franco won a decisive victory in Spain.

Analysis

One of the unique qualities of César Vallejo's poetry—one that makes his work almost impossible to confuse with that of any other poet writing in the Spanish language—is his ability to speak with the voice and sensibility of a child, whether as an individual orphaned by the breakup of a family or as a symbol of deprived and alienated human beings everywhere. Always, however, this child's voice, full of expectation and hope, is implicitly counterposed by the adult's ironic awareness of change and despair. Inseparable from these elements is the poet's forging of a language capable of reflecting the register and the peculiarly elliptical reasoning of a child and, at the same time, revealing the Hermetic complexity of the adult intellectual's quest for security in the form of truth. The poetry that is Vallejo's own answer to these problems is some of the most poignant and original ever produced.

The Black Heralds

The lines of Vallejo's subsequent development are already evident in his first volume, *The Black Heralds*, a collection of sixty-nine poems grouped under various subtitles. As critics have observed, many of these poems reflect his involvement with Romantic and *Modernista* poetry. They are conspicuous in many cases for their descriptions of idyllic scenes in a manner that juxtaposes words of the Peruvian Sierra and the vocabulary of Symbolism, including religious and erotic elements. Vallejo did not emphasize rhyme and rhythm to the extent that some *Modernistas* did, but most of these early poems are framed in verse forms favored by the latter, such as the Alexandrine sonnet and the *silva*. While demonstrating his impressive mastery of styles already worked out by others, he was also finding his own voice.

This originality is perhaps most evident in the last group of poems in *The Black Heralds*, titled "Canciones de Hogar" ("Home Songs"), poems dealing with the beginning of Vallejo's sense of orphanhood. In "A mi hermano Miguel in memoriam" ("To My Brother Miguel in Memoriam"), the poet relives a moment of the childhood game of hide-and-seek that he used to play with his "twin heart." Speaking to his brother, Vallejo announces his own presence in the part of the family home from which one of the two always ran away to hide from the other. He goes on to remind his playmate of one day on which the latter went away to hide, sad instead of laughing as he usually was, and could not be found again. The poem ends with a request to the brother to please come out so as not to worry "mama." It is remarkable in that past and present alternate from one line to the next. The language of childhood, as well as the poet's assumed presence at the site of the events, lends a dramatic immediacy to the scene. At the same time, the language used in the descriptive passages is clearly that of the adult who is now the poet. Yet in the last verse, the adult chooses to accept literally the explanation that the brother has remained in hiding and may finally respond and come out, which would presumably alleviate the mother's anxiety and make everything right once more. The knowledge that the poet is unable (or refuses) to face the permanent alteration of his past may elicit feelings of tragic pathos in the reader.

"Los pasos lejanos" ("The Distant Steps") recalls the poet's childhood home in which his parents, now aged, are alone—the father sleeping and the mother walking in the orchards. Here, the only bitterness is that of the poet himself, because he is now far away from them. He in turn is haunted by a vision of his parents as two old, white, and bent roads along which his heart walks. In "Enereida," he imagines that his father has died, leading to a regression in time so that the father can once again laugh at his small children, including the poet himself, who is again a schoolboy under the tutelage of the village priest.

Many of the poems in *The Black Heralds* deal with existential themes. While religious imagery is pervasive, it is apparent that the poet employs it to describe profane experiences. Jean Franco has shown that in speaking of "the soul's Christs" and "Marías who leave" and of Communions and Passions, Vallejo trivializes religious language rather than attempting to inflate the importance of his own experiences by describing them in religious terms. As well as having lost the security and plenitude of his childhood home, the poet has lost the childhood faith that enabled him to refer in words to the infinite.

In the title poem, "Los heraldos negros" ("The Black Heralds"), Vallejo laments life's hard blows, harder sometimes than humans can stand. He concludes that these blows come from the hatred of God, that they may be the black heralds sent by Death. In "Los dados eternos" ("The Eternal Dice"), God is a gambler throwing dice and may as easily cast death as life. In fact, Earth itself is his die. Now worn to roundness, it will come to rest only within the sepulchre. Profane love is all that is left; while the beloved may now be pure, she will not continue to be so if she yields to the poet's erotic impulses. Love thus becomes "a sinning Christ," because humankind's nature is irrevocably physical. Several poems allude to the poet's ideal of redeeming himself through brotherly love, a thematic constant in Vallejo's work, yet such redemption becomes difficult if not impossible if a person is lonely and alienated. In "Agape," the poet speaks of being alone and forgotten and of having been unable therefore to "die" for his brother. "La cena miserable" ("The Wretched Supper") tells of the enigma of existence in which humans are seen, as in "Agape," as waiting endlessly for spiritual nurture, or at least for some answer concerning the meaning of life. Here, God becomes no more than a "black spoon" full of bitter human essence, even less able than humans to provide needed answers. The lives of humans are thus meaningless, since they are always separated from what they most desire—whether this be the fullness of the past, physical love, God's love, or brotherly love.

Even in the poems most laden with the trappings of *Modernismo*, Vallejo provides unusual images. In "El poeta a su amada" ("The Poet to His Beloved"), he suggests that his kiss is "two curved branches" on which his beloved has been "crucified." Religious imagery is used with such frequency that it sometimes verges on parody, and critics agree that in playing with language in this way Vallejo is seeking to highlight its essential ambiguity, something he continues to do in *Trilce* and *Human Poems*, even while totally abandoning the imagery of *Modernismo*. Such stripping away of excess baggage is already visible in *The Black Heralds*. Antitheses, oxymorons, and occasional neologisms are also to be noted. While the great majority of the poems are elegantly correct in terms of syntax—in marked contrast to what is to become the norm in *Trilce*—there are some instances of linguistic experimentation, as when nouns are used as adjectives. In "The Distant Steps," for example, the mother is described as being "so soft, so wing, so departure, so love." Another device favored by the poet in all his later poems—enumeration—is also present. Finally, traditional patterns of meter and rhyme are abandoned in "Home Songs," with the poetic emotion being allowed to determine the form.

TRILCE

Despite these formal adumbrations and although *The Black Heralds* is not a particularly transparent work, there is little in it to prepare the reader for the destruction of language in the Hermetic density of *Trilce*, which came along only three years later. These were difficult years for the poet, in which he lost his mother, separated from Otilia, and spent what he was later to refer to as the gravest moments of his life in the Trujillo jail. All the anguish of these events was poured into the seventy-seven free-verse poems of his second major work. If he suffered existentially in *The Black Heralds* and expressed this suffering in writing, it was done with respect for traditional verse forms and sentence structure, which hinted at an order beyond the chaos of the poet's interior world. In *Trilce*, this order falls. Language, on which "logical assumptions" about the world are based, is used in such a way as to reveal its hollowness: It, too, is cut loose and orphaned. Abrupt shifts from one metaphorical sphere to another make the poems' internal logic often problematic.

A hint of what is to come is given in the title, a neologism usually taken to be a hybrid of *tres* (three) and *dulce* (sweet), an interpretation that is in accord with the poet's concern about the ideal number expressed in several poems. It is not known, however, what, if any, concrete meaning the poet had in mind when he coined the word; it has become a puzzle for readers and critics to solve. It is notable that in "interpreting" the *Trilce* poems, critics often work out explications that seem internally consistent but that turn out to be related to a system diametrically opposed to the explication and system of some other critic. It is possible, however, to say with certainty that these poems deal with a struggle to do something, bridge something, and say something. Physical limits such as the human body, time, space, and numbers often render the struggle futile.

Two of the thematic sets of *Trilce* for which it is easiest to establish concrete referents are those dealing with the poet-as-child and those dealing with his imprisonment. In poem III, the poet once again speaks in the voice of a child left at home by the adults of the family. It is getting dark, and he asks when the grown-ups will be back, adding that "Mama said she wouldn't be gone long." In the third stanza, an ironic double vision of years full of agonizing memories intrudes. As in "To My Brother Miguel in Memoriam," the poet chooses to retain the child's faith, urging his brothers and sisters to be good and obey in letter and spirit the instructions left by the mother. In the end, it is seen that the "leaving" is without remedy, a function of time itself; it eventually results in the poet's complete solitude without even the comfort of his siblings. In poem XXIII, the mother, the only symbol of total plenitude, is seen as the "warm oven" of the cookies described as "rich hosts of time." The nourishment provided by the mother was given freely and naturally, taken away from no one and given without the child's being obliged. Still, the process of nurturing leads to growing up and to individuation and alienation. Several poems mythicize the process of birth but shift so abruptly to demythicize human existence that the result is at first humorous. In poem XLVII, a candle is lighted to protect the mother while she gives birth, along with another for the babe who, God willing, will grow up to be bishop, pope, saint, "or perhaps only a columnary headache." Later, in *Human Poems*, there is a Word Incarnate whose bones agree in number and gender as it sinks into the bathtub ("Lomo de las sagradas escrituras"/ "Spine of the Scriptures").

In poem XVIII, the poet surveys the four walls of the cell, implacably closed. He calls up a vision of the "loving keeper of innumerable keys," the mother, who would liberate him if she could. He imagines the two longer walls as mothers and the shorter ones as the children each of them is leading by the hand. The poet is alone with only his two hands, struggling to find a third to help him in his useless adulthood. In poem LVIII, the solid walls of the cell seem to bend at the corners, suggesting that the poet is dozing as a series of jumbled thoughts produce scenes in his mind that follow no easy logical principle of association. The poet sees himself helping the naked and the ragged, then dismounting from a panting horse that he also attempts to help. The cell is now liquid, and he becomes aware of the companions who may be worse off than he. Guilt suddenly overwhelms him, and he is moved to promise to laugh no more when his mother arises early to pray for the sick, the poor, and the prisoners. He also promises to treat his little friends better at play, in both word and deed. The cell is now boundless gas, growing as it condenses. At the end, he poses the question, "Who stumbles outside?" The openness of the poem is similar to that of many others in *Trilce*, and it is difficult to say what kind of threat to the poet's resolutions is posed by the figure outside. Again, the poetic voice has become that of a child seeking to make all that is wrong in the world right once more by promising to be "a good boy." Of course, he is not a child at all, as the figure outside may be intended to remind both him and the reader. The result is a remarkable note of pathos tinged with irony.

Many of *Trilce*'s poems deal with physical love and even the sexual act itself. "Two" seems to be the ideal number, but "two" has "propensities of trinity." Clearly, the poet has no wish to bring a child into the world, and sex becomes merely an act of organs that provides no solution to anything. While the poet seems to appreciate the maternal acts performed by his lover, he fails to find any transcendental satisfaction in the physical relationship, even though he is sad when it is over.

An important theme that emerges in *Trilce* and is developed more fully in *Human Poems* and *Spain, Take This Cup from Me* is that of the body as text. In poem LXV, the house to which the poet returns in Santiago seems to be his mother's body. Parts of the body—the back, face, shoulder, eyes, hands, lips, eyelashes, bones, feet, knees, fingers, heart, arms, breasts, soles of the feet, eyelids, ears, ribs—appear in poem after poem, reminding the reader of human and earthly functions and the limitations of human beings.

In many ways, *Trilce* resembles the poetry of such avant-garde movements as Surrealism, Ultraism, and Creationism in the boldness of its images, its unconventional vocabulary, and its experimentation with graphics. Vallejo did have very limited exposure to some of this poetry after he reached Lima; his critics, however, generally agree that *Trilce* was produced independently. While Vallejo may have been encouraged to experiment by his knowledge of European literary currents, his work coincides with them as an original contribution.

HUMAN POEMS

As far as is known, the poems after *Trilce* were written in Europe; with very few exceptions, none was published until 1939, a year after the poet's death, when they appeared under the title *Human Poems*. While Vallejo's life in Peru was far from affluent, it must have seemed easy in comparison with the years in Paris, where he often barely subsisted and suffered several illnesses. In addition, while he did see a new edition of *Trilce* published through the intervention of friends in 1931 and his *Rusia en 1931* did go into three editions during his lifetime, he could never count on having his writings accepted for publication.

Human Poems, considered separately from *Spain, Take This Cup from Me*, is far from being a homogeneous volume, and its final configuration might have been different had it been Vallejo who prepared the final edition rather than his widow. Generally speaking, the poems that it includes deal with ontological anguish whose cause seems related to physical suffering, the passage of time, and the impossibility of believing that life has any meaning. In fact, *Human Poems* examines suffering and pain, with their corollaries, poverty, hunger, illness, and death, with a thoroughness that few other works can match. At times, the anguish seems to belong only to the poet, now not only the orphan of *Trilce* but alienated from other people as well. In "Altura y pelos" ("Height and Hair"), the poet poses questions: "Who doesn't own a blue suit?/ Who doesn't eat lunch and board the streetcar . . . ?/ Who is not called Carlos or any other thing?/ Who to the kitty doesn't say kitty kitty?" The final answer given is "Aie? I who alone was solely born." At least two kinds of irony seem to be involved here. The activities mentioned are obviously trivial, but neither is it easy to be alone. In the well-known "Los nueve monstruos" ("The Nine Monsters"), the poet laments the abundance of pain in the world: "Never, human men/ was there so *much* pain in the chest, in the lapel, in the wallet/ in the glass, in the butcher-shop, in arithmetic!" and "never/ . . . did the migraine extract so much forehead from the forehead!" Pain drives people crazy "in the movies,/ nails us into the gramophones,/ denails us in bed . . ." The poem concludes that the "Secretary of Health" can do nothing because there is simply "too much to do."

"The Nine Monsters" is representative of several features of *Human Poems*. The language is extremely concrete, denoting things that are inseparable from everyday existence. Much of the poem consists of lists, continuing a device for which the poet had already shown a disposition in his first work. Finally, the logic of the systems represented by the items named is hard to pin down, so that it is somewhat reminiscent of child logic in its eccentricity. Again and again, Vallejo's remarkable sensibility is demonstrated beyond any preciosity or mere posturing.

One reason for the poet's alienation is that he sees people as engaged in trivial occupations and as being hardly more advanced on the evolutionary scale than pachyderms or kangaroos, whereas he himself aspires to rise above his limitations. In "Intensidad y altura" ("Intensity and Height"), he tells of his desire to write being stifled by his feeling "like a puma," so that he might as well go and eat grass. He concludes, "let's go, raven, and fecundate your rook." He thus sees himself condemned not to rise above the purely mundane. Religion offers no hope at all. In "Acaba de pasar el que vendrá..." ("He Has Just Passed By, the One Who Will Come..."), the poet suggests that "the one who will come"—presumably the Messiah—has already passed by but has changed nothing, being as vague and ineffectually human as anyone else.

While the majority of these posthumously published poems convey utter despair, not all of them do. Although the exact dates of their composition are generally unknown, it is natural to associate those that demonstrate growing concern for others with Vallejo's conversion to Marxist thought and eventually to Communism. In "Considerando en frío..." ("Considering Coldly..."), speaking as an attorney at a trial, the poetic voice first summarizes the problems and weaknesses of humanity (he "is sad, coughs and, nevertheless,/ takes pleasure in his reddened chest/... he is a gloomy mammal and combs his hair...") Then, however, he announces his love for humanity. Denying it immediately, he nevertheless concludes, "I signal him,/ he comes,/ I embrace him, moved./ So what! Moved . . . Moved. . . ." Compassion thus nullifies "objectivity." In "La rueda del hambriento" ("The Hungry Man's Wheel"), the poet speaks as a man so miserable that his own organs are pulled out of him through his mouth. He begs only for a stone on which to sit and a little bread. Apparently ignored, aware that he is being importunate, he continues to ask, disoriented and hardly able to recognize his own body. In "Traspié entre dos estrellas" ("Stumble Between Two Stars"), the poet expresses pity for the wretched but goes on to parody bitterly Christ's Sermon on the Mount ("Beloved be the one with bedbugs,/ the one who wears a torn shoe in the rain"), ending with a "beloved" for one thing and then for its opposite, as if calling special attention to the emptiness of mere words. It is possible to say that in these poems the orphan has finally recognized that he is not alone in his orphanhood.

SPAIN, TAKE THIS CUP FROM ME

Although first published as part of *Human Poems*, *Spain, Take This Cup from Me* actually forms a separate, unified work very different in tone from the majority of the other posthumous poems—a tone of hope, although, especially in the title poem, the poet seems to suspect that the cause he has believed in so passionately may be lost. In this poem, perhaps the last that Vallejo wrote, the orphan—now all human children—has found a mother. This mother is Spain, symbol of a new revolutionary order in which oppression may be ended. The children are urged not to let their mother die; nevertheless, even should this happen, they have a recourse: to continue struggling and to go out and find a new mother.

Another contrast is found in the odes to several heroes of the Civil War. Whereas, in *Human Poems*, humans are captives of their bodies and hardly more intelligent than the lower animals, *Spain, Take This Cup from Me* finds people capable of true transcendence through solidarity with others and the will to fight injustice. A number of poems commemorate the battles of the war: Talavera, Guernica, Málaga. Spain thus becomes a text—a book that sprouts from the bodies of an anonymous soldier. The poet insists again and again that he himself is nothing, that his stature is "tiny," and that his actions rather than his words constitute the real text. This may be seen to represent a greatly evolved negation of poetic authority, first seen in *The Black Heralds* with the repeated cry, "I don't know!"

Nevertheless, *Spain, Take This Cup from Me* rings with a biblical tone, and the poet sometimes sounds like a prophet. James Higgins has pointed out certain images that recall the Passion of Christ and the New Jerusalem, although religious terminology, as in all Vallejo's poetry, is applied to humans rather than to divinity. While Vallejo continues to use techniques of enumeration—which are often chaotic—and to use concrete nouns (including many referring to the body), he also employs abstract terms such as peace, hope, martyrdom, harmony, eternity, and greatness. The sense of garments, utensils, and the body's organs stifling the soul is gone and is replaced by limitless space. In Vallejo's longest poem, "Himno a los voluntarios de la República" ("Hymn to the Volunteers for the Republic"), a panegyric note is struck.

One of Vallejo's most immediately accessible poems, "Masa" ("Mass"), tells almost a parable of a dead combatant who was asked by one man not to die, then by two, and finally by millions. The corpse kept dying until surrounded by all the inhabitants of Earth. The corpse, moved, sat up and embraced the first man and then began to walk. The simplicity of the story and of its narration recalls the child's voice in *Trilce*, promising to cease tormenting his playmates in order to atone for the world's guilt. In this piece, as well as in all Vallejo's last group of poems, however, the irony is gone.

POETIC CYCLE

It is thus possible to see the completion of a cycle in the four works. Disillusionment grows in *The Black Heralds*, and then alienation works its way into the language itself in *Trilce*. *Human Poems* is somewhat less Hermetic than *Trilce*, but life is an anguished nightmare in which the soul is constrained by the ever-present body that seems to be always wracked with pain. Only in *Spain, Take This Cup from Me*, with the realization that men are brothers who can end their common alienation and suffering by collective action, does the poet regain his lost faith and embark upon a positive course. The orphan relocates the lost mother, whom he now sees to be the mother of all, since all men are brothers. The true significance of Vallejo's poetry, however, surely lies in his honesty in questioning all established rules of poetic expression, as well as the tradition of poetic authority, in order to put poetry fully in touch with the existential prison house of twentieth century humanity.

OTHER MAJOR WORKS

LONG FICTION: *Fábula salvaje*, 1923 (novella); *El tungsteno*, 1931 (*Tungsten*, 1988).

SHORT FICTION: *Escalas melografiadas*, 1923; *Hacia el reino de los Sciris*, 1967; *Paco Yunque*, 1969.

PLAYS: *Colacho hermanos: O, presidentes de América*, pb. 1979; *Entre las dos orillas corre el río*, pb. 1979; *La piedra cansada*, pb. 1979; *Lock-Out*, pb. 1979; *Teatro completo*, 1979.

NONFICTION: *Rusia en 1931: Reflexiones al pie del Kremlin*, 1931, 1965; *El romanticismo en la poesía castellana*, 1954; *Rusia ante el segundo plan quinquenal*, 1965; *Contra el secreto profesional*, 1973; *El arte y la revolución*, 1973.

BIBLIOGRAPHY

Britton, R. K. "Love, Alienation, and the Absurd: Three Principal Themes in César Vallejo's *Trilce*." *Modern Language Review* 87 (July, 1992): 603-615. Demonstrates how Vallejo's poetry expresses the anguished conviction that humankind is simply a form of animal life subject to the laws of a random, absurd universe.

Dove, Patrick. *The Catastrophe of Modernity: Tragedy and the Nation in Latin American Literature*. Lewisburg, Pa.: Bucknell University Press, 2004. This discussion of the theme of modernity as a catastrophe contains a chapter on Vallejo's *Trilce*.

Hart, Stephen M. *Stumbling Between Forty-six Stars: Essays on César Vallejo*. London: Centre of César Vallejo Studies, 2007. A collection of essays on various aspects of the poet.

Hart, Stephen M., and Jorge Cornejo Polar. *César Vallejo: A Critical Bibliography of Research*. Rochester, N.Y.: Boydell and Brewer, 2002. A bibliography collecting works of Vallejo. Invaluable for researchers.

Hedrick, Tace Megan. "Mi andina y dulce Rita: Women, Indigenism, and the Avant-Garde in César Vallejo." In *Primitivism and Identity in Latin America: Essays on Art, Literature, and Culture*, edited by Erik Camayd-Freixas and José Eduardo González. Tucson: University of Arizona Press, 2000. Relates the indigenism of "Dead Idylls" from *The Black Heralds* to the "avant-garde concerns and practices" of *Trilce*, often considered Vallejo's most brilliant work.

Higgins, James. *The Poet in Peru: Alienation and the Quest for a Super-Reality*. Liverpool, England: Cairns, 1982. Contains a good overview of the main themes of Vallejo's poetry.

Lambie, George. "Poetry and Politics: The Spanish Civil War Poetry of César Vallejo." *Bulletin of Hispanic Studies* 69, no. 2 (April, 1992): 153-170. Analyzes the presence of faith and Marxism in *Spain, Take This Cup from Me*.

Niebylski, Dianna C. *The Poem on the Edge of the Word: The Limits of Language and the Uses of Silence in the Poetry of Mallarmé, Rilke, and Vallejo*. New York: Peter

Lang, 1993. In the context of the language "crisis" of modern poetry and the poet's dilemma in choosing language or silence, Niebylski examines the themes of time and death in Vallejo's *Human Poems*.

Sharman, Adam, ed. *The Poetry and Poetics of César Vallejo: The Fourth Angle of the Circle*. Lewiston, N.Y.: Edwin Mellen Press, 1997. Collection of essays examining Vallejo's work from the perspectives of Marxism, history, the theme of the absent mother, and postcolonial theory.

Lee Hunt Dowling

ANNE WALDMAN

Born: Millville, New Jersey; April 2, 1945

PRINCIPAL POETRY
On the Wing, 1968
Giant Night: Selected Poems, 1970
Baby Breakdown, 1970
Memorial Day, 1971 (with Ted Berrigan)
No Hassles, 1971
Life Notes, 1973
Fast Speaking Woman and Other Chants, 1975 (revised as *Fast Speaking Woman: Chants and Essays*, 1996)
Shaman/Shamane, 1977
Four Travels, 1979 (with Reed Bye)
First Baby Poems, 1983
Makeup on Empty Space, 1983
Invention, 1985
Skin Meat Bones, 1985
Helping the Dreamer: New and Selected Poems, 1966-1988, 1989
Iovis: All Is Full of Jove, 1993, 1997
Troubairitz, 1993
Polemics, 1998 (with Anselm Hollo and Jack Collom)
Marriage: A Sentence, 2000
In the Room of Never Grieve: New and Selected Poems, 1985-2003, 2003
Zombie Dawn, 2003 (with Tom Clark)
Fleuve Flâneur, 2004 (with Mary Kite)
Structure of the World Compared to a Bubble, 2004
Manatee/Humanity, 2009

OTHER LITERARY FORMS

Anne Waldman is known primarily for her poetry.

ACHIEVEMENTS

Anne Waldman has written more than thirty books of poetry and has edited numerous anthologies. She was assistant director, and later director, of the St. Mark's Poetry Project from 1968 to 1978. She cofounded the Jack Kerouac School of Disembodied Poetics at Naropa Institute in Boulder, Colorado. Waldman has received numerous grants and awards, including the Dylan Thomas Memorial Award (1967), a Poets Foundation Award (1969), a National Endowment for the Arts Grant (1979-1980), the Poetry Society of America's Shelley Memorial Award (1996), an Atlantic Center for the Arts Residency (2002), and a fellowship from the Emily Harvey Foundation, Venice (Winter, 2007). In 2001, she received a grant from the Foundation for Contemporary Arts; the same year, she was a resident at the Vermont Studio School.

In March, 2002, the University of Michigan officially opened an archive of Waldman's works and mementoes, calling her "one of the most vibrant writers of the post-Beat generation, . . . a performance poet of electric intensity."

Biography

Anne Waldman was born in Millville, New Jersey, in 1945. Before her fifth birthday, her parents, John Waldman and Frances Waldman, moved to Greenwich Village. Her father encouraged her to read omnivorously, but she learned a special love of poetry from her mother, who translated the work of a Greek poet. Waldman graduated from the Friends Seminary High School, where she first read the work of the Beat poets, which, along with her parental influence, was instrumental in her decision to devote her life to poetry. Her studies at Bennington College further reinforced this dedication.

In 1965, while still enrolled in college, she traveled to California to participate in the Berkeley Poetry Conference. There, she met Allen Ginsberg, with whom she was to form a close literary alliance. After graduating from Bennington in 1966, Waldman became assistant director, and later director, of the Poetry Project at St. Mark's Church-in-the-Bowery in New York. In that capacity, between 1968 and 1978, she met many more of the Beat poets in person.

Also at the St. Mark's Poetry Project, Waldman began to give high-energy public readings of her own work and became known as a pioneering performance poet. She published her first book, *On the Wing*, in 1968, and in 1975, her performance poem *Fast-Speaking Woman* was published by Lawrence Ferlinghetti's City Lights.

In the same period, Waldman, whose interest in Eastern religion dates from high school, began to study with Chögyam Trungpa Rinpoche, a meditation master of Tibetan Buddhism. In 1974, Waldman participated with Ginsberg, Trungpa, and others in founding the Jack Kerouac School of Disembodied Poetics at Naropa Institute in Boulder, Colorado. She later came to serve as a distinguished professor of poetics and director of Naropa's Summer Writing Program. Her son Ambrose Bye is a musician with whom she frequently collaborates in poetry performances.

Overall, Waldman's influence has served to extend the boundaries of poetry well beyond the printed page. As a performance poet, she combines in her work an intense political activism, strong feminism, a critique of all gender identity, extreme departure from conventional poetic forms, and ambitiously long poems embracing large subjects.

ANALYSIS

Despite her connection with two generations of Beat poets, Anne Waldman has never considered herself to be one. In fact, her poetic inspiration has virtually worldwide sources; moreover, unlike the largely apolitical Beats, she has been deeply involved in protest politics. Her work is an intense expression of her advocacy for feminist, environmental, and human-rights concerns. She has also written powerful love lyrics and spiritual meditations.

While describing herself as an "outrider" or as part of "a hybrid outsider tradition," Waldman is an avowed formalist, although the tremendous range, vitality and unconventionality of her work, especially her performance poetry, often belies its own structural underpinnings. For political and aesthetic reasons, her poetic practice has been highly inclusive, assimilating the forms of Asia, the ancient Mediterranean, Western Europe, and contemporary America. With the incantatory work of poet Charles Olson as one of her chief inspirations, she delivers her performance pieces in the "vatic" style of a crazed prophet, attempting to embrace the whole of human social experience and even that of other species. Overall, Waldman's influence has served to revivify the oral tradition of poetry and to extend the boundaries of poetry far beyond the printed page.

GIANT NIGHT

Giant Night displays Waldman's exuberant, expansive consciousness of the world and people around her. Her use of meter, a rapid alternation among spondees, anapests, and iambs, reinforces the impression of constant change. Underlying the surface, however, is a profound and paradoxical sense of timelessness. In the title poem, she declares:

> Awake in a giant night
> is where I am
>   There is a river where my soul,
> hungry as a horse drinks beside me
>
> An hour of immense possibility flies by
> and I do nothing but sit in the present
> which keeps changing moment to moment

"What's New" conveys her deep sense of connection with other beings:

> when you sit down and write
> at a big desk
> think of everyone everywhere writing

FAST SPEAKING WOMAN

Fast Speaking Woman was first published in 1975; in 1996, a twentieth anniversary edition was published, augmenting the original text with essays based on her teachings about chant and performance poetry. The title poem is a long "list chant" listing the attributes of a phrase repeated at the beginning of each line. Waldman presents the list as descriptive of both herself and "everywoman:" "I'm an abalone woman/ I'm the abandoned woman/ I'm the woman abashed, the gibberish woman/ the aborigine woman, the woman absconding."

While the "list chant" form was originated by the Indians of Mexico, Waldman's use of it also contains echoes of the Greek poetess Sappho and William Butler Yeats; in addition, she makes reference to Tibetan Buddhism and ancient magical doctrines. *Fast Speaking Woman* is considered an outstanding contemporary example of performance poetry, with the spoken word lending itself to a more complete experience of the poems than that created by the printed page alone.

IOVIS

Iovis, a monumentally ambitious work, was published in two books, in 1993 and 1997. (A third installment was added in 2003 when it was incorporated into *In the Room of Never Grieve*.) Combined, the books exceed six hundred pages in length. The first two books address the themes of male and female energy, history, mythology, mystical and Eastern religion, and politics. Critics were not cordial to the first book, calling it self-indulgent, overlong, "patched together," and obscure. The second part fared better critically, though even appreciative reviewers noted that the work would be best heard aloud.

Waldman's introduction to book 2 announces that the work is not to be judged by conventional, hierarchical standards: "I feel myself always an open system (woman) available to any words or sounds I'm informed by." The poem defies attempts to summarize its prosody or its formal structure; perhaps this indefinable nature can be taken as a feminist statement. Waldman avoids exclusionary feminist rhetoric, however. Indeed, she asserts that both women and men harbor multiple identities. For example: "What is this identification with young men? Are they playful tricksters inside the hag?" In this and many other ways, Waldman attempts to assimilate all of modern experience, from the ineffable to the quotidian.

MARRIAGE

The energetic and lyrical poems in *Marriage* embody the playful contemplation of marriage as a social institution. The work is not a feminist diatribe against that institution, as Waldman enumerates both the happy and the unhappy aspects of marriage. Moreover, she recognizes marriage in all of its contemporary forms, including traditional, same-sex, and nuclear couples at the center of an extended family. Waldman bases her work on the traditional *haibun* form originated by the Japanese poet Matsuo Bashō, which pairs prose poems with similarly themed lyric poems. With her characteristic inclusiveness, she has said that her goal was spiritual revivification of marriage in its diverse contemporary forms. Critics praised *Marriage* as being accessible to the average reader.

IN THE ROOM OF NEVER GRIEVE

In her introduction to *In the Room of Never Grieve*, a collection of new and old poems from 1985 to 2003, Waldman explains the title: "It's the little girl biting the bullet: *I will stay in this room forever, I will be strong, I will never grieve.*" She describes her goal in poetry as being "To reclaim the imagination, to free our language from the stench of manipulation, . . . [to] examine how the mind moves in language that seeks to create alternative ways to live, to survive, and to sing. These are the tasks, the disciplines." She speaks of her books, this collection in particular, as having "efficacious possibility." In a possible reference to deconstruction—one of the many disciplines she has sought to assimilate—she declares her intention to "question the role of language as it plays with its own markers." Collectively, the poems in this collection fulfill this agenda, displaying the evolution of Waldman's thought regarding the major spiritual, aesthetic, and political themes of her work. The collection was sold with a compact disc containing a selection of the live poetry performances for which she is noted.

The new poems in this collection include statements on current events such as the September 11, 2001, terrorist attacks on the United States and the war in Iraq, as well as the third installment of Waldman's epic *Iovis*. Waldman is convinced that poetry can make a defining difference at this critical juncture of history only by escaping its traditional boundaries. She challenges the reader to think: "If the very future of the world is at stake, is it enough to deconstruct, to mystify, to obviate? Would beauty still be the call? Or love?"

MANATEE/HUMANITY

Manatee/Humanity is a contribution to the genre of ecopoetry, the title playing on the similarity of sound between the words "humanity" and "manatee," the name of the animal popularly known as sea cows. The book exemplifies Waldman's interest in Kalachakra, an Eastern spiritual practice promoting empathy with nonhuman species. In incantatory style, she explores the profound subtleties of interspecies communication and meditates on evolution, neuroscience, endangered species, and the varieties of consciousness.

The title poem begins with a line evocative of the motion it describes: "the manatee is found in shallow slow moving rivers." Among other things, the poem is a kind of primer on a less-familiar animal:

> a manatee calf is born every 2-5 years
> a manatee gestates for a year in the manatee womb
> 8,400 miles of tidal waters could be for the manatee

OTHER MAJOR WORKS

TRANSLATION: *Songs of the Sons and Daughters of Buddha*, 1996 (with Andrew Schelling).

EDITED TEXTS: *The World Anthology: Poems from the St. Mark's Poetry Project*, 1969; *Talking Poetics from Naropa Institute: Annals of the Jack Kerouac School of Disembodied Poetics*, 1978 (with Marilyn Webb); *Nice to See You: Homage to Ted Berrigan*, 1991; *Disembodied Poetics: Annals of the Jack Kerouac School*, 1994 (with Andrew Schelling); *Civil Disobediences: Poetics and Politics in Action*, 2004 (with Lisa Birman); *The Beat Book: Poems and Fiction of the Beat Generation*, 1996; *Beats at Naropa: An Anthology*, 2009 (with Laura E. Wright).

MISCELLANEOUS: *Vow to Poetry: Essays, Interviews, and Manifestos*, 2001; *Outrider: Poems, Essays, Interviews*, 2006.

BIBLIOGRAPHY

Notley, Alice. "Iovis Omnia Plena." Review of *Iovis*. *Chicago Review* 44, no. 1 (1998): 117-130. This review from a feminist critical perspective suggests that Waldman's choice of a male mythical god for her title was deliberately ironic given her feminism and shows how Waldman begins by celebrating Jove but then brings in female myths from Najavo and Gaelic culture, which, along with her own story, come to dominate the poem.

Osman, Jena. "Tracking a Poem in Time: The Shifting States of Anne Waldman's 'Makeup on Empty Space.'" *Jacket* 27 (April, 2005). Examines Waldman's concept of the "wakeful state, through language that stays alive." Focuses on Waldman's poem "Makeup on Empty Space," showing how this concept is realized through an "organic" method of collaborative change, with the poem leading outside itself to other ideas and works of art—a poem, a dance, a book, a day.

Sadoff, Ira. "On the Margins: Part Two." *American Poetry Review* 35, no. 2 (March/April, 2006): 51-55. This article discusses several experimental poets' work and literary style, including themes of Waldman's prose poems. Focuses on her dramatic poem "Stereo." Also touches on the stylistic techniques of women poets Lyn Hejinian and Claudia Rankine.

Smith, Larry. "Embracing the Wild Mind." Review of *Outrider*. *American Book Review* 28, no. 3 (March/April, 2007): 19. Explains Waldman's intuitive discovery of structure in action, rather than prescribed poetic form with its "structured coherence." Describes how Waldman's beliefs as a Buddhist and rebel poet, as well as the influence of Charles Olson's "open poetics," led her toward creation by association, intuition, accumulation of imagery, and leaps of the imagination.

Waldman Anne, and Lisa Birman, eds. *Civil Disobediences: Poetics and Politics in Action*. Minneapolis, Minn.: Coffee House Books, 2004. In her introduction, Waldman denounces a "disturbing disjunct or rip in our culture that calls for an articulate active response to the current repressive agenda" and sets her own agenda for poetry to reverse this trend. Supporting this agenda in the volume are essays, interviews, and lectures from poets of many schools and all ages. Waldman herself contributes "Femanifestos" as a handbook for women poet-activists of the future.

———. *Vow to Poetry: Essays, Interviews, and Manifestos.* Minneapolis, Minn.: Coffee House Press, 2001. Besides the dedication to poetry indicated by the title, Waldman, in this collection of autobiography, interviews, and essays, reports on her life as a poet and political dissenter. Contending that "Language . . . arrives, it manifests, it is a relationship," she details her own poetic practice and offers a how-to guide for young writers.

Thomas Rankin

DEAN YOUNG

Born: Columbia, Pennsylvania; July 18, 1955

PRINCIPAL POETRY
Design with X, 1988
Beloved Infidel, 1992
Strike Anywhere, 1995
First Course in Turbulence, 1999
Skid, 2002
Elegy on a Toy Piano, 2005
Ready-Made Bouquet, 2005
Embryoyo, 2007
Primitive Mentor, 2008
Thirty-one Poems, 1998-2008, 2009

OTHER LITERARY FORMS

Although Dean Young is known primarily for his poetry, he has written a collection of essays on poetics entitled *The Art of Recklessness: Poetry as Assertive Force and Contradiction* (2010), which examines various philosophies and theories in writing and teaching poetry, including sources of inspiration and the relationship between a poem and the reader. He also collaborated with several other poets on the collection *Seven Poets, Four Days, One Book* (2009), and his work has been anthologized in *New American Poets of the Nineties* (1991). Young is the cover artist for several of his collections, including *Skid* and *Primitive Mentor*.

ACHIEVEMENTS

Dean Young's third poetry collection, *Strike Anywhere*, won the Colorado Poetry Prize, and his fifth collection, *Skid*, was a finalist for the Lenore Marshall Poetry Prize. In 2006, *Elegy on a Toy Piano* was selected as a finalist for the Pulitzer Prize in poetry, and in 2009, *Primitive Mentor* was shortlisted for the ninth annual Griffin Poetry Prize.

Young received a Fine Arts Work Center Fellowship in Provincetown, a Stegner Fellowship from Stanford University from 1987 to 1988, National Endowment for the Arts Fellowships in 1988 and 1996, a Guggenheim Fellowship in 2002, and an Academy Award in Literature from the American Academy of Arts and Letters in 2007. Young's poetry has been anthologized in the collection *Best American Poetry* in 1993, 1994, 1997, 2000, 2001, 2006, and 2008. Young is most noted for bringing to modern Surrealist poetry a mixture of humanism, humor, and celebration through his accelerated, disjunctive, and expansive treatment of language and theme. In 2008, he was appointed the William Livingston Chair of Poetry at Austin University.

Biography

Dean Young was born Richard Young in Columbia, Pennsylvania, in 1955. In various interviews, Young comments that he identifies personally and poetically with being misunderstood, which is often an underlying theme of his poems. He spent a year in nursing school, but quickly changed majors, and received his B.A. in English in 1978 and an M.F.A. in 1984, both from Indiana University.

Shortly after finishing his Stegner Fellowship in 1988, Young published his first poetry collection, *Design with X*, which drew heavily from his nursing background. Although this collection shows moments of Young's disjunctive surrealism, the tone of the collection is more solemn than that of his subsequent books. In his third collection, *Strike Anywhere*, Young's poems began to fully exhibit his trademark brand of absurdist humor.

Young divides his time between Austin, Texas, and Berkeley, California, where he lives with his wife, novelist Cornelia Nixon. While Young taught at Loyola University in Chicago, his style grew more expansive, esoteric, and humorous while maintaining a resonant sense of the human condition. By 2005, Young had become a member of the permanent faculty at the Iowa Writers' Workshop. It is at this time that his poems began delving more frequently into themes of family and mortality, as a result of his father's death as well as his own health issues. Young has taught at the low residency M.F.A. program at Warren Wilson College in North Carolina.

Analysis

Dean Young's poetry is noted for its ability to incorporate humor with somber moments, high culture with low, and both Romantic and postmodern sensibilities. Young's poems create a collage of seemingly unrelated images, utterances, and moments by combining, through the use of rapid juxtapositions, the strategies of the Surrealists as well as the standup comedian. In a 2004 *Prairie Schooner* review of *Skid*, Hadara Bar-Nadav suggests that due to Young's shifting poetic strategies, the mixing of literary and popular allusions, and strange lists, it is difficult for the reader to know if Young "is simply observing, critiquing, or making fun of his subjects." Frequently, the answer is all of the above. Young's poetry requires that readers learn the various strategies of its specific, often personal, ordering system. Young's poems work to bring form and order to the subconscious and to illuminate both the expansiveness of people's physical and imaginative world and the role of various relationships in those worlds.

The specific subjects in his work may be politics, literature, popular music, and personal tragedy, sometimes in the same poem. However, recurrent themes in Young's body of work center on the abilities of language and experience to misdirect and confuse, as well as the abilities of the reader to bridge the gaps between his abrupt transitions. Young is often held up as a central figure in contemporary Surrealism, as well as a member of the second generation New York School of poetry.

Beloved Infidel

The poems in Young's second book, *Beloved Infidel*, use a variety of cultural icons—Rastafarian musician Bob Marley, modern artists Mark Rothko and William de Kooning—combined with personal memories. In "The Business of Love Is Cruelty," which is ostensibly about a child telling his mother that he hates her, the poem transitions into a social critique and empathetic understanding of Dr. Frankenstein:

> And Herr Doktor,
> what does he want among the burning villages
> of his proven theories? Well, he wants
> to be a student again

The themes of the poems in *Beloved Infidel* focus on relationships, faith, and alienation, as suggested by the collection's title. The poems in this collection mark evidence of Young's developing style of humor. They derive dramatic tension from his ability to make abrupt shifts in subject matter and strategy, while returning to central themes of alienation, family, and an exploration of the human condition. These surreal examinations of the psyche, through the splicing of culture and personal experience, work to create a common ground between the poet and the reader, while allowing Young to maintain his authorial distance. As a result, the reader is left with a distorted but compassionate reflection of the world.

In the concluding poem of the collection, "The Soul," Young analyzes the philosophy of existence, claiming that Christian religion should not focus on "Christ nailed but brought down," but rather "the tenderness of two summoned women." The poem then ends on another note that draws attention to kind human gestures, what Young suggests is the culmination of human existence, "our momentary gentle attendance as someone calls,/ come look at the moon, come watch the waves." It is this "attendance" to the details and minutia of living and Young's ability to place that minutia in the service of the self that brings cohesion and a Romantic sensibility to this collection.

Elegy on a Toy Piano

In *Elegy on a Toy Piano*, Young continues his critique of modern culture and considers the place of art in that culture, with a strong sense of celebratory playfulness, while simultaneously delving into themes of human relationships and the power of the imagination.

These poems use their sense of the absurd to mediate, and often undercut, subject matters of illness and death. In the title poem, "Elegy on a Toy Piano," the speaker begins with a parable of life and death, "You don't need a pony/ to connect you to the unseeable." This statement requires the reader to work at making meaning out of seeming nonsense by constantly scrambling for connections. After a series of non-sequitur statements, the poem ends with a somber finality as the speaker considers:

> When something becomes ash,
> there's nothing you can do to turn it back.
> About this, even diamonds do not lie.

Elegy on a Toy Piano includes many postmodern moments, which both pronounce Young's aesthetic while simultaneously undercutting it. In "With Hidden Noise," Young strings together several metaphors in a surreal collage of images to help define his relationship to his own writing. In the first line of the poem, Young uses the metaphor "I am a teapot and this is my song." A list of "I am" statements continues until the poem ends with the speaker imploring the reader to attempt writing Surrealist poetry "on your own at home."

Although Young's poems often rely on quick non-sequitur transitions, these strained connections are not arbitrary, but a focused attempt to enact what Danielle Chapman, in her September, 2005, *Poetry* review of *Elegy on a Toy Piano*, called Young's project, to examine "how lonely, how confusing, how ridiculous it is to be an imaginative creature in an ever-streamlining culture."

PRIMITIVE MENTOR

The poems in *Primitive Mentor* show Young being both more serious and more playful than in his previous collections. On the surface, many of these poems pay homage to Young's poetic influences such as William Butler Yeats, Arthur Rimbaud, William Wordsworth, and Walt Whitman. On a broader level, this collection deals more with legacy, mortality, and the speaker's and reader's place in the universe. As a result, the poems in *Primitive Mentor* have an undercurrent of pain that is not as prevalent in his earlier collections. However, Young's poems work more diligently than ever to mediate or soften that pain with his undercutting humor. In the first poem of the first section, "What Form Death," the speaker meditates on death, moving quickly between literary references, memory fragments, punch lines, and wordplay until the speaker imagines addressing a relative who is most likely dead as "Dear mustachioed Aunt Gloria who/ gave me 20 bucks to blow on rubber snakes/ and pinball, what became of you?"

The subjects and themes of *Primitive Mentor* tend more toward the overtly political with poems such as "Enter Fortinbras," which draws parallels between the political climate in William Shakespeare's *Hamlet, Prince of Denmark* (pr. c. 1600-1601) as well as the political and cultural climate prevalent in contemporary America. Young rewrites one of Shakespeare's most famous passages:

> The slings and thongs
> of outrageous fortune, well, no need
> to kill yourself over every bomb and extinction.
>
> To be or not to be, what's the big diff?

This collection's penultimate poem, "Exit Exam," shows Young's speaker contemplating human mortality and the afterlife. In the last lines, Young writes of everyone's inevitable death, and contemplates various institutional beliefs and practices surrounding that death:

> will we be petrified or dashed to even smaller pieces,
> will we be released from the wheelhouse
> or come back as hyena or mouse,
> as a cloud or rock
> or will it be sleep's pure peace of nothingness?

Ending on "nothingness" in this typical Young poem, however, is less a resignation to the inevitability of death as it is the solace of an eventual "pure peace," which reaffirms the importance and vitality of the author's own aesthetic of constant momentum and attentiveness.

Other major work

NONFICTION: *The Art of Recklessness: Poetry as Assertive Force and Contradiction*, 2010.

Bibliography

Harris, Peter. "Difficult and Otherwise: New Work by Ruefle, Young, and Aleshire." *Virginia Quarterly* 73, no. 4 (September, 1997): 680-692. This article works to identify a trend toward Surrealism, the use of condensed language and images in contemporary poetry. In the process, Harris examines Young's collection *Strike Anywhere*, as well as collections by two of Young's peers. Although less than a third of the essay is focused on Young, the sections on Mary Ruefle and Joan Aleshire illuminate principles of Young's aesthetic.

Hoagland, Tony. "The Dean Young Effect." *American Poetry Review* 38, no. 4 (July/August, 2009): 29-33. This article works to place Young into the landscape of contemporary poetry by examining his latest work, his influences, and his influence on younger poets. Hoagland works to clarify some common misconceptions about Young's work and establish him as an important voice in contemporary American poetry.

Logan, William. "The Great American Desert." *The New Criterion* 23 (June, 2005). 66-74. In this essay, Logan reviews several new collections by contemporary authors, including Young's *Elegy on a Toy Piano*. This review takes Young to task for his poetic style and connects that style to that of fellow contemporary American poet John Ashbery.

Young, Dean. "An Interview with Dean Young." Interview by Lee Rossi. *Pedestal Magazine* 53 (May/June, 2009). Rossi and Young discuss poems from *Primitive*

Mentor, and Young's various aesthetic concerns, such as his serious use of the joke, his poetic influences, his writing process, and his indebtedness to Latin American Surrealism.

_____. "Surrealism 101." In *Poet's Work, Poet's Play: Essays on the Practice and the Art*, edited by Daniel Tobin and Pimone Triplett. Ann Arbor: University of Michigan Press, 2008. Describes how Surrealism used trauma, confrontation, and destabilization to bring about change. In examining Surrealism and Dadaism, he sheds light on his own poetry.

Roy Seeger

CHECKLIST FOR EXPLICATING A POEM

I. The Initial Readings

A. Before reading the poem, the reader should:
  1. Notice its form and length.
  2. Consider the title, determining, if possible, whether it might function as an allusion, symbol, or poetic image.
  3. Notice the date of composition or publication, and identify the general era of the poet.

B. The poem should be read intuitively and emotionally and be allowed to "happen" as much as possible.

C. In order to establish the rhythmic flow, the poem should be reread. A note should be made as to where the irregular spots (if any) are located.

II. Explicating the Poem

A. *Dramatic situation.* Studying the poem line by line helps the reader discover the dramatic situation. All elements of the dramatic situation are interrelated and should be viewed as reflecting and affecting one another. The dramatic situation serves a particular function in the poem, adding realism, surrealism, or absurdity; drawing attention to certain parts of the poem; and changing to reinforce other aspects of the poem. All points should be considered. The following questions are particularly helpful to ask in determining dramatic situation:
  1. What, if any, is the narrative action in the poem?
  2. How many personae appear in the poem? What part do they take in the action?
  3. What is the relationship between characters?
  4. What is the setting (time and location) of the poem?

B. *Point of view.* An understanding of the poem's point of view is a major step toward comprehending the poet's intended meaning. The reader should ask:
  1. Who is the speaker? Is he or she addressing someone else or the reader?
  2. Is the narrator able to understand or see everything happening to him or her, or does the reader know things that the narrator does not?
  3. Is the narrator reliable?
  4. Do point of view and dramatic situation seem consistent? If not, the inconsistencies may provide clues to the poem's meaning.

C. *Images and metaphors.* Images and metaphors are often the most intricately crafted vehicles of the poem for relaying the poet's message. Realizing that the images and metaphors work in harmony with the dramatic situation and point of view will help the reader to see the poem as a whole, rather than as disassociated elements.
  1. The reader should identify the concrete images (that is, those that are formed from objects that can be touched, smelled, seen, felt, or tasted). Is the image projected by the poet consistent with the physical object?
  2. If the image is abstract, or so different from natural imagery that it cannot be associated with a real object, then what are the properties of the image?
  3. To what extent is the reader asked to form his or her own images?
  4. Is any image repeated in the poem? If so, how has it been changed? Is there a controlling image?
  5. Are any images compared to each other? Do they reinforce one another?
  6. Is there any difference between the way the reader perceives the image and the way the narrator sees it?
  7. What seems to be the narrator's or persona's attitude toward the image?

D. *Words.* Every substantial word in a poem may have more than one intended meaning, as used by the author. Because of this, the reader should look up many of these words in the dictionary and:
  1. Note all definitions that have the slightest connection with the poem.
  2. Note any changes in syntactical patterns in the poem.
  3. In particular, note those words that could possibly function as symbols or allusions, and refer to any appropriate sources for further information.

E. *Meter, rhyme, structure, and tone.* In scanning the poem, all elements of prosody should be noted by the reader. These elements are often used by a poet to manipulate the reader's emotions, and therefore they should be examined closely to arrive at the poet's specific intention.
  1. Does the basic meter follow a traditional pattern such as those found in nursery rhymes or folk songs?
  2. Are there any variations in the base meter? Such changes or substitutions are important thematically and should be identified.
  3. Are the rhyme schemes traditional or innovative, and what might their form mean to the poem?
  4. What devices has the poet used to create sound patterns (such as assonance and alliteration)?
  5. Is the stanza form a traditional or innovative one?
  6. If the poem is composed of verse paragraphs rather than stanzas, how do they affect the progression of the poem?

7. After examining the above elements, is the resultant tone of the poem casual or formal, pleasant, harsh, emotional, authoritative?

F. *Historical context*. The reader should attempt to place the poem into historical context, checking on events at the time of composition. Archaic language, expressions, images, or symbols should also be looked up.

G. *Themes and motifs*. By seeing the poem as a composite of emotion, intellect, craftsmanship, and tradition, the reader should be able to determine the themes and motifs (smaller recurring ideas) presented in the work. He or she should ask the following questions to help pinpoint these main ideas:
  1. Is the poet trying to advocate social, moral, or religious change?
  2. Does the poet seem sure of his or her position?
  3. Does the poem appeal primarily to the emotions, to the intellect, or to both?
  4. Is the poem relying on any particular devices for effect (such as imagery, allusion, paradox, hyperbole, or irony)?

BIBLIOGRAPHY

GENERAL REFERENCE SOURCES

BIOGRAPHICAL SOURCES

Colby, Vineta, ed. *World Authors, 1975-1980.* Wilson Authors Series. New York: H. W. Wilson, 1985.

_____. *World Authors, 1980-1985.* Wilson Authors Series. New York: H. W. Wilson, 1991.

_____. *World Authors, 1985-1990.* Wilson Authors Series. New York: H. W. Wilson, 1995.

Cyclopedia of World Authors. 4th rev. ed. 5 vols. Pasadena, Calif.: Salem Press, 2003.

Dictionary of Literary Biography. 254 vols. Detroit: Gale Research, 1978-   .

International Who's Who in Poetry and Poets' Encyclopaedia. Cambridge, England: International Biographical Centre, 1993.

Seymour-Smith, Martin, and Andrew C. Kimmens, eds. *World Authors, 1900-1950.* Wilson Authors Series. 4 vols. New York: H. W. Wilson, 1996.

Thompson, Clifford, ed. *World Authors, 1990-1995.* Wilson Authors Series. New York: H. W. Wilson, 1999.

Wakeman, John, ed. *World Authors, 1950-1970.* New York: H. W. Wilson, 1975.

_____. *World Authors, 1970-1975.* Wilson Authors Series. New York: H. W. Wilson, 1991.

Willhardt, Mark, and Alan Michael Parker, eds. *Who's Who in Twentieth Century World Poetry.* New York: Routledge, 2000.

CRITICISM

Brooks, Cleanth, and Robert Penn Warren. *Understanding Poetry.* 4th ed. Reprint. Fort Worth, Tex.: Heinle & Heinle, 2003.

Classical and Medieval Literature Criticism. Detroit: Gale Research, 1988-   .

Contemporary Literary Criticism. Detroit: Gale Research, 1973-   .

Day, Gary. *Literary Criticism: A New History.* Edinburgh, Scotland: Edinburgh University Press, 2008.

Draper, James P., ed. *World Literature Criticism 1500 to the Present: A Selection of Major Authors from Gale's Literary Criticism Series.* 6 vols. Detroit: Gale Research, 1992.

Habib, M. A. R. *A History of Literary Criticism: From Plato to the Present.* Malden, Mass.: Wiley-Blackwell, 2005.

Jason, Philip K., ed. *Masterplots II: Poetry Series, Revised Edition.* 8 vols. Pasadena, Calif.: Salem Press, 2002.

Lodge, David, and Nigel Wood. *Modern Criticism and Theory.* 3d ed. New York: Longman, 2008.
Magill, Frank N., ed. *Magill's Bibliography of Literary Criticism.* 4 vols. Englewood Cliffs, N.J.: Salem Press, 1979.
MLA International Bibliography. New York: Modern Language Association of America, 1922-   .
Nineteenth-Century Literature Criticism. Detroit: Gale Research, 1981-   .
Twentieth-Century Literary Criticism. Detroit: Gale Research, 1978-   .
Vedder, Polly, ed. *World Literature Criticism Supplement: A Selection of Major Authors from Gale's Literary Criticism Series.* 2 vols. Detroit: Gale Research, 1997.
Young, Robyn V., ed. *Poetry Criticism: Excerpts from Criticism of the Works of the Most Significant and Widely Studied Poets of World Literature.* 29 vols. Detroit: Gale Research, 1991.

POETRY DICTIONARIES AND HANDBOOKS
Carey, Gary, and Mary Ellen Snodgrass. *A Multicultural Dictionary of Literary Terms.* Jefferson, N.C.: McFarland, 1999.
Deutsch, Babette. *Poetry Handbook: A Dictionary of Terms.* 4th ed. New York: Funk & Wagnalls, 1974.
Drury, John. *The Poetry Dictionary.* Cincinnati, Ohio: Story Press, 1995.
Kinzie, Mary. *A Poet's Guide to Poetry.* Chicago: University of Chicago Press, 1999.
Lennard, John. *The Poetry Handbook: A Guide to Reading Poetry for Pleasure and Practical Criticism.* New York: Oxford University Press, 1996.
Matterson, Stephen, and Darryl Jones. *Studying Poetry.* New York: Oxford University Press, 2000.
Packard, William. *The Poet's Dictionary: A Handbook of Prosody and Poetic Devices.* New York: Harper & Row, 1989.
Preminger, Alex, et al., eds. *The New Princeton Encyclopedia of Poetry and Poetics.* 3d rev. ed. Princeton, N.J.: Princeton University Press, 1993.
Shipley, Joseph Twadell, ed. *Dictionary of World Literary Terms, Forms, Technique, Criticism.* Rev. ed. Boston: George Allen and Unwin, 1979.

INDEXES OF PRIMARY WORKS
Frankovich, Nicholas, ed. *The Columbia Granger's Index to Poetry in Anthologies.* 11th ed. New York: Columbia University Press, 1997.
_____. *The Columbia Granger's Index to Poetry in Collected and Selected Works.* New York: Columbia University Press, 1997.
Guy, Patricia. *A Women's Poetry Index.* Phoenix, Ariz.: Oryx Press, 1985.
Hazen, Edith P., ed. *Columbia Granger's Index to Poetry.* 10th ed. New York: Columbia University Press, 1994.

Hoffman, Herbert H., and Rita Ludwig Hoffman, comps. *International Index to Recorded Poetry*. New York: H. W. Wilson, 1983.

Kline, Victoria. *Last Lines: An Index to the Last Lines of Poetry*. 2 vols. Vol. 1, *Last Line Index, Title Index*; Vol. 2, *Author Index, Keyword Index*. New York: Facts On File, 1991.

Marcan, Peter. *Poetry Themes: A Bibliographical Index to Subject Anthologies and Related Criticisms in the English Language, 1875-1975*. Hamden, Conn.: Linnet Books, 1977.

Poem Finder. Great Neck, N.Y.: Roth, 2000.

POETICS, POETIC FORMS, AND GENRES

Attridge, Derek. *Poetic Rhythm: An Introduction*. New York: Cambridge University Press, 1995.

Brogan, T. V. F. *Verseform: A Comparative Bibliography*. Baltimore: Johns Hopkins University Press, 1989.

Fussell, Paul. *Poetic Meter and Poetic Form*. Rev. ed. New York: McGraw-Hill, 1979.

Hollander, John. *Rhyme's Reason*. 3d ed. New Haven, Conn.: Yale University Press, 2001.

Jackson, Guida M. *Traditional Epics: A Literary Companion*. New York: Oxford University Press, 1995.

Padgett, Ron, ed. *The Teachers and Writers Handbook of Poetic Forms*. 2d ed. New York: Teachers & Writers Collaborative, 2000.

Pinsky, Robert. *The Sounds of Poetry: A Brief Guide*. New York: Farrar, Straus and Giroux, 1998.

Preminger, Alex, and T. V. F. Brogan, eds. *New Princeton Encyclopedia of Poetry and Poetics*. 3d ed. Princeton, N.J.: Princeton University Press, 1993.

Spiller, Michael R. G. *The Sonnet Sequence: A Study of Its Strategies*. Studies in Literary Themes and Genres 13. New York: Twayne, 1997.

Turco, Lewis. *The New Book of Forms: A Handbook of Poetics*. Hanover, N.H.: University Press of New England, 1986.

Williams, Miller. *Patterns of Poetry: An Encyclopedia of Forms*. Baton Rouge: Louisiana State University Press, 1986.

Maura Ives
Updated by Tracy Irons-Georges

GUIDE TO ONLINE RESOURCES

Web Sites

The following sites were visited by the editors of Salem Press in 2010. Because URLs frequently change, the accuracy of these addresses cannot be guaranteed; however, long-standing sites, such as those of colleges and universities, national organizations, and government agencies, generally maintain links when their sites are moved.

Academy of American Poets
http://www.poets.org
    The mission of the Academy of American Poets is to "support American poets at all stages of their careers and to foster the appreciation of contemporary poetry." The academy's comprehensive Web site features information on poetic schools and movements; a Poetic Forms Database; an Online Poetry Classroom, with educator and teaching resources; an index of poets and poems; essays and interviews; general Web resources; links for further study; and more.

Contemporary British Writers
http://www.contemporarywriters.com/authors
    Created by the British Council, this site offers profiles of living writers of the United Kingdom, the Republic of Ireland, and the Commonwealth. Information includes biographies, bibliographies, critical reviews, and news about literary prizes. Photographs are also featured. Users can search the site by author, genre, nationality, gender, publisher, book title, date of publication, and prize name and date.

LiteraryHistory.com
http://www.literaryhistory.com
    This site is an excellent source of academic, scholarly, and critical literature about eighteenth, nineteenth, and twentieth century American and English writers. It provides individual pages for twentieth century literature and alphabetical lists of authors that link to articles, reviews, overviews, excerpts of works, teaching guides, podcasts, and other materials.

Literary Resources on the Net
http://andromeda.rutgers.edu/~jlynch/Lit
    Jack Lynch of Rutgers University maintains this extensive collection of links to Web sites that are useful to researchers, including numerous sites about American and English literature. This collection is a good place to begin online research about poetry, as it

links to other sites with broad ranges of literary topics. The site is organized chronologically, with separate pages about twentieth century British and Irish literature. It also has separate pages providing links to Web sites about American literature and to women's literature and feminism.

LitWeb
http://litweb.net

LitWeb provides biographies of hundreds of world authors throughout history that can be accessed through an alphabetical listing. The pages about each writer contain a list of his or her works, suggestions for further reading, and illustrations. The site also offers information about past and present winners of major literary prizes.

The Modern Word: Authors of the Libyrinth
http://www.themodernword.com/authors.html

The Modern Word site, although somewhat haphazard in its organization, provides a great deal of critical information about writers. The "Authors of the Libyrinth" page is very useful, linking author names to essays about them and other resources. The section of the page headed "The Scriptorium" presents "an index of pages featuring writers who have pushed the edges of their medium, combining literary talent with a sense of experimentation to produce some remarkable works of modern literature."

Outline of American Literature
http://www.america.gov/publications/books/outline-of-american-literature.html

This page of the America.gov site provides access to an electronic version of the ten-chapter volume *Outline of American Literature*, a historical overview of poetry and prose from colonial times to the present published by the Bureau of International Information Programs of the U.S. Department of State.

Poetry Foundation
http://www.poetryfoundation.org

The Poetry Foundation, publisher of *Poetry* magazine, is an independent literary organization. Its Web site offers links to essays; news; events; online poetry resources, such as blogs, organizations, publications, and references and research; a glossary of literary terms; and a Learning Lab that includes poem guides and essays on poetics.

Poet's Corner
http://theotherpages.org/poems

The Poet's Corner, one of the oldest text resources on the Web, provides access to about seven thousand works of poetry by several hundred different poets from around the world. Indexes are arranged and searchable by title, name of poet, or subject. The site also offers its own resources, including "Faces of the Poets"—a gallery of portraits—and "Lives of the Poets"—a growing collection of biographies.

Representative Poetry Online
http://rpo.library.utoronto.ca

This award-winning resource site, maintained by Ian Lancashire of the Department of English at the University of Toronto in Canada, has several thousand English-language poems by hundreds of poets. The collection is searchable by poet's name, title of work, first line of a poem, and keyword. The site also includes a time line, a glossary, essays, an extensive bibliography, and countless links organized by country and by subject.

Voice of the Shuttle
http://vos.ucsb.edu

One of the most complete and authoritative places for online information about literature, Voice of the Shuttle is maintained by professors and students in the English Department at the University of California, Santa Barbara. The site provides countless links to electronic books, academic journals, literary association Web sites, sites created by university professors, and many other resources.

Voices from the Gaps
http://voices.cla.umn.edu/

Voices from the Gaps is a site of the English Department at the University of Minnesota, dedicated to providing resources on the study of women artists of color, including writers. The site features a comprehensive index searchable by name, and it provides biographical information on each writer or artist and other resources for further study.

ELECTRONIC DATABASES

Electronic databases usually do not have their own URLs. Instead, public, college, and university libraries subscribe to these databases, provide links to them on their Web sites, and make them available to library card holders or other specified patrons. Readers can visit library Web sites or ask reference librarians to check on availability.

Canadian Literary Centre

Produced by EBSCO, the Canadian Literary Centre database contains full-text content from ECW Press, a Toronto-based publisher, including the titles in the publisher's Canadian fiction studies, Canadian biography, and Canadian writers and their works series; *ECW's Biographical Guide to Canadian Novelists*; and *George Woodcock's Introduction to Canadian Fiction*. Author biographies, essays and literary criticism, and book reviews are among the database's offerings.

Literary Reference Center

EBSCO's Literary Reference Center (LRC) is a comprehensive full-text database designed primarily to help high school and undergraduate students in English and the humanities with homework and research assignments about literature. The database contains massive amounts of information from reference works, books, literary journals, and other materials, including more than 31,000 plot summaries, synopses, and overviews of literary works; almost 100,000 essays and articles of literary criticism; about 140,000 author biographies; more than 605,000 book reviews; and more than 5,200 author interviews. It contains the entire contents of Salem Press's MagillOnLiterature Plus. Users can retrieve information by browsing a list of authors' names or titles of literary works; they can also use an advanced search engine to access information by numerous categories, including author name, gender, cultural identity, national identity, and the years in which he or she lived, or by literary title, character, locale, genre, and publication date. The Literary Reference Center also features a literary-historical time line, an encyclopedia of literature, and a glossary of literary terms.

MagillOnLiterature Plus

MagillOnLiterature Plus is a comprehensive, integrated literature database produced by Salem Press and available on the EBSCOhost platform. The database contains the full text of essays in Salem's many literature-related reference works, including *Masterplots, Cyclopedia of World Authors, Cyclopedia of Literary Characters, Cyclopedia of Literary Places, Critical Survey of Poetry, Critical Survey of Long Fiction, Critical Survey of Short Fiction, World Philosophers and Their Works, Magill's Literary Annual*, and *Magill's Book Reviews*. Among its contents are articles on more than 35,000 literary works and more than 8,500 poets, writers, dramatists, essayists, and philosophers; more than 1,000 images; and a glossary of more than 1,300 literary terms. The biographical essays include lists of authors' works and secondary bibliographies, and hundreds of overview essays examine and discuss literary genres, time periods, and national literatures.

Rebecca Kuzins; updated by Desiree Dreeuws

GEOGRAPHICAL INDEX

CZECH REPUBLIC
    Seifert, Jaroslav, 186

FRANCE
    Apollinaire, Guillaume, 4
    Aragon, Louis, 15
    Breton, André, 46
    Celan, Paul, 54
    Cocteau, Jean, 63
    Mallarmé, Stéphane, 131
    Reverdy, Pierre, 155
    Stein, Gertrude, 197
    Tzara, Tristan, 210

PERU
    Vallejo, César, 220

POLAND
    Herbert, Zbigniew, 99

ROMANIA
    Celan, Paul, 54
    Tzara, Tristan, 210

RUSSIA
    Esenin, Sergei, 85

SPAIN
    Vallejo, César, 220

UNITED STATES
    Ashbery, John, 26
    Berrigan, Ted, 41
    Cummings, E. E., 74
    Guest, Barbara, 94
    Koch, Kenneth, 110
    Lowell, Amy, 120
    Notley, Alice, 140
    O'Hara, Frank, 146
    Schuyler, James, 165
    Schwartz, Delmore, 175
    Stein, Gertrude, 197
    Waldman, Anne, 233
    Young, Dean, 240

CATEGORY INDEX

CHILDREN'S/YOUNG ADULT POETRY
    Seifert, Jaroslav, 186
    Stein, Gertrude, 197
CONCRETE POETRY
    Apollinaire, Guillaume, 4
    Cummings, E. E., 74
CONFESSIONAL POETS
    Berrigan, Ted, 41
    Schwartz, Delmore, 175
CUBISM
    Apollinaire, Guillaume, 4
    Cocteau, Jean, 63
    Cummings, E. E., 74
    Reverdy, Pierre, 155
    Stein, Gertrude, 197

DADAISM
    Aragon, Louis, 15
    Breton, André, 46
    Seifert, Jaroslav, 186
    Tzara, Tristan, 210
DIALECT POETRY
    Cummings, E. E., 74

ECOPOETRY
    Waldman, Anne, 233
EKPHRASTIC POETRY
    Ashbery, John, 26
    Scwartz, Delmore, 175
ELEGIES
    Berrigan, Ted, 41
EPICS
    Koch, Kenneth, 110
    Notley, Alice, 140
    Schwartz, Delmore, 175
    Tzara, Tristan, 210
    Waldman, Anne, 233

EXPERIMENTAL POETS
    Breton, André, 46
    Celan, Paul, 54
    Cummings, E. E., 74
    Lowell, Amy, 120
    Mallarmé, Stéphane, 131
    Reverdy, Pierre, 155
    Stein, Gertrude, 197
EXPRESSIONISM
    Celan, Paul, 54

FEMINIST POETS
    Notley, Alice, 140
    Stein, Gertrude, 197
    Waldman, Anne, 233

GAY AND LESBIAN CULTURE
    Ashbery, John, 26
    O'Hara, Frank, 146
    Schuyler, James, 165
    Stein, Gertrude, 197

HARVARD AESTHETES
    Cummings, E. E., 74

IMAGISM
    Guest, Barbara, 94
    Lowell, Amy, 120
IMPRESSIONISM
    Lowell, Amy, 120

JEWISH CULTURE
    Celan, Paul, 54
    Schwartz, Delmore, 175
    Stein, Gertrude, 197
    Tzara, Tristan, 210

LOST GENERATION
    Cummings, E. E., 74
    Stein, Gertrude, 197
LOVE POETRY
    Cummings, E. E., 74
    Seifert, Jaroslav, 186
    Vallejo, César, 220
    Waldman, Anne, 233
LYRIC POETRY
    Apollinaire, Guillaume, 4
    Celan, Paul, 54
    Cummings, E. E., 74
    Esenin, Sergei, 85
    Seifert, Jaroslav, 186
    Vallejo, César, 220

NARRATIVE POETRY
    Notley, Alice, 140
    Tzara, Tristan, 210
NEW YORK SCHOOL
    Ashbery, John, 26
    Berrigan, Ted, 41
    Guest, Barbara, 94
    Koch, Kenneth, 110
    Notley, Alice, 140
    O'Hara, Frank, 146
    Schuyler, James, 165
    Schwartz, Delmore, 175
    Waldman, Anne, 233
    Young, Dean, 240

OCCASIONAL VERSE
    Schuyler, James, 165
ODES
    O'Hara, Frank, 146

PARNASSIANISM
    Mallarmé, Stéphane, 131

PATTERN POETS
    Apollinaire, Guillaume, 4
    Cummings, E. E., 74
    Mallarmé, Stéphane, 131
PERFORMANCE POETRY
    Waldman, Anne, 233
POLITICAL POETS
    Aragon, Louis, 15
    Herbert, Zbigniew, 99
    Seifert, Jaroslav, 186
    Waldman, Anne, 233
POSTMODERNISM
    Herbert, Zbigniew, 99
    Tzara, Tristan, 210
PROSE POETRY
    Berrigan, Ted, 41
    Herbert, Zbigniew, 99
    Mallarmé, Stéphane, 131
    Reverdy, Pierre, 155
    Waldman, Anne, 233

ROMANTICISM
    Mallarmé, Stéphane, 131

SATIRIC POETRY
    Cummings, E. E., 74
SOCIALIST REALISM
    Aragon, Louis, 15
SONNETS
    Berrigan, Ted, 41
    Lowell, Amy, 120
SURREALIST POETS
    Apollinaire, Guillaume, 4
    Aragon, Louis, 15
    Ashbery, John, 26
    Breton, André, 46
    Celan, Paul, 54
    Cocteau, Jean, 63
    Reverdy, Pierre, 155
    Tzara, Tristan, 210

Vallejo, César, 220
Young, Dean, 240

SYMBOLIST POETS
Apollinaire, Guillaume, 4
Mallarmé, Stéphane, 131

ULTRAISM
Vallejo, César, 220

VERSE DRAMATISTS
Schwartz, Delmore, 175

WAR POEMS
Apollinaire, Guilaume, 4
Aragon, Louis, 15
Reverdy, Pierre, 155

WOMEN POETS
Guest, Barbara, 94
Lowell, Amy, 120
Notley, Alice, 140
Stein, Gertrude, 197
Waldman, Anne, 233

SUBJECT INDEX

Alcools (Apollinaire), 10
All Soul's Day (Esenin), 90
"All the Soul Indrawn . . ." (Mallarmé), 134
Ancel, Paul. *See* Celan, Paul
And the Stars Were Shining (Ashbery), 37
Anna Snegina (Esenin), 92
Antschel, Paul. *See* Celan, Paul
Apollinaire, Guillaume, 4-14
    Alcools, 10
    Bestiary, 10
    Calligrammes, 11
    "The New Spirit and the Poets," 4
    poem about, 215
Apollinaris, Wilhelm. *See* Apollinaire, Guillaume
Approximate Man, and Other Writings (Tzara), 217
April Galleons (Ashbery), 36
Aragon, Louis, 15-25
    "Elsa's Eyes," 22
    "Poem to Shout in the Ruins," 20
    "You Who Are the Rose," 23
Art of Love, The (Koch), 115
"Art of Poetry, The" (Koch), 115
Ashbery, John, 26-40
    And the Stars Were Shining, 37
    April Galleons, 36
    Houseboat Days, 35
    Self-Portrait in a Convex Mirror, 33
    Some Trees, 29
    The Tennis Court Oath, 31
    Three Poems, 31
    A Wave, 36
    Where Shall I Wander, 37
    A Worldly Country, 38
    Your Name Here, 37

Autobiography of Alice B. Toklas, The (Stein), 207
Automatic writing, 19
Azure (Esenin), 91

"Ballad of the Children of the Czar, The" (Schwartz), 179
Beloved Infidel (Young), 242
Berrigan, Ted, 41-45
    Personal Poems, 44
    The Sonnets, 44
Bestiary (Apollinaire), 10
Black Heralds, The (Vallejo), 223
"Blow, The" (Seifert), 194
Breton, André, 46-53
    Communicating Vessels, 48
    Fata Morgana, 52
    Free Union, 52
    "In the Eyes of the Gods," 50
    "In the Lovely Half-light," 51
    Manifesto of Surrealism, 48

Calligrammes (Apollinaire), 11
Cap de Bonne-Espérance, Le (Cocteau), 68
"Carrefour" (Reverdy), 158
Casting of the Bells, The (Seifert), 193
Celan, Paul, 54-62
    Mohn und Gedächtnis, 57
    Die Niemandsrose, 60
    Speech-Grille, 59
    Von Schwelle zu Schwelle, 59
Chant des morts, Le (Reverdy), 162
"Circus Performers, The" (Tzara), 216
Cocteau, Jean, 63-73
    Le Cap de Bonne-Espérance, 68
    La Danse de Sophocle, 68

Discours du grand sommeil, 69
Opéra, 70
Plain-Chant, 70
Poésies, 1917-1920, 70
Le Prince frivole, 68
Vocabulaire, 69
Communicating Vessels (Breton), 48
Coup de dés jamais n'abolira le hasard, Un. See *Dice Thrown Never Will Annul Chance*
Cummings, E. E., 74-84
"r-p-o-p-h-e-s-s-a-g-r," 78

Danse de Sophocle, La (Cocteau), 68
"Day Lady Died, The" (O'Hara), 152
De nos oiseaux (Tzara), 215
"Death of Guillaume Apollinaire, The" (Tzara), 215
Descent of Alette, The (Notley), 142
Dice Thrown Never Will Annul Chance (Mallarmé), 137
Discours du grand sommeil (Cocteau), 69
Disobedience (Notley), 144
"Dog Named Ego, the Snowflakes as Kisses, A" (Schwartz), 182

Elegy for the Departure, and Other Poems (Herbert), 107
Elegy on a Toy Piano (Young), 242
"Elsa's Eyes" (Aragon), 22
"Enfin" (Reverdy), 162
Esenin, Sergei, 85-93
  All Soul's Day, 90
  Anna Snegina, 92
  Azure, 91
  "Inonia," 91
  Moskva kabatskaia, 92
  Persidskie motivi, 92
  Pugachov, 91
  "Strana negodiaev," 91

España, aparta de mí este cáliz. See *Spain, Take This Cup from Me*
"Et Maintenant" (Reverdy), 163

"Far Rockaway" (Schwartz), 180
Fast Speaking Woman (Waldman), 235
Fata Morgana (Breton), 52
Free Union (Breton), 52

Giant Night (Waldman), 235
Goluben'. See *Azure*
"Guerre" (Reverdy), 159
Guest, Barbara, 94-98
  Miniatures, and Other Poems, 97
  The Red Gaze, 97
  Symbiosis, 96

"Heavy Bear Who Goes with Me, The" (Schwartz), 181
"Her Pure Fingernails on High Offering Their Onyx" (Mallarmé), 135
Heraldos negros, Los. See *Black Heralds,The*
Herbert, Zbigniew, 99-109
  Elegy for the Departure, and Other Poems, 107
  Hermes, pies i gwiazda, 105
  Mr. Cogito, 106
  Napis, 106
  Report from the Besieged City, and Other Poems, 106
  Studium przedmiotu, 106
Hermes, pies i gwiazda (Herbert), 105
Herodias (Mallarmé), 135
Homme approximatif, L'. See *Approximate Man*
Houseboat Days (Ashbery), 35
Human Poems (Vallejo), 228

Igitur (Mallarmé), 137
Imaginism, 88

Imagistes, Des (anthology), 124
"In the Eyes of the Gods" (Breton), 50
"In the Lovely Half-light" (Breton), 51
"In the Naked Bed, in Plato's Cave" (Schwartz), 179
In the Room of Never Grieve (Waldman), 237
"Inonia" (Esenin), 91
Iovis (Waldman), 236

Koch, Kenneth, 110-119
   The Art of Love, 115
   "The Art of Poetry" (Koch), 115
   New Addresses, 117
   On the Edge, 116
   The Pleasures of Peace, and Other Poems, 114
   "The Seasons," 117
   "Some General Instructions," 116
   Straits, 117
Kostrowitzki, Guillelmus Apollinaris de. *See* Apollinaire, Guillaume

"Little Town in Siberia" (Tzara), 215
Lowell, Amy, 120-130
   "On Looking at a Copy of Alice Meynell's Poems," 126

"Main-Morte" (Reverdy), 161
Mallarmé, Stéphane, 131-139
   "All the Soul Indrawn . . .," 134
   Dice Thrown Never Will Annul Chance, 137
   "Her Pure Fingernails on High Offering Their Onyx," 135
   Herodias, 135
   Igitur, 137
   "My Old Books Closed at the Name of Paphos," 134
Manatee/Humanity (Waldman), 237
Manifesto of Surrealism (Breton), 48

Marriage (Waldman), 236
"Mémoire" (Reverdy), 160
Miniatures, and Other Poems (Guest), 97
Mohn und Gedächtnis (Celan), 57
"Morning of the Poem, The" (Schuyler), 170
Moskva kabatskaia (Esenin), 92
Mr. Cogito (Herbert), 106
"My Heat" (O'Hara), 149
"My Old Books Closed at the Name of Paphos" (Mallarmé), 134
Mystery of Small Houses (Notley), 143

Napis (Herbert), 106
New Addresses (Koch), 117
"New Spirit and the Poets, The" (Apollinaire), 4
Niemandsrose, Die (Celan), 60
Notley, Alice, 140-145
   The Descent of Alette, 142
   Disobedience, 144
   Mystery of Small Houses, 143

O'Hara, Frank, 146-154
   "The Day Lady Died," 152
   "My Heat," 149
   "Poem (Lana Turner has collapsed!)," 152
   "Savoy," 151
"On Looking at a Copy of Alice Meynell's Poems" (Lowell), 126
On the Edge (Koch), 116
Opéra (Cocteau), 70

Pan Cogito. *See Mr. Cogito*
Persidskie motivi (Esenin), 92
Personal Poems (Berrigan), 44
Plague Column, The (Seifert), 194
Plague Monument, The. *See Plague Column, The*
Plain-Chant (Cocteau), 70

Pleasures of Peace, and Other Poems, The (Koch), 114
"Poem (Lana Turner has collapsed!)" (O'Hara), 152
"Poem to Shout in the Ruins" (Aragon), 20
Poésies, 1917-1920 (Cocteau), 70
"Poetry and Grammar" (Stein), 205
Primele Poème (Tzara), 214
Primitive Mentor (Young), 243
Prince frivole, Le (Cocteau), 68
"Prothalamion" (Schwartz), 181
Pugachov (Esenin), 91

Radunitsa. See *All Soul's Day*
Raport z oblezonego miasta i inne wiersze. See *Report from the Besieged City*
Red Gaze, The (Guest), 97
Report from the Besieged City, and Other Poems (Herbert), 106
Reverdy, Pierre, 155-164
  "Carrefour," 158
  Le Chant des morts, 162
  "Enfin," 162
  "Et Maintenant," 163
  "Guerre," 159
  "Main-Morte," 161
  "Mémoire," 160
Rosenstock. Sami. See Tzara, Tristan
"r-p-o-p-h-e-s-s-a-g-r" (Cummings), 78

"Savoy" (O'Hara), 151
Schuyler, James, 165-174
  "The Morning of the Poem," 170
  "Song," 169
Schwartz, Delmore, 175-185
  "The Ballad of the Children of the Czar," 179
  "A Dog Named Ego, the Snowflakes as Kisses," 182
  "Far Rockaway," 180

"The Heavy Bear Who Goes with Me," 181
"In the Naked Bed, in Plato's Cave," 179
"Prothalamion," 181
"Seurat's Sunday Afternoon Along the Seine," 183
Summer Knowledge, 183
"Tired and Unhappy, You Think of Houses," 180
"Seasons, The" (Koch), 117
Seifert, Jaroslav, 186-196
  "The Blow," 194
  The Casting of the Bells, 193
  The Plague Column, 194
Self-Portrait in a Convex Mirror (Ashbery), 33
"Seurat's Sunday Afternoon Along the Seine" (Schwartz), 183
"Some General Instructions" (Koch), 116
Some Trees (Ashbery), 29
"Song" (Schuyler), 169
Sonnets, The (Berrigan), 44
Spain, Take This Cup from Me (Vallejo), 229
Speech-Grille (Celan), 59
Sprachgitter. See *Speech-Grille*
Stanzas in Meditation (Stein), 206
Stein, Gertrude, 197-209
  The Autobiography of Alice B. Toklas, 207
  "Poetry and Grammar," 205
  Stanzas in Meditation, 206
  Tender Buttons, 204
  Things as They Are, 203
  Three Lives, 203
Straits (Koch), 117
"Strana negodiaev" (Esenin), 91
Studium przedmiotu (Herbert), 106
Summer Knowledge (Schwartz), 183
"Sunday" (Tzara), 214
Symbiosis (Guest), 96

Tender Buttons (Stein), 204
Tennis Court Oath, The (Ashbery), 31
Things as They Are (Stein), 203
Three Lives (Stein), 203
Three Poems (Ashbery), 31
"Tired and Unhappy, You Think of Houses" (Schwartz), 180
Trilce (Vallejo), 225
Triolet, Elsa, 18
Tzara, Tristan, 210-219
    Approximate Man, and Other Writings, 217
    "The Circus Performers," 216
    De nos oiseaux, 215
    "The Death of Guillaume Apollinaire," 215
    "Little Town in Siberia," 215
    Primele Poème, 214
    "Sunday," 214
    Vingt-cinq Poèmes, 215

Union libre, L'. See *Free Union*

Vallejo, César, 220-232
    The Black Heralds, 223
    Human Poems, 228
    Spain, Take This Cup from Me, 229
    Trilce, 225
Vingt-cinq Poèmes (Tzara), 215
Vocabulaire (Cocteau), 69
Von Schwelle zu Schwelle (Celan), 59

Waldman, Anne, 233-239
    Fast Speaking Woman, 235
    Giant Night, 235
    In the Room of Never Grieve, 237
    Iovis, 236
    Manatee/Humanity, 237
    Marriage, 236
Wave, A (Ashbery), 36
Where Shall I Wander (Ashbery), 37
Whitman, Walt, 114
World War I, 12
World War II, 118
Worldly Country, A (Ashbery), 38

"You Who Are the Rose" (Aragon), 23
Young, Dean, 240-245
    Beloved Infidel, 242
    Elegy on a Toy Piano, 242
    Primitive Mentor, 243
Your Name Here (Ashbery), 37